I

THE street was darkened by a smoky sunset, and light had not yet come on in the lamps near the empty house. Under a troubled sky the old house looked deserted but charged with reality. It was a place, Asa Timberlake thought, where everything had happened and nothing would ever happen again. Its life, with so many changing lives, was finished. Already, he saw, the wreckers were at work on the white columns. Nothing would remain in the end, not a brick, not a splinter of wood, not a tree, not a leaf, scarcely a blade of grass; for a new service station, flaunting a row of red pumps in front of a stucco arch, would presently spring up between a Georgian mansion and a Victorian dwelling in lower Washington Street.

A man in overalls rushed through the open gate, cast a hurried glance at Asa's face, and stopped short in surprise.

"You're Mr. Timberlake? I thought I knew you. My name's Maberley."

"Not Jim Maberley?"

"That was my father. We lost him winter before last, but Grandpa's still holding on, as spry as he ever was. He used to work in your grandfather's old factory. He had a job in the stemming room."

"I'm working there now, and in the stemming room."

"You're kidding. Not in your grandfather's factory? But I recollect hearing something about it. Your folks lost out a long time ago—didn't they?—when the works were sold?"

"Lost out. That's right."

"And you went back to work there. Good Lord! What

will the old man say when he hears of it? He used to think the Timberlakes were the top of creation."

"Tell him I went in at the bottom. That was forty-seven years ago."

"Forty-seven years! You must have been a kid at the start."

"I was twelve. I'm now fifty-nine. Many things slip my memory, but I never forget that twelve subtracted from fifty-nine leaves forty-seven."

"The house went too, didn't it? I've heard about the auction here after . . . after . . . I mean the time Mr. William Fitzroy bid on the place. But I reckon that was all right. He's some kin to you, ain't he?"

"I married his niece, but that was long afterwards."

"You lived on here, anyway."

"Yes, I lived on here."

"Well, I reckon Mr. Fitzroy knows what he's about. It must feel pretty good to stand in his shoes. Some say he's the biggest man in the South."

A quizzical gleam flickered in Asa's eyes. "Some do."

"And he must be over eighty! But you moved uptown, didn't you? It's funny how often I passed by this house without noticing it till we began pulling it down."

"I've a little house in the West End. Not like this one. Not built to stand."

"They're solid, these old buildings. They don't come down easy."

"No, they were meant to last. People had long thoughts in those days."

"Well, I like to see things come and go. I'm always glad when I get a job clearing away something old. You ought to have been here yesterday when that big syca-more crashed. We had a tough job with those roots."

Asa frowned. "That tree had more life than I have, and a stronger hold on it."

"I reckon that's so, sir. I bet that old tree could have told us aplenty if it could have talked."

"Are you cutting down the willow too?"

"You mean that big fellow down yonder by the back wall? No, sir, I tell you that would take some doing. But it ain't in the way yet."

"It will be."

"Sure it will. Every blessed tree seems to get right plumb in the way of business as soon as a town begins to wake up. But I'm all for progress, I am. I like to see things going fast. We've come a long way since Grandpa used to work ten or twelve hours at a stretch and then have to walk up every step from river bottom. An old Ford would have looked like a golden chariot to him, and I ain't joking either! But I can ride to work and come back in my own car as long as I'm able to pay for gas. I tell you, sir, what with automobiles and radios and movies, we've got a lot more to live for than folks used to have. Grandpa says we've got everything to make us happy but happiness. He's old, though, and he don't seem to take to the new ways. Anyhow, I'm right glad I met you, and the old man will be tickled to death. So long!"

He dashed off to his car, while Asa thought, watching him: Yes, we're better off nowadays, only we don't know it.

There was a sound of backfiring. A red light shone out through the fluted leaves on the maples, and several white pigeons fluttered up from the pavement and sank down again. The April wind had turned suddenly, and the last flare of daylight was gilding the street and the houses and the wide arch of sky. Standing there alone with the doomed house, Asa seemed to feel the slow oozing up of the past from beneath the dead levels of consciousness. Was it an illusion of memory, or could he

still hear the echo of that old shot, faint and far-off as the cracking of an icy branch in the woods? Like the echo in a dream, it came back to him. Only, as he reminded himself, there are no echoes in dreams. . . .

More than forty years ago, and it might have been yesterday! He was a boy then . . . but all that was long over. Yet he had known, or thought he had known, every step of his future. Nothing extraordinary. Nothing that an average boy, possessing average endowments, might not set out to achieve. He was not unusual, either in mind or body. This knowledge had been drummed into his head by a competent elder sister. The sense of mediocrity, of an inherent failure to impress people or circumstances, had been, in the rough-and-tumble school of experience, his earliest lesson. Still, he had kept up well in his classes. He was a bookish chap, and learning from books had always been easier than learning from life. At twelve, he had won honors in an expensive Queenborough school. After school, he would naturally have gone to the University of Virginia. After the university, he had expected to find a sheltered place in the Timberlake Tobacco Factory. In these sober expectations, if anywhere, he might have told himself, there was security.

An established house just entering its second century, the Timberlake Tobacco Factory was, or appeared to be, one of the soundest firms in Virginia. Privately owned, it was protected nevertheless from the robber barons of American industry. His father had put both his heart and his fortune into a popular brand of cigarette, the John Smith. Well, the John Smith was still popular. Asa had heard that it sold widely in China. But it now belonged, with the Timberlake Factory and the Timberlake fortune, to the Standard Tobacco Company.

"A gang of pirates, but they've got me," Daniel Timberlake had said, before he had picked up his gun and gone

down beyond the big willow to the foot of the garden. . . .

An inconspicuous figure in shabby clothes, Asa leaned against the sagging iron fence, and remembered. In the paling light he looked a man that one might carelessly pass in a crowd. There was nothing about him to attract a lingering glance, nothing except his closed, sensitive mouth and the amused ironic gleam in his eyes, mocking at life. On the surface there was no shadow of that strong man, the sleeping giant, who so often turned and struggled below the waking stream of thoughts and events. Longing to excel, he had never even succeeded. He had been hampered by not knowing a number of things the average man took for granted; but he was hampered still more by knowing a number of other things the average man had never suspected. Yet, in his silent way, he had known happiness. He had enjoyed even the night school, where he had gone of his own choice soon after his father's death. Then his mother's health had failed and he was needed to help her in the house, which they rented for a modest sum because it lacked many conveniences. After the day's work was over and the downstairs rooms had been straightened for an occasional early boarder, he would get out his schoolbooks and try to study for a few hours before going to bed. But he was always too tired, and night after night he had dropped to sleep under his student's lamp with the green shade.

Well, it did no good to bring back what was over and done with. His father had died long ago, but the big willow was still standing. When Asa, just now, had turned into Plummer Street, he had seen the green mist spraying out against the tarnished light in the sky. A flock of dark birds (starlings, he supposed, though he did not know much about birds) had flashed down, like curved blades.

There was a scent of April in the abandoned yard. A scraggy lilac bush was blooming in the tall grass near the front porch. From one of the vacant windows a scrap of curtain—or was it only a cobweb?—was blown out and sucked back into darkness. Was there a sound of footsteps above? Or had a draft stolen in through an open door?

They will never again build like this, he thought. Dignity is an anachronism. Yes, the old house was going out with its age, with its world, with its manners, with its fashion in architecture.

Suddenly, it seemed to him that stillness was gathering without and within. He stood alone in a lost hemisphere, while time flowed on above, below, around, and beyond him. Muffled discords from the present, now near, now far, rushed toward him, assailed his ears, and dropped back in the tumult. He heard cars speeding, horns blowing, feet hurrying, voices calling, dogs barking, radios crooning, starlings chattering as they settled to roost. Then, while he listened, the sounds dwindled; the moment broke up and vanished. . . .

He was glad, Asa told himself, that his father had fought to the end. Daniel Timberlake had fought against an idea, a mass movement, against an epoch in history. In the long struggle to survive, the age of the individual was over. When he refused to yield his place, the opposing forces had combined to put him out of the way; and by the time they had won the fight, he had nothing left but his life. It was then that the final blow had fallen with a stroke of paralysis. When once he was able to move his ruined body, he had picked up his shotgun and dragged himself down to the big willow, where the sound of the shot was dulled in the noises of traffic.

"As long as I could stand on my feet, I kept up the fight," he had said. "But I could never bear to be wheeled. I'd choose to die with my boots on." There had

been people in Queenborough who had called him a coward; but his wife and children knew better.

Long ruin, Asa remembered, had followed disaster. At a public auction the place had been knocked down to William Fitzroy, who was prudently buying land in lower Washington Street. Then, since bidders had been few and progress was turning in another direction, he had let the house, for a small sum, to Mrs. Timberlake and her competent daughter. After this, until the death of his mother and the marriage of his sister, Asa had lived in the timid and scurrying haste of a boy-of-all-work in a boardinghouse where servants are lacking. Was his later fear of life rooted, he wondered, in his earlier fear of offending his mother's indispensable lodgers?

Well, it had been a good boardinghouse, and he was not ashamed to look back on it. But his schooling stopped, and before he was thirteen he had begun to work in the factory. He was still working there, though he had risen from three to fifty dollars a week. It was the best he could do, for even now he felt himself to be a stranger under the new system. In the old days his father had known the name and face of every man he employed. One and all, he and his men had belonged to a single social unit, which, though often torn by internal dissensions, was held together by some vital bond of human relationship. There had been injustice; there had been greed and oppression; but one had dealt with flesh and blood, not with a list of printed names at the top of a page.

In the present spring of 1938, the heads of the Standard Tobacco Company, who lived in New York and spent the winters in Florida, had never heard Asa's name; and they had forgotten, if indeed they ever knew, that the dingy factory down on Canal Street had been recognized from Queenborough to Peking as the Timberlake trademark. For the past ten years, Asa had looked ahead

to the day when he should no longer be wanted, and when his dismissal would spring on him from some featureless source which was both inhuman and hostile. At fifty-nine, with forty-seven years of faithful plodding behind him, he was as insecure, he told himself, as a drying leaf on a stem. When he had outlived his usefulness, he could expect nothing better than the ignominy of private or public relief. The government would hardly bother about a man who could turn to well-off and well-thought-of relations. What government, however paternal, had learned that the fruit of a family tree may taste as bitter as death?

But he had fighting blood. They could not take that away, he thought, bracing his rounded shoulders, while his heart seemed to turn over. Yet fighting blood had not kept off dependence, and how he hated dependence! How he hated the thought that Lavinia's uncle, that staunch pillar of the Stock Exchange and of St. Luke's Episcopal Church, had provided better dresses for Lavinia's two daughters, as well as a better roof over their heads. That William, who was by nature more just than generous, should provide these things begrudgingly was merely an added dash of bitter in Asa's cup of humiliation. In some inscrutable manner, his self-respect was bound up with the independence he had sacrificed to Lavinia's ill health and his daughters' increasing demands on life. Even when William had displayed a sudden avuncular weakness for Stanley, the younger daughter, who had ripened into a beauty, Asa had found himself resenting the constant slights to Roy, his own favorite. William's benevolence, he knew, could be dismissed as a cold virtue; for he had shown no warmer feeling toward Lavinia, his only niece, than he had bestowed upon the most distant of what he called his "connections."

Nevertheless, in striving to be fair, Asa conceded that it was difficult for anyone to feel tenderly toward Lavinia.

None knew better than he that her temperament was not designed to encourage warmth, even—or was it especially?—in a husband. In childhood and early youth, she had been tormented by men; and after a disappointing courtship and marriage, she had learned to assuage her wounded instincts by tormenting the solitary male whom life had ever delivered into her hands. In the beginning Asa had feared that Andrew, their only son, was also set apart as a victim; but, by some sharp variation from type, he had turned out to be a healthy and cheerful boy, who had escaped through sheer lightheartedness all the perils of environment and heredity.

Why Lavinia should have stooped to Asa Timberlake had always been, to Asa, a mystery. Her family was more prominent than his, in a community where families were still reckoned with, though the nature of the reckoning had altered from intangible to tangible values. As the only niece of a leading citizen who had no closer heirs of his body, she might have found, it appeared to Asa, a more thrilling experiment. But from the day when she first met him and took possession, no trace of mystery had obscured his too palpable reason for marrying her. The sense of failure had hung heavily. He had felt that he was outside life, while he was longing desperately to come inside and to have a share in the process. His unreconciled twenties had been, he understood now, the hardest years in his past. Even his grief for his father, with its burning hatred of social injustice, had begun to die down to ashes. He had felt both inferior and rudderless. Though he had wanted love, he had been afraid of all women who were not maternal and elderly. Then, by a kind of sardonic accident, he had met Lavinia; and her prompt pursuit had aroused that sleeping giant, who was also a poet. His lean identity had filled out and drawn nourishment from her flattery. In sudden exaltation, he had grasped an illusion of personality. The strong man

had come at last to the surface; the strong man had triumphed over adversity.

For a few years, until Lavinia renewed her self-torture, he had imagined that the choice and pursuit had been his alone. He had even convinced himself that he had been in love with her, through that brief, bewildering courtship, when his head had appeared to betray or deny his heart. Only afterwards, when he had grown to dislike his wife (what nonsense people talked about marriage!), he perceived that she had married him solely because the time had come to marry somebody, and there had been no other opportunity within easy reach. . . .

The air was warm even for late April. It couldn't do any harm to rest a bit on the steps. That was a steep pull up Main Street, though it was no worse than hanging on a strap in a streetcar. He used to think he might someday buy a secondhand Ford; but there had always been more imperative needs. Entering the gate, he went slowly up the brick walk, where a solitary pigeon was waddling, and sat down on one of the granite steps. The stone was stained brown and green from the drippings of trees, and weeds had sprouted among the bricks of the walk, which was laid in a herringbone pattern. A black iron urn, once brimming with red geraniums, had tumbled down on the grass. The scent of lilacs grew stronger, and he saw that a purple spray was brushing his shoulder. Through the blue dusk in the street he could see people dining on the terrace of a hotel over the way. An awning was strung with Chinese lanterns, and beneath them rows of red and yellow tulips were blooming. Were those people really as happy, he wondered, as they looked in the colored lights?

Taking off his hat, he put it down carefully in a clean spot on the step. It must be pleasant, he thought, to wear the right sort of hat and not an old one that Andrew had handed on. Not that it mattered beside the major problem of holding fast to one's job when one was no

longer able to hold fast to the lengthening years. For today he was late again. Either his mind had grown slower or the work in his department had become more confusing. The early dinner would be over, and Virgie, who was a poor cook but had her pleasures, would have collected her basket of pickings and resolutely set out toward freedom. He would find on the kitchen table a plate of lean meat and lukewarm vegetables. A pot of bitter coffee would have simmered down on the cold gas range. Everything would be like this, he mused with candid realism, if he were to return to earth after he had been safely buried and insufficiently mourned.

His daughters, who admired the new house, with rooms like closets and with doors and windows that stuck fast in damp weather, would call him an old fogy because he wanted things to wear well and was particular about quality. But he was careful, after painful enlightenment, to keep a discredited sense of values hidden away from his children. Even Roy, the only one who took after him, would, in her brave modern fashion, disapprove of his loyalty to any place so unmistakably left behind by the years. Like all other young persons nowadays, his three children, he thought tolerantly, were convinced that wisdom would live on with them. He had learned long ago that the only sure way to win and keep their respect was to conceal from them how easily his thin defense could be pierced. That was why he had clothed himself in this protective coloring of ironic amusement.

In the beginning his mockery of life had been worn chiefly as a make-believe with his children. Then he had found that the pretense served him well, first with Lavinia and later on with the rest of the world. In the end, he had come to regard his original disguise as a reluctantly acquired second nature. Only when he escaped for a few hours from the conspiracy called family life and went into the country to run free with Jack and Kate

Oliver and the dogs that Lavinia would not allow him to keep, did he feel that another and a real Asa Timberlake emerged from obscurity. For nearly twenty years he had enjoyed this innocent sanctuary; and for two years, after Jack had dropped dead from a heart attack, Asa had known beyond any doubt that he wanted to marry Kate. He wanted to marry her, though she was plain and middle-aged and plump and unashamed, and had never been either pretty or slender. But he knew also that he was still firmly married to Lavinia; and Virginian tradition decreed that infidelity should be an expensive pursuit.

There was nothing, he admitted, to be done about it. And there was quite as little to be done about the new house in Westward Avenue, which dampened his spirits whenever he entered it. Especially when he was tired. Especially after he had found trouble with figures. Was it merely the smell of fresh paint and varnish which would fade away with time, as Lavinia insisted? Or was it the closeness and narrowness and the utter impossibility of escaping from the few persons he loved most? Were human beings really meant to live in houses? he wondered. Were human beings really meant to live together? For thirty years he had lived, day and night, with a wife whom he had loved—if he had loved her at all—only in the beginning for a few months. For at least fifteen years he had lived, day and night, with a wife whom he had grown to dislike. Not actually on the surface, perhaps, but in some secret core of his nature, with the wordless antipathy of his unconscious mind. Yet nobody had forced him to marry Lavinia. Nobody had urged upon him that disastrous mistake. And not even Lavinia could have married him against his openly expressed disinclination. He had married her of his own free and unbridled will, in spite of the agonized remonstrance of his mother and the aloof disapproval of William Fitzroy.

But gathering opposition had merely hardened his purpose. He perceived that clearly when he looked back. At the time he had felt only that he must assert himself; that for once in his life he must act the strong man and repulse interference. A flare of mating instinct had done more than encourage folly; it had actually created self-confidence. So, disregarding alike the forces of prophecy and precedent, he had married Lavinia Fitzroy, the plain daughter of one of the best and meanest families in Queenborough. And though excellence may be seldom or never handed down in the blood, meanness, as his mother had warned him, is a fatal inheritance.

In twenty years his only holidays from his family had been those stolen Sunday afternoons with Jack and Kate and the dogs or, after Jack's death, with Kate and the dogs alone at Hunter's Fare on James River. Though the farm and the two pointers provided his chief pleasure and his only release, he had spent the better part of his life with a woman who hated the country and disliked dogs. Yet, in spite of an inner revolt, he had acknowledged and obeyed the severe rule of right living. He had worn patched clothes, while his children kept up a proper appearance. As a little child, Stanley had been given a coat of white fur; he had never forgotten her angelic face, framed in primrose-colored curls, springing up above the high collar. Well, he had loved his children; he had been, according to his straitened means, a good father; but he would think twice, he meditated, before accepting the world's estimate of family feeling. For it seemed to him that family feeling had stood in the way of everything he had ever wanted to do. Lavinia and family feeling together.

At dinner, he assured himself, his absence tonight would pass unnoticed, unless Lavinia had felt an attack of heart failure or chanced to run out of soda mints or aromatic ammonia. He had not failed to observe that excite-

ment, either nuptial or funereal, possesses a strange effi-
cacy in chronic afflictions. Stanley was to be married next
week to Craig Fleming; and the wedding preparations
were already overflowing the house. Another unsuitable
marriage, Asa told himself, though he had nothing
against Craig, an attractive chap in his way, as a son-in-
law. On the contrary, Asa very much preferred Craig,
who had identified himself with an external world in confusion and was stuffed full of entangled ideologies, to
Roy's husband, Peter Kingsmill, a big, blond, reckless
liver, who made Asa feel that he was deficient in the true
nature of man.

Craig was different, with his light, restless eyes in
a dark face and his mouth of an embittered idealist.
Though he had his charm, Asa had never been able to
think of him except as a weathercock. A flabby liberal,
Andrew called him; but Andrew, as even his father admitted, took a short and narrow view of the liberal outlook. It was true that before Craig had met Stanley, he
held advanced, or what Lavinia, whose vocabulary was
dated, called radical opinions. As a youthful attorney with
a promising future, he was constantly turning aside to defend forlorn causes in the law courts. But, since his
engagement to Stanley, he had become wholly absorbed
in the cost of rent and furniture and crockery. Not that
he was insincere. The trouble was exactly the opposite.
His beliefs were rooted in emotion and assumed the
urgent nature of impulse, as they do when a man begins
to think with his heart and to feel with his head. In his
way, an agreeable way, he was a sympathetic companion;
and the slight limp in his walk increased a certain wistful
appeal.

Yet all this, Asa reflected, might account for Craig's
infatuation, but scarcely for Stanley's. He was not her
sort. No, he was not in the least her sort, Asa repeated.
Was it, he asked himself, merely the quality of unlikeness,

the attraction of the new and the strange? Or had Stanley wanted Craig because she knew he was engaged to another girl? Though both had lived their brief lives in Queenborough, they had met only a few months before and apparently had fallen in love at first sight. The presence of the other girl, one of Stanley's best friends, had served, Asa suspected, only to fan the sudden vehement flame. Even as a baby, Stanley had been animated by some deep motive to grasp at any object that gave happiness to another. Hadn't she always cried for Roy's dolls? And had she ever failed to seize and hold them in the end? There was a tiny scar, no bigger than a dimple, at the corner of Roy's mouth, where her little sister had struck her in a battle over a toy.

With less than three years between them, the two sisters might have belonged to different epochs in history. Did they love each other? Did they hate each other? Had they inherited the conflict of types from a marriage of opposites? He could not tell. No one could tell by observing them on the surface.

"She isn't nearly so intelligent as Roy," he had once remarked to Lavinia in the small hours before daybreak.

Lavinia, an ample figure with the large, loose mind and the comfortable waist of the hypochondriac, had replied tartly: "She doesn't need to be, Asa."

"And she isn't really beautiful if you take her features apart."

"No man," Lavinia had retorted, "will ever take her features apart."

Asa had raised himself in his smaller bed, with the harder mattress and the inadequate springs, while he stared at her thoughtfully. It was odd, he had reflected, how quickly Lavinia resented even an implied criticism of Stanley. In her youngest child, who embodied all that she had longed to be and was not, she had recreated not her actual youth, but that other more vital youth which had

existed in her imagination alone. To touch Stanley was like touching an exposed nerve in Lavinia's ego.

According to her unfailing habit, Lavinia had enjoyed both the last and the right word. After waiting a few minutes, however, she had continued magnanimously: "I don't deny that it is hard on Roy. No young girl likes to play second fiddle. But young girls today don't take things to heart as we used to do."

"I'm not sure," Asa had rejoined, "how much Roy takes to heart. But I'm glad she was safely married before Stanley came home from school."

Though Lavinia had not answered directly, he had never forgotten her look of secret anxiety; yet when she spoke after another pause, her tone was quite cheerful. "I wish Uncle William would not make such a difference between them. It doesn't seem fair that Stanley should have been sent to that expensive boarding school, while Roy was earning her living. But men do things like that."

"Wouldn't Roy rather have had Peter? The marriage seems to have turned out very well, though I'm old-fashioned enough to believe that a man ought to support his wife . . . or . . . at least make the effort."

"That wasn't Peter's fault. Girls today are so impatient."

"Well, she has her job and she's happy. Nothing else matters."

Had he really meant that? he asked himself now. Or was he merely trying to evade a suspicion he had refused to acknowledge? The furtive look had not left Lavinia's eyes when she added, with an air of dismissing the subject, "You ought to know if anyone does. Roy has always loved you better than me."

While he sat there alone this recollection flickered up in a mellow glow. Was it happiness? Was it humility? . . . Looking down at his feet planted squarely on the lower step, he reminded himself, with an effort to be matter-of-

fact, that it was time to have his shoes half-soled again. It was odd, he thought, how frightened he was of the word "happiness." He could never face it directly; instead, he shifted his glance and pretended to himself he didn't know it was there. For it was true that Roy loved him, that she was the only human being in the world with whom he had ever come first. And he had loved her, he told himself, because, though she had had to play second fiddle, she had ended by proving to them all that she was not second best. After her marriage, though they had continued to live in the same house, she had been caught up and borne away by an absorbing devotion to Peter. But she remained a child to Asa, and he thought of her always as the little girl who was too proud to let them know when she was hurt. Lavinia had complained that she should have been a boy, because she ran wild in the street and was constantly losing her hair ribbons on back fences.

Even now, after she was married and settled with Peter in the third story of the new house, her mother said that Roy did not keep her bureau drawers tidy. That did not bother Asa. Disorder was, or appeared to be, the dominant note of the age; and he had learned that one must, of necessity, live in one's age. After all, what was outward disorder but the breaking away from a fixed pattern of conduct? I suppose it's because I've never had a life of my own, he thought, that I am ready to sympathize with almost any sort of breaking away. I am out of touch with my world, but I do not belong with the past. I have never had anything, yet, oddly enough, I seem to be standing among its ruins.

What he liked in Roy was something strong and self-reliant and unyielding, some hard fine grain of integrity. She possessed all the qualities, he told himself, that men have missed and wanted in women: courage, truthfulness, a tolerant sense of humor, loyalty to impersonal

ends. That men have *thought* they missed and wanted, jeered a small satirical voice in his mind. For he doubted, with his rational part, whether men had ever wanted truthfulness in women. Or loyalty, for that matter, to impersonal ends. What men imagined they desired and what they actually desired were as far apart, he knew, as the ideal and the fact. Young people nowadays declared they were different, but they declared it themselves. . . . As for Peter . . . well, Asa couldn't be sure about Peter. How could a man be sure of anything in the midst of confusion? A year earlier or even six months ago, he would have said that Roy and Peter were completely united. Then something had happened, something scarcely more evident than a pause in the rhythm. Probably he would never know what it was. But he had seen the change in Roy's face, and he had felt the sharp stab of a wordless anxiety. In the vacant air her face rose before him, as if it were spun out of the faint afterglow. It was a thin face, delicately modeled, with gray eyes under dark surprised eyebrows, an attractive blunt nose, and a sudden smile etched in with a bright derision. Her small brave head was framed in short blue-black curls, very thick and upspringing. . . .

And Stanley, too, he mused tolerantly, had her points. She was kind to her mother; she was gentle with old people (though she refused to bother about them); she was never out of temper, unless one stood between her and something she wanted. It was a pity that she was more beautiful than Roy, and more vivid. She was taller; she was fairer; she had a skin of pale gold and waving hair which turned to dusky amber in the sunlight. Her eyes, set a trifle too close together, were as changeable as the sea or the weather. Sea-blue, Lavinia called them, but at times when Stanley was hurt or offended, they could look as cold as blue glass. A single flaw in her features marred, for Asa, their young loveliness, though he suspected that,

like many other imperfections in women, this special fault was not without a charm of its own. Her mouth, naturally red and moist and tremulous, had a trick of never quite closing, and in moments of anger or excitement her thrust-out lower lip would give to her face a vacant and hungry look. Like a disappointed baby, said Peter Kingsmill, who found it appealing. . . . But after all, Asa told himself, he was only a father and fathers are notoriously lacking in critical judgment. In a week Stanley would make a romantic marriage; and fortunately, William Fitzroy had lent his big new house in Lakeview Park for the wedding reception. With three children pleasantly settled, Asa thought, a man may be forgiven for wanting a little life of his own.

II

LIGHT flooded the corner. There was a lull in the traffic, and for a few minutes Washington Street appeared almost deserted. It was a good time to go over, Asa thought, while the crossing was still clear. Then an old man with a stout walking stick hobbled into the glare. A woman carrying a bird cage went slowly past. Three small Negro boys, crying a paper in treble voices, trailed on, one after another. Who would believe, to look at it now, that this shabby-genteel neighborhood had been once the most desirable part of the town? Why, he remembered when people had come to board with his mother because her house was in fashionable Washington Street. And after his mother's death Lavinia and he had stayed on, amid gradual deterioration, while property owners invited reluctant mercantile progress to march over from Main Street and take possession. Only a year ago, when business activity had shown signs of turning in this direction, William Fitzroy had sold the lot at a high figure and offered his niece one of a row of commonplace houses he owned in Westward Avenue. Well, Lavinia and the children, Asa hoped, would be satisfied with a house which had no roots, no history, no background, and no safe escape except through the back gate into an untidy alley. But it was right, no doubt, to consider the young; and Lavinia naturally thought first of her daughters and their insecure social position. Family alone, she remarked truly enough, was not the help that it used to be. And, apart from the increasing prestige of the West End, she would be nearer Stanley and Craig, who had taken an apartment in a trumpery building a few blocks away.

To be sure, Roy complained, Westward Avenue was

too far from the interior decorating shop in which she worked, while her husband, a surgeon of brilliant promise, was making a place in his profession. There was no doubt, Asa admitted, that Peter Kingsmill was brilliant, especially in the matter of promise; but in his way, a different way, he was as unstable as Craig Fleming. Was instability, like disorder, Asa pondered, only one of the many confusing signs of the times? Were both the brilliant promise and the arrested fulfillment of modern youth merely outward symptoms of some obscure inner decay? Peter was dominant; he was genial; he was filled with a kind of flaming egoism which appeared to dazzle women; but his father-in-law had decided that, as a husband, he lacked the quality which used to be called character. Though he was only twenty-eight, there had been before his marriage several rumors of romantic or moral entanglements. But Roy had not seemed to care, though she adored him. She was the sort of woman, fortunate or unfortunate (Asa could not decide), who would cheerfully sacrifice herself, not only for a man, but for his career. This was the reason, Asa knew, that she had kept on with her work. And this was the reason that she had refused to take a summer vacation while Peter went on a fishing trip.

Stanley was not like that. . . . Asa lifted his hand and smoothed back the gray hair from his forehead, which was high and a trifle too narrow between jutting dark eyebrows. . . . No one, least of all her father, expected Stanley to be like anyone else. Even William Fitzroy, who was aging more rapidly in fact than in fancy, never refused Stanley anything that she wanted. He had placed her in a better school than Asa could have afforded; and when she had declined to go to college, being endowed with a more potent aptitude than that of intellect, he had sent her abroad for "a classic tour" with Miss Frances Allen, the elderly but still indefatigable English scholar.

Ever since her return last year, lovelier than ever, William had said he felt that she belonged to him, and though he insisted she was throwing herself away upon Craig Fleming, that stuffy intellectual, he had proved he had a lavish hand on the proper occasion. Not only had he given her a generous check and a smart gray sports car, which she had soon learned to drive, but she was likewise providing an elaborate wedding reception. No, we couldn't do without William, Asa admitted; for he knew that Stanley could not have borne to cut her wedding cake in a house smelling of varnish, or to let herself be toasted as a bride in punch instead of champagne.

Starting up from the step, he dusted off the seat of his trousers, while he wondered whether Lavinia would reproach him for the stains of mildew and rust. The crown of his hat was not damaged; but when he glanced down at his shoes in the white glare, he told himself that they were too far gone for half-soling. I didn't know they were so bad, he said to himself regretfully, as he passed down the walk and out of the gate.

Near the end of the block, under a giant mulberry tree, which was already marked for destruction, a deep shadow stirred and drifted forward before it broke up and divided into a larger and a lesser shape. As the two figures advanced quickly, he saw that they belonged to Parry Clay, a colored boy, and his sleek brown dog, Jasper. Asa had always felt an interest in Parry, chiefly, he supposed, because the boy's family on his mother's side had once belonged to the Timberlakes; and Jasper, the dog, was a sterling character in his own right, independent and unafraid, with an animated manner, a friendly tail, and an inquisitive but peculiar sense of humor. He happened, too, to be the kind of dog Asa respected, the best of several good breeds, with strong smooth muscles under a healthy coat, like burnished satin, and the dark, eloquent eyes of a dumb poet. It was

pleasant to recall that five years before on a snowy December night he had found Jasper, a small defiant puppy, curled up in a ball on the doorstep, and that, after feeding him in the kitchen, he had given him to Minerva, the washerwoman, to hide in her basket. I'd never have given him away, he thought now, if Lavinia had let me keep him.

Running ahead of Parry, Jasper sniffed at Asa's legs as he stooped over to pat him.

"That's a smart dog, Parry," he said, as usual.

"Yes, sir, Jasper's a smart dog," Parry replied. He was a delicate-looking boy, very light in color, with a straight, slim figure and an intelligent but moody expression. Unlike the greater part of the Negroes (if, indeed, he could be called a Negro) in Queenborough, he was discontented with his lot and was trying desperately to pick up an education and rise in the world. For several years now Asa had lent the boy books from the old Timberlake library, against the stern opposition of Lavinia, who believed that the colored race (especially when it has profited so freely by white blood) should be held firmly down to its proper station.

After an exchange of civilities, Jasper had hurried on and was turning into the empty yard. A bright chap, Asa thought, watching the dog track a pigeon to a pile of trash under the steps. Thrown into the gutter, yet full of sense and personality. But life was that way. You couldn't tell what made personality, either in man or dog.

Looking round again, he noticed that Parry's eyes were like Jasper's, dark and liquid with meaning. And he had, too, the same eager yet hooded gaze, as if something alive and inarticulate struggled there for expression. Was that what his mother used to call "the Indian look," he wondered, remembering that Aunt Matoaca, Minerva's mother, had been part Indian. But it is queer, he mused, how little we actually know of the Negro race. Our ser-

vants know all about us, while we know nothing of them. They are bound up in our daily lives; they are present in every intimate crisis; they are aware of, or suspect, our secret motives. Yet we are complete strangers to the way they live, to what they really think or feel about us, or about anything else. And the less colored they are, the more inscrutable they become, until, when they have so nearly crossed the borderline, like this boy Parry, they seem almost to speak another language and to belong to another species than ours.

He wished to befriend the boy; yet whenever they met, as they did once in a while, he could find nothing to say to him. It was the new education, he supposed, that embarrassed him. With the old-fashioned illiterate Negro he felt no such awkwardness. Parry's grandmother, Aunt Matoaca, who had nursed Asa's mother through her last illness of several years, had been a born conversationalist and excellent company. She could neither read nor write; but she had the Indian manner of royalty, and he had felt as much at ease with her as with his own grandmother. He was at ease, too, though less completely, with Parry's mother, Minerva, a tall, still handsome octoroon with a pale yellow skin and the noble bearing of women who in youth have carried baskets on upright heads. Minerva had nursed his three children, and she still dealt with the family washing. Since they had moved to the West End, Lavinia, whose hand did not open easily, had consented to pay for the ramshackle Ford which Minerva hired for her trips on Friday evening and Monday morning. For Minerva herself, who had improved her stinted lot in life through industry alone, Asa had always felt more respect than affection. She had never inspired him with the friendship he had shared with her mother, old Aunt Matoaca, who had known her white folks by heart, but had trusted to the mysterious arts of the conjurer when it came to dealing with black folks. It wasn't, Asa as-

sured himself, that he distrusted the more educated Negroes; it was simply that he could not understand them as he had understood, through tradition, the older Negroes of servitude.

"I'm glad you're doing well, Parry," he said. "I saw your father in the post office the other day, and he told me you were at the head of your class."

The boy's sullen face brightened. "Yes, sir, I'm getting on fine." Even when he smiled, and he had a pleasant smile, there was a shadow of bewilderment—or was it apprehension?—in his expression. Was it, Asa asked himself, the bewilderment of being so nearly white? Or was it the darker apprehension of being so little black?

"You'd like to go to college?"

"Yes, sir, I'm trying. I'm trying for a scholarship."

"Maybe you'll want to go North?"

Again that faint hesitation, that hooded glance. "Yes, sir." He stood for a minute silently fingering the cap in his hand. "I'd give most anything to get away. If it wasn't for my folks at home, I'd give most anything."

Asa sighed. "That feeling is in the air. We're all wanting new ways."

Parry swallowed and nodded, while his eyes roved to Jasper. "Yes, sir. I reckon that's so."

"Well, I'm not surprised," Asa said, and indeed he was not. "There isn't much chance for you in the South. . . . But I hope you'll get on." How ineffectual it sounded, and what did it mean anyway? The truth was he couldn't talk to the boy, for there was nothing that seemed to him worth saying. The situation appeared hopeless; and, because it was hopeless, it gave him a sinking sensation in the pit of his stomach. It wasn't easy to tell the young who wanted to go ahead that they must stand back. It wasn't easy to tell a man who craved knowledge that he must turn round and begin to dig ditches. "I'll see what I can do," he added, and knew that he could do nothing.

Parry swallowed again, and then spoke with a gulp, as if the words were wrenched out of him. "I want to rise. I don't want to stay down."

"Will you get a job in the summer?"

"I'm working now with automobiles. I'm a good driver, and I'm learning how to look after cars. Mr. William lets me take care of the sports car he's given Miss Stanley."

"That's good." Why was it, Asa asked himself, that men were so generally reluctant to spend money where it was most needed? For William, with all his wealth, was a little near, and it took a pretty girl, who wanted only fine clothes and cosmetics, to loosen his clutch on his pocketbook.

"I'm studying at night. I'm trying to learn law."

"Don't go too fast. If you go too fast, you'll give out before you get anywhere." Words, words, Asa thought, empty words rattling like husks. He had known several ambitious Negroes, but they had all suffered from an arrested intelligence. They had been too young to understand what they wanted, and by the time they had ceased to struggle, it was all over, the ambition, the restlessness, the unstable endeavor. Some light-colored wench across the street would swing her hips; then a man and his woman would marry on nothing, and begin in poverty to breed like jack rabbits. Aspiration would be subdued in the end to the elementary law of biology.

The boy shuffled his feet on the rough pavement. "If I don't go young, I'll never go at all, Mr. Asa. You have to get away young, or you lose the will. Uncle John was like me. Ma says he wanted to get away. But he's proud now to be a waiter at the country club."

"I know," Asa said, for he himself had been through it all in his time. But he couldn't talk. There wasn't anything to say, and had there been anything to say, he couldn't have said it. The twilight thickened between

them, and he felt that it was the dark thickness of race, that impenetrable obscurity, which was welling up among the intricate ties of human relationship. And through this thickness, which appeared alien and hostile, the boy's eyes, blind with seeking, stared back at him from a face that seemed to be without edges and without structure. All he really knew of Parry was a neat blue suit of clothes, outgrown, no doubt, by the son of one of Minerva's patrons, a well-laundered blue shirt, also a hand-me-down, he supposed, observing the carefully darned collar, a cheap red tie, and black hair without a kink, which might have belonged to a white man or an Indian. But beyond these external details, which were the only obvious facts, he felt the thick silence, not of mystery, but of a vast emptiness.

"Yes, I know," he repeated. "I know, Parry, and I'll do what I can."

"Thank you, sir," Parry answered before he passed on, whistling to Jasper.

When the boy had crossed Washington Street, with Jasper at his heels, and had been swallowed by the shadows on the opposite pavement, Asa looked sadly after the two lost figures. It was hopeless, he thought, for nobody who possessed the power to help would be interested. The best thing ahead of Parry, if he kept his manners and his neat appearance, would be a place as a porter in a Pullman car or a waiter in one of the better hotels. A raw deal, Asa said to himself, while he waited for an omnibus up Washington Street. A raw deal, but, like so many other raw deals in an unfinished world, there was nothing that he could see to be done about it.

III

NO ONE passed him as he walked the long block on Westward Avenue. Only the transparent image at his side, himself and yet not himself, appeared to whisper as it moved slantwise before him in the light wind. Then, suddenly, a small green car plunged from a side street into the glare of the arc lamp, and as it flashed by, he caught a glimpse of a man whose hair shone red in the light and of a girl with amber curls blown back from her neck. That was Peter's car, Asa thought, not in words, but as formlessly as a shifting impression. That was Peter's car, and Stanley was with him. But why should Stanley be with him? And why hadn't they brought Roy? Roy needed air and change far more than did Stanley, who had her own car now, and was independent of Peter, as of everyone else. But how radiant she was! With her upturned face and her streaming hair, she had looked, in that brief glimpse, winged and triumphant.

Well, no matter. He had reached the new house, which was like a house on the stage, unreal, insubstantial, two-dimensional, and utterly without character. It might have stood anywhere in the world. It might have been packed away with any collection of stage properties and unpacked again at the next theater. Crammed into the most narrow possible space between two other dwellings which were exactly like his home from foundation to roof, this house appeared oddly enough to be shuttered, not only against the street below, but against the overhanging dark triangle of sky. The stucco was putty-colored, already stained and streaked, and the doors and flimsy cornices were tinted a dreary brown. But in front there were the flying shadows of maples, and from the small backyard, where the recent builders had neglected

to cut down an old tulip tree, closely woven branches were spilling over the roof.

"It's even worse inside," he said to himself. "It's even worse than it looks out here." Hurrying up the six wooden steps, he slipped his latchkey into the lock and entered a hall so narrow that he could barely turn round, between the small Duncan Phyfe table, a present from William on their wedding anniversary, and the old mahogany hall stand which Asa had inherited from his grandfather. There was no light in the living room but only in the small room beyond, where Stanley's wedding presents were arranged on tables covered with some of her Aunt Charlotte's best linen and lace cloths. Well, there would be time enough for all that. At the moment, he was in search of the food that Virgie had set aside in the kitchen. It takes more than a sandwich at lunch to stay by you, he thought. If I can't get rid of this gone feeling, I'll be having another one of those sinking spells.

Trudging through the dining room, he pushed back the swinging door into the pantry and passed on into the cramped kitchen. Here, after the electricity flashed on, he confronted in miniature the sleek aspects of modern utility. Small to be sure, necessarily circumscribed, like so many things modern, but how exact, how impeccable, how complete in its own degree. For the furnished kitchen with its gleaming pots and pans was a present from William's wife, Charlotte, and William had said pompously: "Even for those in moderate circumstances, there is no excuse in these days to be without the best plumbing." The kitchen sink alone, Asa mused sardonically, would have placed its owner in the best circles. For even Lavinia admitted that nowadays one's social importance was rated more accurately by plumbing than by ancestry.

Pausing in admiration before the sink, he observed that there was not a scratch on the spotless enamel, not a

stain on the bright metal. No leaking taps, no rust anywhere, no smoke smudges, no sagging shelves, no worn
oilcloth, no trash piles in corners, no unsightly garbage
cans, and (heaven be praised!) no black beetles. There
was, indeed, not one of the homely discomforts among
which he had grown up and without which he was lonely.
The walls were blue and white, the woodwork was blue
and white, the rows of imitation china (not even china
was real any longer) were blue and white also, and even
the cup-towels (Lavinia had told him that they came from
the five-and-ten-cent store) were checked in a blue and
white pattern. Yes, there is no excuse, William had repeated, squeezing his heavy figure through the pantry
into the kitchen, there is no excuse for poor servants
when everything they have to do is made easy for them.

Yes, there's no excuse for any of us, Asa said to himself, when things are made easy. But he couldn't feel at
home here. In the old house, whenever he was late, his
supper had been left at one end of the old table in the large
dining room. Nobody had bothered about insulting that
severe Georgian dignity. Here, however, there was no
dignity, there was only convenience, and, as Lavinia insisted, "They must do their best to live up to it." The only
way he could live up to it, Asa had soon discovered, was
by inconveniencing himself. Like modern life in general,
he observed from his prejudiced point of view, convenience was bright, brittle, and unwearable. In the midst
of it all, he felt, there was no middle age. There was
youth in the machine and old age under the wheels, but
there was no middle age anywhere, not even at fifty-
nine.

Removing the cover from a plate on the cold gas
range, he probed with a fork at the slice of corned beef
and the sodden heap of potatoes and spinach. Then,
while he turned on the gas and touched a match to the
jet, he shook his head at the blue percolator before he

emptied the contents down the sink and set about making a fresh cup of coffee. Good coffee, he reminded himself with pride, was one of his few accomplishments, though he still preferred the old-fashioned drip coffee with its heavenly aroma, which he used to make for his mother at the first crack of dawn. After an uneasy night, how they had enjoyed that early coffee, with the doll's pitcher of cream he had borrowed from the jug that was put aside for the boarders. No one, he told himself now, had ever come so near to him as his mother. Not Roy, not Kate, not anyone in the world. Never had he laughed with any other woman as he had laughed with her, pure laughter, without irony, without bitterness. After her death, his sense of humor had been shut in, either by circumstances or by his own adverse nature. Though he still laughed, it was silent laughter; though he still mocked, it was inward mockery.

The door at his back opened, and a faintly derisive voice called, "Scraps again! Oh, you poor Daddy!"

As he wheeled round, fatigue dropped away from him. It was seldom nowadays that Roy remembered to call him "Daddy," and his heart seemed to pause at the childish name on her lips. "Well, I'm used to scraps," he tossed back, with the familiar note of whimsical chaffing. "I've lived on them all my life." That she herself might have looked after his dinner, or at least seen that Virgie had kept it warm, did not at the moment occur to either father or daughter. He had been too well disciplined by neglect, and she was too deeply involved in the vehement problems of youth. "That's a pretty dress," he added. "I like you in blue."

"What, this old thing? I had it last spring."

"Well, it's pretty." She was too thin, he thought, and there was a look of strain in her young face; but she carried her small dark head with a gallant air. "Even if I'm an old fogy, I still know what's pretty."

Darting into the kitchen, while the door swung on its hinges, she perched insecurely on the end of the table and smiled a gay, defiant, and unnatural smile. Her dress was too pale for the strong blue of the walls, and in the hard white glare from the unshaded electric bulb, her face was drained of color, except for the scarlet curve of her lips. "You're becoming a man of mystery, old dear," she said teasingly. "Mother suspects you of committing a pleasure, or at least a movie, on the way home."

"I'd be hard put," he retorted, "to find a pleasure coming up from Canal Street." This faintly ironic mirth was the accepted manner between them, their only durable defense from the world and each other.

"Do you really have to be late?"

"Sometimes—not always."

"Then you'll get scraps. Virgie says she'll give notice if she can't have her evenings."

"Couldn't we spare her?"

"Don't you believe it! Not after I spent a whole afternoon chasing a cook through Jackson Ward, and Mother interviewed thirteen domestic problems. Virgie's a poor cook, but she's cheap, and when they're cheap, they have not only rights but privileges. Her privilege waits at the back gate for her every evening in an old Ford. If she keeps him waiting too long, he honks his horn three times and drives off in a huff."

"Well, we can't expect her not to have a life of her own." He rose, poured out a cup of coffee and poured it back again into the percolator.

"Not on eight dollars a week, anyway. Mother says they used to stay from six in the morning till ten at night for eight dollars a month; but that was before the war or the flood." Her tone was flippant, and he could not tell whether she meant to be mocking or serious. He could never tell with the young, especially with his own children.

[35]

"I suppose some of us are really better off," he said, "than we used to be."

"That doesn't mean you, does it, Daddy?"

"Maybe not. When we married on forty dollars a week, we thought we were just beginning. But I suppose I'm not the sort that's made to get on. Your mother has always held that against me." The softened look in her eyes was too much like pity, and he asked quickly, "Are you tired, daughter?"

She shook her head with a frown. "Oh, I'm all right. I'm perfectly all right."

"Nothing worrying you?"

"Nothing in the world. What could worry me?"

He filled his cup from the percolator and brought it back to the table. "A good many things. Isn't everybody worried, even your Uncle William, who has more money than he knows what to do with, but still not enough."

"Well, I'm not worried. I'm not a bit worried."

"I wish you could stop working."

"I like the shop. And besides . . . besides I couldn't have married Peter if I hadn't kept up my work. Give me one of yours," she added, reaching for a cigarette, "I left mine in the living room."

"You've been smoking too much. That chain-smoking makes you nervous."

"Nervous?" She laughed and drew away while she inhaled quickly. "I don't know what nerves are."

"You will know soon enough if you don't look out." Her natural pallor had deepened in the past few weeks, and there were faint violet circles under her eyes.

"I don't care. I'm not going to look out." She smoked rapidly in short breathless puffs, and then stopped to light a fresh cigarette from the unfinished one in her hand.

"You rush all day and all night too."

"I'm obliged to have a little fun sometimes. I can't just sit at home with Mother in the evenings. And Peter likes going about. He says he needs distraction, after the hospital."

"Why don't you stop work and let him look after you?"

Her eager face hardened, and it seemed to him that she had grown older while he watched her. "I like to work. And I want money. I want to save up enough for a home of our own."

"But Peter might do that. Doesn't he, too, want a home?"

Her lip quivered; and for an instant, he dreaded to see her break down. Then, while he waited for tears, she uttered a forlorn small laugh that tore at his heartstrings. "Of course Peter wants a home of our own," she said. "He'd adore having one."

"Well, he must be making enough now. It means a great deal having you with us, but I prefer having you happy. Your mother and I don't spend much, and we can manage without your help."

"What would you do?" she asked derisively. "Take in other lodgers?"

"We might even do that. But we'd find a way, somehow."

"When Mother doesn't come downstairs, and Virgie must have her evenings? I suppose you'd do the cooking."

A dry sound, between a gasp and a laugh, broke from him. "If I did, it would be better than Virgie's. But I'd do more than cook, daughter, to make you happy."

She turned hurriedly away, but not before he had noted the tremor of a sob in her throat and a moist gleam in her eyes. "But it mightn't make me happy," she said. "Happiness is a queer thing . . . or perhaps I'm queer. . . ."

"I'd do more than that for you, Roy," he repeated,

and felt ashamed of the tenderness in his voice. How the young, nowadays, despised tenderness!

For the first time she looked at him directly, and the bright challenge in her smile moved him with its pathos. "You're an old dear," she said flippantly, "but I'm afraid the lodgers wouldn't appreciate the kind of coffee Grandmother used to make. They'd just as soon stir up a spoonful of powder in a cup of hot water."

"You may laugh as much as you like, but I'm serious. I don't like the way you're looking, and I'm going to speak to Peter about it."

"Oh, you mustn't." Fear ruffled her voice. "You mustn't speak to Peter, Daddy."

"Why not? Why shouldn't I tell him your mother and I can manage alone?"

"Because it would hurt him. Peter isn't to blame."

"I'm not so sure of that. I—"

"But he isn't, and I won't have him hurt. He can't afford a change now. He has so many expenses. And it is important for him to put up an appearance. It means so much for him to have an office in the best neighborhood. After all, it wasn't his fault that we came here."

"I see." He would have pretended to see anything if only to quiet her fear. "And I won't speak to Peter. But I doubt whether it's ever wise for two families to live together, especially when one is just starting out and one is almost ending. It puts too heavy a strain upon family affection." It was like trying to see through a fog of words, he thought, and he felt vaguely irritated because he did not know where he was looking or what he expected. But there was tension in the atmosphere, something strained and secretive and disturbing. If only Roy would speak plainly and tell him why, in spite of her gay mockery, she looked troubled and anxious.

"Oh, we're all right," she said impatiently. "I suppose we don't scrap any more than other families. And after

Stanley's wedding there won't be so many of us. I only wish," she added passionately, "that she could be married tomorrow."

"Isn't next week soon enough?" It was unlike Roy, he told himself, to be so unstrung. Could she have quarreled with Peter? No, that was unlikely. In the two years they had spent with Roy's parents, first in the old house and then in the third story of the new house, he had never heard so much as an angry word pass between them. Some husbands might have been spoiled, but Asa had always assumed that Peter was different. A man as dominant as that commanded adoration.

"Oh, yes, yes," she said now. "But I can't help wishing the wedding could be tomorrow."

"A week longer can't matter, dear, not really."

"No, not really. It's just that I'm sick of the noise and the fuss and the—oh, and the . . ."

"You've been doing too much. But as long as you're happy . . ."

"As long as I have Peter."

"Well, you have Peter. So that's that." The most appealing thing in youth, he thought, is a timeless quality, a constant susceptibility to life. How vulnerable it is, and how resentful of the thing that has wounded it! His love for her was a sudden stab in his heart. Neither of his other children (not Andrew, who was average and proud of it, nor Stanley, who was an ardent changeling) had ever seemed to him, as Roy did so often, the embodiment of his old longing for release and for escape. Her very mockery was a tonic, for she mocked openly at all the images which he had feared and obeyed in his conscious mind.

"Yes, I have Peter," Roy said almost fiercely. "But he's free. Peter knows he's free."

"Free?"

"I mean I'd never hold him. He knows I'd never hold

[39]

him if he wanted his freedom. We've always understood that. It isn't like the old way of marriage. Neither of us believes in that old way. Both of us are perfectly free to change if we wish—if we . . ."

Free! Free! There were moments, and this threatened to be one of them, when the eternal patter of inexperience wore on his nerves. After all, what was freedom and who was ever free, in a world which entangled you at the instant of birth? The social web, he thought, was worse than unyielding; it was inescapable. For fifty-nine years, and as far back as he had wished for anything but the moon, he had hungered for freedom. And he had never even known what freedom was like; he had never had so much as a glimpse of its features. After the first few months of marriage, the impulse toward liberty, if not the visible form, had been his earliest thought on waking and his last thought when he lay down at night. And yet if Lavinia had said to him, as Roy said to Peter, "You are free," what difference would it have made? Freedom, he knew, was not a thing that could be packed into a phrase or a word. The intangible web was still there. It was stronger than impulse, because it was woven not of a single strand, but of an intricate multitude. Like every other unsatisfied and continuously thwarted human being, he had struggled against a conspiracy of tradition and of custom, of reason and of economics.

"That's fine, darling," he said presently, "even though I'm not sure it's sensible." He poured out a second cup of coffee while she slipped down from the table.

"I know, Daddy; but I hate being sensible."

"Why didn't you go out with the others?"

"Somebody had to stay with Mother. She almost had a heart attack when we left her last night, and you hadn't come in."

"Where's Stanley?"

"Aunt Charlotte telephoned for her. She has something

to show her . . . a lace cloth . . . or something. I told her I'd unpack the other presents."

"How did she go?"

"In her car. Peter says she's a good driver."

"And where's Peter?"

"He had an emergency call, but he's coming straight back. Craig is going by to get Stanley, and Andrew and Maggie are coming to look at the presents. You'd think Maggie was getting married again. She takes such an interest."

"And you don't, Roy?" he asked, as she went ahead of him through the swinging door.

While he stopped to switch off the light in the kitchen she glanced back at him with a cool little laugh. "Oh, yes, I do, but I wish it were over. There's Mother's bell again. You'd better go up and find out what she wants. If Uncle William comes, I suppose she'll expect to see him."

"Is he coming tonight?"

"I don't know, do you?"

"I know rather less than nothing about William—or about Charlotte either."

"Well, Aunt Charlotte is right enough. She isn't nearly so soft and silly as she looks. But there's too much of Uncle William. He seems to get all over the place."

"Still, my dear, we are living under his roof."

They were standing at the foot of the staircase, and when he turned on the bottom step and looked down at her, she raised her chin with a spirited gesture.

"Well, it *is* his roof, isn't it?" he repeated.

"The thing I dislike most about him," she burst out resentfully, "is that I ought to be grateful to him. I despise having to be grateful."

"I know. It's easy to feel that way. If we refused to take what he gives, we shouldn't have to be grateful. I sometimes think," he added seriously, "that the people I envy most are those who have no appearances to keep up."

"You mean the people who haven't any children?"

"Well, even the most unworldly men and women are still worldly for their children, aren't they?"

"Poor Daddy," she said lightly. "You might have done very well for yourself if you hadn't had us."

He shook his head, with a return of his quizzical smile. "Eccentric as it may sound, my dear, I'd rather have had you."

"I wonder . . ." she began and then broke off with a laugh. "I suppose it is easier," she continued after a pause, "when the bottom drops out to drop with it. Mother is always saying that the bottom has dropped out of everything."

He chuckled under his breath, as if he were afraid Lavinia might resent an improper sense of humor. "A great tradition is an expensive luxury," he said. "Falling back on the past may lend inspiration, and it may also lead to gradual hardening of the arteries."

IV

LAVINIA looked up from Mr. Wodehouse's *Young Men in Spats,* which she was languidly reading, because somebody had told her it was a cheerful book and did not deal with the poor. "What an odd sense of humor the English have," she remarked. "It doesn't seem real."

"I heard your bell," Asa said. "Do you want anything?"

She gazed at him with the calm but foreboding expression which presaged either a reprimand or a heart attack. "Virgie didn't come back for the tray, and she hasn't given me my digitalis. She gets flightier every day she lives."

"Was she ever worth her salt?" he asked irritably, while he picked up the tray from the small table beside Lavinia's daybed. In the morning her front sitting room was the sunniest place in the house, and in late afternoon the beams of the sunset flooded the twin beds in the adjoining bedroom. Glancing through the doorway, he could see the two beds with the night table between. At precisely nine o'clock, unless William and Charlotte had kept her up, he would turn down the beds and help her into the one with the comfortable springs and mattress and the quilt of pure eiderdown.

"You're late again," she said in a resigned voice.

"I can't always be on time." With the tray in his hands he waited, in subdued exasperation, between the table and the door.

Her large, heavy, composed face, in which disposition had long since triumphed over contour and feature, appeared to him to hang there, like a moon in a sullen sky. She wore her soft, thin hair strained back from her high forehead, and the added length of countenance gave a

deceptive appearance of intellect to her thick dark eye-brows and to her humorless, slightly bulging eyes, which in a dim light reminded Asa of faded Malaga grapes. Her spreading figure, unconfined by an old-fashioned wrapper of purple challis, seemed to fill the entire space of the couch.

In the past twelve years, ever since an eminent special-ist had advised her against any and every exertion, she had discovered that a physical malady may be turned, by a prudent farsighted woman, into a moral support. After forty years of unavailing struggle to make over a world of which she disapproved, and a personal destiny which she resented, she had found, as other rebels against fate have learned before her, that only from com-plete surrender can one win freedom in security. As a strikingly plain girl in a society where a modest amount of feature was regarded as necessary, she had suffered inwardly from romantic fantasies and outwardly from a neglectful father and a morbidly malicious younger brother. Though the idea had never entered her slow but expansive mind, the years of sheltered invalidism had been the least unhappy part of her life. Now, at last, in the ample leisure of hypochondria, she had transferred alike her fantasies and her longings to her favorite daughter. All the beauty she had been denied in youth, all the emotional ecstasy she had craved and missed had been miraculously fulfilled through the simple extension of her maternal ego. In Stanley she could live more in-tensely and more abundantly than she had ever lived in herself.

"I'll take this down and come back," he said.

"Please take my thermos bottle too. Virgie forgot to fill it."

Going into the bedroom, he picked up, from beside an open Bible, the rose-colored thermos bottle and found a place for it on the crowded tray. "Is this all?"

"Where are the girls? Nobody's been near me since dinner."

"Roy is unpacking Stanley's presents. She says Charlotte telephoned for Stanley."

"She didn't tell me. I wonder why she didn't tell me?"

"You can find out when she comes back. Craig is going to bring her home."

While he carried the tray down the back stairs to the kitchen, Asa told himself gratefully that his legs at least were as good as they had ever been. He was fortunate, he supposed, to be underweight and not over tall. It was easier on the legs, especially when one was kept going up and down a steep flight of stairs. As he passed through the front hall on his way back, he saw that the lights had been switched on in the living room, which looked gay and cheerful with the dim blue walls and the brightly flowered chintz Roy had picked up as a bargain. In the small room adjoining, he could see Roy bending over a box as she unpacked the silver. How lovely her movements were, he thought, watching her, and how seldom anyone noticed the beauty in movement or the grace in a flowing gesture. His mother had prided herself on her walk and on what used to be called her noble bearing; but his mother had been dead now for nearly thirty years, and only Minerva, their washerwoman, had retained a noble bearing.

Lavinia laid the book aside and turned to her more congenial knitting. "I hate to make so much trouble," she said regretfully, "but, after all, as Dr. Buchanan says, it is harder on me than on anyone else."

"That's true, my dear. Anyway, it isn't hard on Buchanan."

"What did you say, Asa?"

"Nothing. I was only asking if there was anything else."

"Not until you bring me my malted milk. Unless, of

course, Uncle William and Aunt Charlotte would like to see me."

"I wish you could get out of these rooms, Lavinia. It must be depressing never to get out."

"Of course, it is depressing, but you know what the doctor says."

"Are you sure that Buchanan isn't just another old fogy?"

"He's known me all my life, Asa. He understands my constitution."

"All the same, I believe it would do you good if you made an—effort."

The word, he perceived instantly, was unfortunate, for Lavinia, in common with other victims of that uncertain organ, the heart, resented bitterly the suggestion that an effort was commendable. Since she was never acrimonious, however, she reproached him, not in words, but with the patient gaze of an aging Madonna. "I'm going to Stanley's wedding if I have to be taken in a wheelchair," she said mildly.

"Well, you mustn't strain your heart," he replied hurriedly. After all, he supposed Buchanan really did know what was best. Damn it, he had said the wrong thing; but then he always said the wrong thing to Lavinia. The room felt suddenly stuffy; and moving to the window, he looked out on the darkening leaves of the maples. It couldn't go on forever, he thought, nothing went on forever. A change would come next year, or maybe tomorrow. So many things might happen; so many things must happen if only one waited. William was an old man, and when William died, Lavinia would be wealthy, and he himself would be free. There was time still for a little happiness at the end. There was time still for a life of his own, for a few years of freedom with Kate and the two dogs and the broad river at Hunter's Fare.

Through the outer husk of his mind he became aware

that Lavinia was speaking. "Asa, are you easy about this marriage?"

He turned sharply, while a pricking sensation ran over him. "No, Lavinia, I am not ever easy about any marriage."

Lavinia dropped her knitting and stared at him with eyes which seemed bottomless but empty. "I've been worried for some time, but I did not say anything because I tried to hope for the best."

His forehead puckered. "Tell me the worst." He knew she enjoyed hurting him, but his defensive irony, he told himself, was invulnerable.

"It's nothing definite. Only I've a feeling . . . a feeling . . ."

He shook his head. "Well, I've a feeling, too, but a feeling isn't evidence."

She picked up her knitting and put it down again. "Of course you wouldn't have noticed it," she said, "but Stanley isn't really in love with Craig."

"The devil she isn't!"

"Please, Asa."

"Then why is she marrying him? Nobody is making her do it."

"That's what I've been trying to make out. But she won't talk to me. She won't tell me anything."

"So far as I know, she is the only one who approves of this marriage—if we except Craig."

"She was mad about him in the beginning . . . or she behaved as if she were. I suppose there was an excitement in taking him away from Gertrude Bolton, and he is good-looking. Don't you think he is very good-looking?"

He nodded impatiently. "Yes, oh, yes. But I'm not strong on pretty men."

"He isn't a sissy. Craig isn't a bit of a sissy."

"Well, I've nothing against him. If I had to choose, I'd pick him any day rather than Peter."

[47]

"Oh, so would I. I could never understand Roy's infatuation for Peter. But I believe she's just as much in love today as she was when she married him."

"That we'll never understand; and, thank God, we don't have to try. The whole younger generation looks to me like a sum that doesn't add up."

Lavinia sighed. "I used to think I understood Stanley."

"Well, you didn't. We don't understand any of them . . . not the first thing about them."

"When I try to talk to her seriously, she puts me off or goes out of the room."

"What I want to know is why she's marrying the fellow."

"When I ask her, she laughs and says she's crazy about him. You know how wildly they talk. But I have a feeling that she's grown tired of him since the excitement has worn off. The trouble is that Craig gives way to her all the time. He has lost his head completely, and of course that's a fatal thing when one is in love."

"I imagine it would be, with Stanley. Don't you think, though, you'd better have it out with her before it's too late?"

"Is it ever too late nowadays? They talk of marriage, even Roy, as if it could be done over as easily as a permanent wave."

"No matter. You'd better have it out with her before she goes any farther. There's no use my speaking to her. Now, if it were Roy . . ."

"Do you think Roy would have listened to you if you'd advised her against Peter?"

"I do not. Nor against anything else that she wanted. Yet Roy's fine, through and through. She's as square as a man."

"Do you think she's happy?"

He hedged abruptly. "Who is happy?"

"Who is?" she repeated, and shook her head. "I sup-

pose some people are. But the young are trying to build happiness without any foundation."

He gazed at her reflectively. After all, Lavinia might be a fraud, but she was nobody's fool.

"Do you think we older ones did any better? Whose mess are we cleaning up now?"

"But we were young when we made it. Don't the young always make a mess of the world? Only children seem to be different from us. They won't even wait to do things over. They are always running away from life."

"Not Roy. Roy isn't like that. She's straight, and she's thorough. But I know what you mean. We were muddled, too, but we stayed to finish what we had begun."

"They don't, nowadays. They lack"—she hesitated for the right word and breathed deeply—"they lack staying power."

"Well, they're our children. We didn't make them, and we didn't make ourselves. It seems to me"—the corners of his eyes wrinkled—"that there's nothing we can do about it. That's the bell. I'd better go downstairs, hadn't I?"

"Not looking like that."

"What's wrong with the way I look? You don't expect me to change?"

"It won't hurt to brush your hair and make yourself tidy. What on earth have you been leaning against?"

"Stone. I've been sitting on some stone steps."

"And that suit was cleaned only last week."

"It will brush off. I can brush it."

"But there are green stains. I can see them. Why in the world did you have to sit down on dirty steps?"

In a minute, he told himself, she would begin to peck at him, after he had put up with enough, and more than enough, for any day in the year. "For pleasure," he replied tartly. "That was my only motive. I sat down for pleasure." As he turned away and went into the

bathroom, he heard her smothered ejaculation. "I some-times think, Asa, that you act like this just to make trouble."

Maybe so, maybe so. He washed his face and hands, and when afterwards he brushed his thinning hair, he frowned slightly at the reflection in the mirror above the gushing taps and the porcelain basin. That was not, he admitted without prejudice, the face he would have chosen. The strong man in the depths should have assembled a harder collection of features, as well as a firmer stand of hair on the chest. What he saw was a brown, hollowed face, puckered about the eyes, with a tight, sensitive mouth, and a faintly sardonic gaze which gave away nothing. His skin was breaking up, his hair was going gray; and what had he ever had in return? A little freedom for our generation might have spared us great misery, he thought; the young today have so much freedom that they do not know how to enjoy it. But what good had ever come of the emotional starvation and the moral tyranny he had endured with Lavinia? What pur-pose had they served, except perhaps as a warning ex-ample to a generation that ignored all warnings and every example? For the sake of a past tradition he had spent nearly thirty years doing things that he hated and not doing things that he liked; and at the end of that long self-discipline, when he was too old to begin over again, he had seen his code of conduct flatten out and shrivel up as utterly as a balloon that is pricked. And yet the denial of one's nature, he told himself, is not the worst. The worst is to feel that the moral universe, the very foundation of all order, has trembled, has toppled over, has vanished.

For an instant he stared blankly at the secretive face in the mirror; and while he stood there, he was visited by a feeling that never before had he ever really seen the fea-tures at which he was gazing. Then the uneasy sensation

passed as quickly as it had come. He fastened his clean collar, carefully knotted the blue and gray striped tie, and went back to Lavinia.

"That must be Andrew and Maggie," she was saying. "They are making so much noise. If they want to scream, why don't they turn off the radio?"

"I thought that bray was William's."

"Oh, Asa, why will you?"

"What's wrong with a bray?"

"It isn't respectful. Uncle William is a grand old gentleman."

"He is. Are you sure you don't want anything?"

"No, I'll wait till you come up. Stanley may have something to tell me, and, anyway, I may doze off if they don't make too much noise."

She reclined there on her comfortable couch, imperturbable, exacting, serenely centered in her own egoism, which embraced her dream life in Stanley. Was she really a dull woman, as he had always believed, or was she diabolically sagacious under all the pretense? Though she rarely left her room, whenever she did so it became a public occasion; and her influence had rayed out, and extended very far beyond her household into languishing moral causes and browbeating social reforms.

"Then I'll go down and try to help Roy. She has all the work to do."

"Of course it's hard on her." Lavinia breathed a martyr's sigh and picked up her book. "But, after all, Stanley is getting married, and a girl doesn't get married but once."

"Oh, doesn't she?" he retorted grimly, as he went out of the room. No, it couldn't last. Nothing ever lasted forever. Kate and the wind over the river would still be there when all this had dropped into the bottomless past.

V

WELL, here we are!" William was mumbling. "Well, well, well! oh, well, well!" Such was the playful tone which he imagined young girls expected from men in the prime of life.

The small living room appeared to be crowded; but then, as Asa reflected, William and Charlotte made a crowd even when they were alone. William Fitzroy, the wealthiest and therefore the leading citizen of Queenborough, bore himself with the air of superiority which only a very wide margin of vested interests can confer. His manner diffused, as a citizen, a sense of immediate importance and, as a sustaining member of St. Luke's Episcopal Church, a pious hope of future immortality. He was a hugh unwieldy man, whose paunch had once been rotund, but was now, since he had dieted for a stomach disorder, rapidly falling into flabbiness. His head was immense, pear-shaped, and almost entirely bald, except for a straggling fringe at the back of his neck. He had long, angular legs, and his large, knobby feet splayed out from his lean ankles as if they did not quite belong to him. Though he wore expensive shoes, made by the best bootmaker in New York, he was a martyr to fallen arches. Yet, so triumphant is the victory of will over circumstance that, in spite of these and other physical impediments, he remained at eighty not only a prop to the failing world of industry and finance, but a congenial, or at least an urgent, companion of adolescence. Completely sane on the subject of business or speculation or the distracted state of public affairs, his major faculties, or so it appeared to Asa's bird's-eye view, had begun to soften dangerously concerning the youthful female figure. Even

in public he seemed to lose control of his hands as soon as
a young girl came within reach of his arms.

"Well, well, are you saving a kiss for your old uncle?"
he demanded, with a sly wink at Stanley. "But you
aren't going to turn your cheek, not after that check, are
you?"

"Oh, Uncle William, you're simply wonderful!" Stanley gasped, twisting lightly out of his moist embrace. "That
check was too marvelous."

"Liked it, did you? Well, I reckon it won't be lasting you
long."

She tossed her charming head. "But there's always
more where it came from."

"What's that, you minx?" William brayed in delight.
"Do you hear what she says, Charlotte? You'd better keep
a close hand on your pocketbook."

On the far side of the room, which was still very near,
Charlotte was bending over the flat silver Craig's father
had given to the bride. "Very pretty," she said in her
agreeable voice. "I always liked that pattern." She was an
amiable old woman, with a pleasant expression, who had
been very handsome before she had fattened out of her
small features and her once slender figure. Nothing remained of her now but an unfailing appetite and a mountain of smooth and unworried flesh, which was inclined
to bulge generously in the wrong places. She had once
been an ashen blonde, and when she smiled there was
still a flash of sunny blue in her eyes. For years Asa had
suspected that she was by no means so simple as she pretended to be, and then suddenly, when William was ab-
sent one day, he had seen her display actual intelligence
and a firm hand with an emergency. After this, he had
observed her more narrowly, and had detected the
lurking sagacity in her glance and the firm traces of character underlying her puffed face.

Stanley had darted across the room, and his eyes fol-

lowed her. Something was wrong. Tired probably. Hadn't Lavinia said that a wedding was always a strain, and that most brides were nervous wrecks when they set out for their honeymoon? But Stanley was prettier than ever, he thought, in this primrose-colored wisp of a frock, which made her look like a spring flower. Though Craig kept close to her side, it struck Asa abruptly that Craig was not included within her range of vision. Yet Craig was extraordinarily attractive tonight. You noted a striking contrast between his light restless eyes and his sallow skin and sharply edged features.

I wonder where Peter is, Asa thought; but Peter came in almost immediately, a picture of vital energy with his healthy skin, which flushed easily from heat or cold, his thick reddish hair, rising in a slight crest from his forehead, and his conquering manner, which irritated Asa, who had never conquered anything except himself. He's good-looking, but there can be too much of a good thing, Asa thought. His skin is too tight over his muscles. It must be especially elastic to stretch like that and not burst. And he has the hands, but not the temperament, of a surgeon. I wonder, after all, if hands, strong, delicate hands, are the more important. I wonder . . .

Until now he had missed Roy, but he saw presently that she was still in the small room, unpacking the silver. She looked tired, he thought, and checked an impulse to tell her she was wearing herself out. There were lines between her winged eyebrows and the corners of her mouth drooped. She's too young to look so worn, he decided. Or was it only the hideous white shades which made the electricity as searching as sunlight? Everyone appeared ghastly, except Stanley, who bloomed with excitement or happiness.

But something was wrong; the thought tugged at his heart. Voices were too high. Everybody was talking at

once, and Roy's hands were trembling as she picked up
and dropped and picked up yet again a hideously em-
bossed silver vase.

"That's pretty," William croaked, as he held up the ornament. "Now, that's what I call handsome."

"It will do nicely for flowers," said Charlotte, who
would have encouraged anything, even senility, so long as
it made William happy.

Stanley laughed. "Isn't it all simply thrilling?"

"Remember to telephone me as soon as your dress
comes," Charlotte insisted. "It's lucky for you that we
haven't any daughters of our own, or I could never let
you wear my own wedding veil."

"Oh, how wonderful," Maggie sighed in ecstasy. "That
marvelous rose point!"

"It's so lovely of you, dear Aunt Charlotte. I want you
to help put it on me." The most charming thing in
Stanley's face, Asa told himself, was the way her smile
seemed to begin first in her eyes, so deep and changeable
in color, and then to ripple on and linger in an edge of
light on her lips. Here again, as with Peter's hands and
temperament, he thought, was an occasion when the substance and the pattern were not in complete harmony.

"You'll soon be rid of us, Father," a voice said at his
back; and there were Andrew and Maggie, the happiest
pair, Asa had long ago decided, that he had ever known.
Yet he never looked at Andrew, whom he regarded indulgently as perfection of the commonplace, without
wondering whether his son also harbored a second self,
repressed but rebellious, beneath his ordinary exterior.
No, the settled smugness of Andrew's geniality proved
beyond a doubt that he accepted the universe at its own
exorbitant value. When one observed him, alert, hearty,
continually bandying a smile or a jest, and noted his
smoothly parted fawn-colored hair and his undistin-
guished nose and chin, one saw at a glance that he was

designed for contentment in any average scheme of things in general.

"You oughtn't to tease Father, as good as he's been to us," protested Maggie, who had made herself popular by always telling people what they wanted to hear. Small, plump, neither pretty nor plain, and excessively kind-hearted, she was a favorite with everyone, including Asa, and for exactly the same reason. No one, not even her husband, had ever heard her utter a disagreeable word, and seldom a true one. But, as with most persons who see only the best, her vision was usually shortsighted and often inaccurate.

"Well, you know he's glad to get us off his hands. Who wouldn't be?" Andrew chaffed, while Asa told himself that the bantering tone struck a false note in the oppressive air of the room. Or was it only that he himself was feeling his fifty-nine years and letting his nerves play a trick on him?

"Not Father." Maggie patted Asa's sleeve with a hand as soft and light as the paw of a kitten. Though his daughter-in-law was more flattering to him than any of his own children, she seemed to him now, as he looked at her, to be well-intentioned but insignificant. Tonight, his mind was occupied by some undercurrent of life, as if he were involved in a play within a play, in some secret yet violent drama of smothered antagonism. He glanced round inquiringly. Had anyone else in the room felt this charged atmosphere, this thickening of the air, as when a storm gathers but does not break? No one apparently had felt the faintest disturbance. It was his talk with Roy, he supposed (he was always sensitive about Roy), and then Lavinia's veiled hints and mysterious evasions, that had started him off at this tangent of apprehension. Long before his marriage, even as a boy, he had known a queer susceptibility as to what people were thinking or were trying not to think under the surface.

[57]

William had followed Stanley, while he made a mumbling effort to secure her undivided regard. Charlotte was placidly examining a lace tablecloth. Craig Fleming, hastily smoking one cigarette after another, leaned against the wall in one corner and stared moodily at Stanley, as if his gaze were drawn by an invisible thread toward her face. Sitting on the floor behind a table, Roy was still unwrapping pieces of silver, as if her life or her happiness depended on getting the task over. Once, Asa noticed, her busy hands dropped apart, while she turned her head and glanced casually, without expression, from Stanley to Craig and from Craig to Peter, who was pretending to listen to William. At every lull in the mingled sounds Maggie, who imagined that by screaming cheerfully one could make people enjoy themselves, would open her unpainted lips and emit a series of unmeaning ejaculations. No, there was nothing unusual, Asa reflected; but it was not right. Standing there, he saw the room, saw the persons and objects, as if all were bathed in a fluid quality of suspense. He was a normal parent; he loved his children, especially Roy; and some natural or unnatural perception in which Lavinia had seemed to share warned him that the happiness of these children was threatened. By what? By whom? From what unseen antagonist? He could not answer these questions. He refused even to imagine what the answers would be. All he admitted was that Lavinia and he had drawn closer together in the face of a danger so impalpable that they hesitated to give it a shape or a name. Lavinia, whom he disliked, stood alone with him in defense of an idea which did not exist as a reality, and perhaps had never existed. Lifting his eyes to the ceiling, he watched a swarm of gnats, so fine as to be almost invisible, whirling in a ball round the light. Against the porcelain globe these gnats, he thought idly, were like a golden net. From the open window, through which they had drifted, a timid breeze

stirred gently, fluttered the transparent curtain, and then dropped, sighing, back into the shadows.

"Peter!" Roy called sharply. "Do be good and bring us something to drink. Aunt Charlotte takes only ginger ale."

"Oh, don't send Peter. He's helping me," Stanley protested.

Peter, who had started to the door, halted abruptly and glanced from his wife to her sister. For an instant, no longer, it seemed to Asa that two wills met and clashed. Stanley can have no motive, Asa told himself, but the daring test of her power. Her mystery, like her charm, is nothing more than the secret wildness of youth. . . .

"You'll get us something, won't you, Father?" she asked in a caressing voice. "Scotch and soda for Uncle William, but rye highballs for the others."

"And ginger ale for Aunt Charlotte and the girls," Asa added. "But the whiskey is Peter's. The best I have is beer in the icebox."

"Oh, you're welcome to my whiskey," Peter broke in eagerly. "The Scotch isn't so good as Mr. Fitzroy's, but the rye was a prewar bargain."

"That's a long time," William said. "So I think I'll try the rye with plain water, and just a thimbleful, anyway." His genial temper was suddenly dampened by the recollection that whiskey had been forbidden him.

"Beer for me, Mr. Timberlake," called Craig, who was looking a trifle disturbed—or was it merely pensive? "Do you need any help?"

"None in the world, my boy. I shouldn't know what to do with it."

Well, he was glad that his daughters did not drink whiskey. He was glad that drinking as a revolutionary gesture had gone out with prohibition. As he crossed the hall on his way to the pantry, he was followed by an empty tinkle of laughter.

"Isn't this simply swell?"

"But what can you do with it?"

"Oh, anything."

"Anything?"

"Yes, anything."

"Uncle William, she says anything."

A scream from Maggie, and quickened movement from the radio. "That's simply adorable. Oh, Uncle William, will you really? What on earth should I do without you?"

"It looks as if you couldn't get married without me, doesn't it?"

"You ought to give her away. She really belongs to you."

"Oh, Andrew, but Father must give her away."

"I know, Maggie, of course, Father . . . I was just thinking of all Uncle William has done for her. . . ."

"Well, who has ever done as much for any of us as Daddy?" That was Roy's voice, with a deepened undertone which threatened an outbreak of anger. "Hasn't he worked like a slave for us, without thanks, ever since we were born?"

"Now, I say, Roy, what's stung you?"

Roy wasn't herself. Asa could tell that by the jarring edge to her tone. Yet he might have known she would fly to his defense. He could trust her not ever to let anyone except herself be unjust to him.

"Now, now, children, don't quarrel," Charlotte said soothingly. "Andrew was only joking."

"I don't care." Roy's tone was still ruffled. "He oughtn't to joke like that."

It was safer, anyway, to be in the pantry, Asa thought, while he separated cubes of ice and placed the whiskey and the ginger ale on the largest tray he could find. Peter's whiskey, even the best, of which he was inordinately proud, could not compare with William's old

Bumgardner or William's bourbon; yet, oddly enough, William would prefer to drink Peter's, just as he enjoyed rowdy gatherings of young people more than he did his wife's dinner parties, where the food and drink were superlatively good, but older company predominated. Why was it, Asa asked himself, arranging glasses and bottles over the Venetian scene which decorated the tray, that rowdiness had become so popular alike among old and young? In his mother's time, even after her fallen fortunes, nothing stronger than Madeira and thin biscuits would have been served on such an occasion. But nobody, not even those persons who had valued ceremony in the past, had any patience nowadays with the graces of living. For graces, like manners, made pauses and postponed activities, whereas all that the present appeared to want was to go faster and faster. Acceleration, not beauty, was the strange god of our modern worship. Already he could hear them asking if he would ever return. In a minute Peter or Roy would come out to look for him, and he had not as yet discovered Virgie's hiding place for the tin of Uneeda biscuits.

There was a knock at the kitchen door, and he paused to wonder whether Virgie could have parted so soon from her privilege. But when he opened the door, he found Minerva, the washerwoman, with her basket of clean clothes on the step at her feet.

"I'm glad it's you, Minerva," he said. "I was afraid it might be Virgie."

"I ain't Virgie," replied Minerva, who spoke with bilingual emphasis, slipping under stress from English idiom into the full flavor of African dialect, "and I'm right glad I ain't. I couldn't get here any sooner with these clothes," she explained. "That old Ford broke down just when we'd started the engine, and I had to wait till it was fixed.

What are you doing out here, Mr. Asa? The kitchen ain't the place for a gentleman."

"Maybe I'm not a gentleman, Minerva."

"Go 'way from here, Mr. Asa. That ain't the right way to talk."

"Anyway, I'm a better cook than Virgie, and I'm not bragging."

"Have you got company tonight?" Minerva inquired, as she eased the heavy basket down in the corner behind the door.

"The girls have. It's the same old bunch, and they want drinks."

"You ain't goin' to carry in that waiter, Mr. Asa. I reckon your ma would have a fit if she could see you toting a waiter."

"Well, she won't see it, though you've forgotten how many I toted when I was a kid."

"Naw, sir, I ain't forgot, but you're a gentleman grown now. You wait till I get off my hat and find me an apron. I'll be right back in a minute." She passed into the servant's room jutting off from the kitchen, and returned immediately without hat or apron. "There's a whole parcel of aprons in the press," she said scornfully, "and not a clean one among 'em. Do I look right enough as I am?"

"You look like a disinherited princess, Minerva. There, they're shouting again. You'd better hurry, or we'll have the whole pack in the kitchen."

"I'm going, Mr. Asa, I'm going as fast as I can." With a regal air, she picked up the tray and swept through the pantry and the hall into the living room. Yes, Minerva was a remarkable woman. Had her skin been white instead of pale yellow, she might have become a power in the community, or perhaps a recognized genius on the stage. I'm glad she saved me, he thought. I don't like

waiting on people, and that hullabaloo gives me a headache. There's no doubt about it, I was not made for a mixer. . . . The sentiment might be antisocial, but it seemed to him that human beings were at their worst when they were enjoying themselves. On the whole, he preferred his fellow mortals when they were more repressed and less natural. But the next minute, it seemed, Minerva was back in the kitchen and had put on her hat.

"Some more young folks have come in," she said. "They certny can raise a rumpus, but they ain't saying nothing a-tall. You've got mighty fine children, Mr. Asa, and I'm proud I was their mammy. Stanley looks as pretty as a picture, and poor Mr. Craig, he's a real nice gentleman."

"Why do you say 'poor Mr. Craig,' Minerva?"

Minerva bit her lip and glanced out into the darkness. "Oh, well, Mr. Asa, he ain't even married yet," she replied vaguely, "but he sure is a nice gentleman."

"He is, and they're fine children, all of them. I've always had a soft spot for them—especially for one."

"Roy favors your ma. She always did, even when she was little."

"Yes, there's something about her, but she'll never be the beauty my mother was."

Minerva shook her head. "The Lord don't make 'em like that any longer. I can recollect just as well the way Ma used to let me peep in the door when young Miss was all dressed up to go out in the evening. She'd look like she was made of roses, and she was smelling like a rose too."

Asa blinked his eyes as if to blot out a memory. "She used to come in to tell me good night after I was in bed. I can see her now, all in satin and lace, with a lace scarf over her hair. But I don't like to think of it. She had a mean life at the end. . . ."

"That's so, sir. She certny did come down after your pa

went." Minerva looked at him pensively before she straightened her hat and hung her knitted bag over her arm. "I reckon I'd better be getting along now."

"Well, you've good children, too, Minerva. I saw your boy Parry as I was coming home by the old house. You've got a good husband and good children."

"Yes, sir, the Lord has used me mighty well. That He has, Mr. Asa. But I can't feel as settled as I'd like to about Parry. He's got ideas in his head, and I ain't never seen anything come of ideas but trouble and worse trouble."

"You mean he's ambitious?"

"That's it, sir. That's what it is. He ain't satisfied with the old ways, like most of us colored folks. He's setting out to be different. He ain't satisfied to be a waiter, or even a letter carrier. He's bent on being a lawyer."

"I shouldn't worry. He's young yet."

"He's young, Mr. Asa, but he's bent."

"By the time he's ready, he may find an opening. There are plenty of colored lawyers and doctors now, you know, and some very good ones."

"You can't go to college on nothing, sir, and what with so much sickness and burying, right after that bank failure, Abel's savings have pretty near dribbled away. We'd help Parry if we could, Mr. Asa, but we just manage to scrape along as it is and keep our insurance paid up."

"Well, things are changing all the time. Anyway, I think he ought to go ahead if he wants to. I shouldn't try to stand in his way. By the time he's finished school, we may be able to help him. I'll speak to Mr. Fitzroy about him." But even while he uttered his hopeful words, he knew that any speaking to William would be worse than useless. "And there's Craig Fleming," he added, with greater confidence. "Mr. Craig might be able to show him a way."

"I'll tell him what you say, Mr. Asa, and I certny do thank you, sir." She smiled back at him before she went out of the door and down the flight of three steps into

the backyard. Yes, Minerva was a fine woman, he thought. There weren't many like her, white or black, left in the world today. . . .

Standing in the doorway, he looked out into the ugly yard, and beyond that, through the open gate into the alley, where the dark shape of a cat was slinking under the light. Then the gate shut after Minerva, and he lifted his eyes to the faintly stirring leaves of the tulip tree. His head ached and he felt alone and apart, without knowing why. There was nothing unusual in this. All his life he had felt loneliness, but the feeling had taken a sharper edge since he had moved into the new house. At fifty-nine it was not easy to adjust oneself to strange surroundings, to unfamiliar habits, to different standards, or, rather, to an absence of standards. I shall never feel that I belong here, he thought. I shall never feel that I belong anywhere. And perhaps I do not. Perhaps I have always been out of step with my time. In a little while now, all his children would have left him for lives of their own, and he would be by himself with Lavinia. Roy, who had stayed with them as long as she was happy, had talked tonight of wanting a home for herself and Peter. And that was natural, he knew. She was a good child, the only unselfish one in the lot, and he did not wish her to be put upon by the others.

Well, he ought to be going in again, he supposed; but he dreaded the return to noise and glare and the suffocating sense that he was in the midst of an invisible conflict. For there was a conflict. He couldn't put his finger on the spot, but he could feel that it was there. Of course none of them would ever tell him the truth, not even Lavinia, who relished truth whenever the form of it was plain and unpalatable. But something strange and distant had looked at him from Roy's eyes, as if she were trying not to see an object that stood directly in front of her. I never liked Peter, he said to himself. I never thought it

would last. But Lavinia was right. At the bottom of it, whatever it was, there was this elementary nonsense about freedom. This incessant chatter about having no responsibilities, only privileges. As if any marriage could rest permanently upon privilege. Where would he be tonight if Lavinia had possessed only a privilege, without a right, over a husband? Not here. No, certainly not here.

The image of Kate sprang into his mind, and he saw her, alone, except for her servants and the two pointers, while the roving scents of the April night drifted in through her windows. That was what liberty would have meant to him had he ever possessed liberty. But liberty, of course, was only a word among other words. How long had he been here, he wondered. An hour? Or half an hour? Or even two hours? Not that it mattered. They wouldn't miss him. But somebody was going, for he heard the front door open and shut, with a slam which reverberated through the dining room into the kitchen. . . .

"Daddy!" That was Roy calling. "Daddy, where are you?" He heard her running footsteps in the hall, and presently she slipped through the swinging door from the pantry. "They've gone. They've all gone."

"They went early."

"Aunt Charlotte felt a pain somewhere. You know how frightened she is of that pain."

"Yes, I know." For years Charlotte had lived in fear of cancer, but whether or not there was a physical reason, Asa had never discovered. All he suspected was from watching her hand flutter helplessly to her heart whenever a sudden pain seemed to clutch at her bosom. Lavinia insisted that the trouble came from overeating, and that cancer in the breast did not begin with a pain; but Charlotte's mother and an aunt had both died of that malady, and neither Lavinia nor a celebrated specialist in

New York could banish the dread of such an inheritance.

"Did the others go too?" Asa asked.

Roy sighed and stretched out her arms. "Every one of them. Maggie and Andrew went because it's their nurse's night off, and Stanley and Craig have gone to the country club with some boys and girls who stopped by for them. There's a dance, and you know how Stanley is about dancing."

"And I know, too, how Craig isn't about dancing."

Roy laughed. "That doesn't matter, does it?" she mocked.

"Well, where's Peter? Why didn't you and Peter go with the others?"

"He had to look up a report in his office. Dr. Cullender is coming for a consultation at nine o'clock." She frowned and brushed the crisply curling hair back from her forehead. "Of course, I knew you were in hiding, but I couldn't help laughing when Mammy brought in the tray. She has the only stately figure I know."

"Yes, I may be a better cook than Virgie, but I'm not equal to Minerva as an ornament."

"What were you doing, Daddy?"

"Just sitting. It's a relief sometimes just to sit."

"You're all in, that's the trouble." Her frown deepened while she looked at him. "You didn't have a supper fit for anybody to eat. There's a whole bottle of milk in the icebox, and I'm going to make you drink every drop of it."

"Your mother has to have her hot milk later."

"She doesn't have to have this. There's some left over from morning. Isn't one of your headaches coming on?"

"Yes, a little, but it will wear off after I get to bed."

"Well, wait a minute. I'm going to give you some aspirin." She was gone in a flash, and in a flash, or so it seemed to him, she was back again with two aspirins in her hand. "Here, take ten grains and sip your milk

slowly. For once in your life you're going to have the top of the bottle."

Obediently, he swallowed the tablets and sipped the milk, which was agreeably rich and staying in quality. "I feel better already," he said presently, "but I don't know what your mother will think."

"She needn't think. She can have Ovaltine. Something," she added, desperately, looking him straight in the eyes, "has got to be done about it."

"About what?"

"About you."

"Oh, I'm all right, dear. I was feeling a little gone inside, that was all."

"It isn't all." There was a sharpened edge to her voice, and her eyes looked larger and darker because of the shadowy circles. How slender she was, with her straight, well-knit figure, which had barely a curve over her small pointed breasts. "Something," she repeated in a fierce undertone, "has simply got to be done." Turning away, she sank down on the doorstep.

"But I'm all right now, Roy."

"I don't think of you for months at a time, Daddy, not really think. Then, suddenly, I look at you in a new slant of light, and it's just as if I'd never seen you before. I see then what a mean life—what a perfectly rotten life —you've had from the beginning."

"I haven't, darling, I really haven't. I've had a lot more than most people."

Smiling faintly, she stared at him with the unflinching courage and the candid irreverence of modern youth. While he returned her look, he thought fantastically that this was one of the special attitudes of the present with which he was able to sympathize. Nothing was permanent. Life created itself and dissolved in the moment of passing.

"More of what, old dear?" she tossed back.

He tried to think of a true, or at least a safe, answer. "More of—of everything. I've had good children, haven't I? Children make up for a great deal." But this wasn't sound, he knew; there was a lack of sense—or was it logic?—somewhere.

"Do you suppose, Daddy," she asked flippantly, "that even the idiot who first thought of that bromide really believed it?"

His head was aching again, and he rubbed his forehead as if he were rubbing away an inner disturbance. "Well, I rather like my children, Roy. Don't you?"

"Not—not terribly."

"Have you ever thought what my life would have been if I hadn't had you?"

"Oh, me!" She threw out her hand. "You would have had other things. Think how nice it would have been to have the top of the bottle every evening."

He looked at her gravely. "My top of the bottle, darling, is your happiness. So long as you're happy, I can be satisfied."

Her face changed so subtly that he wondered whether a flitting shadow had darkened it. But the shadows of leaves did not move into the circle of light, and through the open door he could not see any stars. "Then don't worry, dear old thing," she said. "I *am* happy. I am as happy as—as the night is long."

He shook his head. "You're not, Roy, and I wish I could do something about it."

"Well, you can't." Her voice hardened. "There is nothing in the world to do anything about. I can take care of myself. I can manage my life."

"You may think so, but I doubt it. After all, you're too young to know much of the world."

"Oh, I know it. I know it all right."

"As a little thing you used to have what we called a sunny disposition. You were different from Stanley."

[69]

"Well, I'm sunny still." She laughed and made a mocking face at him. "Can't you tell, just to look at me, Daddy, that I'm sunny?" She sprang up from the doorstep and turned back into the kitchen. "There's Mother's bell. We'd better be going. Good night, Daddy dear." Before he had locked the back door and put out the lights, she had flitted from him into the hall. A few minutes later, as he passed through the dining room, he heard her calling up the stairs. "Yes, we're coming, Mother. We're so happy about everything in the world that we had to wait and talk it all over."

VI

"YES, my Lord, You sure have used me well," said Minerva; for she was a grateful soul and had established cordial relations with the Almighty. As the ramshackle Ford snorted and creaked and wheezed and bumped down Westward Avenue, she leaned back on the sagging seat and told herself that this was the best of life. It was a blessed relief to rest her feet, instead of having to tote the clothesbasket on her head, as she used to do when her folks lived in the old house. Not that she minded working; but her legs, especially at the knees, were not all that they used to be. If it wasn't for her legs, she often said to herself, she'd feel as spry as she ever did. And her husband was just like her. After serving as a letter carrier on the same round for more than thirty years, his joints had begun to go back on him. Then a gigantic, but not unfriendly power called Government had found for him a place inside the post office. Everybody had a good word for Abel, and though he had been appointed by the Republicans, the white folks on his route had prevailed upon the Democrats not to turn him away.

Here they were at last, swinging under the thick maples into Granite Boulevard. All the quality lived in those big houses, except the upper crust that had moved out into the country; and she was riding along right in the middle of them, bumping on with the stream which raced toward the green light at the corner. It would have taken her an hour or more to lug that heavy basket on and off the streetcars, besides carrying it along the squares where no streetcars could run. Yes, ma'am, she was surely pleased when Miss Lavinia, who was as close as the bark of a tree, had agreed to pay for her trip in the old Ford that Brother Jacob Moody had bargained for on

its way to the junk heap. Brother Jacob was old, but he was right handy with automobiles. "All she needs to make her go is some better bowels," he had said. He was a great one for poking fun at you.

They were having a party in that big house on the corner. Minerva loved a party, no matter who gave it. White or colored, it made no difference, so long as it was a party; but colored parties were best, because white folks had never really learned how to have fun. They couldn't give themselves over to a good time, the way colored folks did. White folks wanted too much, that was the trouble. They went to so much bother to have pleasure that they were worn out before they began to enjoy it. No, ma'am, that wasn't the way to get the best out of life. That wasn't the way, by no manner of means. The more things you'd try to take on, the harder it was to get right down to the bottom of happiness. But even colored folks in these days had forgotten how to be happy. They couldn't be like her old mammy and pappy when they were alive—satisfied to make happiness out of a little or nothing—just from patting and shouting, just from looking on at a wedding, or even a funeral if the hearse had nice plumes on it. Nobody ever had to tell her mammy and pappy to go out and enjoy themselves. They did it just by living and not studying about it.

Young folks, white or black, weren't like that any longer. Colored children were asking for silk stockings, the same as the quality. They wanted to know what was what, and they talked a lot of big foolishness about being as good as the best. Parry had been at the top of his class, and now he was saying that he wanted to go to Makepeace College and then to the university in Washington. Well, she thought a heap of Parry, but she wasn't easy about all the notions he'd got in his head. She wasn't sure you were a bit better off when you knew more than was good for you. Her children weren't nearly so happy as

her old mammy had been, and her mammy and pappy didn't have a speck of book learning. They couldn't even read their own names that were written down for them.

No, she wasn't easy. Learning might mean only more trouble, and sweet Jesus knew she'd had a peck of trouble, and brimming over. Of course, she had always held herself proud. Not that she was stuck-up or put on airs, as the low-down trash said of her; but she'd always held herself proud. She'd never talked the way the colored trash talked, nor the white trash either, for that matter. She'd picked up nice talk and nice ways while she waited on her white ladies. When her children started with school, she'd studied their books with them every night till she taught herself to read and write all the easy words. She'd even tried going to night school for a while; but after washing and ironing and cleaning and cooking all day, she was too tired to stretch her eyes and fuss over print. Still, she'd learned right much by setting her mind to it. She could tell almost any word if it was short, and she was able to write real nice letters to her kinfolks down on the old place in the country. She could talk proper, too, like white folks, when she took pains; but when she thought all by her lonesome self, she had to think natural, the way colored folks did. . . .

The big new houses were left behind now. The Ford, snorting more wildly than ever, was lurching into a less fashionable part of the town, where tired men in shirt sleeves were sitting on porches and noisy children were roller-skating out on the pavement. It was late for those children to be out, but their mothers, jabbering over front fences, had no minds on them, not even on that teensy bit of a boy (he couldn't have been a day over two) that plunged straight from the curbstone all but under their wheels. If Brother Jacob hadn't swerved away so quick and sideswiped that car in front, they'd surely have gone over him. . . . A few fine houses were still left here,

but they were old, Minerva thought, and waiting for the new time to get rid of them. Shadows, like running water, flowed under the elm boughs, as the Ford lumbered along over cobbles, and turned presently to the other side of Broad Street and on through the market, where everything but the smells was asleep.

Here the level of the city appeared to be sinking slowly, little by little, from a state of former affluence to the bare features of poverty. Houses were crumbling, fences were sagging, window sashes were empty, weeds and crabgrass were sprouting among the sunken bricks and over the fallen steps. But if the background had dwindled away, the human elements had strengthened and multiplied. People swarmed everywhere. For a few blocks the faces were white, and then, farther on, the failing lights had transformed these same faces into shades of black, brown, yellow, or cinnamon. The Ford had to slacken its creaking speed, and snort between every puff and blow of the engine. Children of many varied colors raced, plunged, darted, crawled amid the welter of dust and trash, filthy newspapers, and old rinds of vegetables.

"Praise the Lord, I don't live in this part," Minerva exclaimed, and Brother Jacob nodded his grizzled head over his right shoulder. "Praise de Lawd!" he rejoined fervently.

"We've a heap to be thankful for, Brother Jacob. The Lord has been good to us."

"Dat He has, Sister, dat He has. Praise de Lawd!"

"The Lord's mighty good to poor folks, Brother Jacob."

"He sho' is, Sister Minervy. He sho' is."

"I'm certny glad I've got my religion, Brother Jacob. I wouldn't take a mint of money for my religion."

"Dat I 'ouldn't, Sister. Dat I 'ouldn't. De pity wid w'ite folks is dat dey ain' got de true religion."

They had passed through the worst now. The market

was behind them, and the Ford lurched, wheezing, into a quarter where the better class of Negroes had houses. Long before the Civil War, Hill Street had been a fashionable neighborhood. A dignified old dwelling still stood here and there; but for the most part, the new frame houses, hastily built because of crowded conditions, were small and simple and cheap, and the sidewalks in front of them were paved insecurely. Yet the street was respectable, and now the screaming children, out of bed at the wrong hour, seemed almost as remote as the prosperous West End. Even the roar of traffic had lulled, until it was barely more than a far-off rumble of sound.

The narrow frame house, painted gray within a gray paling fence, at the end of the block was the one Abel had bought and paid for, thank the Lord, out of his savings. When she counted up her blessings at night, the first one she thought of was that Abel had bought and paid for their home. There was a big backyard, too, and that was the second blessing, because Abel had a born hand with flowers and made a pretty penny raising jonquils and ragged robins and asters and zinnias and marigolds, to sell in the market. No matter whether it was spring, summer, or fall, he'd be sure to have something blooming to take by the market. He had some right nice roses, too, coming on. Miss Lavinia said she'd never seen such fine Sunset roses as Abel had raised last year. And there was a Paul's Scarlet Climber the neighbors had flocked in to look at. She hoped the flowers would do well again this year; but Abel was already worrying about this new Japanese beetle. Nobody ever heard of Japanese beetles in the olden time, Abel said; but if they kept on getting worse, they'd soon be eating us out of house and home.

The front door stood open. A friendly light streamed over the shallow porch and the short brick walk. As the car puffed and creaked and finally stopped, Jasper's

cheerful bark was lifted in welcome. An instant later, his sturdy little shape darted out of the house and rushed down to the closed gate. Yes, this was home, Minerva thought. It was true that the good Lord had never forgotten her.

She stepped out of the car and smoothed her dress over her strong, straight figure. "You certny gave me a nice ride, Brother Jacob. I sure did enjoy it. Won't you come in," she added politely, "and rest a bit before you go on?"

"Naw'm, I reckon I'd better be gittin' along back. But I'se jes' as much obleeged to you, all de same."

"Well, I sure did enjoy it."

"Thanky, Sister Minervy. Hit wan't no trubble a-tall, nary a mite."

"You're a lucky man to have a car for your own, Brother Jacob."

"Yas'm, I know I is. I sho' was born lucky. But I ain' never let up f'om tormentin' de th'one till I done git it."

"You won't forget to be here the first thing Monday morning?"

"Naw'm, I mines me er dat. I ain' gwine ter furgit you."

The Ford rattled off, and Minerva, watching him uneasily, said to herself: "I reckon he's mighty old. Brother Jacob is mighty old to be so spry at the wheel. He's so old that he don't know himself when he was born."

When she opened the gate, Jasper, who had been clawing frantically at the palings, flung himself upon her and then bounded in whirls ahead of her up the walk. In the small, clean living room, overfurnished with odds and ends her white friends had discarded, Parry was studying under a student's lamp with a green shade, which had belonged to Mr. Asa a long time ago. Away from the light, Abel was leaning back, fast asleep, in a lumpy upholstered chair, with his head resting on a tidy Aunt Matoaca

had crocheted out of spool cotton when she was night nurse to her old Miss. Since the family on both sides had been thrifty and saving, nothing had ever been thrown away as long as it held together; and the small square room contained the art treasures of several forgotten periods. There was a heavy rosewood sofa, discarded as out-of-style, a table with carved rosewood legs and a white marble top, and a crippled ebony *étagère,* which had been mended with black walnut. On the walls several speckled engravings depicted children in sentimental attitudes of virtue or piety, and the narrow ledge of the mantlepiece was crowded with photographs of the Timberlake and Fitzroy families. On the marble-top table, beside an enormous Bible with gilt clasps, which had been a wedding present to Abel from the Baptist church he attended, a slender vase held several remarkably fine Darwin tulips. After leaving the post office, Abel had worked till dark with his flowers, weeding the beds of perennials and preparing the soil for seeds of the heavenly blue morning glory, which he beheld in an ecstatic vision running over the clematis arbor at the foot of the yard. He was sleeping now the sleep of happy exhaustion, and Minerva walked softly in the hope that, since he was growing a little deaf, he had not heard her when she came in.

"You're back early," Parry whispered, while Jasper sat primly on his sleek brown tail and gazed up at her as eagerly, she told herself, as if he were waiting to hear what she had to tell him. "That dog certny has a lot of sense," she said under her breath, "and I declare he's getting exactly like you, Parry, all big eyes in a narrow face, only he don't look nearly so dolesome."

"Did you see the presents, Ma?"

"No, I ain't seen 'em yet."

Parry sighed. "Haven't, Ma."

"I know, son. I mean haven't, but I'm tired. I can't

think pretty when I'm done-up." As she looked at him patiently, the idea crossed her mind that life was a simpler matter for the uneducated. Minding her talk, first with Abel, who had had schooling when he was young, and then with Parry had kept her hands full ever since she was married. But ain't it so? she found herself thinking perversely. Ain't it the gospel truth that life was easier for her mammy and pappy in the olden days when words were just words and not parts of speech?

"Why didn't Miss Stanley let you look at them?"

"Some folks were there. But Mr. Craig spoke to me real nice. He wanted me to stay and look, only I said I'd be back again the first thing Monday morning."

"Who else was there?"

"Mr. Andrew and Miss Maggie, and a few young things ran in on the way to somewhere. Then there was Mr. William and Miss Charlotte. I declare, son, I never saw anybody wilt away like Mr. William has. He looks to me as if he wasn't long for this world."

"It's that doctor in New York. The cook told me he wouldn't let him eat anything."

"Well, I don't hold with that," Minerva said. "I never yet seen no good come of starving yourself. Mr. William used to poke out so hearty in front, and now he's slunk up to almost nothing."

Though she sighed, the sigh was merely a passing breath over her settled contentment. No matter where she went or what she saw, she was always glad to get home again. She loved the little house, with everything that it contained, as if it were human. Every inanimate object had its own personality; she knew each one through and through, she often told herself, and when she cleaned and scrubbed and dusted and polished, she felt that her loving ministrations were understood and accepted by some secret identity beneath the surface of wood or marble or brass. If only, she thought, she could

deal with Parry as successfully as she dealt with her house. Parry was a smart boy, everybody said that about him; but it had always worried her that, even as a teensy child, he wanted, as Old Miss used to say so often, marrow in his bones. And God Almighty knew, you had to have marrow in your bones, and plenty of it, if you didn't mean to get trampled on.

"That's because he's on a diet," Parry was saying, "but the doctor says if he keeps it up, he'll be better than ever."

"I reckon it's a stomach complaint," Minerva said. "They starve you 'most to death with a stomach complaint. I noticed," she added, "he put his whiskey right on the table and didn't touch it. But he didn't seem a bit down in the mouth. I heard him telling Miss Maggie he felt like a new man since he'd lost forty pounds."

"He might lose a hundred and not miss it. Did you see Mr. Asa?"

"He was in the pantry fixing drinks. I took them in for him. I didn't want him to be stooping to wait on young folks. If it's the last word I speak, Miss Lavinia don't treat Mr. Asa right. He used to be real good-looking, but now he's getting kind of wizen-faced." She sighed and looked thoughtfully at her sleeping husband. "I certny do set a heap of store by Mr. Asa."

But Parry was thinking, naturally enough, of his own problems. "Did he say anything about me?"

"He did, son. He said you're a bright boy and he hoped you would get on."

"But he didn't say how. He didn't say how I'm to get on."

"No, he didn't say how, son."

Abel opened his eyes with a start and sat up, very straight, in his old winged chair. "I dropped off," he said. "Did you notice those Scarlet Beauties? I just picked a few of 'em."

"Yes, I noticed 'em. I wish Mr. Asa could see 'em."

"There's plenty more in the bed, but I don't like to pick 'em. I'm going to work all day Sunday on those borders."

"Ought you to do that, Abel? The Lord might not be pleased."

Abel shook his head. "I know what pleases the Lord, Minervy, I've known the Lord all my life."

It was true, she thought proudly. Abel was a good man; he knew what was right. But, no matter, her religion took her to church, and it was true, also, that she wouldn't take a mint of money for her religion.

Abel yawned, and Jasper, sitting by his side, barked imperatively; for it was after his bedtime and the door to the bedroom was shut. "Do you have to go back to put Miss Stanley's car away, son?"

"Mr. Craig said he'd leave it at the garage. I like Mr. Craig." Parry got up and opened the door for Jasper, who barked again and ran in to jump up on the foot of the bed.

"I declare, the sense that dog has got," said Minerva.

"Everybody likes Mr. Craig," Abel assented. "I never heard a word against him, except that he thinks the wrong way in politics. He's a smart lawyer, they say, and he's always ready to help somebody."

"I wish he'd help me," Parry rejoined moodily. "He's a lawyer, and he might tell me how to get on in the law."

Minerva shook her head doubtfully. "I wish you could get rid of that notion, son."

"Well, I can't," Parry rejoined irritably. "I can't get rid of it, and I don't want to."

"There, there, Minervy," Abel said soothingly. "The boy will have to be happy in his own way. It's easy as does it."

"All I'm thinking of is what's best for him," Minerva answered, while her glance wandered from Abel's placid

face—a fine face, too, she told herself, and good enough for anybody to look at—to Parry's downcast and slightly sullen features. "And I ain't sure that being a lawyer is best for anybody. Mr. Craig's a lawyer, and the Lord knows he don't look so pert, not even though he's going to marry one of the children I raised. Stanley gets prettier every day, too, but that don't seem to make Mr. Craig any brighter." She sighed and shook her head again. "Something ain't right up there. I can't make out what it is, but sure's you're born, something ain't right."

"Did you see anything wrong?" Abel asked wonderingly.

"Not a thing. Not a thing in the world. But I can feel sometimes when I can't see, and I felt it all in my bones. Something's gone wrong up there, but they ain't a-telling."

"What about Mr. Asa?"

"He didn't say nothing, but he was looking the way he gets when he's clean wore out with 'em all."

"Did you have a word with the bride?"

"Who? Stanley? I ain't had a chance yet, but I'm going to see all her wedding things when I go up on Monday."

"Well, I'd leave worrying alone," said Abel. "You can never tell how weddings are going to work out, and it don't do a bit of good to keep worrying. Anyway, it's all settled now, and it's got to be. If Miss Stanley ain't minded to marry him, there's nobody making her."

"That's so, I reckon, Abel." Minerva bent over the bowl of tulips with a caressing touch. "What will be, will be, and I'm making a bit to-do about nothing. But I felt what I felt. I felt it in the air, and I felt it in Mr. Asa when he talked to me. Well, here's Jasper back again! He's coming to hear what we're fussing about."

Parry's face cleared. "Mr. Asa likes Jasper," he said. "I reckon he's sorry now he ever gave him away."

"He couldn't help himself," Minerva explained. "Miss

[81]

Lavinia has always been so set on not having a dog in the house, she wouldn't even let him keep that little rangy terrier he had when he was married. You recollect, don't you, Abel, the state Mr. Asa was in when she made him give Benny away?"

"No, ma'am, it was too long ago."

"Well, I was waiting on his ma then, and I can't never forget her telling me that she didn't believe Mr. Asa would have married Miss Lavinia if he'd known the way she'd be about Benny. The day before the wedding he took Benny down to Mr. Jack and Miss Kate Oliver, and as long as Benny lived, Mr. Asa used to go down to see him regularly every Sunday. That was the way he started seeing so much of the farm."

"Mr. Jack's dead now." Abel spoke sternly, for he was a Baptist and a Fundamentalist in morals.

"Yes, but Miss Kate is just the same. I see her sometimes when she comes up to shop. She's the salt of the earth, is Miss Kate."

"It's a pity Mr. Asa didn't pick her out first," Parry said.

"She was married to Mr. Jack before he ever laid eyes on her. All the same, if I do say it, I don't see how Mr. Asa could ever have put up with Miss Lavinia all these years if he hadn't had some place to go. She'd have worn him to a frazzle but for Miss Kate."

"Well, I hope he'll have a show some day," Abel said. "He's had a measly life, I reckon, except for his children." He rose, stretching himself. "I'm kind of stiff in my joints, and I'm going to lock up and try to get a good sleep."

"Don't you bother to lock up," Minerva said. "I want to look out-of-doors just a minute."

After he had dragged himself upstairs to bed, groaning occasionally under his breath, Minerva went out on the front porch and stood gazing thoughtfully into the

glimmering darkness. In the sky, she could see the immense glare of Broad Street reflected, and she could hear the broken noises or the faint humming of traffic. While she stood there alone on the porch, she felt that her peace was vaguely disturbed by an incident she had not been able to put out of her mind. I ain't a-telling, she thought. No, Lord, I ain't a-telling.

A shuffling sound approached her on the pavement, and she recognized the tapping of old blind Uncle Elisha's stick. "Good night, Uncle Elisha!" she called cheerfully, and he answered in a plaintive singsong voice, "Nighty, Sister!" Day and night were both the same to him, she knew, but he never missed his stroll every evening before he went to bed in his cellar under the cobbler's shop on the corner. He eked out a scant livelihood by helping to mend shoes; but the church looked after him in a fashion, and some of the colored families in the neighborhood gave him whatever scraps they could not make into soup. He slept in a cellar and lived on crusts, but he would hang on to his life as long as he could.

A few bright stars were shining over the church steeple, but some mare's tails streamed out toward the west, and it wouldn't surprise her if the sky clouded over before morning. The air was so summery, she could hardly believe it was April, and that, too, she told herself, was one of the sure signs of falling weather. She wondered whether Mr. Asa would go down to the country day after tomorrow, and decided that Miss Lavinia would not let him have a Sunday off if she could find a way to prevent it. Anybody could tell just to look at Mr. Asa that he was henpecked. To be sure, Abel said it was his own fault and he ought to have shown more backbone about standing up to his wife; but it's hard to stand up to a sick woman when you're married to her and can't pay her doctor's bills. . . .

She glanced up at the sky and then down into the

shabby street. No, ma'am, I ain't a-telling, she said to her-self, not a soul alive, not even Abel. I ain't a-telling. Not that there was anything she could catch hold of, only the little she had seen had been full of disturbance. Trifling as it was, she couldn't, no matter how hard she tried, worry it down in her thoughts. And it wasn't tonight. What happened was last Friday, after nightfall, when she had gone up to carry back the clean clothes. She'd been upstairs to leave the basket with Miss Lavinia, and there wasn't anybody a-tall in the room but Mr. Asa and Roy. There was nobody else in sight anywhere. They were talking kind of cheerful when she went in, but somehow they didn't sound natural. It was a noise all right, but it didn't sound to her like voices talking. So she didn't stay long. She could feel that queer something in the air again, with everybody pretending it wasn't there, or didn't mean anything if it was. She could tell that Mr. Asa was worn-out, what with Miss Lavinia picking on him about this and that every minute. He had that pinched look she knew so well, as if his nerves had been drawn through a keyhole.

Yes, ma'am, she'd said her say and got out of the room as quick as she could. She went right downstairs, easing herself along softly, because her bunion was killing her. At first she wasn't studying about a blessed thing but sparing her bunion. Then when she came down in front of the parlor door, she was wonderstruck by the sight of Mr. Peter and Stanley staring at each other and not saying a word, just as if they were waiting for something to happen. Stanley was sitting on the arm of the sofa and Mr. Peter was standing there, stock-still, looking down on her with all his eyes, as if he was ready to eat her up. They weren't speaking a word, but they didn't need a morsel of talk to tell what they were thinking. She wasn't meaning to spy on them, but she was afraid to move, be-cause she didn't want to let on she was waiting there at

the foot of the stairs. She couldn't see Mr. Peter's face, except sideways, but she could tell by the way he stiffened up that he was holding himself in. Then, the very minute she was minded to steal away, Stanley gave a kind of gasp and ran into the little room next door, where all the presents were laid out. But Mr. Peter didn't turn his head, and he didn't go after her. He just stood there, like he was under a spell, till she had run out of sight. Then he stooped over and passed his hand, kind of slow and soft, over the arm of the sofa where she'd been sitting. God Almighty knows what he was up to; but he stood there stroking the sofa as if he was stroking a real flesh and blood arm. He didn't do it but once. After that, he drew himself up and let out his breath in a whisper between sighing and singing. Minerva reckoned he'd turn round the next minute; but before he could catch sight of her, she'd bestirred herself, bunion or no bunion, and had scooted away.

That was all. There wasn't a thing in the world to tell, and whether there was or not, she wasn't a-telling. If trouble was headed this way, it would get here soon enough without helping it on. Not a word, not so much as a speck of a word, passed between 'em. But, never mind, she knew what she knew; and she'd felt the sort of sultriness that whips around in the air when a thunderstorm is all but ready to break.

VII

"ROY, is that you?"

"Yes, Mother, do you want anything?"

"Aren't you late?"

"No, I came in a little early, but I've had a bath and a change."

"Have you seen Stanley?"

"Not since this morning."

"Did she seem all right then?"

"All right?" Roy repeated vaguely, as she came to the door. "Oh, I suppose so. I saw her only for a minute before I went to the shop. But we've had a terrible day. We're furnishing a house at Virginia Beach for a woman who doesn't know what she ought *not* to want."

Mrs. Timberlake put aside the slumber robe she was knitting of russet and orange yarn, and turned a resigned yet apprehensive gaze on her daughter. "It must have been tiresome," she remarked, "but I haven't had an easy day myself. Not a soul has been near me since breakfast."

"Well, I had to lunch downtown. We were in a terrific rush, but Stanley ought to have looked after you."

"I haven't laid eyes on her. She hasn't been near me since right after breakfast."

Roy made an impatient gesture while she slipped a thin blue dress over her head and settled it on her shoulders. "Well, I can't take on my own job and Stanley's, too," she replied irritably. "I'm not to blame for Stanley, thank goodness."

Christian fortitude, as Lavinia was fond of saying, demands an attitude of repose. Heaven alone knew how much effort, especially that branch of effort which is regarded as noble endeavor, she had been spared by simply lying down whenever she saw it approaching. So,

without lifting her head, she murmured softly, "Won't you wait just a minute, dear?"

Reluctantly, with a step that dragged slowly, Roy came into the room, while her mother sank deeper and flatter among the pillows. "I was just going to finish dressing. I want to brush my hair before Peter comes in." An hour before, hurrying up the block in the April breeze, Roy had felt with a quivering gladness, as if wings were rushing within and without, all the expectancy and delight of youth in the spring. Now, the thrill of joy had died as swiftly as it flamed up, and her spirits drooped as she crossed the room and looked down on her mother's supine figure.

"There's no use asking me anything about Stanley," she said.

"It isn't about Stanley, Roy. It's about you. You haven't been at all like yourself."

Roy laughed. "Maybe I'm only more myself."

"You aren't looking well."

"Oh, I'm all right. Don't begin to worry about me."

"How can I help it when I see you getting thinner and paler every day?"

"Well, it's nice to be thin, and I can soon change my color. Is that all you wanted to tell me?"

Lavinia looked at her gravely. Yes, the child had character, she reflected, and breathed a sigh of thanksgiving because the postwar generation had grown old—or at least middle-aged—and decrepit before her daughters grew up. Difficult as it was to stand character when it was opposed to one's principles, it would have been still more trying, she reflected, to contend with the absence of character. In a husband, for example, if one intended to stay married, character might still be considered an indispensable attribute. Though she acknowledged that life and marriage had both been disappointing, and that this failure was the cause—or at least the occasion—of her physi-

cal malady, she found satisfaction, if not happiness, in being simply a mother. Long ago she had accepted the fact that she and her children could never learn to speak the same or even a familiar language. Yet her antagonist, she was shrewd enough to perceive, was not a generation, but time itself; and she knew that in the endless conflict with time no woman wins an ultimate victory.

"There is something else I wanted to ask you, dear," she said slowly. "Has Stanley said anything to you about her marriage?"

"So it was about Stanley?"

"Well, has she?"

"Said anything? Isn't she always saying something about it?"

"Has she said anything to make you think she's unhappy?"

Roy laughed again, but more flippantly. "She wouldn't to me, would she? We've never talked to each other, except, of course," she added slowly, "to say things we don't mean."

"That's what I can't understand," Lavinia sighed hopelessly. "Two sisters, and so near the same age. You used to be so fond of her when she was little."

"That was when she was little."

"I know you think I never notice anything, lying up here by myself"—Lavinia's voice trembled—"but I can feel things even when nobody tells me."

"You feel . . ." Roy began impatiently and broke off.

"I have a feeling that Craig is not the right man and that Stanley is unhappy."

"Well, she's going to marry him in five days."

"I wish she wouldn't. Much as I dislike a sensation or gossip, I'd rather she'd break it off now than spoil her life."

"She won't spoil her life, Mother. She'll only spoil Craig's—or—"

"Oh, Roy, your own little sister!"

"Anyway, we've got to decide for ourselves. Stanley knows what she's doing."

"She hasn't the slightest idea what marriage means. She may be very unhappy."

"Does that really make so much difference? Aren't most people unhappy?"

"That isn't like you, Roy. What has come over you?"

"Nothing. Only I rather like Craig. . . ."

"Well, I like him, too," Lavinia assented, "but I can't help regretting that he is so much taken up with the lower orders. Heaven knows, I'm not a snob, and I realize it's the fashion nowadays to climb down and not up; but all the radicals you see in the newspapers look so untidy, and I'm afraid when he gets middle-aged he will never want to brush his hair or wash his face."

Roy smiled and pushed back her dark curls. "By that time we may all be going unwashed. But you needn't worry about Craig and the lower orders. Stanley will take care of that. The worst thing about Craig is that he's sentimental. For all his hard-boiled theories, he's positively mushy about Stanley. I like Craig," she repeated after a minute, with a ripple of scorn in her laugh, "but, good Lord, how I hate mushiness!"

Regarding her thoughtfully, Lavinia asked herself with a pang of self-reproach why she had felt so little need to protect her elder daughter from life. Was it because Roy's defiant gaze and the gallant carriage of her head, with its spirited poise, seemed to reject any offer of help? Perhaps Asa was right when he said she was finer than Stanley, but this fineness, Lavinia reflected, made fewer demands upon the heart or the nerves. A hard little thing, she told herself from the safe shelter of platitude, but as honest as day. It may be true that her father understands her better than I do. I don't know. I don't know anything, she sighed heavily, and gave up without

an extra exertion. After all, the only way to face life, she decided, was with a paradox, by turning your back on it.

"I won't keep you, dear," she said. "Run away now and dress."

"I'll come in again later. There's Stanley now. You'd better ask her what you want to know."

She darted out into the hall and then upstairs to her rooms on the third floor. Lavinia heard the doors overhead open and shut, and she was still listening to Roy's light footsteps, when Stanley came in, bringing a glow of both natural and artificial brightness.

"Poor Mother, have you had a good day?" Stopping in the middle of the room, Stanley threw a quick glance at the long mirror on the wall, which reflected her leaf-green dress and the burnished luster of her hair. In the last beams of the sunset her small oval face appeared to swim before her mother's eyes with the shallow vagueness of light. Only her large radiant eyes, of that unusual shade of greenish-blue, and the flying curves of her eyebrows were strikingly vivid. It is a pity about her mouth, Lavinia thought regretfully. The child would be really beautiful but for the petulant droop of her lower lip.

"How nice you look, dear, in green," she said. "No, my day was rather lonely. Nobody came near me."

"I couldn't get back any sooner. Uncle William made me stay to lunch, and then I had so much to do."

"It doesn't matter, darling." Lavinia yearned over her as if she were on the verge of a complete separation. "Nothing matters if you're really and truly happy."

Stanley tossed her hat on the table and shook out the curls on her neck. "Oh, I'm happy."

"If only I could feel sure of that."

"Well, anyway, I know what I'm doing."

"You don't sound as if you did, and you don't act as if you did."

"I can't help that, can I? I can't help how I sound and act."

For a minute or two Mrs. Timberlake did not reply. Then she said, more gently than ever, with the invincible patience of martyrdom, "If you aren't perfectly sure of your own heart . . ."

Stanley's laughter vibrated with an overtone of hysteria. "Sure of my own heart! Oh, Mother, that must have come out of a play when you were young!"

"Well, if you aren't sure of yourself, it would be better to break off everything before you go any further. Nothing can be so bad as ruining your whole life."

"It won't ruin my whole life. Marriage isn't one's whole life."

"It's the better part of it, anyway. It's very nearly the whole of one's happiness or unhappiness."

"Maybe it used to be in your day, but it isn't now."

"Some things don't change, my child, and love is one of them." After all, the only real security was in the commonplace.

"But it does, Mother, everything changes. Think of the way women used to suffer in marriage. Just imagine any of us doing that now!"

"Don't women still suffer in the wrong marriage?"

"Not if they have any sense. Nothing can ruin your life so long as you're free to get up and run away."

"Is anybody free, darling? I can't see that love is any different from what it used to be."

Stanley thrust out her hand as if she were pushing something away. "Well, we don't have to take it so seriously."

Mrs. Timberlake sighed again. "Don't you young people believe in anything, Stanley?"

With a wholly charming gesture, the girl stooped and kissed the top of her mother's head. "We believe in

knowing what we want," she answered brightly, "and in going after it. We have a right to be happy."

Hearing this perpetual refrain of youth, which seemed to her to have lost nothing in the past thirty years, Mrs. Timberlake asked gently, "Is Craig what you want?"

"Well, isn't he? Wasn't I mad about him from the very first minute? Didn't I feel that I simply couldn't live without him?"

"Do you still feel that way?"

Stanley had dropped down on the foot of the daybed, and she sat now swinging her slender feet in green slippers. "Oh, I suppose so. How does one ever know from day to day what one feels?"

"But it isn't too late yet if . . ."

"Oh, yes, it is. It's too late," Stanley cried out sharply, and burst into tears. "It's too late for everything. It's always too late."

"My child, my precious child!" Mrs. Timberlake bent over and clasped her passionately, as if she were holding her back from some threatened disaster. "It is not too late. It is never too late," she declared, with valiant dissimulation.

Stanley drew away, wiping her eyes on the fringe of her mother's shawl. "I'm just tired," she murmured. "I'll be all right in a minute."

"I don't wonder, poor child. You must be tired out. But let me talk to Craig, darling."

"Talk to Craig!" Her laugh sounded so natural, while the tears still dampened her lashes, that Mrs. Timberlake asked herself if her whole attitude could be merely a childish make-believe. Even as a baby, Stanley had been unpredictable.

"Let me tell him that . . . that you . . ."

"That I . . . that I . . ." Stanley echoed, and waited in smiling expectancy.

"That you would rather wait until you are sure of yourself. You don't know what marriage means, Stanley. You are still scarcely more than a child."

"Oh, I know. I know more than you think."

"You like to say that, but it isn't true. I don't know why girls today have a horror of being thought innocent."

"Because it sounds so silly. That's why."

"No girl of your age, my dear, can have any real knowledge of life. In ten years you may be a different person and may want an entirely different husband from Craig."

"Well, I can leave him if I want to. We both understand that. Nobody believes that marriages are made in heaven. Roy will tell you the same thing. Yet Father is always saying how loyal Roy is."

"She is loyal, and she adores Peter."

Stanley's sea-blue gaze was suddenly veiled and distant. "I wonder . . ."

"You know she does. It's true that Peter isn't exactly the kind of man I'd have chosen for a husband or . . . or a doctor, but the marriage has turned out much better than I expected." Mrs. Timberlake looked impressively at Stanley, who, silent now, sat interlacing her young fingers, with their pointed bright red nails and their lovely half-moons of white. The child must spend hours on them, Lavinia thought irrelevantly; and added, aloud, in her most maternal accents, "They are perfectly suited."

Without raising her eyes, Stanley unclasped her hands and bent over to straighten the strap of a slipper. "I wonder . . ." she repeated in a voice that was almost a whisper.

"But, of course, they are nearer the same age than you and Craig. Six years is a safer difference than ten."

"I wonder . . ." Stanley sprang to her feet and

turned to look at herself in the mirror. "Craig is coming up to see you. Did you tell him he might?"

"Yes, he asked me last night. It isn't that I'm not fond of Craig, you know. I believe he'd make a better doctor than Peter."

"He hasn't the hands. Peter's skill is all in his hands, Craig says."

"Is that his step? It sounded almost like your father's."

"They both drag the left foot a little, and it isn't a bit unattractive. Well, I'll leave him with you, only remember there's no use interfering."

She opened the door, ran lightly into Craig's arms, and then, as she released herself and fled on, called back playfully: "Don't believe a word Mother says to you, Craig, darling. She's trying to break up our happiness."

Yes, he is attractive, Mrs. Timberlake told herself, if only he could be made to brush his hair properly and straighten his tie. She liked his dark harassed features, with the sharpened bony structure beneath, and that light roving glance which appeared to see everything and rest nowhere. His smile, too, was engaging, and, she supposed, his general air of dishevelment was in keeping with the new fashion of rowdiness. In her heart she had always been sympathetic to Craig, though she felt strongly that he was not suited to Stanley, who skimmed so lightly over the shifting surface of life. Lying there day after day, month after month, year after year, Lavinia had been forced back upon her own mind for companionship, and almost to her surprise, she had discovered that it contained unsuspected resources. Craig was the only one of her acquaintances who shared with her a liking for serious discussion, in a community where talking pictures and trivial gossip were the popular diversions. The dearth of conversation which appears inevitable between

husband and wife had naturally restrained her from ex-
changing ideas with Asa Timberlake; yet there were moments, however brief, when the thought crossed her
mind that if she were not married to Asa, they might
have found a good deal to talk about.

"Stanley is very nervous, Craig," she said, as she held
out her hand and wondered how she should ever begin.
But begin what? After all, was there anything in the world
that she could say to him?

He nodded gravely. "I'd noticed it."

"She's been going too hard. It's a pity that brides will
wear themselves out."

He sat down close to her sofa and looked at her inquiringly. "I suppose so. I haven't had much experience."

Yielding to a sudden impulse, Lavinia leaned over and
put her large, soft hand on his arm. "Do you think she is
happy, Craig?"

"Happy?" He shrugged his shoulders. "That's a good
deal to ask, isn't it?"

"Well, you are, aren't you?"

For an instant, he simply stared at her. "Good God!"
he exclaimed presently. "Do I look it?"

She shook her head. "You do not. But it isn't easy to
tell anything by the way you look. Your face isn't con-
fiding."

"I can't help that. It's the way I was made."

Before replying, she gave his arm a sympathetic pat.
"I've been very much worried," she said, carefully picking
her words. "Especially in the past week or two, I've been
very much worried. I have wondered whether it wouldn't
be better to postpone your marriage till . . . till . . ."

"Till what?"

"Till you're sure you aren't risking great unhappiness."

He was silent for so long that she decided he had re-

fused to answer her question. Then, just as she was on the point of speaking again, he moved his arm and let her hand slip away. "Wouldn't the breaking off—for I suppose you really mean breaking off—mean great unhappiness?" he asked in a voice that vibrated with pain—or was it resentment?

"But wouldn't it be worse to go on unless—unless you are both sure of yourselves?"

He laughed angrily. "Well, I'm sure, for one."

"And is Stanley?"

The shadow of a storm appeared to sweep over his face. "I don't know, and that's the truth. I used to think so. I used to think she was—well, as far gone as I was—or almost. But, if you ask me now, I don't know."

"What does she say?"

He swallowed hard, as if he were forcing down a lump in his throat. "I haven't asked her. I'm afraid to ask her."

"She is still too young."

"She was happy at first. I know she was happy at first."

"Yes, I thought so. All of us opposed this marriage, her uncle and I were firm against it. We felt that she hadn't really found herself, and that when she grew up, she would regret it. But she wouldn't listen to us. She was bent on having what she wanted." She sighed hopelessly. "You can't do anything with children today."

"I hoped we'd grow together," Craig said in a tone of savage bitterness.

"But you aren't alike. You haven't a single idea in common. Not," she corrected herself hastily, "that Stanley has many ideas."

He assented moodily, while Lavinia thought, No, men haven't changed, nor, for that matter, has emotion or appetite.

"But she never seemed to care what I believed in," Craig was saying moodily. "She was sweet about every-

thing. She didn't mind my being what you call radical. She was satisfied just to be worshiped."

"I know," Mrs. Timberlake said sympathetically. "She likes being loved, and she hasn't really any serious interests."

"That didn't matter. I wanted her just as she was. And it's only five days ahead," he burst out passionately. "In five days we are to be married!"

"You love her like that?" The bleak despair in his eyes seemed to clutch at her heartstrings. Poor boy, she reflected, though she disliked men and enjoyed hurting Asa, poor boy, what will become of him?

"From the first glance," he answered desperately. "I've never had another thought since I first looked at her. It was just as if—as if all my bones went suddenly soft."

Too soft. Yes, that was the trouble, she told herself wearily. You can be too soft with women, and with men, too, for that matter. Human relationship, to endure, must be woven of tough fiber underneath the gentler emotions. Deep down below her conscious mind, she knew that her own marriage would have been happier if Asa, in his oversensitive nature, had a touch of the barbarian at play. "Poor boy," she murmured aloud. "It is hard on you." Then, after a wondering pause, "But your convictions—your social theories, I thought they meant so much to you?"

"They did once. I used to think I'd spend my life working for a better social order. I really believed I was interested in aggregates, not in individuals, till . . . till a thunderbolt struck me. After I met Stanley, all I could think about was wanting her."

"Poor boy," Lavinia repeated soothingly; for it was the kind of pause, she felt, which demanded either a prayer or a recurring phrase.

Yes, he was weak, she conceded. Any man was weak

who sacrificed his convictions or his purpose in life for a woman, especially for the painted shell of a girl. Though she adored Stanley, she had, even as a mother, no illusions about her daughter.

"What must I do?" he asked abruptly. "I want her to be happy. I'll do whatever she—whatever you . . ." He bit off his words and looked at her with a despairing hesitation.

"Tell her that. Go and ask her what you must do."

"She wouldn't answer. She wouldn't even listen. You saw her just now. You know how she hates to be pinned down."

"Yes, I know. That's the way she is. She can't help it."

"I'd give my life for her. I'd give up all that I believed."

"But that's the wrong way. Can't you see it's the wrong way? The only way to keep love is by holding on firmly to something else." Lavinia knew, she told herself with conviction, because she had tried his way in youth and so had lost everything. She had tried to run away from reality, and she had found that the only road away from life brought you back again in a circle. "You will have to work it out between you," she said. "I can't help you. Nobody can help you but yourselves. And don't forget that in five days it will be too late to wish you'd done differently."

He stood up and straightened his shoulders. "I'll go to her now, but it won't be any use. After all, I may be mistaken—we may both be mistaken . . ." His voice was stronger and a light shone in his face. "She may not have changed. She may still care as much as she ever did."

Lavinia's eyes followed him as he left the room. He turned to smile at her before shutting the door. What a boy he was still, and how entirely unfitted for marriage! He doesn't know women, she said to herself. He doesn't know the first thing about women. If only he had sense

enough to stand by his convictions and to leave love alone—at least until he had spent his passion on philanthropy, or revolution, or whatever it was that had once possessed his soul undividedly.

VIII

YES, Father is right, Roy said to herself, Peter and I would be happier by ourselves. Picking up a comb from the bureau, she ran it through her hair, while she glanced from the low ceiling to the pattern of blue morning glories on the walls. But what in the world would poor Father do with only Mother and Virgie? she thought, after a minute. She hated the two cramped third-story rooms, which were hot in summer and insufficiently heated in autumn and winter. She could never have stood living up here, she decided, except for the sense of separateness from the rest of the house—and the plentiful windows which looked out, in front, on the young maples and, at the back, on the crooked boughs of the old tulip poplar.

Why was it, she wondered, that she and her father had always stood so closely together within the family circle, and yet a little apart from the rest of the family? Her earliest recollection, very dim and remote, was of his sitting by her bedside day and night when she had scarlet fever. He had stayed away from the factory and shut himself in with her when quarantine was imposed; and she had refused to take her milk, Minerva had told her afterwards, except from his hands. Until she met Peter, her father had been nearer to her than anyone else, and she had thought resentfully of his endless drudgery and the monotonous round of his drab-colored life. But, more recently, ever since she had suffered from this gnawing fear of a disaster she never defined, she had thought of nothing but the constant ache at her own heart. People may say what they please, she thought bitterly, but unhappiness makes the soul shrink and dwindle.

Crossing the room, she stopped by the open window and looked down on the pavement, where the few passersby appeared to be swimming slowly upstream, through fluid shadows. In the middle of the street, sparrows flocked in a brown cluster, which broke and scattered before the approaching wheels of a car. The noise of horns and brakes floated up and mingled with the cries of children, piercing, yet as thin as the sound of distant bells chiming unmeaningly. Out of the mist of light in the west, pigeons swooped down, and then up again, in retarded long rhythms. Less than an hour before, she had felt the heightened consciousness which is almost, if not quite, ecstasy. The world, the street, the sky, and her own heart had been suffused with joy. Why had it come like that? she asked herself; and why had it gone?

Breaking into her thoughts, she heard Peter's step on the stairs; and while she listened, the rapid beating of her heart seemed to stifle her. After two years of marriage, his return at the end of the day could still start again in her nerves that urgent whisper of excitement which quivered and then died.

She heard his hand on the doorknob. In another second, the door had opened and shut, and he came quickly into the room, to stop short, as if in astonishment.

"I didn't know you'd come in," he said, with a breathless laugh. "I have no sense of time, and that's all wrong for a doctor." As she went toward him, he put his arms about her and brushed her cheek with his lips.

His kiss felt like a leaf, like a dead leaf, she thought, watching him with eyes that were bright and wistful. His kiss was as stiff and dry as the brushing of a dead leaf. Yet, while the thought was still in her mind, she was aware again of his power over her, of that responsive vibration. Do I love him too much? she asked herself. Is

love always pain when it is more than the heart can hold? Or was it only that she knew, without admitting the knowledge, that he was slipping beyond her? Was her distraught longing merely the agonized involuntary clutch of emotion at an endangered part of her life, the most precious and necessary part, which was broken away?

Drawing a little aside, she searched for some reassurance in the face that was more familiar to her than were her own features. She saw the thick fair hair, red in the shadow, which sprang upward in a slight crest, as if blown by a wind; the dark heavy brows beetling in a frown over nearsighted brown eyes; the large strong nose, with wide nostrils; and the vigorous sweep of the jaw, as well as the generous but irresolute curve of the mouth, which seemed nowadays to have coarsened a trifle, above the square and firmly modeled chin, with its surprising cleft in the center. She saw these things, but what she felt, without seeing distinctly, was the vital force that enkindled his look. His animal well-being diffused the glow, and the warmth, and the physical combativeness of pure energy. Or was it simply that she imagined this because she was in love with him still? Was it because—oh, well, but there was no use in wondering!

"I came as soon as I could, " she answered slowly. "I hoped—"

"Then it is later than I thought. I must hurry away again."

"I hoped we might go out. I thought you might take me somewhere. I thought . . ." She bent her head, hiding her eyes.

"I wish I could. But I've got to go out of town. Bellamy called me just as I was leaving the hospital. I'm in the devil of a hurry." He went into the bathroom, and a minute later she heard water gushing and the clatter of the soap dish against the porcelain. When he came out,

he was running a comb through his hair. "I can't find my collars. I don't seem to have any clean collars," he said irritably.

"You didn't look. They're in the second drawer. Are you obliged to go before dinner?"

"I can't wait. It's an emergency case, out of town. Bellamy is going with me."

"Where is it? Are you sure that you'll have to spend the night?"

"No, I'm not sure. I'm not sure of anything. We're going to Lynchburg. I'll get back if I can." He seemed in desperate haste, and for a minute she watched him hurriedly stuffing clothes into a small suitcase. His shoulders, she noticed, twitched as he turned his back on her, but his strong, steady hands were not trembling.

"Let me pack it for you," she said at last. "You aren't taking the right things."

"Oh, that's all right." He pushed her aside while he fastened the suitcase. "It doesn't matter, really. That's all right, I say," he added in a prickly tone, when she would have helped him. I don't know him, she thought, suddenly chilled. I don't know him, and he doesn't know himself any better than I do. He never used to be like this. He never used to be prickly to the touch. She ought to be quiet and composed, she told herself, after the true wifely tradition; but she couldn't be composed when she was tingling with anxiety and when her pulses were drumming her into a conflict of doubts.

He had put down the suitcase by the door and was changing into a fresh blue shirt. "I like you in blue," she said as casually as she could.

He glanced down. "Yes, it's blue, isn't it?"

"Didn't you know? Did you put it on without looking?"

"I wasn't thinking about it."

"But your tie matches. You always like things to match."

"Things to match," he hummed, in a jazz tune, beneath his breath. "Yes, I like things to match." He smiled at her in the old way which he had forgotten or lost, and she felt that a veil had suddenly dropped between her and life. Without and within there was this faint humming, which approached and receded in the room, in the sky, and in her own senses. A thought throbbed with a pang in her mind: I couldn't live if he stops loving me. I couldn't . . . I couldn't. . . .

"Oh, Peter, I'm tired of living with other people. Let's go to ourselves. I'd rather be poor by ourselves."

His smile faded, and he looked anxious and older. "Why, I thought we were all right," he said gently. "I thought you liked being here."

"But you hate it. You didn't want it in the beginning."

He nodded gravely, trying, she could see, not to hurt her. "That was in the beginning. I've got used to it, now."

"We ought to have gone. We ought to have gone to ourselves at the start."

His eyes were moody as he stared at her. "Well, it wasn't my fault. I wanted a home of our own. I was all for it when we were engaged."

"I know." She choked over the word. "It was my fault. It seemed to be letting Father down, somehow. But it's different now. This house is so small. Father says they can manage . . ."

He shook his head, and she watched his mouth twitch with annoyance. "I've got used to it, I tell you, Roy."

"Do you mean you'd rather . . . you'd rather . . ." Her voice quivered and broke.

"I mean, I'm used to it." He turned away to the mirror. "I wanted to begin differently, but I've settled down. I'm used to things as they are."

"But I'm not. I want to be alone with you. I'm never really alone with you. There's always somebody else. And

[105]

I hate this new house. I just pretended I didn't. But it's so—so thin, it's just like living in paper walls."

"Well, then, there is not much to do before you get free." He swung round with a laugh. "You know how much freedom means to us."

"Yes, I know." An ache, like a cold shudder, had seized her throat. What did it mean? What did anything mean? "We're free. Of course, we're free as—as air."

He slipped into his coat and then, after he had gone to the door, turned back quickly and kissed her on the cheek. "You're a good sport, Roy," he said, almost humbly. "I like a good sport."

For an instant she clung to him before her hands dropped away from his arm. "What does freedom matter as long as we love each other?" she asked with a catch in her voice.

"It doesn't matter a bit, really, only we used to talk about it for hours.

"That was before . . . before . . ."

"Well, but we meant it, didn't we?" He sounded as if he were jesting, but she couldn't be sure. "We meant every word of it."

"Yes, we meant it." She drew herself up with a gallant gesture.

"And we still mean it." Though his tone was gay, his eyes brooded unhappily.

"Why, but of course we mean it. I remember there were to be no strings to our marriage. Even when I was little, I hated anything with a string to it." Her smile remained bright and firm.

"That was your idea always."

"And yours too. We both felt that way. We both still feel that way," she corrected herself, on a note of mocking defiance. For it doesn't do any good to whimper, she thought, not any least good in the world.

"Well, thank God, my dear," he said, "I didn't marry a womanly woman."

Her smile had not broken. "They did make things difficult." Then the question that she had tried to bite back on her lips broke out in a sharp despairing cry: "Oh, Peter, what has happened? Why are you so unhappy?"

Standing there in the narrow space of the half-open door, he looked back at her without speaking; and she felt that this silence was surrounding them in waves and cutting them off, alone on an island in time, as if the present moment were separated forever from both the past and the future. It was her life, she knew, and yet it seemed to have no part in life as a whole. But was it only the silence? Was there something else, some fear, some antagonism, some repulsion, surging there in a deep tidal movement between them?

"What an idea!" he said presently. "What have I got to be unhappy about? And you're the best thing that could happen to anybody. If I'm a coward, Roy, I've only myself to blame."

The door closed slowly, then opened and closed again, as if he were hesitating outside in the hall. An instant later, she heard his rapid footsteps turn away and begin to descend the stairs, while she went over to the front window and stood watching for his car in the street. The sudden hush in her mind seemed to her like the breathless pause in a storm between the lightning and the crash of the thunderbolt. It's nothing, really, she said to herself, leaning over the windowsill. The little leaves on the maple stirred faintly; the branches swayed in the wind; and down below in the street a film of shadow flowed onward in ripples. Most of the pigeons had gone home to roost; but a single lonely bird floated down from the trees and then swept up again into the paling sky. Of course, it's nothing. It's nothing but . . . but . . . oh, I

love him too much! Anything too much is always a pain. A sob shuddered through her, while she struggled against it. But why can't people ever say what they mean? Why isn't there any meaning in marriage?

Was this true only of marriage, or was it life itself that was meaningless? Even the spring before (she was twenty-one then, and had been married a year), she had said proudly that, whatever the future brought, she could take it. She had believed that the weak alone are defeated, that any dependence on something outside oneself is an infirmity of the past. Well, she could still believe that. She wouldn't go back to the old ways again. Not for anything in the world would she exchange her lot for her mother's. Yet it was true that when fear came, Roy felt bereft, with nothing to cling to, while her mother could find support either in God or in surrender to circumstances. Anyhow, I am real and she isn't, Roy thought bitterly. There is nothing real about Mother except her pretending. She turned away from the window, and pushing her hair from her forehead, she lifted her soft girlish chin in direct challenge to life. I, she was thinking, I am real, no matter what happens.

IX

WILLIAM FITZROY was old, but he was not yet too old to feel young in April. He had then his hours, surrounded by pretty girls, when he felt that he was scarcely more than a boy. And he had, too, those other hours, alone in the night, when he understood that the greatest tragedy of all is to linger on among futile years after one has finished with life. He had finished; but he was still empty. Dreaming or awake, he knew that he had never had what he wanted; and he knew, also, that in an old man's dreams is a hungering not ever to be satisfied.

Sitting on the terrace in the late sunshine, he had complained of the chill breeze from the river, and Charlotte had fussily brought him into the library and touched a match to the small wood fire in the immense fireplace. While he meditated now upon the inadequacy of things in general and of marriage in particular, he glanced at his wife, as she sat on the other side of the hearth, knitting a baby's blanket of pink wool. Married for more than fifty years! and she might as well have been a casual woman who had nudged down into the seat beside him, while they rattled over a rough road in an omnibus. He had understood Charlotte, of course. Women, especially wives, he reflected, are easy to see through, since they lack that vast inner area of waking and sleeping dreams; but he told her as little of the truth about his hidden self as he would have confided to the first attentive stranger he happened to meet.

He still liked his wife; he admired her disposition; and no one, not even a husband, could fail to respect her; but there was growing upon him, since he had entered that second youth, which a benevolent Providence has denied to women, a suspicion rather than a conviction that mar-

riage is not enough. And though it was true that the outward man, if not the inward Adam, had been designed for imaginary infidelities alone, he still cherished the delusion that a moral nature had inclined him to financial instead of feminine conquests. Because of failing health, and because in part, no doubt, of a sympathetic blonde in New York, his pursuit of pretty girls, in Queenborough at least, had now relaxed into the mere harmless vanity of the aging and impotent.

Like all other successful men of his time and place in the South, he had seen, as a child, the ruin of his family fortunes and the complete reversal of a social system. His struggle had been hard and long, and in the severe process his nature also had hardened. One thought alone troubled him, if we except the itching disturbances of his dreams, and this was the painful knowledge that, no matter how tightly he clung to his possessions, the time must inevitably come when death would loosen his clutch, and all that he had ever owned would slip away from him. His fine new house, as bad as money was able to make it, would pass on to strangers, or, worse still, to relatives who had never owned anything that was worth having.

Glancing round the spacious library, where the handsome sets of books were never taken out of the formidable modern yet still Jacobean bookcases, he sighed regretfully because possessions, like the spirit of the possessor, are not incorruptible. The house, he mused behind his evening paper, had cost him a small fortune, because, naturally, the plan of it had been left to the costlier architects and its furnishing to the more expensive interior decorators. All William had insisted upon was that the place should equal, as he said, the price he was paying for it; and this insistence had borne much opulent fruit both within and without, inasmuch as two formal gardens, one

Italian and one Japanese, now enhanced his surroundings. "Which garden do you prefer?" a landscape
gardener, brought at great expense from New York, had
inquired; and William had replied haughtily, for by this
time his avarice had collapsed in its weakest spot, "What's
the matter with having both?"

So he had both, and with them, a profusion of varied
flower beds arranged in geometrical patterns, which the
landscape gardener described as "floral background."
Gardeners and decorators, William soon discovered, were
all partial to "backgrounds"; and since the term sounded
expensive, he decided that an investment in such purely
ornamental values might in time yield a profit.

Leaning back on the plum-colored velvet cushions of
his chair, he let his predatory gaze wander searchingly
over the walls of the room. Then, abruptly, his eyes narrowed to mere slits of light, while he stared at the imposing bookcase behind his wife's yellowish gray head.

"My dear, have you been at that bookcase?" he asked
testily. "The row on the third shelf from the top is
uneven."

Charlotte bounced on her cushions. Whenever William addressed her as "my dear," she had learned what to
expect. "No, William, I haven't been near it."

"Has anybody been dusting those books?"

"Why, no, William. Fanny wouldn't think of taking
out the books unless I was watching her." Though no
one, least of all her husband, would have attributed to
her such an organ, Charlotte possessed, in reality, a mind
of more than ordinary dimensions. It is true that feminine dissimulation, combined with the flattening influence of marriage, had subdued its activities; yet her
rational part continued to exercise, in discreet silence,
both passive intelligence and a critical faculty. "It may
have been Craig," she murmured, in the apologetic tone

[111]

she had employed for fifty years with but moderate success. "He was down here quite a while yesterday when Stanley was upstairs with me."

William snorted over his paper. "That's who it was then. He can never leave books alone."

"Books alone," echoed his wife, who had acquired the wisdom of the parrot, and knew too well the unhappy consequences of disagreeing with her William.

"You can never tell what he's up to." William's tone was becoming irascible. "There's a screw loose somewhere, and, to save my life, I can't see why Stanley is throwing herself away. The truth is," he snorted explicitly, "I never could stomach the fellow."

Charlotte nodded in assent; on the subject of Craig she had no wish to argue with William. "It is one of those queer infatuations nobody can see any reason for. Stanley isn't very bright, but she is unusually headstrong."

"Well, she's bright enough. Too much sense only makes trouble for a woman." A smile, sly, furtive, and as it appeared to his wife, a well-oiled smile, had puckered his large loose mouth. He was recalling Stanley's young face, colored like a rose, he thought tenderly; for there was a strain of poetry in his mind, though neither the poetry nor his mind moved in a modern direction. His wife could observe his thoughts as plainly as if they were exotic goldfish swimming in a glass bowl; but she continued to regard him with the serene tolerance of the completely disillusioned.

"I hope it will turn out better than we expect," she remarked, as she picked up a loop of wool.

"It won't." William rustled his paper. "Ten chances to one, a marriage turns out exactly as you expect, unless," he added concisely, "it turns out worse."

"Anyway, we needn't worry about Stanley. I can't imagine a situation when she wouldn't come out on top. I suppose that's because she's so pretty," Charlotte added,

with one of her sagacious flashes of insight, "and because men make most of the situations in life."

"The little imp!" William said, but he said it gently. "What was it Craig called her the other night? He's a satirical ass, but he hits the nail on the head sometimes."

Charlotte, who knitted without looking at her needles, did not answer immediately. At the moment, she was busily wondering how women could have survived marriage throughout the ages if knitting had not been invented, and probably by a man. The ubiquitous cigarette, which scented the modern institution so strongly, appeared to her an inadequate substitute. For knitting composed the mind; knitting served the necessary means of evasion; knitting constituted not only an escape, but a tangible protection from husbands. Not that she meant to be harsh upon husbands in general. Even William had his good points as a provider; and in her sensible way she was really attached to him, as one becomes attached to a bed, however uncomfortable, in which one has slept, or tried vainly to sleep, for more than fifty years. To be sure, though he had supplied her with every luxury she did not want, he was disposed to be near about ready money; and there were frequent occasions when she would have preferred fewer rings on her fingers and a little change in her pocket. But one can't have everything, she reasoned, and after all, she was able to manage. Early in her married life, she had learned that the ways of circumventing a husband are many and varied. They required diplomacy, it is true; but what with one thing and another, whether it was a secret negotiation with butchers or an adroit subtraction from the household accounts, she had contrived to keep a tidy sum put away as a nest egg.

"Something about a savage," William was muttering. "Something about the old savage and the new freedom . . ."

"I thought it was the old siren, William, and the new freedom. Of course, he was chaffing. Craig is simply distracted about her."

"Maybe so. Maybe so," grumbled William, who did not take kindly to any correction. "But I've missed her about today. Busy with her new finery, I reckon."

"Yes, she hasn't been in. Roy called up to ask if we'd seen her. She sounded worried about something."

"Worried?" William turned from the financial to the editorial page, and prepared to inform himself on the state of human behavior. "Well, there's plenty to worry her. All she's got to do is to pick up a newspaper and glance over the market. Bless my soul, Charlotte, the radio isn't on. I thought something was wrong."

With an obedient sigh, Charlotte rose from her chair, and holding her knitting in one hand, moved cautiously to the radio, which began after a minute to blare out an immelodious torrent of sound. "I sometimes think it gives me a headache," she said, raising her voice.

"Headache? Pish! Tush! I don't know what's come over women today. They're nothing in the world but a mass of nerves. What's that about Roy?" he shouted above the tumult. "You were saying something about Roy."

"Only that she sounded worried. I may have imagined it." Pushing her chair farther away from the radio, Charlotte settled herself on the cushions and passed a weary hand over her forehead. Why, she wondered pathetically, were men so fond of noise, and of discords in particular? It was like trying to talk in a high wind. A pain as sharp as the thrust of a needle stabbed into her bosom and was gone in an instant. It was nothing, the doctor said, the merest twinge of neuritis; but her florid face turned pale, and she remembered, as if it were yesterday, the dreadful years when her mother and her aunt lay dying of cancer. "I'm fond of Roy," she added, at a higher pitch. "She's an honest little thing, and she's very attractive too."

"Yes, she's honest," William assented, without enthusiasm; for honesty, though commendable in principle and in its place, is not an endearing quality in women.

"I felt she never had a fair chance," Charlotte rejoined, absentmindedly counting her stitches. "I mean, everybody has always made such a difference between her and Stanley."

William scowled. "If Stanley takes my fancy, I can't help it. There's something about Stanley."

"I know." His wife nodded patiently, while she looped the wool over her finger. "Yes, there's something taking about her."

"I can tell you what's wrong with Roy." William dropped his paper and thrust out a long admonitory forefinger, which, though rheumatic in the joints, was still eloquent in gesture. "She's too modern. And I can tell you what's wrong with the whole modern outlook, from *a* to *izzard*. There's not an ounce of religion in the younger generation . . ." He broke off, spluttering slightly, while the radio spluttered still louder and then stopped short as if it were winded. "Not an ounce," he bellowed, gathering his voice, as Charlotte clapped her hands to her ears.

"Religion?" his wife echoed, in confusion, as if the idea were new to her. Yes, it was true, she supposed, though she had never thought of the young as needing religion, because they always had so much else. For the elderly, especially for the elderly with husbands who were even more elderly but refused to admit it, she considered faith indispensable. How could I ever have stood William, she found herself thinking, if I hadn't had something to fall back on? Not, she repeated, that she wasn't attached to William, and proud of him, too, after the inexplicable fashion of wives; but there was no use in denying that God had helped her to stand him.

William, who had been grunting irritably to himself,

burst out presently in an explosion of anger. "I never could make out what anybody sees in him. I mean, that fellow Craig, with his rattlebrained, stuffed-up, crackpot ideas. Talks of liberalism, when all he wants is to take away what I've got and hand it over to some trifling half-wit who never lifted a finger except to light a cigarette or cast a vote."

When he had exhausted his wind, and not till then, Charlotte murmured gently, "That was before he met Stanley. All he thinks of now is giving Stanley everything that she wants."

William started to grumble again, but in the middle of the snuffling noise, he was seized by a sudden jovial humor. "Well, it will take a better living than he'll ever make to do that. But what does she see in him? I ask you that. What can anybody see in him?"

"He's attractive in his way, I suppose. The girls were all silly about him at first. They thought him so romantic." She paused, smoothed out the baby's blanket over her plump knees, and added impressively, "His father is well-off, isn't he?"

"So-so. Nothing to brag about. Made his money in oil, and then let most of it slip through his fingers. Hadn't sense enough to hold on to what he'd got." Stopping between breaths, William drew out a white silk handkerchief and snorted into its ample folds. "The trouble with the fellow, sir"—he always addressed her as "sir" when he was in a scolding vein—"is that he has no guts. . . ."

A shadow rather than a sound made her turn quickly to find that Beavers, the new English butler, had materialized, like the spirit of Empire, beside the radio, which had become prophetically ominous over the European situation. Though Beavers spoke in his usual smooth undertones, his low voice was audible above the international jeremiad. Having received the message, Mrs. Fitzroy passed it on to her husband, who had plunged

back behind his paper. "Beavers says Parry Clay asks to speak to you."

The paper was lowered sufficiently for a bald head and a pair of bushy eyebrows to emerge above it. "If he's anything to say, let him come in, Beavers."

"Yes, sir. Thank you, sir." Beavers faded obsequiously into air, while his mistress reflected, I'll never get used to English servants; they don't seem quite human. The thought was still in her mind when Parry slipped noiselessly into the room. Or was it only the rage of foreign oratory that made everything else soundless by contrast?

"Come in, Parry," she said kindly. "Mr. Fitzroy will speak to you." If only he wouldn't look so dumb and sullen, she said to herself, for William liked cheerful Negroes. But was the boy really a Negro? she asked, startled, while her trained perceptions skimmed lightly over ethnological problems. Parry's father looked as white as William, or more so, because ill health had darkened William's skin and pouched the loose flesh under his eyes. Somewhere, a long time before, white blood had come in on both sides of the Clay family, and after once coming in, apparently, it had never quite departed. But white blood, though Charlotte had heard that it was less sanguine than black, would not necessarily make the boy appear so gloomy and—well, yes, vaguely tragic. He looks lost, she told herself pityingly, for hers was a generous heart. He looks confused and lost, as if he were trying to find his way. She wished she could help him; he had a good face, she decided, in spite of his brooding expression.

"Well, Parry," William said over his paper, "is there something you wish to see me about? I hope there's nothing wrong with Miss Stanley's car."

Though his tone was not unpleasant, it was edged with finality. Hearing that familiar accent, William's wife told herself that whatever the boy wanted, he would not

find it in her husband. While she fumbled for an instant over her knitting needles, she felt devoutly thankful that she had not been alive in the ages of slavery. And she felt doubly thankful, she added after a pause, that William had not been alive in the ages of slavery. For there were traits in William to which the solemn marriage ceremony had never reconciled her completely, and the chief of these, she had decided long ago, was William's unfortunate manner with the poor and with animals.

They waited in silence for Parry to answer, while he stood there, in his clean striped shirt and neatly patched suit, as if some hostile element in the room had turned him into wood. His dark, melancholy eyes looked enormous, she thought, and curiously opaque, as if the light splintered back without sinking into the pupils. I believe he is frightened, she said to herself. He is frightened of William. But she had watched the effect of William upon the helpless too often to wonder about it.

"What is it, Parry?" she prompted, fearing that William might become testy again and make it harder for everybody. "I hear you have taken honors at school, and I know your father and mother are proud of you."

Light appeared to grow rather than flash in his face. She watched it deepen under the skin while his features became surprisingly animated. He is like a foreigner, she decided, in astonishment, for she had never looked upon colored people as foreigners. A respectable foreigner, she added hastily, as if she were being unfair.

"Yes, ma'am," the boy replied, and then rushed on, reciting words he had patiently committed to memory. "It's about the school I came. I'm sure to take a scholarship for next year, the teacher says, but that's only for the classes, and if I can go on to Washington, I thought Mr. Fitzroy might lend me the money to live on. I'll pay him back. I'll pay him back every cent as sure as I live."

Leaning slightly forward, Mr. Fitzroy regarded him

indulgently; and to Mrs. Fitzroy, who had learned to interpret her husband's every look and gesture, it appeared to be the indulgence of established refusal. She stirred uneasily, while she looped the wool over her finger, and the knitting needles clicked on more rapidly, as if they were running a race with the minutes.

"But I thought you had had schooling enough," William said placidly. "You can read and write and do sums, I suppose."

"Yes, sir, but I want to get on. I want to go to college and then, if I take another scholarship, to Howard University. Pa could have helped me but for the bank failure last year. . . . But I'll pay back every cent of it, sir."

The race slackened and paused for an instant, while Charlotte glanced up over her knitting. "It's remarkable how well the boy has done," she said, with the desperate courage of pity. "His teacher thinks he ought to be helped." Of course, she told herself as she broke off, she believed in keeping colored people in their place, wherever that was or wasn't, but she did think they might have their own lawyers and doctors. When it came to that, she didn't know two finer characters than Minerva and Abel, but William would say that they belonged to the old school and had never tried to be "uppity."

Her husband turned his frosty glance on her and continued as evenly as if there had been no interruption, "I am glad to have a good report of you, Parry, but I hope you won't let your head get chock-full of tomfool ideas about education. Your race doesn't need lawyers. There are too many white lawyers already, and if any of you get into trouble that's not your fault, your white friends are always ready to help you out. The best thing you can do is to turn your hand to some suitable work. There's room for a good waiter or porter, or you might find a job as a postman, though that's less easy, I imagine, than it used to be. But take my advice and don't get fancy ideas in your

head. There's too much education, anyway. Too much foolishness out of books and too little old-fashioned religion." He cocked a suspicious eye over his paper. "You go to church regularly, I hope?"

Parry did not reply. He merely stood there, in a kind of downcast immobility, while the animation drained slowly out of his face and figure, and even out of the new blue cap which hung, limp as a rag, in his relaxed grasp.

"You go to church, don't you, Parry?" Mrs. Fitzroy repeated.

When she spoke, he looked at her with a bewildered expression, and it seemed to her that he plucked himself by force out of the little space he had filled in the room. A few minutes before she had turned off the radio, and she now found herself longing for the calm nasal tones of the announcer or even for the furious clamor of oratory. Then, while her thoughts jerked into place, she became aware that William was still speaking his mind.

"If you aren't afraid of work," he was saying, "I'll see what I can do. I'll pay you for looking after Miss Stanley's car in your spare time, but I haven't any money to throw away on tomfoolery."

"Yes, sir," the boy said. Then, glancing at Mrs. Fitzroy, he added, "Yes, ma'am," under his breath, before he turned and disappeared as soundlessly as he had come.

Like a startled rabbit, Charlotte huddled on her cushions, and then bounced up impulsively. "Wait a minute, Parry," she called. "I've something to send your mother."

"Where're you going, my dear?" William asked, as if he had not been listening.

Without answering him, she waddled, as she always did when she forgot herself, across the room, past the radio, which William had turned on again, and out into the hall. Her purse was in her knitting bag, for she had learned to be prepared for William's denials, and not a

little of her pilfering from the household accounts was animated by justice or charity. She couldn't do anything with William, she knew, but in small ways she had been able occasionally to outwit his designs.

When she reached the servants' dining room, however, the boy was not there, and Beavers, moving softly in the pantry, said that he had hurried through without stopping. Fumbling in her bag, she thought, I might have given him a little money, but it wouldn't have been enough . . . And now there's William. I'll have to face William. . . .

There was a ring at the door as she scurried back into the library and ignored William's peremptory, "What's that? Where've you been, eh?" While she flopped down in her chair, and nervously wound up her ball of pink wool, she said in a voice which was drowned by the radio, "I wonder if that can be Stanley and Craig?"

But it was only Asa, and the first thing she noticed about him was that he seemed worn-out (there was a fagged look in his eyes that reminded her of a jaded horse), and he was shabbier—or was it more seedy?—than usual. Well, he had a hard life. Anybody who married Lavinia must have expected that. She had always been fond of him, and tonight her sympathy brimmed over in the hope that William would offer him a glass of sherry or a drink of his old Bumgardner. "So it's you, Asa," she said, vaguely motioning to a chair, while, for the hundredth time, it seemed to her, she stopped the radio. "You look tired. Wouldn't you like something? We thought it might be Stanley and Craig."

Asa shook his head, and she felt that the movement had rippled out in circles through the air of the room. Could there have been an accident? she wondered; there was so much careless driving. Or was Lavinia having an actual instead of a sham heart attack?

It was a moment before Asa answered, and his voice,

when at last he spoke, was so flattened in tone that it might have come from an inanimate object. So a piece of furniture might have spoken, she found herself imagining, if furniture had a voice. "No, I came to ask about Stanley. Didn't she spend last night with you?"

A growl broke from William, while his wife looked up in anxiety. "She was coming, but something must have prevented. William and I were just saying how much we had missed her." She clipped off her sentence and looked at him expectantly. "Haven't you seen her tonight?"

"That's why I came. I haven't seen her. I thought she might be here. I thought Roy might have misunderstood. . . ."

"You mean you haven't been home?"

"Home? Oh, yes, I've been home."

"Wasn't she there?"

He shook his head, while the amused gleam in his eyes was washed out by a mist of pain. "She hasn't been there since—since yesterday."

"But where is she?" William was beginning to boom as he did when he was agitated. "Good God, man, what has happened?"

"I don't know," Asa replied soberly, and Charlotte reminded herself that, poor and unimportant as he was, he could not be bullied by William. He's the quiet kind, she thought, but he's stubborn enough to dig in his toes and hold his ground against everybody. "I don't know," he repeated. "I'm trying to find out."

"When did she go out? Was she in her car?"

"She went out in her car yesterday afternoon. Virgie says she was taking some dresses to be altered. She had a suitcase . . ."

"Where's the car?" William's flabby face seemed to have withered, and his large mottled hands, covered with coarse reddish hair on the back, were twitching over the newspaper.

"The car's in the garage. The dressmaker called up the house this morning and asked us to send for it."

"Where is she, then? God alive, she's got to be somewhere!"

"Of course, she's somewhere." Charlotte spoke in the firm unsweetened tones she reserved for a crisis. "She can't possibly be lost. If she'd had an accident, we should have heard from the hospital."

"She called a taxi. . . ." Asa uttered the words as if they were wrung out of him. "Mrs. Dayton says she had her call a taxi, and went off in it." He hesitated and added in an expressionless voice, "She took the suitcase."

"But the dresses were to be altered."

"They weren't altered. She didn't open the suitcase."

"But somebody *must* have seen her." Charlotte's whisper drained away with a moaning sound. Yet, in spite of her horror of mystery, she could tell herself that she did not really love Stanley. William loved her in his peculiar way, which, strangely enough, seemed to her gluttonous (yes, that was the only word for it), but his wife had never loved the child, not even when she was an adorable smiling baby in a cap and coat of white fur. It was William, notwithstanding his thick husk of vanity, who would be hurt by what happened, or did not happen, to Stanley. For William loved his niece as an old man loves the remembered ecstasy of his youth.

"Why, I saw her myself," William growled, knotting his forehead until his eyebrows hung like tufts of dried grass over the blinking anger in his eyes. "I saw her as I was coming out yesterday afternoon. I was later than usual, and it must have been six o'clock . . . or maybe half past. She was on her way downtown in Peter's car. Peter was driving, and, bless my soul, I noticed him because he almost ran into a truck at the corner of Seventh and Washington. Grazed it by an inch! I called to Baxter to stop when the car skidded into the gutter. Rattle-

brained driving, if ever I saw it, sir! What I can never understand is how a man who drives like that should be able to cut up people without killing them. But they're all rattlebrained now, the whole bunch of them. I was just saying to my wife when you came in that all this modern racket (and Stanley's no better than the rest of 'em) sticks in my gizzard. . . ."

"Then Peter must know where she was going," Charlotte murmured. "Why don't you ask Peter?"

Asa smiled faintly, but his smile was scarcely more than an ironic flicker over the stiffened mask of his features. "We can't ask him. He hasn't come back."

"Not come back? Where's he gone?" thundered William.

"He had a call out of town. Dr. Bellamy, I think he said, called him to operate. He told Roy he might not get home till this morning. But this morning he didn't come. He has not come tonight."

"It's half past nine now." William drew out his watch and looked at it indignantly. "It's a quarter to ten."

"He may still come," Charlotte suggested feebly.

"I don't know." Asa's gaze wandered round the room and came to rest on her bulging figure, seated like some emblem of domestic security on her plum-colored cushions. "I called up Bellamy . . ."

"Well? Well, I said, sir!" William's face had flushed from gray to purple, while he lifted a shaking hand to pluck unsteadily at his collar button.

Sliding from her chair to her uncertain feet, Charlotte hurried out of the room and returned with a glass of water, which she held to her husband's lips. This is the only thing, except his own flesh, that could hurt William, she thought. If anything has happened to Stanley . . .

"He couldn't tell me," Asa answered slowly. "He didn't know. He said he hadn't asked him to operate out of town. . . ."

"Hadn't asked him? Do you mean . . ."

Asa moistened his lips, but they were still so stiff that he had to wait a minute before replying. "I don't mean anything. I don't know anything. I'm in a . . . in a . . ."

William's features were suddenly convulsed, as if he were choking. "You've got to mean something!" he burst out. "Damn it all, sir, you've got to mean something!"

The explosion left Asa unshaken. He was the color of wood that has been left out-of-doors in bad weather, Charlotte found herself rambling, and the smudges under his eyes looked as if they had been rubbed in with charcoal. Men are so helpless in trouble, she thought with a sigh. Why is it, when they spend all their lives facing facts, that they should never have learned how to meet an emergency?

"I thought you might have heard something," Asa was saying.

"But you can't think they're together!" Charlotte cried out. "You can't think she's gone off with—with Peter."

Asa shook his head again. "I can't think. I've stopped thinking."

"But Stanley couldn't. She . . . she isn't . . . she isn't like that."

"I don't know what she's like." Asa's voice was hard and level. "I don't know what anybody is like."

"She's like all the others," William stormed, while Charlotte understood as she watched him that, for the first time in her uneasy marriage, she had seen her husband stripped to the bone, stripped even of that masculine vanity which he had worn always like a protective layer of fat. "But if that girl . . . By God, Charlotte, if a niece of mine . . ."

"Don't, William. Please, William." An impending nameless fear had yielded to the immediate horror of an apoplectic stroke under her very eyes. "You will make yourself sick."

A smothered gurgling and rumbling issued from William's throat. "I tell . . . I tell you . . ."

Asa stood up and straightened his shoulders. "I'll go now," he said quietly. "There doesn't seem to be anything else I can do."

"Where's Craig?" asked Charlotte, with her apprehensive glance on her husband.

"Craig?" It was the first moment that any of them had thought of Craig. "He's waiting for me outside. He brought me out in his car."

"What does he say?"

"He doesn't say anything. What is there for him to say? But I'm not thinking of Craig. I'm not thinking of Peter, damn him! I'm not thinking of Stanley! I'm thinking of Roy!"

His voice broke with anger, and turning away before they could stop him, he rushed out of the room and through the hall to the front door.

With more anxiety than pain in her eyes, Charlotte stared after him. "We didn't give him a drink, William," she said. "And I never saw a man who needed a drink more."

X

WAS he tired of waiting? Has he gone back without me? Asa asked himself, as he stumbled down from the terrace and on through the April starlight in the Italian garden. Well, they were all alike, young people nowadays. They knew no law but their own impulses. It is hard to be young in the present, they told him; but isn't it always hard to be young? Though not nearly so hard, he added at once, as it is to be old. . . . "I can't find the car," he said aloud, feeling tired and angry, and as if he had caved in through the middle. "He must have gone off and left me to get home as best I can."

But no. Rounding a group of three cypresses, he saw the lights of the car at the end of the avenue, and a few minutes later Craig's profile was outlined as sharply as if it were a projection from darkness. Black as night, he looked against the electric lamp in the road. Until Asa reached him, he neither spoke nor moved. Then, at the sound of his name, he tossed a dead cigarette from his fingers and put his hand on the wheel.

"I was afraid you'd gone," Asa said, as he scrambled over the stones and into the car. "She hadn't been there. They don't know anything."

Craig did not answer. His face seemed to be molded of hollows, dark hollows among which the shifting lights from the road sank and were absorbed. It might have been a skull beside him, Asa thought, a skull bared of flesh and yet curiously animate. Once, when he glanced round, the light roving eyes looked as shallow as glass in their sockets, and as empty of all expression. He hasn't spoken three words, Asa told himself. He seems to have lost the power of speech—or never to have possessed it. Yet speech, not action, had been Craig's natural expres-

sion. He had been enslaved by words, so long as words were only the vehicle of impersonal forces. Now, when to speak would mean tearing out a part of himself, he was overwhelmed by a kind of dumb agony.

The pity is, Asa thought, that he's futile. Like all the rest of us, like our world, our time, our code of living, he has no direction; he is incapable of any permanent motive. Ideas may matter to him, but they do not matter enough. He has never known what he believed. Or is it that he has never really believed anything? Feeling has eaten him through and through, and there has been nothing hard and strong in him to resist it. They are all like that, and so am I, Asa told himself, only they have the freedom for destruction, and I was kept always in chains. I may have lost my beliefs, but the empty forms of my beliefs are still holding me. And Roy would have nothing left, not even these vague impressions, to live by. Oh, Roy, Roy . . .

But Asa couldn't think of her. There were things that wouldn't bear thinking about. Anybody but Roy might have been hurt, Roy, the core of his heart, he thought, repeating a phrase he had read somewhere. He loved Stanley as he loved Andrew. Stanley was his child, but not, he hesitated, watching Craig's reckless hands on the wheel, the core of his heart. Aloud he said: "We'd better go straight home. She may have got there before us. After all, so many things may have happened."

Craig nodded, without turning his head. "That's what I've been telling myself."

The car shot out of the side road and turned in the direction of Queenborough. They sped past a service station, past a second service station, past a row of small houses with unkempt yards, past a butcher shop, a green-grocer, a corner drugstore, and the unsightly stumps of what had once been a fine row of maples. How we hate beauty, Asa meditated, diverting his thoughts. How we

hate order. . . . Yes, it was true, as he had said to Craig, anything might have happened. The car—Peter's car—might have broken down. She might have decided to spend the night with a friend. The telephone may have been out of order. But he must keep his mind on the bare facts; he must refuse to imagine. Glancing round, he asked himself what Craig was feeling. What was he thinking? What was he imagining? Carved out of bone, Craig might have been, with that lean, blank face jutting out between flashes of light and darkness, arrested, immobile, solitary. A changeable face which had been petrified into a look of mortal despair; into a look which was caught and held fast before it could break up with surprise or pleasure or anguish. He was keeping it back, too, that incredible probability—the thought they evaded and denied even while they acknowledged its truth.

What could she have found in Peter? Asa wondered. What is there about him that is different from Craig, or from the rest of us? A few months ago, she was apparently infatuated with Craig; but she had drained him dry in the end, and the end, after all, was barely more than the beginning. Then it was that she had turned to Peter, for excitement, for renewal, for an inexhaustible charm against tedium or satiety. Or had the sight of Roy's happiness (Asa flinched from the question) aroused a secret destructive instinct, which still survived, under the sham called civilization, in most men and women? Not that anything mattered now. Digging for reasons could help nothing and prevent nothing. The reason had lain there all the time, while they set up ineffectual pretenses and trusted vainly to a philosophy of evasive idealism. A collection of good impulses, of right intentions, without the necessary balance of power. . . . "Look out!" he called sharply, for they had grazed a truck and just missed a dog in the road. "Look out, or you'll kill something!"

Craig laughed on a jarring note. "I'd like to kill something. But not a dog. I've nothing against dogs."

They were speeding down Granite Boulevard, and Asa waited impatiently for the abrupt turn into Westward Avenue. Ever since they had started just now, his mind, running in a narrow groove like a tunnel had seen a triangle of light in the distance. Was it in another life or only a few hours ago that he had set out to find Stanley? First, the telephone to the hospitals; then the dressmaker's and the garage; then to Fitzroyal, the Fitzroy place in the suburbs. It seemed to him now that these hours had nothing to do with reality, no part or place in the flux and reflux of time. Things like this don't happen to people like us, he thought stubbornly. They simply don't happen.

Aloud he said, "They may be waiting at home for us now."

"Or in a hospital."

"But we telephoned."

"She may have been brought in later."

"But we should have had word."

"Not if they didn't know. Not if she is unconscious."

"But someone must have been with her."

"She spends the night out so often."

"Well, we'll be there in a minute. The house looks all right."

"There's a light in the living room."

"And in her mother's room upstairs. If she's come back, she will be with her mother."

"God!" said Craig under his breath, and then over again in the same deadened voice, "God!"

The car stopped with a jerk. Holding his latchkey in his hand, Asa ran up the steps and opened the door. Behind him, he heard Craig breathing in short gasps, and each breath sounded as if it were struggling to break free in a spasm of pain.

The hall was dimly lighted, and there was a single lamp turned on in the living room. At the noise of the slamming door, a figure appeared on the staircase, and because the dress was green and the glow behind it merely a faint shimmer, Asa imagined for an instant that it was Stanley.

"Here she is!" he cried. "Here is Stanley!"

Craig's breath was suddenly suspended, and then went on again with a shudder. He did not speak; but the figure on the upper landing descended slowly to meet them, and Asa saw that he had mistaken Roy for Stanley. She moved as if she were frozen into stillness, and her features wore a graven look, remote and inaccessible, as if she were withdrawn from a share in any of the things that happened around her. Her lips were tight and straight, but they were vividly reddened, and the look in her tired eyes was still bright and defiant. A thought jerked through his mind. She can face anything that comes. She can face anything without giving way.

"You looked like Stanley in that green dress," he said. "Has Stanley come back?"

A bitter little laugh answered him. "Did you expect her?"

"We hoped she might. . . ." How foolish the phrase sounded! "We hoped. . . ."

Roy laughed again, and it seemed to him that the only living thing left in her was that derisive voice.

"Mother wants to see you," she said. "And you, too, Craig. She's had a letter. It came by special delivery, just after you went out."

"A letter? Then there wasn't an accident?" He had to make some sound, Asa told himself; yet every word he uttered only added to his helplessness, his sense of inward futility.

"Oh, no, there wasn't an accident." She turned back up the stairs, and went on ahead of them to the second

floor and into her mother's room. Her shoulders were straight; her head was high; but she moved blindly, as if she were walking in her sleep and had left her direction to some safe instinct. Her remoteness, he knew, was merely an attitude, a protective barrier which she had placed between her and life. Beneath the stonelike surface she was still vulnerable to disaster.

Lavinia was lying inertly back on her pillows, which had been raised to support the weight of her head. There was despair in her face, and she held an open letter in her relaxed grasp. "I've heard from Stanley," she began, and burst into tears. "But I cannot believe it. Oh, Asa, I cannot believe it. . . ."

Asa seized the letter, which was very short, and read it with a glance, while Craig stared down over his shoulder. With the words whirling in black specks before his eyes, Asa could hear that hoarse murmur, like the panting of a man who has run a hard race and lost.

"Dearest Mother,

"We can't keep on like this any longer, Peter and I. I am sorry to hurt you, and to hurt Roy and Craig, but we can't go on, except with each other. When we feel this way we have to be together, and nothing else matters. I could never have made Craig happy, but Peter and I were made for each other.

"I hope Roy will get over it and live her own life. She is so strong and brave, but she and Peter are not the least bit alike.

"Darling Mother, I do hate to hurt you,

"Stanley."

"Nothing else matters," Asa repeated slowly, and choked over a lump that felt as hard and dry as a cinder.

"Damn him!" Craig cried out in torture. "Damn them both! Damn everybody!"

"Craig!" Lavinia wept reproachfully, and broke into louder sobs. "My poor child, what will become of her?"

Asa looked again at the letter. There was no date and no address; it had been posted, apparently, when the train stopped in Washington, or when they stopped there in Peter's car. While the paper shook in his hand, he felt that his empty stomach had turned suddenly and he might be sick without warning. I've eaten nothing since breakfast, he said to himself, and there's a black chill inside me. His ribs seemed to be closing together, but, after an effort, he was able to summon his mind back from the edge of a void.

"It's Roy I'm thinking of," he heard a hollow voice saying, and recognized it as his own. "He has ruined Roy's life."

Roy, who had been standing by the window, turned quickly and came over to him. "But he hasn't, Father," she said, and there was a bright edge of steel in her tone. "We were both free. I wouldn't have stood in his way. He knew I'd never have held on to him. He had a right to go if . . . if . . ." The edge of steel snapped in two.

"Roy!" her mother gasped, struggling to raise herself. "Roy, do you know what you're saying? Asa, do you hear what the child is saying?"

"I heard, Lavinia. What she says won't do any harm—or any good either."

With a quavering moan, Lavinia sank back again. "That's the cause of it all. Roy has always encouraged Peter in his . . . in his . . ."

"There, there, Lavinia." Asa turned from Roy's frozen brightness to the tragic gloom of Craig's features. "That doesn't help anybody."

Craig, who had said nothing since Lavinia rebuked him, burst out with an inarticulate exclamation, as if he had lost both the power of speech and the verbal pattern of thought. The sound, so burdened with misery, was like the long-drawn cry of an animal in a trap.

Startled, they looked at him, and Asa said, "You're ill, Craig. Don't you need a drink?"

Craig gazed at them stupidly for an instant. Then he answered deliberately, as if he were speaking words in a foreign tongue. "Yes, I need a drink. I need two drinks. I need three drinks." Huddled in his clothes, his long, loose figure seemed to have shrunk and dwindled down to the bony structure.

"Then we'll go downstairs." Asa caught his arm at the elbow and drew him away. "There's nothing we can do. Nothing but telephone William and Andrew."

At this, Lavinia collected her strayed faculties. "William will know what to do," she said. "Tell him to make some

excuse for the newspapers. The wedding was to have been in four—no, three days. Everybody . . . everybody . . ."

"For God's sake, stop talking," Craig called back from the hall. "It's the time for drink, now."

"Don't mind him," Asa said warningly. "He's off his head, poor devil. Somebody ought to look after him."

As he followed Craig out of the room, he turned and glanced back at Roy, who looked tearless and stricken and yet, in some odd way, unbreakable. An instant later, while he descended the stairs, he heard Lavinia's wailing lament, "Oh, Roy, this will kill me! How can I live through it?"

Well, he would go back as soon as he could get rid of Craig without hurting his feelings—if any feelings were left in that skeleton. What feeble folk are human beings in a crisis, he told himself, especially modern human beings. They made crises, and then, having made them, they lost control and began to call on the invisible Powers.

Craig had switched on the light, and the dining room and pantry were flooded with the soulless glare of electricity. He had already brought out the glasses, and he waited impatiently while Asa found a bottle of whiskey and a half-emptied syphon of soda water.

"No water," Craig said. Then after pouring the whiskey into his glass, he pushed it away from him and looked up angrily. "It isn't Peter's, is it?"

"Good God, no. Uncle William sent this down. There isn't any of Peter's."

Craig's fingers were shaking, and the glass had to be held to his lips for the first swallow. When he had tossed off the whiskey in a gulp, and was holding out his glass for refilling, he began to ramble on more coherently. To Asa's astonishment, the drink, which would have paralyzed him almost at once, appeared only to sober Craig

and to steady his nerves. "You'd better take a bite," Asa said, offering some cheese and biscuits he had found in a cupboard. "If your stomach's as empty as mine, it won't stand it."

"I could do with another drink."

Asa withdrew the bottle. "You can't get into a car with all that whiskey inside you."

"I don't care. I don't care a damn what happens to me."

"I'm not thinking of you. I'm thinking of the people who get in your way."

"I'm sober. I'm perfectly sober. I don't even feel it."

"You may in five minutes."

"You think I'm drunk? Good God, you couldn't make me drunk if you tried."

"I'm not trying. How much had you had before you came for me?"

Craig shook his head. "I don't know. I've been trying to get drunk, and I can't. Do you know what that means? I want to get drunk, and I can't . . . not on whiskey . . ."

The young fool has no stamina, Asa thought. He could never hold his breath underwater. Asa remembered he had once asked his father what kind of man dominated a crisis in history, and that Daniel Timberlake had answered: "The man who can hold his breath longest underwater." But Craig, for all his fine impulses, would always be swept away by emotion. He would never subdue or separate the conflicting motives, either within or without. A generous chap, but ineffectual to the bone, Asa told himself, a true child of a dying age, one of the predestined victims of life. If only Craig had been stronger, he might have held Stanley, who was parasitic by nature and would instinctively cling to the victor. But he had lacked the insight to perceive that Stanley could surrender to nothing weaker than the touch of brutality.

Over his glass, which he had half-filled, Craig was looking at Asa in sardonic despair. "I'll have to spend the night in that apartment, I'll have to spend the night in the midst of all the things we picked up together."

"Wouldn't you rather stay here?" Asa grasped his arm as if to drag him back from some act of blind desperation. "You may sleep in the spare room. I'll get it ready." But he was thinking: And Roy will have to spend the night among Peter's things. God damn him! As soon as I can shake Craig, I'll try to move some of those things out. Or I can sleep up there and make her stay with her mother. Her mother will need her.

"No, I'll leave my car and walk home. I can't kill anybody in three blocks on foot."

"Well, I've got to eat," Asa said grimly. "If the skies fall, I've got to eat." After rummaging in the icebox, he brought out a collection of beef scraps which Virgie had saved for hash. "Take a bite of this." He put the dish on the table and began cutting the crust from a loaf of bread. "You need something solid."

"I don't want anything. I'm as sober as—as hell. Hell doesn't get drunk."

Dragging a chair to the pantry table, Asa placed a slice of beef on the crust and began eating ravenously. "A vacuum won't help you," he said. "You can't think with a vacuum."

"I don't want to think. There's nothing to think about."

"You can't live with a vacuum."

"I don't want to live. There's nothing to live for."

"Maybe so," Asa nodded. "But it isn't easy to die. And, anyway, you never know how good scraps can taste till your stomach has caved in." Taking the bottle from Craig, he measured out a moderate drink and squirted into it a dash of soda water from the syphon. That hit the

[137]

exact right spot, he said to himself, when he had tossed off the drink; and the exact right spot was somewhere in an undistributed middle. There would be no hash for breakfast; but Virgie would find an egg for Lavinia, and Roy and he could always make out on next to nothing. "I feel a new man," he said aloud. "It's amazing how much one's courage depends on the pit of the stomach." Was all stamina really physical? But no. He had seen too much starving fortitude to admit that.

"I'd as well be getting on," Craig said. "Not that it matters."

"Don't let go, Craig. Try to hold on. Nobody knows what the future may bring." Did one always, at the end, fall back upon platitude?

"Nothing that I want. Nothing that will make any difference."

"You're young. You have the only two things that really matter, youth and health." Since he was no longer empty, Asa said to himself, it was easier to feel hopeful. But the platitude was true, after all. Youth could never stay beaten. Youth has no finality. If only he doesn't try to find a way out! He is too confused, poor devil, to see where he is going.

"Here's to youth and health!" Craig grinned mockingly. "Anyway, I'm not drunk. I can walk a straight line."

"I wish you'd stay,'" Asa urged; for he was worrying over what might happen in that empty apartment.

"Sorry, but I'd rather not."

Following him to the front door, Asa watched anxiously while Craig hurried on through patches of light and darkness to the next crossing. He walked, as he had said, a straight line, with his shoulders erect and his bare head flung back. Perhaps the whiskey would take effect later on. Or it might be that his mental agony was immune from any form of physical intoxication.

Another ruined life, Asa thought, glancing up at the indifferent heavens. And God only knows why!

XI

AS ASA closed the door and shot the bolt into the socket, he reminded himself that Lavinia was waiting for him to bring her a cup of milk. Not even the ruin of four young lives could alter the inexorable logic of custom. Meals must still be served and eaten, or left uneaten, at the usual hours; one must still undress before going to bed and dress again after getting up; and all this irksome tyranny of little habits would presently dissolve and mingle in some thick deposit of days, months, years. The slow dust of time would drift in and settle; one would cease to remember and go on again as if nothing had altered.

In the kitchen he touched a match to the gas jet and put on the milk in a blue saucepan. He was still stirring it aimlessly, when the door into the pantry swung open and Roy came in.

"I've just given Mother some Veronal. She may get quiet after she's had her hot milk."

"I'm heating it now. Craig stayed some time. He's a broken man, Roy."

Roy's lips hardened. "He would be. He's the brittle sort." Her face, under the light, was like a waxen mask, and her dry-eyed gaze reminded him of the unblinking detachment of the dead. He dropped the spoon and put out his hand to her. "I'd give my life if I could spare you this, Roy."

She flinched away, as if his tenderness hurt her. "Don't pity me," she said harshly. "I will not be pitied."

"But I must suffer with you."

"You mustn't. I don't want you to suffer with me."

"I'm your father, darling. How can I help it?"

She shook her head obstinately while she drew farther

away from him. "I won't get soft. If I let myself get soft, I'm done for. . . ." As he looked at her in silence, she added in a metallic voice, without modulation or cadence, "I have to face things my own way. Nobody can help me. I don't want help. I don't want pity. I'd rather die than be pitied."

"But I can't let you go, my child. I must keep as close to you as I can. I can't see your life ruined without having my heart broken. . . ."

She turned on him fiercely, though he could see the cold despair in her eyes. "Why will you and Mother never really grow up? Nobody talks that way any longer. My life isn't ruined. Nobody could ruin my life. . . . And I won't have them hounding Peter. He knew he was free to leave me whenever he wanted to. We had agreed to that when we were married. He knew I'd never try to hang on to him. I despise women who hang on to men. . . ."

"It was more than marriage, darling. There was responsibility, and integrity, and—"

She laughed scornfully. "Words, words, and they mean nothing. They have never meant anything. But I don't care. I will not have Uncle William and you and Andrew hounding Peter. . . ."

"But Stanley?" A spark flickered in his eyes at the picture of himself on anyone's track, even Peter's.

"You needn't worry about Stanley. She will always be taken care of. There will always be some man, or more likely two men, to look after her."

"She's weak, Roy, and you are strong. The weak have always had the strong to protect them. But the strong must protect themselves or go under."

"Well, I'll save myself. Nobody, not even Peter, is going to spoil my life. As for Stanley . . ."

She broke off; and he said unhappily: "The hardest thing for me to believe is that family feeling no longer means anything, for better or worse. It has done harm

[141]

enough, I know, but at least it held things together when the world rocked. Anyway, the family as a unit now seems to be only another habit that has played out."

"Well, I'm not obliged to love my enemies because they happen to be related to me."

"You'll let him marry her?"

"I have nothing to do with it. He is living his own life."

"He can't unless you give him his freedom."

"He's free now. I'll never stand in his way. Craig is a lawyer . . ." Her laugh pierced his heart. "He may be glad to arrange it."

"Don't, Roy! For God's sake. I can't bear it. . . ."

"Poor Father." Her voice wavered, but the next instant she had regained control of it. "If you love me, you must leave me alone. I have to work things out in my own way. I have to save myself as I can. It may not be the right way, but it's mine."

That was only the truth. Her enemy, he knew, was within the heart; for she was at the mercy of some antagonist more hostile than the mere abstraction called life. Her own will must bear her up; she must fight her inner conflicts in solitude. She belongs to another age, he thought; she is a part of the future, and I am still encrusted with the outworn shape of the past. I cannot share either her joy or her grief; all I can do is to stand aside and sympathize from a distance. She is stronger than any of us, and finer in many ways; but she lacks tenderness—or is it merely imagination? She is riding a single virtue, the new gallantry, too hard—perhaps to self-destruction. Who knows? He felt that he had come suddenly to the brink of a precipice; and he could not see into the gulf that divided two hemispheres. Was it light there? Was it darkness? Was it another dawn? Or was it but a quite old ending masked as a new beginning?

"I know," he said, "and, Roy, I understand —only . . ."

She slipped from his grasp. "You'd better stir the milk. It's scorching."

Grimly, but with a thudding heart, he dipped the spoon into the saucepan and began to stir very slowly, as if life or death were contained in Lavinia's cup. Then, lifting the saucepan from the flame, he carefully poured the contents into the small pitcher beside the cup on the tray. A few drops spilled over into the saucer, and he wiped them off before he picked up the tray and started to the door. "Will you stay with your mother tonight," he asked, "and let me sleep upstairs?"

Without looking at him, she made a gesture of impatience. "I've got to face things. I can't face things that way."

"But you'll sit by her till she's quiet?"

"If she'll stop talking." Irritation ruffled her toneless voice. "If she won't stop talking, I'll want to murder her."

"Didn't the Veronal help?"

"I didn't wait to see. She wanted her milk. You'd better take it up before it gets cold."

She held the swinging door open, while he went through with the tray held in front of him. "Don't let yourself get too hard, darling."

She smiled and shook her head. "Hard things don't break easily."

Looking back over his shoulder as he went out of the kitchen, he caught the flash of cold disillusion which lit up her features and now faded into a sullen reserve. There was nothing to answer, he told himself in an anguish of pity. What answer could there ever be to life's betrayal of youth?

Lavinia had been put to bed by Roy, and she was now dozing, mercifully benumbed, in a state between two borders of consciousness, the dream and the actuality. Walking softly, he crossed the room and spoke to her in a whisper. "Are you awake, Lavinia?"

Raising her eyelids, she moaned under her breath, "I feel sick."

"Well, drink your milk while it's hot. It will make the Veronal act quicker." Slipping his arm under the pillows, he lifted her head and held the cup to her lips, while an erratic thought skimmed through his mind. Damn it all, I wasn't made for a nurse. . . . A smell of mustard from a plaster at the back of her neck stung his nostrils, and for an instant, evoked by an illusion of memory, the head on the pillow became the head of his mother. Then the phantom receded, and he looked down in resentful pity on the face of Lavinia. With that look, he knew that he was bound to her only by an empty form which he lacked either the courage or the cruelty to break. For the rest, there was nothing. He had ceased to love her; he had ceased even to like her. She was less, or more, than a stranger to him; she was an intimate enemy.

"My poor child!" Lavinia was moaning between swallows. "What will become of her?" Her head rolled back on the pillows, and she appeared to be falling asleep. Then starting up in an effort to spring out of bed, she cried frantically: "I must go to her, Asa! Somebody must go to her."

"Try not to think, Lavinia," he said, reproaching himself. "We can't do anything before morning."

"Have you telephoned Uncle William?"

"I haven't had time. I couldn't leave Craig alone while he was trying to drink himself into a stupor."

"Then Andrew doesn't know?"

"I'll call up both of them as soon as you've dropped off. There isn't anything they can do tonight."

"Poor Craig," Lavinia sighed, "he loves her."

"Yes, he loves her, God help him."

"I can't find it in my heart to be hard on her, Asa. She is only a child. . . ." Her voice trailed off until it was scarcely more than a breath.

"Stop talking, Mother," Roy said. "If you don't stop talking, the Veronal won't do any good."

"You're so strong, Roy. I don't know what any of us would do without you."

"For God's sake, stop talking!"

"I feel so wretched. I feel that I don't want to live. . . ."

"Well, you aren't dying, but you'd better be quiet."

"I'm suffering with you, too, my child." Lavinia's voice sounded as if she were rambling in her sleep. "Don't think that I . . ."

A spasm of anger distorted Roy's features. "Then you may as well stop. I can do my own suffering."

Pushing back the chair by the bed, she went over to the window and leaned out to meet the approaching rain.

"It's so close," Lavinia complained drowsily. "The air's so heavy I can't get my breath."

"Yes, it feels like summer," Asa said. "The rain will help. There'll be rain in a minute now. Roy, you'd better put down that window."

"I don't mind," Roy answered, without turning. As the rain came down in a singing rush against the street lamp, she held up her face to the windblown shower.

"Come away, Roy. You'll be soaked."

"I don't mind," Roy repeated again, without turning; but when he touched her arm, she followed him back to the bed and sat down by her mother.

"It will be soon over," he said, "and everything will be better after the rain."

"After the rain," Roy echoed tauntingly, "everything will be better."

As the sedative began gradually to take effect, Lavinia's voice rose, and wavered, and was swallowed up in the outside violence of the storm. A branch had blown down from a maple; the light at the corner was darkened; leaves were torn off and hurled down in drenched

clusters from the swaying trees. "My poor misguided child, what will become of her?" Another pause, and then a lower moan, "My poor child . . ." A longer silence broken by a still feebler moan, "My poor misguided . . ." Then an inarticulate sighing into unconsciousness.

"Are the windows down upstairs?" Asa asked in a whisper.

"No, I left them open," Roy replied listlessly.

"Then it must be raining in. Stay with your mother till I come back."

Roy looked at him vacantly, as if raining in were the last thing that mattered. Except for an almost imperceptible turn of her head, he would not have known that she heard him; but as he passed her on his way out of the room, he saw that the hands lying in her lap were nervously clasping and unclasping.

Once outside the door, he hurried up the narrow stairs to Roy's bedroom, where the floor was splashed with water and the wind was twisting the soaked curtains. As he went over to lower the window, the brown muslin curtains whipped in his face, and he was obliged to struggle against the gusts before he could shut out the storm. When at last all the windows were shut, he mopped the floor with some bath towels; and then standing up with the dripping towels in his hands, he looked about him for any signs of Peter's possessions that might be safely removed. He must have known he was going, Asa thought angrily. He must have taken most of his things away before Roy came in. For an instant, alone in the room, he felt that his heart was bursting with rage; and he knew, with a blinding flash of insight, that it was in the nature, if not in the will, of every man to do murder. Below the disintegrated surface of character, he had discovered that there was a bottomless abyss of dark impulses. I didn't know it was in me, he thought. I wonder if all other men are like that in the depths?

Opening the closet door, he took down the few clothes, mostly heavy suits, that Peter had left. When he had bundled them over his arm, he stooped to pick up several pairs of half-worn shoes, while the thought darted through his mind that every pair of old shoes was endowed with a curious semblance of personality. I must get rid of these before she comes upstairs, he said in a furious whisper. I must get rid of everything he has left. At any minute, Asa knew, Roy might become suspicious and follow him to the upper floor; and the mere idea brought out a creeping shudder, as if a caterpillar were crawling slowly down his spine. Carrying his armful into the spare room at the end of the hall, he threw the clothes on the bare mattress of the bed, and went back to collect the toilet articles from the bathroom. But Peter's shaving things were not there; even his toothbrush and powder and soap had been taken away with the razors. Damn him! Asa burst out, while he picked up a box of used neckties and threw it on the pile of clothes in the spare room. As he soon learned, however, swearing could not do any harm. He couldn't reach Peter. He couldn't touch him. He couldn't cause him so much as a single bad moment. In other years men had been killed for less than this, and a passionate regret surged up in him that the final authority of what his father had called "the Code" no longer survived, and that righteous killing had, long since, become as out-of-date as offended honor. Then, the next instant, that hidden imp of satire in his mind assured him Peter would have been the inevitable victor in any nature of combat, whether moral or physical.

He had flung a discarded quilt over the mound on the bed, and was just shutting the door on confusion, when he heard a step in the hall below, and Roy's head emerged from the dim well of the staircase.

"You stayed so long, Father," she said in a resentful whisper. "What have you been doing?"

"The floor was soaked. I had to wipe it up."

Together they went into her small sitting room and then into the bedroom adjoining. One object, he noticed, he had overlooked, a bag of tobacco from which Peter had recently filled his pipe. But, even while he hoped that she would not see it, she picked it up indifferently and tossed it into the wastepaper basket.

"I wish you would stay downstairs tonight, Roy. In the morning we may have better news."

"Better news?" He flinched from her mockery. "What news would be better?"

"I can make up my bed for you . . . or your mother's daybed in the sitting room."

Her temper flared up. "Mother is driving me wild."

"Try not to feel that way, darling. She is your mother."

"That isn't my fault. I didn't ask her to bring me here."

"But you've always been fond of her."

"I'm fond of her still, I suppose, but I can't stand her. I can't—can't—can't stand her."

He sighed and gave up the struggle. It was true, he repeated to himself, she must save herself in her own way. "Take something to make you sleep," he said, turning as he was about to go. "I'll bring you one of your mother's tablets."

"I don't want anything. I don't want to sleep."

"You will wear yourself out."

"I want to wear myself out."

"At least you'll stay at home tomorrow. You won't go back to work in the morning."

"Why should I stay at home? Why shouldn't I go back to work?" Her laugh cut into his nerves. "I'm going out as soon as the shops open, and buy a new hat. I'm going to buy a red hat."

There was nothing to answer. There was nothing to do or even to think. Without a word, he went over to the

bed and turned down the coverlet. After he had smoothed the sheets and shaken the crushed pillows, he took up her blue thermos bottle and started again to leave the room. "I'll bring this back a little later," he said in a tone he tried to make unemotional, "and I'll leave a tablet on your bed table. You may need it in the night."

She did not answer, and as he turned away, he felt his pity struggling, like a breathless thing, in his throat. Had he ever, even in his thwarted youth, suffered this agony? Did every man live over his own mortal pain intensified in his children?

Lavinia was lying quietly, sunk in a hollow between two pillows, and at first, while he listened to her shallow moaning, he could not tell whether she was awake or asleep. Bending nearer after an instant, he saw her features, exposed and unguarded, as if sleep had washed away her last frail protection against the nature of facts. Her face appeared puffed and discolored and oddly foreshortened. What had he ever seen in her? he found himself thinking. When he looked back on it now, the whole of his life and marriage seemed merely ridiculous. A man wouldn't stand for it nowadays, not in this irresponsible age. A whiff of mustard floated up from the bed, and it seemed to him that he breathed in the very odor of melancholy. Unbidden, a motiveless idea flitted into his mind and then out again before he had grasped it. She can't live forever. Some time . . . some day . . . The thought was cut in two with a stroke, or rather, there was no beginning and no end to the wordless vibration of this thought. . . .

Lavinia stirred and put out a clutching hand. "Are you here, Asa?"

"Yes, I'm here. Try to go back to sleep."

"I can't stop thinking. I can't stop thinking of Stanley. I keep wondering where she is and what she is doing."

"I know, but it doesn't do any good. You'll only make

yourself ill again." Though he spoke soothingly, his mind was swept by what he felt to be some external delirium in events. His inner recoil seemed to be merely a wave set in motion by some agitation without. "Whoever suffers from this affair," he added, "it isn't going to be Stanley."

Lavinia was crying softly. "I shall always feel that she is my baby. I can still feel her in my arms."

Leaving the bedside, Asa crossed the room to the window and flung up the sash. The storm was over, but the broken clouds scudded low over the western horizon. Here, even in the city, the country scents of wet grass and earth were blown into the room, into the house, into his aching mind. As he leaned out of the window, he seemed to drink in waves of the fresh darkness. Down below, he could see a luminous patch where the light gathered on the dripping boughs of a maple. It is no good bothering about what cannot be helped, he thought. Even if I'd had a chance, I might never have done any better. A man who knew how to get on would have made something, he supposed, out of nothing. A man who had confidence in himself might have governed his children. But he wasn't so sure about that. He had seen too many successful persons come to grief through their children. Perhaps Roy, with her flippant gallantry, was right. Every human being, parent or child, must save himself by his own strength if he is to be saved. . . . Or was Craig nearer the truth when he insisted that a human being cannot stand alone, and that humanity must rise or sink, not in parts, but as a whole? Craig had believed that the chief end of life was, not man, but humanity. Yet Craig had loved Stanley; and that lonely passion had destroyed him. No, Asa told himself, man is not a rational animal. He may have invented many social philosophies, but he remains incurably biological.

XII

THE worst of all, Roy thought, was when she had turned a corner, thinking of nothing in particular, and had seen the man with broad shoulders and light hair leap down from a small car at the curb. Like a miracle, it had seemed to her, that one moment. Some secret pain in her heart gave a last shuddering beat, and was over, was ended. It wasn't true, what had happened. The brisk air was brimming with surprise, and with delight, and with a startled sense of renewal. He had never gone—or he had come back again. . . . Then the man stopped. He glanced up from the engine of his car, and casually looked at her with the eyes of a stranger. Yes, that had been the worst of all, except the constant dreaming and the waking—except the muffled slowness of time. Now in August she could look back, over a leaden unruffled stream of hours, toward those blank days in April. He had gone in April; and since then there had been no word but a message of unashamed happiness from Stanley to her mother. Nothing more. Nothing ever again as long as Roy lived. . . .

But all that was over. Her life was her own, and she would not let it be spoiled. For there was no fairness in love. There was no fairness in having one's whole heaven and earth overturned because one man, among all the millions of men in the world, had ceased to care, had found her wanting in whatever he needed for happiness. But wanting in what? Where was the lack in her? How could she give all of herself, and yet find that all of herself, to the last heartbeat, was not enough? In the beginning, she had probed the wound deeper and deeper. Alone in the night, she had driven her burning pride, her rage of thwarted longing, far down into the very depths

of her agony. But only when she was alone in the night. Through the intolerable days she had relentlessly governed her thoughts. Down to the shop in the morning, back again to the house and her mother in the late afternoon. Decorating places for other people to live in: furniture, wallpaper, chintz, carpets, and curtains. Once the work had interested or amused her; now she might as well have been playing with cinders. Yet nothing had really happened, she said to herself over and over. You couldn't lose anything that had never belonged to you. And, after all, she knew how to live the kind of life that she wanted. No man, not Peter, not any other, could ruin what was her own. Round and round, wearing a red hat which cast a shadow over her haunted eyes, she went bravely through the interminable days, weeks, months. No matter what it cost her, she would tear out the pain and trample it underfoot. She would rise above it by her own will, she told herself grimly.

In those first months, she missed his physical presence as a man misses a wounded arm that has been cut away. She missed him waking and sleeping; she missed him when she went out and, most of all, when she came in again. Even after he had ceased to live in her heart as a lover, he still lived on as a constant enemy in her nerves. It was as if passion had deserted her conscious mind and taken root in the vital center of instinct. I have forgotten, she would say, and the thought would turn to a clutch of fear in her breast. For memory, like a vulture, was waiting to swoop down and devour her frail pretense. She could feel the dark wings sweeping up from the depths below, and tracking her down through the labyrinth of her dreams, hanging poised and watchful, not ever very far away, not even after she had escaped through the hidden door, where neither thought nor fear could follow her and survive.

All day she could keep the door closed against memo-

ries; all day she could defend her mind against the treachery that was hope. But, alone in the night, after she had resisted sleep as an enemy, she would drop back into the tormented world of her dreams. Living fragments of the past pursued her with the vividness, not of nightmares, but of insane realities. For in her sleep she was always with Peter; and the beginning of her dream was an amazed sense of peace, harmony, fulfillment, perfection. Then, at its highest point, the dream was suddenly shattered, and broken fragments would whirl in a delirium of pain through her consciousness. Why was it always like that? Was it the way of life or merely a mad act of delusion? A hollow curve? Nothing or everything? She did not know because, just as clearness approached, the vision melted and vanished. From her dream, as it broke and dissolved, she would awake in terror and sink back into the ebbing moment of time; and always, night after night, the slow waking was torture. While she was still asleep, the memory of pain, like a charged wire, would begin to vibrate in her nerves, quivering first in her elbows and knees and then up through her limbs toward her resisting mind. The throbbing fear, the insistent message of grief, was as sharp as the backward rush of blood into a throat that has been hanged. What is it? she would ask herself in the uneasy pause between sleeping and waking. Something has hurt me. I cannot remember what it was. Then gradually the cloud would lift, and the hammering beats of her heart would bring the recollection to life. At the same hour of dawn, varying not so much as a minute, day after day, she would awake sobbing because she had not forgotten, because she was beginning a new tomorrow, with all the cruelty of life still undefeated. While the day broke, she would lie weeping. Not until the sun had risen and she heard a noise in the house below, could she struggle to her feet and start again her early morning battle with despair and remembrance. And all

the while (slipping into her bath, drying herself quickly, brushing her hair, and selecting a summer frock from the closet), the woman people called Roy Kingsmill would weave an unuttered conflict of words:

"I have forgotten."

"Not in sleep, never in sleep."

"In the day I do not think of him."

"But you dream of him. Your dreams bring him back again."

"When light comes, I can put him out of my mind."

"Not always, not everywhere."

"Always and everywhere."

"Not in the street. Not when you see glimpses of him in the people you pass."

"But they go on; they pass by."

"They pass by. Your hunger for him does not. It stays and remembers."

"There has been so short a time, only a few months."

"Time is always long, except to the happy."

"I shall be happy again. I shall be happy and free."

"You still hope. There is no freedom in hoping for what never comes."

"Love is not everything."

"Love is all that you want."

"But I will not be defeated. . . ."

Every morning it was like this, an endless sequence, an unbroken weaving of thought and of impulse, of will and of emotion. While she dressed to go out, she would move in response to this continuing unspoken rhythm. Then, at last, as she shut the door behind her, she would shut in the other half of herself. Let me forget, she would pray as she descended the stairs. Let me forget until night.

If only her father had cared less. If only she could be spared the intolerable pity in those secretive and amused eyes, which nowadays were no longer amused when they looked at her. She did not want pity. She wanted

sternness, inflexibility, even that lost sardonic humor. What she needed most, she knew, was to be told, and told, and to be convinced also, that in the midst of a world toppling over in ruins, desire for a single human being had become not merely unimportant but wasteful. Once, Craig might have told her this. He might even believe it again, she thought, and began wondering about Craig. Was he also fighting to save himself from hatred and bitterness? Or had he already given up and gone under? It would be easier to talk with him than with her father, whose wordless sympathy seemed to be draining the little strength she had left. Even ridicule would have been more bracing than pity, because ridicule, pointed the right way, would demand nothing, not even acknowledgment. A core of flint, she thought; I want a heart, not of flesh and blood, but of flint. And then: I am hurting Father, I know, but this also I cannot help. Only by being cruel myself am I able to escape from cruelty. For the first time, she perceived dimly the reason underlying her mother's maladjustment to life. It was necessary, she saw, to enter into the nature of pain, which was cruelty, before she could overcome and destroy it. The one thing that could help her would be to banish the thought of love, to stifle forever the quivering nerve of her memory, and to persuade her aching flesh that she had lost nothing through losing a love which was in itself but less than nothing.

When her father made early coffee, he would bring Roy a cup; and her whole body would seem to awake, and then turn to stone, at the casual sound of his voice. "I heard you stirring"—did he mean crying?—"and I've brought you your coffee."

"You didn't make it just for me?"

"I made it for your mother and myself. She always wants her coffee the first thing."

"I couldn't drink it if I knew you'd got up so early and made it just for me."

[155]

"Bless your heart, darling." His tone sounded too sprightly. "I shouldn't have thought of that."

"Did Mother talk all night?"

"Not after midnight. She quieted down when she'd taken her Veronal and hot milk."

"I wonder how you stand it."

A gleam of laughter would flicker again in his smile. How tired he looked, in his faded blue and white cotton pajamas under a drab-colored bathrobe. He looked old and patient for his years, and yet, in some queer way, indestructible. Seeing him like that, stripped alike of his dignity and his conventional clothes, she might have wondered, had she found time to worry over anything outside herself, whether he did not possess some deep instinct for survival which had been left out of his children.

"Well, I'm getting on, you know," he would answer. "As a man gets older, I suppose he becomes more or less of a pachyderm."

"I wish you didn't look so—so terribly patient."

"Patient? Good Lord, you don't know me! If I had a chance, I'd smash up the whole business. But wouldn't you like to stay in bed this morning? I'll bring up your breakfast."

"No, I'd rather get up. Is it time yet?"

"It's not yet six. I knew you weren't asleep."

"No, I wasn't asleep. These early hours drag so slowly."

"Didn't you sleep at all?"

"Oh, yes, I slept. I slept some."

She would raise herself in bed, sipping the fragrant coffee. "You do make the best coffee. And a little cream does help, doesn't it?" But she was only playing for time, she thought wearily: I can't talk to him. I haven't anything to say, about anything. Then this would give her an idea, and she would murmur between sips of coffee, "I do wish Mother would try to stop talking."

"To wish that does not do any harm." His eyes would smile between crinkled eyelids.

"But she never will."

This would make him chuckle under his breath, as if, with his queer streak of humor, he found it amusing. "She is mortal. So I shouldn't say never."

"It's like—it's like a disease."

"A compulsive neurosis, so young Buchanan calls it. He thinks it may get better in time."

"What does that young man know about nerves?"

"More than his father does, I believe. Don't all you young ones know more than your elders? Anyway, he came yesterday, and your mother approves of him."

"Oh, I know. She told me about him, but I wasn't listening. I never listen when I can help it."

"That's right. It's the only way. But your mother is nobody's fool, my dear. She has a fund of hard common sense."

"You needn't say it. I know." Then he would take her empty cup, while that intolerable misery twisted and turned and struggled in the vacancy of her mind. If only he would go away! If only she could live among indifferent and unpitying strangers!

"I'll see you at breakfast, daughter."

"Yes, I'll be down to breakfast."

"It's still early. Turn over and try to take another nap."

"I'll try." Oh, Daddy, Daddy, can't you see that it is killing me? You are my father; but what do I know of you? Do I really know you any better than I thought I knew Peter? She and Peter had loved each other; they had imagined that love would outlast life; they had believed that marriage would bring happiness. How had that belief ended? Peter, whom she had loved, was no more to her now than any other traveler she might meet and pass on an unfamiliar road. He was as unreal as the fleeting

resemblances that mocked at her from strange faces, from frail gestures or outlines, which fled always a little farther away and which eluded her at the next corner. After her father had gone, and the sound of his footsteps had stopped in her mother's room, she would lie listening to the rattle of milk wagons returning and the steady clop-clop of Bill, the old chestnut horse. One pigeon and then another, and presently a disordered flock of light and dark wings would sail slowly in circles over the houses. From her bed she could watch the mounting flight toward the sky, and then the fluttering indecision of the birds' descent to the ground. Sometimes, she knew, they would wait in dignified rows along the back fence until her father had thrown out cracked corn from the kitchen doorway. Father is good, she thought without emotion or interest, but what has goodness ever done for him? Has he ever really had anything that he wanted? Closing her eyes to the tender green on the trees and the sky beyond, she would sink back into a stillness of the mind which was not so much sleep as a suspension of all thinking and feeling. Thought and sound would mingle and approach, would recede into emptiness. She had forgotten. All or nothing was, for the moment, over and done with. Then, after a long silence, while she lay there with closed eyes and ears, she would feel again the muted discord within, the old familiar vibration.

"What had I left undone? If only I could know why it had to be."

"The why began before you were born. After that, nothing matters that was ever done or left undone."

"Was there some fault in myself? When I gave everything, why was it never enough?"

"Everything, when it is poured out, is never enough."

"But I will not be defeated. . . ."

Even her mother's selfishness (if only her mother could keep quiet) was not so harassing as the unspoken

sympathy of her father. For it was possible to shut her ears to her mother, and to treat her lamentations over Stanley as if they were a hymn or a prayer in church. But, in some deeper part of herself, Roy was always aware of her father. She could not simply plunge down into her inner misery, and pretend him away. His pity might hurt her, it might exasperate her; but it never left her indifferent. There was a nerve of sympathy between them, a mental or emotional connection which ran below the uneven surface of family life. It's because I feel sorry for him that he hurts me, she thought. He loves me too much, and it is all wasted. I don't want anybody to love me too much.

The tension was less with her mother, because the tie between them was superficial. Stanley had always been the favorite, and as a child, Roy had been aware of a ruffled and uneasy strain in her mother's maternal affection—or instinct. Was it jealousy in herself? Roy had wondered. Was it envy? Was it the simple recoil of her earliest emotion toward life? Not until her childhood was over had she discovered in herself a deep-rooted antipathy to her mother's habit of mind.

"Try not to be so hard, Roy," Lavinia would plead vainly.

"But I like hardness, Mother. I like almost anything better than sloppiness. Most of our trouble in the South comes from sloppiness. Sloppy thinking, sloppy feeling, and sloppy workmanship."

Moaning tearlessly, Lavinia would stare at her with pale bulging eyes. Her elder daughter had become an embodiment of that realistic point of view against which Lavinia had fought as far back as she could remember. Even now, that stern principle, rising in a tide over the modern world, was nibbling at the sands of her evasive idealism. Always, she told herself, she had been driven from one stronghold of faith to another. Sentiment had

failed her; chivalry had failed her; feminine weakness and sex compulsion had alike failed her; and it now appeared that her last lonely refuge, of hypochondria, was about to be undermined.

"I've done the best I could, Roy."

"Oh, Mother, for God's sake . . ."

"I feel for you until it almost breaks my heart."

"I don't want you to feel for me. All I want you to do is to stop talking."

"You were always hard even when you were little."

Roy laughed. "And I'm going to be still harder. Just watch me."

"You thought Stanley was my favorite because she is beautiful. But it wasn't that. She was so soft, that's why I petted her."

"Can't you stop thinking about her?"

"Stop thinking! Why, I don't know where she is or who is looking after her. Her clothes are still packed away upstairs, and I don't know where to send them."

"She'll let you know quick enough when she wants them. And somebody is looking after her. You may count upon that."

"I can't stop loving her just because she's weak —or—or even bad," Lavinia sobbed. "After all, she is my baby."

But Stanley was more than a baby, Roy thought; she was a fantasy clothed in flesh and made living. For Lavinia, who had craved charm and beauty, had been endowed with none of the qualities that appeal either to the vague beneficence of chivalry or to the sharp greed of sex. In the reclining posture which she had preserved for so many weary years, she appeared not feminine and languishing, but merely massive and irremovable. As a chronic invalid, she seemed to diffuse less the delicacy of sentiment than the flabbiness of decay. Poor Mother! Roy would say to herself, if only pretenses could last!

When Maggie came in, the stale air would freshen, and the tone of living would become less dramatic and more natural. For Maggie was a practical soul, who, since she had worked for her living, had been chivalry plucked of its more brilliant feathers. In the beginning, Lavinia had opposed Andrew's marriage; but her opposition had melted away as soon as she had made the agreeable discovery that Maggie was the only member of the family who enjoyed her conversation, and who accepted her moth-eaten interior grandeur seriously. Maggie made few demands on intelligence, and had learned long ago that her wishes would be noticed almost as infrequently as they would be gratified. She had sprung from an obscure family, and was, by instinct as well as by education, a diligent climber. With the ingenuous eagerness of a simple mind, Maggie, who was lively, energetic, and "a good manager" on a small income, would ecstatically wander about for hours in Lavinia's own special dreary province of shadows within shadows. For all her healthy zest, Roy wondered, was Maggie animated by a perpetual craving denied? Was her flight into delusion merely an escape from Andrew and the ordinary? Her marriage was highly successful. She and Andrew were a devoted couple, and they were inordinately proud of their three commonplace children. Maggie's nursery, like her house, was well-ordered, and Andrew's pockets were permanently bulging with infant scribblings. One, perhaps two of the children, he was convinced, were budding poets, though he never read poetry, or maybe novelists, though he never read novels. Did it simply mean, Roy asked herself, that human companionship, even at its best, is never enough? After all else had been given, does life still demand its share of self-deception?

Part Second

Years of Unreason

I

THE omnibus swayed, creaked, bumped over a rock, and lumbered on toward the next service station. I hope nobody else will get in, Asa said to himself, glancing round at the empty seats. In twenty minutes more, I ought to come to the crossroads.

Kate would meet him there in her muddy Ford, as she did every Sunday when he was not kept at home by Lavinia or by the absence of Selina, the colored maid, who came on Virgie's afternoons off. For twenty years and more, these Sabbath flights into the country and freedom had been the solitary pleasure, apart from Roy's infrequent companionship, in a life which, from its beginning, had been starved for delight. At first, he had gone to see Jack Oliver, his only intimate friend; but since Jack died, Kate had gradually taken her husband's place in Asa's affection. Kate was the one human being with whom his hidden cave dweller had ever come out boldly under the open sky. His feeling for her was friendship, he knew, but it was friendship exalted to a major emotion. Whenever he thought of her, it was not as a possible lover but as a great companion. He had always, in the ancient language of chivalry, "respected" her. While Jack lived, he had continued to adore him as passionately as a smaller boy adores an older champion. In the last year, however, Asa had understood that he wanted more from Kate than these few Sunday afternoons at Hunter's Fare. What he wanted was to spend his life with her and with the things they both loved—the fields and woods and streams and all the friendly animals on the farm.

Sitting there among vacant seats, he played with his

[165]

desire, as a man toys with a bright, improbable dream. Someday, in a near or distant future, before old age had smothered him in ashes, Lavinia would cease to need his services, as she had long ago ceased to value his company. William was old as well as rich, and no matter how desperately he clung to his possessions, in the end he must leave them. Since he gave to charity with an even stronger reluctance that he gave to his relatives, it was natural to assume that a proper share of his fortune would pass on to Lavinia. And when Lavinia was wealthy enough to afford more competent nursing than a husband provided, Asa told himself with a leaping heart, he should be discharged from his task. She would be glad to get rid of me, he thought without resentment, if she were able to put a trained nurse, or even two of them, in my place. With the coming of the day, if it ever came, Lavinia would set him free to spend his westering years with Kate on the farm by the river. Let people say what they chose. From the chains of public opinion, he told himself thankfully, he was already released.

The road was swathed in October dust, but in the meadows on the right a triangle of silvery bloom opened fanwise within a dark border of woods. From the burning brushwood, blue wings of smoke soared up to melt into the deeper blue of the sky. On the farm, he knew, there would be the bittersweet tang of wood smoke and crushed apples mingled with the wilder scents of earth mold and ripened grass and sunshine on life everlasting. . . .

I've a whole afternoon, he thought. I must taste every drop of it. A flock of crows, bronzed by sunlight, flapped and dipped and floated slowly over an old cornfield. His gaze followed them dreamily. Light and darkness . . . a singing wind . . . an escape from the present. For, in spite of his effort, he could not harness his mind to the moment before him. He could not break away from the

past; he could not ally himself with the future. Something, he admitted reluctantly, was dragging him back.
Even if he were free to choose (and Andrew said that di-
vorces were as easy as talking, and as lightly regarded), he
wondered if he could ever bring himself to stand up to
circumstances. He still belonged to his children, though
two of them (and these two the most gifted) had made,
it seemed to him, a frightful havoc of their own
lives. . . . The crows mounted in orderly ranks, flapped
in a wide circle over the cornfield, and then swooped
down to research among the stubble. And over all—over
the band of woods, the bronze-colored shocks of corn,
the gauzy meadows, the rising and falling crows, the
swaths of October dust in the road—there was something
else, something vague, shimmering, fire-tinted, a mist
and yet not wholly a mist, advancing and retreating and,
as it retreated, calling to that lost hunter in the heart. It
was the spirit of autumn. But the call isn't true, he told
himself. It is only the false echo of a summer that is
ended.

And freedom? Was freedom also nothing more than
an echo? With his eyes on the landscape, which seemed to
start and move and fly away as he rushed on, he was
enveloped in the many humiliations and little miseries of
the past six months. Watching Roy's drawn features as
she grew paler and thinner under her smiling mockery,
he had felt that, day by day, the distance between them
widened. She had steadily rebuffed him; she had denied
him her confidence; she had met every approach with an
instant withdrawal. "I must help myself in my own way,"
she had repeated. "I can do without sympathy." On the
morning after that terrible night, he remembered, she
had gone to work as usual, and had patiently and desperately matched wallpaper and chintz. At lunch, she was
wearing a new red hat, with a becoming slant over her
dark eyebrows; and he noticed at the first glance, that the

color of her lips was deeper and the gloss on her hair more lustrous. Yet, hour by hour, or so it seemed to him, her face had hardened beneath the artificial brightness, and the air of gallant youth had diminished. Well, it was the modern way, Asa told himself, and certainly it was an advance upon the classic manner of the deserted woman. Whether or not it invited sympathy, one could scarcely fail to respect a defeat that had been turned into victory. Yet when William, persuaded into generosity by Charlotte, had offered to send Roy to Europe, she had tossed back airily: "I don't need a change, thank you. I'm all right as I am. Peter and I understand each other, and he hasn't treated me badly."

William, he uneasily recalled, had scowled with anger. "If she's going to stand up for that—that scoundrel," he fumed, "I'll wash my hands of the lot of you." Yes, that was a mistake, Asa told himself. On her mother's account, it was a mistake to repulse William. "I'm sorry you said that, Roy," he had remarked on the way home. "Your Uncle William means well, and he can do so much for you."

"But I don't want him to do anything for me," she had retorted almost fiercely. "I don't want anybody to do anything in the world."

"It wouldn't hurt you to go abroad. It might even help."

She had laughed bitterly. "Not unless I could go where there is fighting." Then she had stared at him. "I'm going to stay here and stand my ground, no matter what happens. And I'm not going to let people pity me or abuse Peter."

That was magnanimous, no doubt, Asa reflected now; but it was imprudent. Peter had been faithless; he had been cruel and selfish, not only to her and to Stanley, but to others who had trusted and believed in him. Asa could find no inclination to defend Peter; and he knew that in

estranging William, who still bore the bruises of Stanley's ingratitude, Roy was not forfeiting material benefits in the future, but was putting herself in the wrong with her family and her friends. It was not agreeable, even for a doting father, as Lavinia called him, to have one's sympathy thrust back and disclaimed. Loving her as he did, he might pretend not to feel hurt; but William had shown plainly that he was affronted. William had always preferred Stanley because her nature was soft, not firm, at the core and because, too, she was as innocent of moral judgment as she was untroubled by convictions. But I loved her, too, Asa thought, for these same reasons. Even when I saw through her shallowness, I was still susceptible to its charm. Well, but love is a queer thing at best, and it seldom thrives, apparently, upon the highest part of us. We love from little motives, not for large reasons; and yet motives no bigger than mice may dart into a man's universe, and nibble away the strongest foundations of belief or honor or even world revolution. It was characteristic, of course, that William's tougher fiber should respond to the attraction of weakness. That was now and would always be, Asa supposed, the primary instinct of man—or was it merely the instinct of sex? Not that it mattered. He couldn't help Roy by thinking. He might worry all day with the thought, as a dog with a marrowbone, but it would still be there after he was worn out by his worrying.

But Roy? What was she thinking in that withdrawn mind of hers? Why was she holding off sympathy, thrusting back tenderness? "I must save myself alone." That was all. And perhaps that was everything. Perhaps she was really saving herself from future disaster. He brooded over the possibility, but the memory of her stricken eyes, when she imagined herself unobserved, tortured his mind. Yet even that look of natural anguish, he found easier to bear than her false gaiety—her laugh that

rang shrill and hollow. She was rarely at home now, unless Lavinia summoned her to witness a heart attack or a recurring deathbed scene. "False angina," Buchanan had called Lavinia's spasms, but, watching her while she struggled for breath, Asa had doubted the medical judgment. The pain at least was true, and pain, he had learned long ago, was the sharpest reality. For a few hours, while her mother demanded her presence, Roy would sit by her bedside. Then, as soon as the worst was over, and Asa or Selina or Virgie had supplied the necessary remedies, she would spring up in nervous haste and rush out of the room and the house—anywhere, day or night. Her work was going well; for Roy had never let herself shirk, he reflected with pride. As an interior decorator, she was beginning to be sought after in Queenborough, and her salary, as manager of the shop, had been increased in September. For a while, after Craig, with a kind of pleasurable self-torture, had arranged for the divorce, she had appeared to think of nothing but work. Day after day, she would linger on at the shop, and then come home with her arms filled with samples to be studied and matched or contrasted at home. Then she had flashed about in a new excitement to dances and screen pictures; but this stage had passed quickly. It was noticeable that since August she had turned to Craig, whom she had met somewhere by accident, as one turns for comfort to the only person who understands and has endured a similar agony. Because he had suffered under the same cruelty, he must have learned how to bear it—or at least how to dull the severest pang of the torture.

In the beginning, she had seen Craig only at long intervals; but within the last month or two they had been often together, and Craig had dropped into the habit of calling at the shop and driving her home in the afternoon. They were not unsuited to each other, Asa mused

now, while the omnibus rocked and lunged onward. It was possible that, given time and opportunity, they might grow together in sympathy. Both were oversensitive, and both were inclined to take life and love too dangerously for happiness. In these ways they were so much alike that they might have been designed for each other. He wondered if fate, with an overpointed cynicism, had yet again staged one of its many ironic tragedies, when it entangled their destinies with the helpless and frail passion of Peter and Stanley? Asa had never doubted that this vehement passion was fugitive, or that it would in the end burn away in its own fire.

Even so, before the next turn of events, what could Roy and Craig save from destruction? In the past month they had seemed to enjoy a new comradeship with each other, and Asa had watched hopefully while Craig's look of sultry anger grew less oppressive. Sometimes, when they were alone downstairs or just coming in from the street, he would hear them laughing together, and, to his anxious ears, their voices would sound cheerful and natural. A few days ago, he might have told himself that with complete confidence. But only last night, on his way downstairs at three o'clock to heat a cup of milk for Lavinia, who could not sleep, he had glanced upstairs and had seen a thin crack of light under Roy's door. Stealing softly up to the third story, he had caught the sound of smothered sobbing; and for several minutes he had hesitated, with his hand outstretched to the doorknob. Dividing them, there was only that crack of light; yet when at last he had turned away, the hall had appeared bottomless, like a well of uneasy darkness. He knew that she would reject both his love and his pity. She would resent any intrusion into the private world of her sorrow. I'd give my right arm to help her, he had thought. I'd give my right arm if I could take all her burden on my own shoulders. . . .

They were approaching the next stop, and the driver had swerved on a sudden to avoid a file of geese perking down the roadway. In a few minutes, Asa would see the old Ford with Kate in the front seat and Pat and Percy, the two pointers, waiting, alert and expectant, beside the car. With this picture in his mind, he told himself that, but for these rare interludes, he could never have borne the thirty years of his marriage. They meant a release, not only from the atmosphere of invalidism, but also from that subjection to material values which, to an accepted failure in life, was still more repugnant. A change, for even a few hours, had been to him like an anodyne in an incurable malady. When the afternoon was over, and not until then, he would return to the familiar hated drudgery of the stemming room, as well as to the sickening fear that this drudgery, which he hated, might soon be denied him. To be thrown on the contemptuous charity of William would be, he decided, more humiliating than any drudgery, either with or without the security that might keep Asa alive yet a while longer.

The omnibus had swerved again; and the sharp turn threw him out of his seat. There was a white mule ambling leisurely across the road toward a distant and more desirable pasture. Straight ahead, he could recognize the big oak, with a bluish tinge in the veins of its wine-colored leaves. For two hundred and fifty years that oak had been rooted in the square at the crossroads; yet Kate told him it was now threatened by the political axe of the highway department. Her casual tolerance of everything and everybody (since God must shoulder at least a share of responsibility) had yielded to a rare flash of moral resentment. "Politicians!" she exclaimed angrily. "Politicians would murder an ancestor to pay for a vote!" There she was, very erect, in her mud-caked car, wearing the old brown woolen suit, with the ugly felt hat slanting forward over her honest bright brown eyes. As he

stepped down from the omnibus and walked toward her, he felt that the whole world was transfigured by the flushed air of October. She was not beautiful; she was not even pretty (though at fifty she carried her years lightly), but she was the one thing in a disappointing life that he wanted unchanged. Her warm smile, as genial as autumn, flooded his heart. By a miracle, he felt the sense of defeat and his timid acquiescence in William's and the world's judgment had vanished. While he held her large, warm hand, which was burned as brown as the soil, he was shot through by an excitement which was not the thrill of joy alone, but a feeling of sanity, of rightness, and of a spirit replenished. The pointers were on him now, overpowering him with their unrestrained welcome. Then, as he took the seat at Kate's side, Pat and Percy scrambled into the back of the car, and immediately he was aware of two cold noses nuzzling behind his ears.

"It's a perfect day," she said. "I'm so glad."

"Yes, that's fine. I was afraid it would rain."

The car turned into the straight sandy road, and they drove on in silence, because the time for speech had not come. Their meetings were always like this, and the first few miles gave him the rest and the change of heart that he needed. Even the pointers had stopped nuzzling. He knew that behind him they had poised themselves on their haunches. He knew also it had been good to see them again. He could never be happy without the companionship of one or more dogs, but he supposed Lavinia was within her rights when she forbade them the house. And no civilized dog would consent to develop a kennel personality.

The sandy road sank down into a narrow stream and ran on again in a long, slow stretch through the powdery bloom of the meadows. There was a faint humming in the air, barely more than a whisper of sound, as if invisible wings flashed and turned in the sunshine. Closing his

eyes, he drew in a languid breath of the life everlasting, so vague, yet so haunting. Then, raising his eyelids, he gazed over the October landscape into the veiled distance of the horizon. Light was everywhere, without and within, and he felt that the flash of wings turning was merely a projection of happiness. For this was happiness. . . . He looked at Kate and, with her eyes on the road, she smiled in complete understanding.

"Are you rested?" she asked, and her voice was a murmur.

"I'm always rested down here. Being with you rests me."

"With me and the dogs."

"That's right. With you and Pat and Percy and things that grow in the fields. The best tonic I know is the smell of the earth."

"You've had a hard week."

"Every week is hard, now. I think my nerves are going back on me."

"You need a change. I can't remember that you ever had a vacation."

"I've had these Sunday afternoons. The trouble is that I'm getting on. You can't argue with time."

She glanced at his downcast face. "I wish you could come more often. This is the first Sunday in three weeks."

"It seems longer than that. All the time it gets less easy to break away. Roy goes off for weekends. I don't like to leave Lavinia alone."

"Has she been worse?"

"I don't know. The doctor says not."

"Does she talk about Stanley?"

"Every hour of the day. She just lies there and worries about her."

"Does she ever hear from her?"

"Once in a long while. There was that letter I told you

about, when they were so happy together. One has come since I saw you."

"Is she as blissful as ever?"

"Lavinia thought so."

"And you?"

"Well, I wasn't quite sure. Maybe I was thinking too much about Roy." What was it, he asked himself, that had made him wonder at the time whether Stanley's letter was as natural as Lavinia imagined? He had never told Lavinia, and he hesitated even now before telling his suspicion to Kate. How much, in mere point of fact, had he ever told Kate? To save his life, he could not remember. That meant that he was growing old (though sixty seemed young enough to him, nowadays), but he supposed he was older than most men of his years. He noticed that he had begun to repeat himself; his father used to say that repeating oneself was the first sign of senility. Yet he could remember quite clearly things that happened when he was a boy, and even when he was hardly more than a baby. His Aunt Mary Gracie, for instance. She had died when he was less than three years old; yet he had never forgotten her. He remembered distinctly the time she opened a paper bag and gave him a stick, with a curved handle, of red and white peppermint candy. "I wonder . . ." he began aloud, and added, "I'm growing more forgetful."

"You aren't old enough for that yet. You're tired out. that's all. What you need is a rest."

He raised his hand to brush away an imaginary cobweb. A real rest, he reflected, was something he'd never had, not since his father died, anyway, and that was more than forty—it was nearer fifty years ago. "I'm damned tired," he said, "of being sorry for people."

At the worried tone in his voice Pat, the elder pointer, pushed a chill nose against the back of his neck. A lone turkey gobbler was strutting across the road, and the car

slowed down until some twenty pounds of feathered dignity had gone by.

"I know," Kate said presently. Her voice was crisp with vitality, and this crispness was bracing.

"All my life, at least since Father died," he burst out, "I've had to be sorry for somebody. I never did anything I wanted to do, because always somebody was so much worse off than I was. I'm fed up on pity now. I've just about come to the end of being sorry for other people. . . ." He laughed with his quizzical accent. "The truth is that my sympathy has gone flat. I can't even feel sorry for Roy, because losing a lover appears so unimportant beside losing a job. I saw a man lose a job yesterday, at sixty-nine, with nothing ahead but the poorhouse, and it seemed to me that losing all the lovers in the world would matter less. I suppose I was wondering whether my turn would come next. . . ."

She threw him a cheerful smile. "Well, there's always a job on the farm," she answered. "A farm always needs an extra man."

A sudden glow irradiated his features. "I'm looking ahead to that. There may be a little happiness yet before—before I'm too old to know what it feels like. . . ." A chain dragged within; but there was still happiness somewhere in the future—somewhere in the distance. . . . "It may be only a notion, but it keeps me going," he added aloud. "When I find myself getting too anxious about Roy, I begin to think that something has got to happen, sooner or later."

"I thought Roy was more happy."

"So did I, for a few weeks; but it isn't easy to tell about Roy. Last night, when I went down to heat Lavinia's milk, I heard her walking about and sobbing in her room. She had gone out with Craig to some lecture. I suppose she turned to him because he has been hurt in the same way, and it looks as if she'd taken up with his ideas, more or

less. After all, I imagine a world revolution, or the hope of one, would be as good a solace for a broken heart as anybody could find."

Kate nodded. "Misery has made more revolutions than either philanthropy or economics. Anyway, I'd be glad to see Roy interested."

"I thought she was interested in her work. She is getting orders all the time. In a few years she should be making a good income. But it looks as if that isn't enough." He smiled, and his voice softened. "She's a generous little thing. If I'd let her, she'd give all she makes to me or her mother."

"Couldn't she help with a nurse for her mother?"

He shook his head. "I can't see her ground down to powder as I was. Besides, Selina is there now whenever Virgie is off, and I come on duty as soon as I get home."

"But it's killing you."

"Good Lord, no. I'm as tough as a pine knot. The trouble with me today is that I heard Roy crying last night. I can't put it out of my mind. I can never keep her out of my mind when she is unhappy."

Kate turned to smile at him, and a wave of energy rushed through her, as if she had summoned all her cheerfulness and her faith in life. "Roy is splendid," she said emphatically. "I think she is finer than we used to be in our youth. I wonder," she added slowly, "if we were ever a match for the generation of today at its best."

"Only it is, or seems to be, so seldom at its best," he retorted. "But what I'm afraid of is that Roy has become too hard, and even bitter in spots."

"That's natural, and it will pass. I couldn't sympathize with her if she didn't feel bitterly. But give her time."

"She seems really to like being with Craig, but of course it may be merely a bluff. I don't know what they can find to talk about; but he brings her books, whether she reads them or not, and they go to meetings and to

movies together." He drew in his breath sharply, while he watched a buzzard sail slowly nearer before it shot down with outspread wings to the earth. "I wonder what is wrong with the world nowadays."

Kate laughed, and her gaiety, he thought, was like music. "The same old Adam, I suppose. Human nature. I don't like human nature, but I do like human beings."

"It's all so illogical. Why couldn't Peter and Stanley, and Craig and Roy, have paired off in the beginning? Why do all of us, every last one, have to go through hell to find out what we really want?"

The car had jerked up before the red gate of the farm, and he got down to open it. While he held back the gate, she drove through, and the pointers bounded out, racing ahead up the white road bordered by cedars. Some years ago, the procession of cedars had led for nearly a mile; now the older trees were either standing dead or else they had fallen and rotted. The few that were still left cast an elegiac gloom into the long avenue; and around them, under the open sky, the wild autumn meadows swept away to the dark range of pines in the distance. "I can't afford to keep up the place," Kate was saying, "but Jack and I always liked it as it is, trodden down by the years. The farm brings in very little, but it has given us something we could never buy."

They drove on, with the pointers racing ahead, until Kate drew up before the square white porch, where the paint was peeling away in flakes. "Will you come in for a drink?" she asked. "Or shall we have our walk?"

"Let's have the walk first. I want to go down through the fields to the river edge."

"In a minute. I'll tell Martha." She went into the house; and turning away, while Pat and Percy leaped and circled in front of him, he crossed the ragged lawn, beneath dappled shadows of elms, and stood waiting for Kate to come out. The river path, trailing across the meadows, was lost

in billowing waves of asters, goldenrod, and life ever-lasting. There was no wind, and the October sunshine, pouring down from the stainless blue of the sky, kindled the variegated bloom into a running flame, misted over with smoke-colored pollen. It can't last, he thought. Time comes, time passes. But what was time? An element or an illusion? Flow or duration? And how deep was the gulf that divided yesterday from today, or today from tomorrow? The scene was so breathless, so drowned in stillness, as if in a well of being, that it seemed to him his pulses had ceased their vibration. Not only time but life itself was suspended. Nothing moved. Nothing passed. The drifting pollen, the bird on the wing, the flower on the weed, the ripened seed in the flower, the bronzed leaves on the elms, the shadows asleep on the grass—all these things were as motionless as is the pause between the flow and ebb of a tide, or the breath between the thought and the spoken word. . . .

Then, suddenly, movement stirred in the air above, and again the scene came to life. A straggling line of crows wavered in curves out of the sky, while below them, their shadows skimmed so close to the ground that the meadows appeared to move and breathe with them in slow pulsations of light. "Yes, it had to change," he said aloud to himself. "Everything changes. Nothing is ever the same again."

"But it may be better," a voice murmured behind him, and there was Kate, bareheaded and smiling. "We'll take that little path where the meadowlarks are flying up from the weeds."

The amused gleam flashed into his eyes, and he felt, without knowing why, years younger. If only he could be with Kate always, he thought; and he wondered why nothing one really wanted ever came except in snatches, except by accident.

They went out from the shadow of the elms, and

turned into the hidden path that led downwards. Pat and Percy wheeled and romped in the meadows, dusting the bloom from the life everlasting and chasing the whirring wings of the larks. A drift of wood smoke curled up from a pile of brush near the barn, and as they approached the old orchard the air was pungent with the smell of crushed apples. As he glanced at Kate and met her laughing eyes, a sense of comradeship, as deep and mellow as the autumn light, stole into his mind and heart. But I am happy, he thought suddenly, in surprise. This is happiness. . . .

II

AS ASA went up the steps and drew out his latchkey, a
clock somewhere in the city struck ten slow strokes,
which seemed to sink into the night and leave a pool of silence behind them. An instant later, when he entered the
house, he felt that he had stepped back into emptiness.
There was no one downstairs; but the sound of voices
from Lavinia's room reminded him that Charlotte had
promised to sit with her until he came in. I hope I haven't
kept her too long, he thought, and then defiantly: I have
a right to an afternoon off once in a while. The few hours
of happiness had altered his mood, and he felt that his
energies were braced for resistance.

"Here is Asa now," Lavinia remarked, a trifle queru-
lously, as he entered. "He looks as if he had had a good
time in the country." Fortunately, she had never suffered
from jealousy, partly because of a firm conviction that,
whatever her husband's failings might be as a bread-
winner, he had been born, as she said, "without that
other side to his nature," and partly because she felt that
Kate also was lacking in what Lavinia regarded as the
wrong kind of appeal.

In the softest of the winged chairs, Mrs. Fitzroy was
enthroned, like some immense seated idol of benevolence. The reflective twinkle in her eyes had always en-
deared her to Asa, and he wondered now, clasping the
plump cushion of her hand, how she had endured her
half century of marriage to William's curiously perverted
sense of humor. Yet, after a glance at her placid features,
one might imagine that she had thrived under browbeating and had been agreeably puffed up by inhibitions.

"I'm glad you've had your day off, Asa," she said in a voice which was singularly sweet and low. "I hope you enjoyed it."

"Enjoyed it?" He looked round him, as if he were trying to find the right answer. "Oh, yes, I enjoyed it. I mean . . ." he began, and broke off because he did not know what he had started to say. Some wave of impulse, which had swept out of darkness and flooded his mind with sound and light, had already subsided. Words were only syllables strung together, he thought; they have been used so often that they are as dry and empty as old wasps' nests. What he treasured in his memory was a single burning ray of experience, the knowledge that, for a little while, he had lived, not according to a rule of custom, but in obedience to some involuntary and unconscious upheaval of pure instinct. Yes, I was happy, he mused, with that sense of surprise which continued to repeat itself as a recurring phrase. I have been happier than I thought I could ever be. But why? He had had only the fields and the white roads leading somewhere—nowhere—and this comradeship, which, if it were not ecstasy, was more satisfying than ecstasy.

"Uncle William has had a letter," Lavinia said.

"A letter?"

"From Stanley. It came yesterday."

"What did she want?"

"She wants him to send her car on to Baltimore. Peter is in the hospital all day, and she is bored and unhappy with nothing to do."

Asa stared at his wife blankly. "Did she say that?"

Lavinia glanced toward Charlotte, who nodded emphatically. "Oh, more than that. It seems that Peter is working very hard. He has a position in a hospital. They say that he has a really brilliant technique. . . ."

Asa smiled. "I've heard that before. Didn't Craig say his skill was a matter of touch and go?"

[183]

"Yes, I remember." Charlotte beamed. "Poor Lavinia would suffer so much less if she could see that everything has its humorous side."

"Even running away with your sister's husband," Lavinia said grimly. "No, I cannot find that amusing."

"Not that, but the way Stanley seems to have lost sight of the—of the tragedy. I hope," Charlotte added, lowering her voice, "that Roy has forgotten as quickly."

"Where is she?" Asa asked. "I mean Roy."

"She went out with Craig. There was a Sunday meeting somewhere about something—but it wasn't religious. Only it must have been unpleasant, or they wouldn't have gone. Only horrors are able to arrest their attention."

"Well, if horrors divert them," Asa rejoined in a tolerant tone, "why worry? And if nothing else can be said in favor of evil, at least it does provide the one inexhaustible topic."

"Yes, I know," Lavinia assented wearily. "Anything is better than brooding—especially for Roy."

"What does William say?" Asa sat down in front of Charlotte as if he were worshiping. "I mean, about sending the car."

"He hasn't said anything yet, but you know how William is about Stanley."

"Nobody could have been more generous," Lavinia insisted.

Charlotte grasped the wings of her chair with hands which were astonishingly strong in spite of their softness. On the third finger of her left hand, guarding her heavy gold wedding ring of more than fifty years ago, she wore a magnificent emerald set in a thin band of platinum. "Well, you know how old men are about young girls," she replied amiably; "and I will say for Stanley that she has always been very nice to him. He is out of patience with her now, but when she tries, she can twist him round her little finger." Charlotte looked as soft as a featherbed,

[184]

and just as expressionless, Asa thought, gazing up at her from a lower seat. She was fat and dumpy and utterly without style of form or feature; but she had dignity; she had a supine force; she had even a presence. In her mild fortitude, she will outlast William, Asa prophesied mutely. He may hector her, but her unruffled softness will wear him down in the end.

"If she wants the car, I'd like her to have it," Asa said. "It may keep her out of mischief."

"Yes, she can't have many friends," Charlotte assented. "She's not the kind to make friends with other girls, and yet she never liked to be left by herself. It's a pity that she can't get to know people," she continued after a minute. "We have several very good friends in Baltimore, but—oh, well, one never knows. . . ."

"I can't imagine what she does with herself all day." Lavinia's tears had become a matter of habit, and nobody noticed them. "She can't have money for shopping. But after all we went through, it is settled now. They are married, thank heaven, and they will have to spend the rest of their lives somewhere. I suppose we can't expect Peter not to go on with his career. Only I do wish he wouldn't leave her so much alone. Young people today aren't brought up to stand loneliness."

"I was wondering," Charlotte murmured, as she so frequently murmured with William; for all families have traits in common which seem to hold them looped together. "I was wondering if something oughtn't to be done about Roy."

"But what?" Asa looked slightly startled.

"I've always felt," Charlotte resumed, "that she behaved splendidly. It is all so different from the way wives used to cling and make trouble when we were young."

"But making trouble used to bring results," Lavinia wailed. "And what on earth can we do for Roy that we haven't already tried?"

"It seems to me, we take too much for granted." Charlotte's tone had dropped to a whisper. "We've fallen into a way of expecting Roy to be wonderful just because she is different from us."

"Well, but what can we do for her?" Asa demanded, and the note of resolution in his voice made Charlotte glance at him keenly. The mere mention of Roy's name, she said to herself, appeared to touch some secret spring in his nature. "She doesn't want any help. She told me that she had to save herself in her own way." Though he spoke with pride, he was thinking, in a tremor of apprehension: But is she saving herself? And for what?

Charlotte stirred uneasily, and her bulk, rolling slightly as she moved, filled out and overflowed the wide wings of her chair. "Well, I wasn't really thinking," she answered. "The idea just crossed my mind like that—" She snapped her thumb and forefinger while the emerald flashed a green light on her hand. "You know what a difference William has always made between the two girls."

"Wasn't that because . . ." Lavinia's question trailed off unfinished.

Charlotte nodded. "Yes, Stanley made an effort to charm him. Men are not ever too old to wallow in flattery."

"She is very fond of him," Lavinia retorted defensively. "She thinks he is—he is . . ."

"Anyway, she was always nice to him, and she brightened up that big empty house when she ran in and out. That's why he gave her a car of her own— He hoped she would come oftener."

"And did she?" Asa's eyelids narrowed as they did when he was amused in spite of himself.

"Come oftener? I don't know. You see, he'd just given her the car for a wedding present when . . . when . . ."

Lavinia shivered slightly, as if a chill draft had blown

through the room. "If he sends on the car, I might put in the rest of her things." Her lower lip, which was like Stanley's, quivered, and she bit into it sharply. "Her winter clothes are all here, and I think Peter's are too. Asa, do you know where Peter left his heavy things?"

"I told Virgie to pack them away in the spare room. The night after he left, I bundled them in there on the bed." He made a sudden gesture, as if he were sketching something in the air. "I'd like to get rid of them, damn him!"

"Why, Asa! What will Aunt Charlotte think of you?" Lavinia protested; but Charlotte, when he caught her twinkling eye, appeared to think very well of him.

"I hope he'll let Parry drive the car up to Baltimore," she said. "Then he could take anything we want to send." She stood up and straightened the chiffon scarf on her shoulders. "Parry's a good boy," she continued, "and as bright as a new pin. I wish William would help him with his education. It does seem hard, when so many half-wits are pushed through college."

"I don't see what good it would do him," Lavinia rejoined indifferently.

"Maybe you're right," Charlotte admitted, "but I can't help feeling sorry. If he went North, nobody would ever guess he was colored," she added with one of her amazing flashes of independence, "and at least somebody white, and probably quite a number of them, must be responsible for his complexion."

Lavinia bridled uneasily; for there were occasions when she felt that Charlotte, who was her aunt only by marriage, was too indelicate for the superior taste of the Fitzroys. "All that was so long ago," she murmured evasively.

"I know. That's what William says. It's wonderful the way you Fitzroys all think alike. But Abel Clay's family

did belong to the Fitzroys for a good hundred years and more, and Minerva's mother was the mammy of Asa, and of his father before him."

Asa's mouth twitched as it did when he was moved. "Your Aunt Charlotte is right," he said. "I hate to see anything good wasted, and Parry has a good mind. Craig told me he was astonished to find how much law the boy had picked up just by reading at night. He seems to have an extraordinary memory for words—or, I suppose, it may be merely for sounds." He turned his head and looked out into the night. "Good God! When I think of the power of money. . . . If he were all white and poor, would he be any happier?" His mind had gone suddenly blank, but something, smothered yet alive, was struggling in a dark corner. What is it, he asked with a malicious twist, that I am longing to do? Overturn the shape of things as they are? Challenge the dumb tyranny of circumstances? Well, someday I shall blow up, he thought, and then I shall be done for in earnest.

"No, but it would be easier to help him," Charlotte answered. "Men like William wouldn't mind my helping him if he were all-white. Even now, he likes my giving odd jobs to Parry, but there isn't enough paying work for them all, white and colored."

Asa frowned. "It's hard for everybody. These are not easy times, though we've known worse and come through them. The difference is that in worse times, we had something to stand on and to hold by. Even in Reconstruction and afterwards, we still believed in ourselves."

Charlotte laughed in a low chuckle. "If we hadn't believed in ourselves, we couldn't have hated the Yankees. It was hating, my mother used to say, that kept her alive. Hate was her one vital possession, she told me, and her last and only affirmation to life."

"I thought," Asa rejoined lightly, "that they called it

moral indignation. Well, anyway, the faculty of moral indignation isn't all that it used to be, and I doubt whether
it ever exerted an undue influence in human affairs."

He remembered his own poor place in the factory,
with a hungry mob waiting to oust him at the first sign
that he was giving way, that he couldn't keep up with the
herd. His father would not have submitted so easily, but,
then, in his father's day, children as well as conditions
were different. Or were they? . . . It is bad for the
young, too, because they are struggling in a time when
there is room neither for youth nor age. No room for
youth! But I'd rather drown myself, he thought, than be
dependent upon my children—upon any children today.
Not that Roy wouldn't divide her last crust with me, and
Andrew too, for the matter of that. He might begrudge
all that he doled out to me; but he would not fail to live
up to what the Democratic Party or the Relief Adminis-
tration expected. No, it isn't that, Asa thought. It is simply that I'd rather be dead than have to fall back on the
best or the worst of my children. I'd far rather sell pencils
in the street or go to the City Home. . . .

"That must be William," Charlotte said warningly, for
the doorbell was ringing. "He told me he would stop for
me." She flinched as if from pain, and her hand shot to
her bosom. That fear is with her day and night, Asa
thought. Even if the danger is over, for she is past sev-
enty, and the doctor had said that the old were seldom
afflicted, the fear still prowls in her consciousness.

"Maybe he will come upstairs," Lavinia called after
Asa, who was hurrying down to the front door.

William entered with his usual air of property well applied, and consented somewhat glumly to ascend to the
second floor. He wore a look of general displeasure, and
Asa surmised that the letter from Stanley had disturbed
him more than his wife suspected. The stairs creaked

under his ponderous tread, and it seemed to Asa, absurdly enough, he told himself, that there was a threatening sound in his footsteps.

While he went back into Lavinia's room, following slowly behind the heavy old man, Asa felt that a subtle change had passed not only over the human figures of Lavinia and Charlotte, but even over the furniture and the bowl of wilting red dahlias on the table. It was as if the sense of property, like some invisible symptom, had altered the atmosphere and the background, as well as the waiting attitude of the two women. Lavinia was sitting up on her daybed, and holding out her hands in a gesture of welcome. Charlotte had moved out of the largest and softest chair, which she left vacant for William. By some curious freak of light or shadow, Asa seemed to discern a faint ripple in the scene, as if a mood had come and gone almost too quickly. Are they afraid of him? he asked himself. Are we all afraid of him, because we feel that he owns us, body and soul?

"This is so good of you, dear Uncle William," Lavinia sighed as he kissed her.

"I just stopped for Charlotte," he replied in the surly tone of a man who cannot be cajoled. "I suppose she told you I had a letter from Stanley. After the way she's behaved, she'd had the impudence to ask me to send her car on to Baltimore."

Lavinia sank back on her pillows and pressed a handkerchief to her bluish lips. "She's always been devoted to you. I used to think she cared more for you than for any one of us."

William snorted. "And she had her reasons, I'll bet. All she wants from any man is what she can get out of him."

"No, no, Uncle William. She is really fond of you. She admires strong men who have done things in the world."

"Ha!" William exclaimed, and then again after a brief pause, "Ha!"

"Yes, she is devoted to you." Lavinia pressed in the point. "You must not forget that."

William appeared to relax slightly. "Maybe so and maybe not. Anyway, that sports car isn't much use shut up in my garage. I offered it to Roy, but she wouldn't touch it, and I can't say I blame her. But what's the matter with Roy, I'd like to know? Independent as the devil, with her everlasting 'I can look after myself, thank you.' All these modern half-baked theories seem to have turned her head. Letting her own sister run away with her husband, and taking it all on the chin. Bought a red hat, too, the very next day, didn't she?" He caught his breath and glared round at his wife. "When you asked her what steps she meant to take, didn't she tell you she'd just stepped out to buy a red hat?"

"Yes, William, but if you'd seen her eyes when she said it! Don't you think she was brave to try to keep up her spirit?"

William puffed out his lips in a sighing whistle. "It was brave," he admitted, "but it wasn't womanly. I like a woman to be womanly."

"The red hat did make a difference," Charlotte continued mildly. "I don't remember just how—but it seemed to sound a note—well, like a—challenge."

"Oh, I'm not complaining of Roy," William retorted. He looked round for a chair and sat down stiffly in the one from which his wife had just risen. While he settled himself comfortably, he uttered a low growl and glanced from Charlotte to Lavinia, as if he suspected they were trying to get something for nothing.

Standing a little aside, Asa found himself thinking idly: Yes, it's true, owning things is the curse of the world. William is an unattractive old man, with a bald

yellow skull, crisscrossed by a network of fine veins, like the haphazard scratching of hens; a pendulous jowl; and a loose-lipped, sensual mouth under a bushy moustache, which is yellow-white at the ends. Yet his very ugliness, after the queer habit of extremes, is impressive. It does not detract, apparently, from his self-esteem or from his enjoyment of life.

There was a rumor, no doubt exaggerated, that he maintained a galaxy of mistresses, all very blonde and young, in New York; though in Queenborough he was careful to observe the proprieties; and he worshiped, beside his wife, every Sunday in St. Luke's Episcopal Church. Well, money isn't everything. Asa repeated the convenient formula of the shabby genteel, while he turned away and stared vacantly out of the window. Money wasn't everything, even to William, who would have liked, one suspected, to buy something more lasting than platinum blondes; and it wasn't everything to Charlotte, who, though the price of her jewels might have endowed a small hospital, was still the victim of an incurable dread. No, wealth could not buy happiness, but it could make unhappiness more comfortable; and even a broken heart, Asa reasoned, cannot afford to despise comfort. Freedom, too, it could buy, he thought resentfully, freedom to cast back favors and reject obligations.

"I can't see that there's much to choose," William was grumbling, "between the two men she took up with. Nincompoops, both of them. You couldn't get one ounce of guts if you made sausage of the two together. I'm not saying, mind you, that the girl deserves any better. She's like all the rest of her empty-headed generation."

"Roy has pluck," Asa said irritably. "And so had my mother. It isn't the generation, it's something else. When I think of the way my mother was brought up, and of all—of all . . . ." While he stood there, frowning moodily at William, two memories drifted into his mind and rip-

pled out again, as frail and fugitive as broken images in
running water. He saw his mother bending over his crib,
with roses in the coils and loops of her bright hair, and
clouds of lace streaming over her white shoulders. Then,
scarcely had this recollection dissolved and vanished,
when it reassembled in the figure of an old and haggard
woman scrubbing the tracked floor in a gray dawn, when
the cook had not come. Oh, my God, he thought, shaken
to the inmost depths of his being.

"Perhaps it's only the surface that's changed," Charlotte said soothingly. "We may talk differently, or even
act differently on the outside; but underneath, I doubt
whether young people are really so changed."

"On the surface," Lavinia repeated as brightly as if she
were proclaiming not a well-worn platitude, but an undis-
covered verity. "I'm sure that it's all on the surface."

"Well, I'd never choose a hard surface on a woman,"
William chuckled under his breath, and then a dash of
his jocose humor enlivened his tone. "I like 'em tender,"
he added, relishing his own wit, "and I like 'em plump."

Charlotte started to speak, but the next instant she
altered her mind and bit back her words. Instead,
she turned her unpolemical glance on Asa; and he understood that fifty years in the thorough training of
wifehood had taught her to value peace above firm
convictions.

"Stanley may be undisciplined," Lavinia remonstrated
gently, "but she has a sincere feeling for you, Uncle William." If he failed to swallow this bait, she told herself, it
would not be because she had stopped casting it on the
troubled waters. After a pause, in which she hoped the
tempting morsel had gone down, hook and all, she added
persuasively, "Do you remember the way she used to run
in and out of your house just for a glimpse of you?" Her
tears overflowed, and she tried unsuccessfully to find
her handkerchief, which Charlotte retrieved from un-

der her pillow. "Poor child, she is alone now, among strangers. . . ."

William blew his nose furiously. "Well, maybe the car will help to keep her out of another—another . . ."

Staring at him in an unfriendly silence, Asa saw with astonishment that he was actually moved. In the sacred cause of property there were few crimes of which William was not capable. He could grind down a living wage to powder, or, to gratify some deep-seated instinct, he might exercise an unscrupulous power over a debtor. Yet any light scrap of fluff, Asa told himself, who thought it worth her while to play upon William's senses, could wring tears from his hardened eyes and persuade him to feather her love nest. I wonder how much of his anger with Stanley, for all its air of moral indignation, is mere jealousy in a perverted form?

"Well, Charlotte, we'd better be going home," William mumbled, shuffling his feet as he rose. "I'll see what I can do about that car. Not that she ought to have it."

"You're so good," Lavinia began, and then, detecting from his glazed eye that the epithet was inadequate, she hastily supplied an imposing substitute. "You're so wonderful, Uncle William. I know Stanley will be overwhelmed by your kindness."

"Tell her it's the last thing she's going to get from me, the last blessed thing. Tell her she needs a sound whipping more than she needs a car, and in the old days she'd have had her deserts." His sly chuckle held a lustful note.

"It must be nearly eleven," Charlotte said, prodding him gently. "Lavinia ought to have been in bed long ago."

"Oh, I put it off as long as I can," Lavinia replied. "I sleep so badly that I go to bed late, and Asa always sits up reading until I've dropped off. Then you'll let me know," she added pleadingly, "when the car goes. I'll have their winter things packed tomorrow."

"I'll try to get it off in a day or two," William answered.

"Maybe I'll have that boy Parry drive the car up to Baltimore. He's a careful driver, I'll say that for him. Now, you'd better get to bed right away, and don't let that husband of yours sit up stuffing his head from books. Books! He'd be better off today, and so would you, if he'd never had a book in his hands after he learned reading and writing. Look at me! I never read a book through in my life, and has that kept me from taking an important place in the world? No, sir, I tell you the ideas people get out of books have made more trouble even than drink."

Bending over reluctantly, for she was no longer young, he brushed Lavinia's flabby cheek with his moustache. "All right, then, I'll see what I can do about it, and I'll let you know." With an abrupt command to his wife, he turned away and stalked pompously out of the room. A few minutes later they heard his spluttering complaints in the hall below; but by the time Asa and Charlotte had hurried after him, he had opened the front door and was waving impatiently to Bradley, the chauffeur. "Are you going to spend the night, Charlotte? Never saw such a woman for dawdling. Doesn't know the meaning of time. Doesn't even know the difference between day and night."

Yes, he was almost repulsive, without a single redeeming trait, Asa thought, watching him as the car rolled away, but a pillar, nevertheless, of a respectable world.

III

STANDING in the doorway, Asa looked out under the thick boughs to the white glare on the corner. There was a faint wind in the branches, and the shadows were stirring on the pavement. Leaves were falling, turning, drifting. Even in the city he could taste the bittersweet flavor of autumn. At Hunter's Fare, he knew, the wind from the river would have sprung up; colored leaves, blanched by moonlight, would hurtle over the grass to the house; the earthy scents of smoke and wood mold and cider would be strengthened by the fresh darkness. Inside the house, Kate would be lingering over her book (for books overflowed the tables and chairs and were piled up in corners), and Pat and Percy would have their run out-of-doors before they went on guard for the night. Peace is there, he thought, in that house, with that friendship. Love comes, love goes; but comradeship is woven of an indestructible element. I'm sixty, he said to himself with a sensation of panic. I'm sixty, and my life is slipping away empty. He would soon be an old man. In ten years more he would be over the top . . . in twenty years more he would be as old as William, with nothing to show for it. He was married; he had children; he had worked for over forty years; but he felt, at the moment, that he had less than nothing to show for it all. Then his mood shifted. I've had Roy, he said to himself. I shall always have Roy. While the thought was still in his mind, it seemed to evaporate. Had he really meant anything to Roy in her unhappiness, or even when she was happy? There were times when he felt that, in her anguish of mind, she would sooner turn to anyone else. That can't

be true, he thought. I will never believe it. For, with Roy estranged from him, he could see only that the bottom had dropped out of his universe. Kate was still there; but even Kate could not fill the place Roy had left empty.

A small sports car sped down the street, swept on through the glare at the crossing, and stopped in front of the house. A minute later Craig and Roy ran across the pavement and up the steps to the door.

"What are you looking for, Father?"

"For tomorrow. Your Uncle William and Aunt Charlotte have just gone."

"Gone? Then we came at the right moment."

"You must have passed them up the street."

"Maybe so. We weren't watching."

"Well, come in. Aren't you coming in, Craig?"

"Of course, he's coming in. He's coming in for a high-ball. Have you any whiskey, Father?"

"I don't know, my dear. I forgot to go to the ABC yesterday." What he meant, though he could not bring himself to say it, was that he had not the price of a bottle. In the old days, before Peter's flight into freedom, it was Peter who kept the sideboard stocked with whiskey and gin.

"I'm sorry I forgot too," Craig said lightly. "I'll remember to bring some tomorrow."

Roy tucked her hand under her father's arm and waited until he had fastened the door. Then she tossed her hat aside and led him into the dining room. "Well, if you haven't, Mother has. Uncle William brought her a bottle of Scotch yesterday, and we'd better look before I go rummaging in her closet. Mother hides things in the most ridiculous places. She suspects us all, even poor Virgie, of secret drinking. I'll probably find this Johnnie Walker tucked away in her hatbox or behind the shoes in her closet." While she ran on, she was searching on the shelves of the sideboard, and after a brief hunt, she drew

out a bottle of bourbon. "You left it here, and I put it away for you," she said to Craig. How intimate her tone is, Asa thought, but aloud he said only, "You don't drink, do you, daughter?"

Roy made a mocking face at him. "Of course I drink, old dear. Who doesn't?" But, after all the fuss about whiskey, he noticed that she did not touch it, and Craig took only a small drink. They don't know what they really are, these young people, Asa thought, but they obey an inner compulsion to make themselves appear worse. Was all their drinking, as well as their bad manners, which they called honesty, nothing more than bravado?

"I must keep a clear head," Craig was saying. "I have to go home and write an article."

"An article on what?" Asa asked. "What are you reforming now?" He remembered how liberal and advanced Craig had been before he had met Stanley, how eager to overturn every barrier in earth and sky, and to make everything, good or bad, different.

"Reform? Good Lord, no," Craig replied. "We've left reform miles behind us. You can't reform human nature."

"Maybe not. But it has been possible in the past, now and then, to reform human behavior, and even to change, or at least control, human appetites."

"The whole trouble with your generation," Craig retorted in his most irritating superior manner, "is that you depended too much on the past. You imagined history proved something." He smiled and diluted his whiskey from the syphon in front of him; and his smile, as Asa had told himself so often before, was still charming, whether or not one admired his manner or agreed with his views. The recent cloud had lifted from his high forehead, and his eyes sparkled with a light brilliance. Yet wasn't his charm, like his mind or his temperament, woven of immediate impressions and intuitions? It comes

[198]

and goes as a mood does, Asa thought, and it has nothing more constant than a mood to fall back upon. Craig must have looked like this when Stanley first knew him; it was her influence that had hardened him, as faces are hardened under a frowning sky. Watching him in this altered light, Asa had a swift feeling that he had learned to know Stanley better. He could understand at last why she had fallen in love with Craig in the beginning, and he understood also why in the end she had fallen out of love. There was all the difference between the man who is master of himself and the man who has surrendered to a magnetism that he resents. She had set herself, Asa mused, to the task of making over a lover, and she had come at last to despise, perhaps even to hate, the thing she had made. With all his fine points, Craig had been as wax in her hands, and Stanley, who worshiped power, could never forgive where she dominated.

"Did you find a place to go?" Asa asked, wondering whether they thought him the nuisance he felt himself to be at the moment. "Aren't Sunday meetings always a background for sermons?"

"Nobody called them sermons, because everybody talked at once," Roy answered. She threw an encouraging smile at Craig over her father's shoulder. "But Craig said the best things. He's fine when he begins to speak."

"About what?"

"Oh, about everything. About the housing problem and the way people are made to live and the right to happiness . . ." She spoke lightly, but he decided, while he listened, that even if she were not wholly serious, she was probably serious enough. If only she could learn to accept life and love less deeply, she would be happier in the future. Yet she took them so deeply, he told himself, because she placed nothing above them. Though she had broken with the past and the fragments of tradition were still scattered about her, could she ever find a refuge, or

even security, in the things that are timeless? Or was she, like so many of her age and way of life, driven by forces she could not understand toward an end which was only a name?

"Well, I'd better see about your mother's milk," he said. "I'm glad of this new interest. By the time you've read all the books Craig is lending you," he chaffed, "you may be able to teach your old fogy father to feel at home in his world."

"But you do think that things ought to be different," Roy said almost reprovingly.

"Different. Oh, Lord, yes. I'd change everything, if I could, beginning with the electron and ending with human nature. You may not believe it, but I've never had a high opinion of things as they are."

"Well, you're a lot more radical than the rest of us." Craig ran his hand untidily through his thick dark hair. "All we want to do is to make the world a little more decent."

A warm glow was suddenly shed into Asa's mind; for somewhere in his buried life the embers of his romantic youth were still flickering. He knew how youth felt; he could even feel with it. In everything except the rational and physical parts, he thought, in all the fantastic dreams and the lost horizons, he was still as young as he had ever been. So short a time ago as this Sunday afternoon, he had watched the larks whirring up from the autumn fields, and had grasped the sense of delight before it escaped him. I never had that in youth, he thought. It was what I've always wanted, but I never felt it before.

Aloud he said presently, "Perhaps I'm not so old as I look, my boy, or is it so unintelligent?"

"Oh, you're all right." Roy beamed on him affectionately, but there was something lacking, he felt vaguely, in her reassurance.

"Right you are!" Craig repeated, tossing off his whiskey and water.

They were kind to him, Asa knew; they were trying to make him feel that they wanted his company, that he was not in their way. Yet he knew also that, in spite of the struggling youth in his heart, he could not speak to them in their own tongue. Not a generation but a mental hemisphere separated the two angles of vision. Youth and middle age had never looked at the same landscape; they did not see the same objects. I'm in sympathy with them, he said to himself, and added in the next breath: But they haven't learned the first thing about order. They don't know how to reason. They have fine ideas without a string of logic to hold them together. They have made a cult of loose thinking, of disarrangement and rowdiness. Even the dandy of our day, he thought, with his eyes on Craig's rumpled head and limp collar, might have given a lesson in method to the popular tough guy of the present. Then, after a moment: But this boy has something the dandy lacked, and that—well, I suppose that is—we'll call it, anyway, the human touch. . . .

Upstairs, while Lavinia was sipping her hot milk, he heard Craig go out and the front door shut after him. "I'd better run down and lock up," he said. "Roy always forgets something."

"She never seems to think that locking up matters," Lavinia assented. "They all behave as if being murdered in your beds were a part of the day's work."

"Well, I'll finish after her," he replied, glad to escape while Lavinia was still awake.

Downstairs, he found that Roy had remembered to bolt the door, but Virgie, in the carelessness of her genial race, had neglected to lock up at the back of the house.

"You liked the meeting?" he asked, trying to arrest and keep the look in Roy's face, which was eager and

interested. There was a warm dusky red in her cheeks, and her gray eyes were luminous.

"Oh, well, there was a lot of talk, but it was amusing."

"And what did they talk about?"

She laughed. "About the state of the world, and what ought and ought not to be done. . . ." Her voice trailed off into vagueness. "Craig talked very well."

"About the state of the world, and what ought and ought not to be done," Asa repeated.

"Sometimes they looked as if they wanted to fight, but that was when they talked about voting. It was rather exciting when they began to quarrel. I didn't know Craig had it in him."

"Had what in him?"

"Oh, I don't know . . . grit, pluck, spunk. Uncle William would call it guts, only he doesn't think that Craig has any."

"Well, I'm glad you like Craig," Asa said. "I think there's a good deal more to him than your Uncle William suspects."

"He's nice to go about with. He sees things."

"What kind of things?"

"I mean, he notices. He can see the color in the sky, and he knows that the change from baseball to football isn't the only way to tell when it is autumn. Some men don't know any more than that about seasons. There's Andrew . . ."

"Andrew is a fine boy in his way. He's never given your mother or me a moment's anxiety."

She shrugged her thin shoulders. "Well, all I said was, there's Andrew . . ."

She was thinking of Peter, he knew. Though Peter had disappeared from her outward life, he was still present in her thoughts, and perhaps in her emotions. "I knew you'd like Craig," Asa said hurriedly, "as soon as you began to see more of him. It may sound absurd to

you, but Craig and I have a good deal in common. You needn't think because I wear a hat and keep my shirt on that I approve of the universe."

"Well, you've never said anything."

"Maybe so, but I've been thinking like blazes."

She put her hand on his arm. "You've had a mean life, poor old dear. I wonder if all lives look mean when you come close up to them." Her tone had altered now; the happier moment had gone by. He thought of her eyes, eloquent with laughter when she came in with Craig. Then, as she started to move away and glanced back at him, he saw that the light had died. They looked haunted, those eyes.

"Good night, Daddy."

"Good night, my darling. Sleep well."

But neither of them, he knew, would sleep well. She would be caught up again in the old horror of desire and repulsion, of memories more vivid than life; and he would sink back into the helpless pity which is as intolerable as physical pain. If only he had something to offer her! If only he could believe! But he had fallen, he told himself, between an age that was slipping out and an age that was hastening in; and faith in life, which had once been an active conviction, now survived, when it survived at all, merely as a fixed habit of mind. I can't help it, he thought stubbornly. I can't help my antiquated sense of responsibility for things I can do nothing about. I can't help harboring the absurd notion that there is a dignity attached to the state of man. Yet he could reflect, on his way upstairs to Lavinia's room, that it was splendid to be young and magnanimous and irresponsible. . . .

Toward the end of the week, at six o'clock one morning, when he was making Lavinia's early coffee, Parry stopped to pick up the suitcases, which were waiting in a row on the doorstep. As Asa was filling the percolator, he heard a car stop by the alley gate, and Parry came

through and knocked at the kitchen door. Asa had not seen the boy for several months, and his first thought was, Parry looks as if he'd been having a hard time. There were hollows under his eyes, and his expression was more sullen, as if it had fed on a grievance. But when he smiled, his face lost its moodiness, and his features were brightened by a flash of intelligence. He was dressed in his Sunday suit of navy-blue serge, with a new striped shirt and necktie, and a good felt hat which Peter had given him a year ago.

"I was afraid I'd have to wake you up, Mr. Asa," he said.

"Oh, I'm an early bird. I never get much sleep after daybreak."

Parry grinned, and the animation made him appear careless and happy. "I've been getting ready most of the night. Ma pressed my suit for me while I was going over the car. I want to stop in Washington long enough to see the Lincoln Memorial."

"Have you ever been to Washington?"

"No, sir. I've never been out of Queenborough, except down to the beach on an excursion."

"Well, I'm glad you have the chance. Have you had breakfast?"

"Yes, sir. Ma got up before day and cooked some for me. It's a good morning, so Pa's been tidying up his borders."

Asa nodded. "That's a nice garden. I wish I had as good a backyard." Why was it, he asked himself again, that he could never feel perfectly at ease with the boy? There was something about Parry, who was neither white, brown nor black, which appeared to defy grouping or classification. There was a kind of unconscious pathos which disturbed the older man and awakened, strangely enough, an obscure and illogical sense of contrition, as if he himself were to blame for some act of injustice in

which he had taken no part and of which he had not been aware. The trouble with the boy was that he had no place anywhere; he did not belong in any unit. He stood wistfully between two hostile elements. He remained outside the life of his age; yet he was living intensely in every nerve and sinew.

"How are you coming on, Parry?"

"Just the same, sir. I can't see much ahead of me."

"You've started back to school, haven't you?"

"No, sir. I got the scholarship, and I'm taking the classes at college. I go out every morning and come home to sleep. I'm doing a part-time job at night in a service station, and Ma and Pa are helping me save up for the university in Washington. But I don't seem able to do enough studying."

"Well, I hope you'll work it out. Have you all the money you need for this trip?" That wasn't what he had meant to say, but it was the only thing that had come into his head. He wanted to help the boy. He knew too well the loneliness of being apart from life; yet all that he could think of was to ask him if he needed a few dollars. Craig would say that one should not consider individuals, but aggregates; yet an aggregate remained for Asa merely a collection of individuals.

"Yes, sir, I've got aplenty. Mr. William gave me some money for my board and oil and gas, and Ma fixed me up a lunch for two days."

"I hope you'll enjoy it." Asa drew out his shabby pocketbook and unfolded a dollar note. "Maybe you'd like to go to the movies tonight." A pang of something like self-reproach seized him. Was he trying to stay a hungry mind by offering it a paper dollar?

"Yes, sir. Thank you, sir." Parry folded the dollar and put it into his purse before he stooped to pick up two of the suitcases. "Is there anything I can do for you, Mr. Asa?"

"Nothing but get there safely. Miss Stanley is waiting for her car."

"I'm a good driver. That's why Mr. William is sending me."

"You've an uncle in the North, haven't you?"

"That's Uncle Amos. He went to New York, but he says it's harder getting on in the North than in the South. Rent and food are way over your head in Harlem. And there aren't any jobs for colored people up there. He's back now, working in a tobacco factory. I wonder if it's any use trying, Mr. Asa."

"I shouldn't give up, Parry," he replied presently. "Nothing is easy."

"Yes, sir. I reckon that's so." As Parry looked round, a ray of brightness shone for an instant in his face, as sunshine wavers and vanishes under a cloud. "I'll get on somehow."

With a suitcase in each hand, he went out of the door and down the walk to the car. After he had packed them away in the back, he returned for the others and carried them away with him. Then the slight figure in the neat blue suit passed through the gate into the alley, and a few minutes later there was the sound of the car starting. Pausing in the open doorway, Asa gazed after him with a vague feeling that something ought to be done about life, but he didn't know what it could be. Then he turned back to the gas range and lifted the bubbling percolator from the flame.

IV

ALL her life had been ruled by chance, Roy thought, while she watched the white and gray pigeons flutter down past her window. The whole of existence appeared to her as a vast accident. She had first met Peter because she had turned a strange corner and had driven down an unknown road toward disaster and heartbreak. If that had not happened, if she had turned in a familiar direction, or if he had not passed her and looked back at one particular instant, then they might have lived out their lives in Queenborough without ever meeting each other.

But the moment of that first meeting was there, ringed round by an unfading glow, preserved in some imperishable element, deep down in the stillness of thoughts which lived on after thinking and feeling were over. And it will be there, that moment, she told herself, when I am old or dead or a mere handful of blown dust. Neither will nor desire, but accident, had created an image that would outlast both will and desire. But now it is over, it is finished forever, she said to herself, looking out of her window down to the pavement, where the pigeons moved in a dream among moving shadows. Even if the bare outline persists, I have left all that was vital behind me; I shall never remember, except when I am asleep. She would keep no share in the past; she would refuse to acknowledge its power of survival; she would deny not only its truth, but its unwanted existence. I will not remember, she said, glancing round at the room, which remembered.

For what, after all, had bound her to Peter? What was the meaning or the nature of a love which had seemed to

touch the heights, as well as the depths, of her being? They had had nothing in common, she saw now, denying while she reflected, nothing but that quiver of the nerves and the flesh, that surprise, that wonder, that eager sense of something precious which hitherto had been missing from life. Beyond this, scarcely a belief, a liking, a shared interest. But that alone had been everything, and now that also was nothing. And she had forgotten. But, oh, Peter, Peter, what pain, what bitter anguish there is in forgetting!

And Craig too. His unhappiness and his need of her had been the result of a chance meeting. After Roy's divorce, he had abruptly disappeared. He had avoided the Timberlakes' house, and not one of them had heard any word from him. Andrew, whose friend he had been, said that Craig had moved out of the apartment, without leaving a message or an address for his letters. "I'm afraid he's taken to drink," Andrew had said regretfully, "but he can't stand it. He's the sort of chap who can get drunk on anything. Even ideas fly to his head. I wish," he added indignantly, "that Stanley had chosen to play ball with somebody else. Craig was too good for her."

"I wonder if Peter is," Roy had retorted scornfully, driving the blade into her heart. "But, I suppose she'll marry every sort till she finds just what she's looking for in her bed."

"Roy, how can you?" Lavinia had remonstrated; but Andrew had exclaimed with boisterous admiration, "That's right, Roy. I call that sporting!"

For an instant, the fresh wound had seemed to draw out the agony; then the relief faded and the throbbing ache was renewed. It doesn't do any good, she told herself. Not any good in the world. . . .

That was in August, and the next day, late in the afternoon, she met Craig as she was passing through Jefferson Park. The day had been one of torrid heat, and

the shadows aslant the graveled walks looked as if they were emblazoned on silver. A little earlier, when she had just come home from work, Aunt Charlotte had asked her to motor out into the country; but she had dreaded the long conversation, and after a bath and a vain effort to rest, she had slipped into a chiffon frock and come out-of-doors into the grassy square at the intersection of Westward Avenue and Granite Boulevard. The leaves on the maples, yellowing in the sun and edged with a reflected transparency, hung as motionless as if they were cut out of brass. Underfoot, were all the sordid and disfiguring signs of an overheated humanity; a litter of newspapers, read and dropped from the benches; eddies of dust scattered by dragging feet; watermelon seeds, shreds of orange peel or half-rotten peaches; and here and there a broken toy or a tattered balloon, which children had thrown away.

It was better indoors, Roy said to herself, and then pausing abruptly before a slouching figure on one of the green benches, she exclaimed, "Craig!" in a horrified tone. He sprawled there against the back of the bench, his long legs crossed over the concrete curb, and the distraught wretchedness in his gaze fixed upon vacancy. The planes of his face, she thought with sudden pity, had shrunk into hollows and angles, as if the inner padding of flesh had withered between the skin and the bone. Poor Craig, he had deserved better than this. Why had this happened to him, when his nerves were so near the surface that one could almost watch them as they writhed and twisted in pain? He was finer than Stanley; he was finer than Peter; and because of his better nature, he was predestined to suffer.

"Craig," she repeated gently, touching his arm.

At her touch, at the sound of her voice, a quiver ran through his features while he lifted his sunken head and looked into her face. His strange eyes, flashing from dark-

ened sockets, held a savage loneliness, and she wondered whether he had been drinking too much and too
long. But his tone, when he spoke, was quite steady and
so flat and dull that she understood he was drunk only
with despair or with emptiness. To her horror, she saw
that he was beginning to look neglected and shabby. Who
would have recognized in him the Craig who had loved
Stanley, who had become, for her sake, an exile from that
world of theory which was the native atmosphere of his
mind? He was, as he had always been, Roy thought, out
of touch with the naked structure of facts, or with any
stable pattern of living.

This was the cause of her old impatience with him,
and with all visionaries. But she knew now, while she
gazed into his defenseless eyes, that if this inner vision
was his weakness, it was also, in a measure at least, his
strength. He was the finer because of his detachment
from an imperfect scheme of existence. He was—she
groped for the right word—nobler. Yes, that was the flaw
in her thinking: a discarded epithet now needed to be
revived by a generation which had rejected nobility.
Though Craig accepted the new social labels, he still harbored the old moral antipathies. While he thought with
the confused present, he was linked emotionally with
those higher passions which distinguish between right
and wrong, not only in the mass, but in individual relationships. Otherwise, why should he have demanded both
love and loyalty in Stanley, who was capable only of self-
delusion? Ironically, Roy remembered her mother's classification of human beings into persons of good or bad
blood. How easy living, and especially loving, must have
been when people believed, or even acted as if they believed, in such fetishes. All that "good blood" had ever
done for Craig was to leave him stranded on some uncertain level between the has-been and the not-yet. He

would always be attractive, she thought, tracing the bleak contour of his face, but the type had worn thin. It was too brittle to stand the barbaric thrusts of the actuality.

"I didn't know you at first," he said, rising and grasping her hand.

"But I knew you," she answered, playing for time until she could collect her faculties and think of something to say. "How are you, Craig?"

"I'm fine. How are you?"

"Fine too," she laughed mockingly. "That's nice, isn't it?"

"Yes, that's nice." While he spoke, she could see his thoughts groping, groping through vacancy.

"What," she demanded, "have you been doing?"

His glance dropped from her face and wandered over the bleached grass and the graveled walk. "Doing? Oh, everything. . . ."

"Well, sit down and tell me about it." Why, she wondered irritably, should she bother? It was no concern of hers; Craig was no concern of hers, however she looked at him. No, I can't be bothered with him, she told herself, I'll speak only a word or two. It wasn't fair that Stanley, who was without depth, should have been able to ruin Craig, who had more depth than a man needed for happiness. But, at least one could talk with him, Roy thought with relief, as if her overcharged mind were suddenly eased of its burden. She could talk with him, because he was the only other human being who had suffered with her, pang for pang, from the same cause. She longed, with a bursting heart, to pour out a torrent of words. Only, what was there left for her to speak?

He dropped on the bench beside her and turned his ravaged face—ravaged and drained, as she thought—toward the sunset. The light flared and sank in his eyes, while she watched the reflection of an unforgotten agony waver and vanish. But it may have been merely the trem-

bling shadows of the leaves in which a faint breeze had quivered and died. "I've been thinking of you, Roy," he said.

"Why didn't you come?"

"I wanted to, but I couldn't. Once I got as far as the corner."

"Where have you been? Andrew said you weren't at your office."

"I've been moving about. I've been trying to shake things. Do you know what it means, Roy? Does anybody know what it means?"

"Can you ask that," she cried savagely, "of me?"

Interest dawned in his look. For the first time, he appeared to fasten upon her his wandering attention. "Then you know it's living in hell."

"As if I didn't know . . ." Her voice broke, while a tremor of aversion ran through her nerves. A woman might suffer, a woman must suffer through love, she thought; but a man should be different. A man should be strong enough to rise above the regrets and denials and betrayals of life. She liked a man to be victorious in conflict, to trample down and destroy the enemies of his happiness. Peter had been like that, and she had loved Peter. Aloud, she continued after a pause: "It's not fair that they should spoil our lives. They are not worth remembering."

"Shall we ever forget them?"

"I *will* forget him." She flung out her hand as if she were threatening a shadow. "Every hour I'm moving farther away from him."

"What do you do with yourself? Are you still decorating your houses for new lovers?"

"I work harder than ever. I pretend to be interested. If only I can pretend long enough, it may come true. I do things with my hands, but never, never, when I can help it, do I let myself think of him."

[213]

"Can you help it?"

"In the day—almost. But at night it is harder. Dreams are hardest of all."

Terror—or was it merely the image of a thought? —leaped into his eyes. "She never leaves me alone," he muttered. "God damn her, she never leaves me alone."

"You must keep her away. You must not let her come back. Oh, Craig, you must keep her away!"

A spasm convulsed his features, but it was soon over. Heaven be praised that he did not burst into tears. Had he cried, she could not have forgiven him; she could not have forgotten. "I've tried everything," he answered. "Nothing does any good, not even drink. I can't get drunk enough to do any good."

Have you tried working? Have you really tried?"

He shook his head stubbornly. "I've wanted only to put an end—"

"And all for her!" The anger in her voice scorched him. "Can't you see she isn't worth any of it? Can't you see—oh, you poor blind fool, can't you see?" Inflamed by resentment, she flashed round on him. "If you give a thing like that power over your life, you're no better than she is. You're a man of straw, and I'll not be bothered with you."

Without rising, he stared up at her in bewilderment. "You can't fight a running fire with words," he said. "Do you think I like this? Do you think . . ."

"Then why do you stand it? Oh, but you do like it." Her eyes blazed. "You *like* being hurt. There's a kind of pleasure . . ."

"Do you like it yourself?"

"I fight it, but you don't. You simply lie down and let the misery wash over you." She had tossed her hat on the bench, and everything about her, from the scornful curl of her lips to her dark waving hair, appeared to spring

upward, alive and glowing, in the flame of the afterglow. The greenish light under the leaves shone in her eyes; and it seemed to her, as she gazed at him, that the whole scene was dissolving and swimming in a circular motion, as if they stood together in the depths of the sea. His features wore the distorted and unreal look of a drowned face that is seen under an ebbing tide.

"Don't go," he pleaded, for the moment had broken in two, and she had stooped to pick up her hat. He raised his hand to his eyes, as if brushing away a delusion. "You might help me. You are the only person alive who might help me."

Her impatient gesture seemed to tear his words in pieces and scatter them on the ground. "I must help myself. That is all I can do."

"I'd like to see you again."

"What's the use? I can't bother. It's true, what I told you. I believe there's something in you that enjoys being hurt."

"You mean, by Stanley?" His lips quivered with pain.

"As long as you still love her or hate her. Which is it?"

He shook his head. "I don't know."

"Well, I don't enjoy being hurt, and I'm going to stop it."

She turned away, but he followed her. "Let me see you again, Roy."

"Our door is open."

"I want to see you alone. You shake me up. You do me good. But I couldn't stand your mother—not yet."

"She was fond of you. So was Father."

"That's why I can't stand them. But you never really liked me."

"I did. I liked you well enough—but, oh, I don't know—You talked so much about social responsibility, and you let yourself be pulled to pieces by any passion that was lying around. Your ideas were fine, but they

were all—well, just air plants." She broke off and looked at him. "Do you suppose anybody has ever been saved by a theory or helped by a sermon?

"I'm the last person on earth to answer that. I've lost everything I ever believed in."

"It may come back. Some day, when you're not expecting it, everything may come back. Even Uncle William, who thinks your views are all poppycock, admits that you meant well."

"Damn it! That's my curse. I mean well, even now. I'm a member of that forlorn company, the men of goodwill."

Her lip curled. "I don't know about goodwill, but I'm not going to be beaten."

"You aren't a misfit, and I am. I have always disappointed people, ever since I came into the world at the wrong time and cost my mother her life. In the beginning, my father couldn't bear the sight of me. Then he started trying to make me over into something I was not intended to be. He wanted me to be the last Southern gentleman of the old school. So he sent me to the University of Virginia, where I went native—or roughneck. Then he thought he'd make me an intellectual by sending me to Harvard. And Harvard turned me into a communist. Tough on the old chap, you know. I used to think him a pompous ass, but I've come to see he has something—I don't know what it is. He'll be ninety-three his next birthday, and he's never been broken—he's never even been bent. He's had three wives, and as a boy of fifteen, he ran away to finish a war and rebuilt the family fortunes after Sheridan went by. He got on, too, without what we call a higher education, and without the help of any benevolent Red Cross or committees for devastated regions. Yes, he has something. I see all that, though we can't be together for five minutes without going up in the air. . . . Still, there's something. It may

be only that he's kept the simple values we've got rid of. He's primitive enough to believe there's some meaning—some kind of center in the mess of things. . . ." Craig choked back a laugh. "A queer bird to be still alive! Caught in a wheelchair, but holding on tight."

"It's a pity you are his only hope."

"Yes, he needed another son—or a dozen of them. All my sisters are quite splendid examples of petrified Southern ladies. Well, that's that." He turned on her fiercely. "Is there anything," he demanded, "that will kill love?"

Her eyes mocked him. "Only another love. It takes love to kill love." Yes, that was true, she thought with a flash of startled insight. Passion alone could destroy passion. All the thinking in the world could not make so much as a dent in its surface.

"Let me see you soon, Roy," he asked again. His eyes softened in the flushed light, and his relaxed figure stiffened. "There is so much we want to say to each other." Was he, she wondered in silence, deliberately trying to whip up a new emotion? Well, no matter, she was sick of emotion. Yet it was true; they had much to say to each other. Suddenly, it seemed to her that her heart was swollen to bursting with all the things she could not say to anyone else. Only to Craig, who was enduring life's cruelty, could she pour out the stifled rage in her own heart. Only to Craig . . .

"If you knew, Roy . . ."

"If I knew! Do you think there's anything you feel that I don't know?"

"Then come back tomorrow."

"There isn't any use. I can't stand any more. I can't take on anything else."

"You can help me. Good God, it's hell on earth, I've told you, and I'm trying to get out of it."

"But you aren't trying."

"You don't know. Nobody knows. I'd do anything —anything to fill up that emptiness."

Her anger had faded, and she gazed at him with dispassionate eyes. "Can't you make yourself look less—less trampled on?"

"Does it matter a damn?"

She frowned. "It matters two damns. How long has it been since you had a haircut? Your clothes look as if you'd been left out in the rain."

A dark flush welled up in his thin cheeks. "I don't know. I haven't thought of it."

"It's time to think of it. A man has to stand up, or pretend to. The first thing I did was to buy a red hat. Men miss a lot because they aren't allowed to wear red."

"I might wear a red necktie."

"Yes, that would help. Red has courage in it. Anything is better than the drabness of misery."

"It matches my face." He laughed frankly, while a glimmer of admiration enlivened his features.

"Well, change it and see."

"Will you come back tomorrow? I'll bring the car, and we can go somewhere we've never been. Do you mind my not coming up to the house? I feel, somehow . . ."

"Mind?" she taunted him flippantly. "I am standing on the edge of a precipice, and you ask me to excuse you for catching my elbow. As if it mattered any longer what is done, or isn't done, by other people!"

"Then you'll come to the corner? I'll be waiting there whenever you say."

"Yes, that's better. I couldn't stand having to explain things to Mother. Her window looks down on the front." Still, she hesitated. "I'll come," she added presently, "if you'll promise me to go back to work."

"I'll promise anything. What's a promise?"

"And you'll keep it?"

"I'll even keep it. I'll go back to that office, but I can't promise you any clients."

"But somebody is there."

"I suppose Appleby is still on the job—if there's any job left."

"And you'll take the first case into court? You have to help yourself if you expect me to help you."

"Then I'll do it. I'll do anything if you won't leave me alone."

Attractive but ineffectual, she thought as she looked at him. Could she do anything with such weakness? Was it worthwhile to bother? Was she only making more trouble for herself in a world which already contained an abundance? Would this unpromising association prove to be as futile or as disappointing as most human ties? Life had taught her the bitter lesson that her will was independent, but her emotion could be too easily and too deeply involved. Pity alone drew her to Craig; yet she had learned that pity could become in itself a destructive force.

Well, it was too late. She had been touched by Craig's appeal, and she had silently made her decision. "Come a little before six," she said, "and I'll go with you unless Mother has an attack."

All that was in August, when the days were long and hot, and the trees were in full leaf. Now it was October. The dusk closed in earlier, and leaves were falling.

V

THE day was Sunday, and light was pointing with long thin fingers over the huddled roofs. Roy heard her father on his way downstairs, and she hoped he would bring her a cup of coffee; since autumn came and the night had grown longer, he had fallen out of that agreeable habit. I suppose he thinks I'm asleep, she thought, because once or twice I've pretended to be when he came upstairs. She had planned to motor out into the country with Craig, and Maggie had promised to sit with her mother until Asa came in. But late last night Andrew had telephoned that he and Maggie and the children were all asked to spend the day on a James River plantation with one of the more important members of his company.

"Of course, they must go," Lavinia had assented plaintively. "If Asa would rather not stay with me, I am quite able to be left by myself."

"But you can't be left alone in the house," Roy had insisted. "I thought old Mrs. Bredalbane was coming to see you."

"You can't count on her, Roy. She's eighty, if a day, in spite of trying to dress young, and she grows flightier all the time."

"Well, there's Aunt Charlotte or Mrs. Littlepage."

"Charlotte may drop in after supper, but she is obliged to go somewhere with William, and of course Louisa Littlepage is tied up with a visiting lecturer."

"Then why can't we keep Selina all day? Father needs a breath of fresh air."

"Selina wouldn't stay on at any price. No colored servant will give up her Sunday afternoon."

"Oh, I'll stay," Asa had said, and though he had spoken reluctantly, still he had spoken.

Had he really minded so much? Roy asked herself now. Did people who were growing old care when they missed things? Did they enjoy and suffer as intensely as young people did, when having or not having meant either happiness or a long hunger? He liked the woods and fields, but he couldn't actually suffer, she imagined, whenever he gave them up. He couldn't possibly care for that nice Mrs. Oliver in the way he might have cared for a woman when he was young. She was sorry he had to stay at home on a fine day, but it wasn't, of course, as if it mattered a great deal. Anyway, she could never know, because, with a father and daughter, there was always a kind of primitive reticence. Or was this true of all human beings when time flowed between them?

The sunshine had grown stronger. Over the greenish steeple of a church, a single flight of birds shot with an arrowy swiftness through the golden air. When I see beauty, she thought, suddenly desperate, I feel that I must have love, or I shall die. If I can't have love, I would rather see ugliness. . . .

Shutting her eyes to the sunlight, she tried to think of her work, of the new orders, of the samples of wallpaper and chintz. But it was no use. The colors tumbled together, green, blue, red, orange, purple, and shifted into a kaleidoscopic design. When she was up and dressed and walking about, she could keep a firm hand on her thoughts; but lying in bed, unarmed and relaxed, she could no longer cut off the rapid stream of impressions. Though she shut her eyes to the blue sky and the flight of birds and the fire-colored maples, the morning brightness still poured in and troubled her mind. Only in love, only perhaps in the fulfillment of love, she told herself, could one find freedom from restlessness.

Craig had come to mean more to her. But how much?

[221]

Her thoughts hesitated, quivered, and rushed back again to that meeting in August, and over the many hours and days they had spent together since then. Gradually, he had grown to depend on her, and even more gradually, she had grown to accept, and at last to value his utter dependence. His weakness, she knew, was a bond between them, awaking some obscure and perhaps thwarted impulse to protect. There was none of the shock and the delicious violence of first love in the emotion she felt; yet it might be, she understood, only the more constant for the lack of that fugitive ecstasy. It doesn't fill my life, she thought, but it colors the drabness.

Almost every afternoon since midsummer he had called for her at the shop; and they had spent every Sunday motoring or roaming on country roads. As she grew to know him better, she became more sensitive to his charm and his magnanimous impulses. It would be easy to love him if she had never . . . but, oh, Peter. . . .

She sat up quickly reached for one of Craig's books lying upon the bedside table, and opening it at random, she read, without fear and without hope, the apocalyptic prophecies of Mr. John Strachey: "This bloody road, too, must no doubt be traveled. But as each of the concluding scenes of the last act of the tragedy of Capitalism is played out, more and more millions of the American people will grasp the purport of the whole play . . . They lack nothing on earth for the building up of an incomparable civilization upon the American continent. For them there is no question of undertaking the desperate, if heroic, process of laying the foundations of the industrialization of a continent—the task which the Russian workers are accomplishing."

Well, perhaps; but the prospect did not excite her. It would take more than a bloody road, she thought derisively, more even that the last act of Capitalism, to excite a woman who had been abandoned by her lover. . . . Sud-

denly, it seemed to Roy that she felt the narrow coils of identity, of the warped personal element, strangling her consciousness. If only there were something larger and deeper than self in which one might plunge and sink, and so become a part of the whole. If only . . . but every way, even that strange bloody road, would lead back in memory to what had been happiness—to what had been Peter. . . .

When she came down to breakfast, her father had just finished his Sunday morning cereal with cream. On weekdays the supply of cream was restricted to a gill for Lavinia; and Asa, who liked all rich and succulent food, had come to look forward to his Sabbath indulgence.

"Good morning, daughter." His proud and tender gaze enveloped her. "That's a pretty frock."

"I bought it yesterday."

"It looks well on you. Would you call it russet or sorrel?"

Roy laughed as she sat down and smiled at Virgie, who was smiling back over the cereal. "Neither. It's dusty cinnamon."

"Well, it looks like autumn. You've a fine day for an outing."

"It's a pity you have to stay in."

He nodded. "Oh, well, I may get a walk before Virgie goes." His eyes held the long steadiness of one who has ceased to expect.

"Did Mother have a bad night?"

"She was restless at first, but after that she slept fairly well."

"That's why you didn't make the coffee."

"Did you miss it? I wish I had known. I came down about dawn."

She looked at him while he tapped his egg. "Poor Father, you ought to have had something more."

"But I've had oatmeal, my dear, and an egg."

"Oh, I didn't mean that. I meant more of—well, more

of life. You ought to have had millions." Self-reproach ruffled her thoughts. He looked tired and gray and shabby, and the puckers around his nearsighted eyes were deeper than ever.

"My darling child, it's hard enough to keep decent on nothing. There's Craig's car. He has come early."

"Yes, he wants a whole long day out-of-doors. I wish you were going too."

"Do you, daughter? Well, so do I. But don't worry about me. You and Virgie must make the most of your freedom. Is it the same follower, Virgie?"

"He sholy is, suh, ef'n I kin manage to keep a holt on him. De young dey ain't easy to ketch, an' I ain' nevah yit had no truck wid an ole man. Dar's Mr. Craig at de do' now. Mustn't I let him in?"

"Ask Miss Roy. He's her young man."

"Mustn't I ax 'im in ter breakfust, Miss Roy?"

"Yes, you'd better ask him. He's probably forgotten it." As Virgie bustled to the door, Roy turned her head and waited expectantly, with a welcoming smile in her eyes. "Come to breakfast, Craig," she called. "We've a long day ahead of us, and it's going to be a happy day."

"And we haven't an idea where we're going." He held her hand for an instant before turning to Asa. "That's the best thing about happiness. It doesn't have to know its direction."

He looks cured, Roy told herself, with a sudden warmth at her heart. I believe he is really cured.

"What will you have, Craig?" Asa asked. "Oatmeal first?"

"Dey ain' no mo' cream," Virgie said, with sepulchral gloom. "Dey's aigs and dey's middlin'."

"That so?" Craig replied hastily. "Well, I don't want oatmeal. I must keep my youthful figure. How about another cup of coffee? I've had two already."

"Dat's too many, Mr. Craig. You is gwinter git de

cawfy habit." Virgie had sprung from a lower class than
Minerva's, and she was still African beneath her dark gin-
gerbread skin. "I reckon I'd better weaken it some," she
added, lifting the percolator.

"Not on your life! You wouldn't believe it, Virgie, but
I've drunk as many as five pots of coffee in one night."

"Naw, suh, I 'ouldn't, but, ef'n you ax me, you is
gwinter be as yaller as a pumkin. I kin tell jes' ter look at
you, Mr. Craig, dat yo' skin ain' natchel." After filling his
cup, she carried the percolator back to the kitchen, where
they could still hear her grumbling under her breath as
she added more water. "Dere's a heap a things dat ain't
natchel in dese yer times."

"Are you ready?" Craig asked, looking at Roy.

"As soon as I get my hat and speak to Mother. I suppose I'd better wear a hat, hadn't I?"

"Not for me," Craig replied airily. "I never wear one."

"Bring a coat anyway," Asa called after her as she ran
upstairs. "There was a sharp frost last night."

"It's a fine morning," Craig said. "Are you going out?"

"Not out of town." Asa's voice flattened suddenly, for
he remembered that he must telephone to Kate, who
would come to the crossroads. She would be sitting there in
her mud-splashed Ford when the omnibus stopped and
the few passengers alighted. Her smile would waver and
disappear, and she would call Pat and Percy, who would
be waiting beside the car. Their eyes, disappointed and
questioning, would turn at the sound of her voice, and
they would ask in their wordless language what had happened and why he had not come? Recalling his mind with
a jerk, he added hurriedly: "It looks as if the war scare
had passed over."

Craig nodded gloomily. "I wonder how many people
are disappointed?"

"More than you'd think. . . . Mass murder is a popular
sport."

"I'd think a good many. That war would have come at the right moment for me. But maybe I can get to Spain, anyway." When Craig smiled, even moodily, Asa could understand why first Stanley and then Roy had felt his queer magnetism. Not a normal attraction, yet, in some odd way, compelling. Was it because he seemed to express the two opposite extremes of his age: the restless discontent and the hopeless search for perfection? Intense but shallow, Asa said to himself, for it appeared to him in the cool wisdom of middle age that modern youth had no passion; that it had only passions. . . . "Did you ever wonder," Craig was still rambling on, "why we can't have the sort of life that we're fitted for?"

"Isn't that because we only imagine we're fitted for it? And don't we imagine so simply because we've never had it?"

"Maybe you're right, but—oh, well, what do we know of ourselves anyway?" Craig bent his head sideways, listening with an abstracted expression, while a door upstairs opened and shut, and Roy's voice was heard answering her mother. "What do we really know about anything?" he asked impatiently, and from his look, from his tone, he might have been speaking across an unconquerable isolation. "If we don't understand ourselves, how can we expect to understand other people? Take men and women, for instance. How on earth . . ." There was a sound of running feet, and Roy came in, wearing a small brown hat with a speckled cock's feather perched jauntily on one side.

"I wonder if he can be falling in love all over again?" Asa asked himself.

Craig rose and held out his hand. "I've wanted to see you, Mr. Timberlake."

"Well, you've only to come. I'm here when I'm not down at the factory." Following them to the door, Asa

called cheerfully, "Don't stay too late, and take good care of her, Craig,"

As the car started off, he stood in the doorway looking wistfully after it. The sunlight was a flying spray in the wind, and while he breathed in long drafts of air, he watched the sweeping gray and black wings of the pigeons. Suddenly the leaves parted overhead, and a ray of sunshine flashed into his face and lit up the cool ironic gleam in his eyes. On the edge of darkness, an unapprehended thought, barely more than a mist of sensation, wavered and vanished and wavered again. Am I here or there? he wondered. Can a man have two separate selves? Can he be in two different places at the same time? What does it mean anyway? Or does it mean nothing? I am standing here, in this doorway, in this street, in this windy emptiness of October. Yet a part of me, the more real part, is miles away with Kate, following the river path, where meadowlarks are skimming over the life everlasting. But this is solid, he thought, this is real; and the other is only an image in the mind, a figment of unsatisfied longing. Still, who knows what is real? Matter is solid, but it can be broken in two; it can be burned into ashes. He had merely to separate his dual life, dividing the life of circumstance from the life which he knew as his own, and his whole relation to the universe shifted and altered. The strong man within and the average man without, he felt, standing there in this one moment, in this autumn brightness, were not different aspects of a single personality; they were two detached and unrelated identities. . . . Then the beam of sunlight flashed on; the leaves fell together across the margin of blue; the instant of illumination faded and died. He was still what he had been from the beginning, an exile who had not ever known his own country, an atom without a universe. And the others? Were they any happier than he, except for that

[227]

perilous youth, which escaped from their grasp even while they were trying in its name to conquer the world? What of Craig, who wanted to reform a whole social system, but could not keep a rein over his own instincts? What of Roy, who was capable of greatness, and craved only the second best? If he were out of step with his time, so, he told himself, were the others; they also were apart from today and would be left behind by tomorrow. The wind stirred the branches; drops of sunlight sprinkled his face; the flicker of amusement shone again in his eyes. Everything at which he looked, the street, the houses, the film of golden dust, everything was faintly colored by the smoky blue haze of October. . . .

A bicycle wheeled round the corner, and the pigeons scattered and rose, while a messenger came from the curb to the door. As Asa reached out his hand for the letter, his glance darted to the address on the envelope, and he saw, with a start of uneasiness, that the writing was Stanley's. But the letter was for Lavinia, and he turned slowly into the house and walked with a dragging step up the staircase.

Lavinia was still in bed, and her untouched breakfast tray was in front of her. When he gave her the letter, she opened it eagerly, and then waited to put on her spectacles before she began to read. "I hope nothing has happened. I hope she can't be going to have a baby." She unfolded the sheets of paper and bent over the sprawling and blotted lines. "No, it isn't that, thank heaven. But she is unhappy. Oh, Asa, she says she is very unhappy!"

"Well, anyway, she's had what she wanted."

Lavinia dropped the letter and pushed it toward him with a trembling hand. "Remember how young she is, Asa."

"I'll remember."

"No matter what she has done, she is still our child."

"That may be the trouble." He looked up from the

page he was reading. "Well, anything would be better than what you feared. It strikes me that the offspring of Stanley and Peter would have the devil to pay."

Lavinia sighed and fell back on her pillows, while he went over to the window and read the letter by the pale golden light that sifted in through the maples.

"Mother darling:

"I am so unhappy that I simply must talk to somebody, and you are the only person, except Uncle William, who has ever really and truly understood me. For the last few days I have cried all the time. Even when I am driving by myself out of town (there is not anything for me to do but drive by myself) I can feel the tears rolling down my cheeks, and I know people must think I am crazy or on my way to a funeral.

"But, oh, Mother, if you could only know what I have had to put up with since I came away. Not having any money is the worst, but it is just a part of what I have been through. At first, I was so madly in love with Peter that I seemed to be living in a dream and was driven by something that was too strong for me. If you have never been in love that way, you cannot imagine what it is like or how terribly it can hurt. I felt that Peter and I were made for each other, and he felt so too—at least in the first few months—before Roy set him free, and we were married and knew we'd have to be together for all the rest of our lives. In the beginning, Peter could not bear to be a minute away from me, but we were no sooner married than we started having the most dreadful quarrels. It was not my fault. Don't you remember you used to say that I had the sweetest disposition of any of your children? But I never dreamed that Peter's temper could be so violent. He flies into a rage over the simplest thing, and I cannot do or say anything without upsetting his nerves. Heaven knows, I have tried hard enough. I have even

[229]

bitten my tongue trying not to answer back when he begins to storm at me. But nothing does any good. It is just plain temper with him. He does not seem able to get on with anybody, and he is always in a scrap with some of the doctors at the hospital. I know that, because when I broke down and told Dr. Blaford about it, he said I ought to make Peter have himself thoroughly gone over and checked up—that *something* was wrong *somewhere*. But I told Peter this, and it made him perfectly furious. He pretended I was trying to get rid of him. After all I have given up for him, he seems to blame me for everything. Yet he will not hear of my leaving him. When I threatened to go home, he said that, after ruining his career, I was doing my best to send him to the devil.

We had it all over again last night, and he began to shout that he could not live with me and he could not live without me. God only knows how it is going to end. When I think that just a very few months ago, I imagined that love was all I needed to make me happy. Tell Roy, if she knew what I had suffered, she couldn't hate me any longer. I cannot help feeling that I have saved her from having to stand Peter's craziness—if he is really crazy.

"Write to me, darling Mother, and will you ask Uncle William what he would advise me to do. He sent me a wonderful check by Parry, and I begin to cry whenever I think of his goodness. We have scarcely anything, and that little goes to pay for our bare living.

"Your unhappy but loving daughter,

"Stanley."

"Yes, it's a mess all right," Asa said, as he gave back the letter.

Lavinia sobbed under her breath, while she read over the first and the last page. "I can't understand Peter," she murmured. "Shouldn't you think that a surgeon ought to have more command over his nerves?"

[230]

"Or his muscles. But I never thought that Peter was cut out for a surgeon—or even for a physician. He lacks what we used to call a healing presence."

"But he seems so big and strong."

Asa laughed. "There's more to a man than mere bone and muscle."

"Aren't big men usually stolid? Look at Uncle William."

"If you don't mind, my dear, I'd rather not."

"You sound so bitter, Asa."

"I've always sounded bitter, Lavinia, about your Uncle William. I suppose I owe him too much."

"When you say things like that, it makes people think that you resent his success."

The twinkle in Asa's eyes was clouded by anger. "I resent that kind of success, anyway. It killed my father and my mother, and it helped to make a failure of me." But what was the use? he asked himself angrily. What, in God's name, was the use?

"I am sorry, Asa." Lavinia was gazing at him with wounded sweetness. "I know you are sensitive."

"I'm not sensitive." His voice rose and fell and trailed off into a murmur. "I'm hard-shelled. I'm a public enemy. But I'll be darned if I'm a pious humbug like William."

"Asa." Calmly, without a rising inflection, Lavinia's voice bore down on his outburst. "Asa, there is nothing to get so worked up about. I was only trying to make you see . . ."

"All right, I see. So stop trying."

"You never used to be like this. I don't know what has come over you." She put her hand to the spot which literature, if not life, has assigned to the heart. "Can there be something wrong with your blood pressure?"

"You'd better get dressed, Lavinia."

"In a minute, but before Selina comes up, I want to

ask you about Stanley. Don't you think we ought to take her away from Peter?"

"Good God, no. After we've taken her away, what are we going to do with her?"

"She would have to come here."

"And wreck Roy's peace for a second time?"

"Well, after all, Stanley is her sister."

"Stanley ought to have thought of that sooner."

"I blame him far more than I do her, Asa. She is young and helpless."

"She's young, but I'm not so sure that she's helpless. And I don't care whom you blame, or how many."

"I'm trying to make you fair to her, Asa."

"Fair to her? I tell you I'm afraid of her. I'm afraid of her making me unfair to other people. Oh, it isn't her fault, I know, but she was born to make trouble. I sometimes think she has no real existence apart from her effect upon other people. Look at the way William goes flabby whenever she cuddles up to him. . . . And if you want to know the truth, I couldn't stand up against her myself—not with that face, not with that injured innocence."

Instead of stopping her, the accusation appeared merely to turn her thoughts in a more hopeful direction. "Do you mind my showing her letter to Uncle William?"

"It's your letter. You may show it to anybody you please but Roy. Now, if you don't want to miss your sermon, you'd better get started and turn on the radio."

VI

"WHERE shall we go?" Craig asked, without looking round, and Roy answered, "Anywhere, anywhere that is away."

Away from people, away from the present, away from having or not having, away from wanting or not wanting. She gazed eagerly beyond the white streak of road into the shimmering distance. "Anywhere," she repeated. "I could go on forever."

"It is a kind of escape." He slowed down and smiled at her, with the wind blowing through his hair and his eyes wistful and dreamy.

"An escape from what?"

"From ourselves, from our lives. Out of everywhere into nowhere."

"Isn't that poetry?"

"I don't know. I hadn't thought."

"But that's what I want. Something I've never had, something I've never known." Her eyes sparkled; there was a dark flush in her cheeks.

"Something . . ." he began, and stopped, with his gaze fixed on the road ahead.

Watching his sharp, thin profile, which looked, in the brilliant light, a little unearthly, she said to herself: Yes, he is interesting up to a point, but what is there beyond? When that point is reached, would one find nothing or everything? But is it always like that with people? she wondered. Must one go on forever experimenting and failing, seeking and missing, finding and losing? Was it a perpetual beginning again whenever one came to the end? I want certainty, she thought, but most of all, I want love. Some women may live without love, but I cannot. When love goes, I slip down again into emptiness.

Craig bent his head as if he were listening, and she asked herself: Is he really here? Is he something to hold by? Or when the wheel comes up again, will he also turn to mist and evaporate? She had been hurt once too deeply; the wound was not healed; but someday the memory would drop back into the past. I have forgotten, she forced herself to say over and over. I am making a new life. A hot vapor stung her eyelids; there was the taste of salt on her lips; her throat ached with the hard strain of forgetting. Suddenly, as if by a blow, she saw through her tears the autumn landscape tossed apart and together. I hate you, Peter, she thought. Oh, how I hate you!

The car came to a stop, and Craig leaned toward her and touched the hand on her knee, the hand that had felt the nearness of Peter. "Happy, Roy?" But he knew. He knew as well as if she had spoken aloud.

"Yes, happy." It had begun as a valiant pretense, this will toward happiness, and then, as the months had gone by, the resolve had seemed to impress itself not only upon their own minds, but even upon circumstances. By repeating that they were happy, they had been able to create the semblance of happiness.

Still looking at her intently, he lifted her hand and pressed it against his cheek. "Is there anything better than this freedom and this friendship?"

She smiled at him, without answering in words. The strain was eased in her throat, the hot mist had melted away from her eyelids. It was more than comfort that she felt; it was a kind of still happiness, a sense of reconciliation—but with what? If only it would last! If only the moment would not spin on as soon as it had fulfilled itself! She liked the warm touch of his hand on hers. For an instant, she felt a thrill of emotion, faint and breathless, as if it were the troubled murmur from a storm that was over. Then the quiver passed; the response faded. Is it

real? she asked herself. Whether it is real or not, it is better than loneliness.

"You mean a lot to me, Roy," he said. "You know that."

Had he read her thoughts? She flushed and turned her eyes away from him. "We both needed to talk," she replied slowly. "I suppose we did need each other."

"God knows we have talked! But it means more than just talking."

"Well, it helped you."

"And you?"

"Oh yes," she replied lightly. "I enjoy the sound of my own voice."

"Don't be bitter. You aren't bitter, are you?"

"I don't know. Father thinks I am. But I'm not bitter about you."

"Or about anybody. We've stopped all that. We're not trying to monkey with the facts of life. They're there, and there's nothing to be done about them."

"I know. We've said all that a hundred times."

"Well, we mean it. We're going ahead with our lives and our work. Nobody can stop us."

She nodded, thinking of that August afternoon in Jefferson Park. Had he really forgotten his despair and defeat?

"You've helped me a lot," he repeated, and fumbled vainly for a new way of saying it. "If it hadn't been for you, I couldn't have come through the last months. I couldn't have got on my feet again." So he remembered. He had thrust the past aside, but it was only dead; it was not buried.

"Nobody could look at you and not want to stand up and face what is coming."

"You don't have to say it."

"But I want to. I want to tell you that I'm no longer running away."

"You're all right, Craig," she said brightly. "I mean that. You're as right as can be."

"That's where you come in, my dear."

"Well, I'm glad, though I'm Daddy's daughter, and I suppose a bit skeptical."

"You're fine, Roy, and so is your father. He may be a misfit like me, but he knows his way a long sight better than does that colossal boob, your Uncle William."

"Uncle William is good to us, in his way."

"Because he gives you a scrap of his millions. And how did he make them?"

She laughed. "I shouldn't know if you told me. But he's a grand old gentleman."

"So I've heard." His mouth twisted into a wry smile. "He's also the last great captain of industry."

"I don't care." She tossed her head defiantly. "Father is worth a hundred Uncle Williams."

"Then can't you see what I'm trying to do? Can't you see, Roy? I am trying to make, or help to make, a world in which men like your father will no longer be at the mercy of men like your Uncle William."

"I do. I can—" Then, suddenly, the shadow of a thought darkened her steady gaze. "But men will never make a world in which women like me will no longer be at the mercy of women like—well, like Stanley."

Silence, cold and heavy as a stone, dropped between them. Why, oh, why had she said that? she asked herself, glancing round at the quivering sunshine and the autumn haze over the meadows. Yet the outburst had brought with it a sharp sense of release. Some pressure within was overcome, and she felt strong and defiant.

For an instant, while he looked away from her, he did not speak. Then he turned slowly toward her, and she saw the deep tenderness in his eyes. "I know," he answered gently. "I know, my dear."

As she smiled up at him, she felt, with a kind of shock,

that the moment of complete sympathy was almost too intense to be borne. Two living forces, she felt, the past and the present, were fighting together. But it is only pity or passion, she told herself, and I despise both pity and passion.

He straightened himself abruptly and put his hand on the wheel, though the car did not start. "It was your Uncle William's advice," he said casually, "that started me on my downward road. He noticed that I was beginning to shoot away from the type, so he advised my father to improve my manners by sending me to the University of Virginia, and to improve my mind by sending me to Harvard. You see, my family was a clinging vine on tradition, and when tradition rots away, the clinging vine topples with it."

"Uncle William despises tradition."

"The devil he does! Not when he can make anything out of it. Forty years ago he began buying worn-out estates and selling them, for five times their value, to Westerners who wanted family graveyards."

She tossed the subject aside. "I wonder why you stayed on in Queenborough."

"I'm blessed if I know! My father says I'm bone lazy. Anyway, I'm always meaning to do things and never getting through with them." The car sped on, and he continued, after a pause, without turning his head. "When I was at Harvard I had a first-rate offer from a firm in New York; but I was fed up on corporation law, and I suppose I was beginning to feel tough. Then Charley Appleby got an idea that we might as well go in together on Main Street. Our only reason, if we had one, was that we were free to follow our noses, and both of us liked mint juleps better than whiskey sours."

"You never told me this before."

"Didn't I? Well, it wasn't worth telling. There's been so much else we wanted to say. There's the war in

Spain. . . . I always meant to get into that war sooner or later. . . ."

"I wish," she sighed wistfully, "that there were a war in Spain for me."

"There used to be castles in Spain."

"There are no castles left now. But I'd be satisfied with a cottage if only—"

"I thought you were all right here."

"Oh, I am. I'm all right."

"How is the shop?"

"Fine. We are decorating the new Crenshaw place, in Hampton Gardens."

"You like working?"

"I don't know. It fills my life from nine in the morning till five in the afternoon. That's the best part of my day."

The hills were presently slipping past them, folded range on range against the dim blue horizon. Far ahead, the mountains were russet with sunshine or purple with the slowly drifting shadows of clouds. Here and there, as they climbed higher, friendly villages dotted the valleys or nestled in a deep cleft of the Blue Ridge. There was the tang of frost in the air, the roadsides were gay with asters and goldenrod, and now and then a scarlet or wine-colored branch arched out of the forest. "It's one o'clock," he said. "We'd better have lunch in Lexington."

"No, I'd rather stop over there, at that little road-house with the big willows."

"Is it too cold out-of-doors? There's a table under the willows." He turned out of the road and stopped in front of a conspicuous service station dwarfing an inconspicuous restaurant.

"No, it's warm in the sunshine. We've followed the summer."

When they strolled over to the table, a long-limbed, loose-jointed mountaineer with brown eyes and tawny

hair came out of the house and spread a checked blue and white cloth over the table. "The season's mostly over now," he explained, "but a big tourist party about cleaned us up an hour ago. Will you be content with just a snack?"

"Will a snack content you, Roy?"

"If it means coffee and bread and butter. Valley coffee is good."

"Yes'm I can give you coffee," replied the long-limbed man, "and I've got wonder bread and fresh butter that's just come out of Mrs. Moore's churn. She still churns twice a week."

"What about an egg?" asked Craig.

"Not an egg left, sir. I wasn't counting on so many tourists, and I didn't lay in enough eggs and bacon to tide over the weekend. I've got some sandwiches of store ham, but they were made day before yesterday."

"No, no store ham. You'd better be putting on the coffee and slicing the wonder bread—and be sure," Craig called after the man's slow mountain stride, "to bring plenty of butter."

As the man disappeared into the kitchen, they sat down in splint-bottomed chairs and smiled at each other over the coarse checked cloth. The pale boughs of the willows, almost bare of leaves, hung motionless over their heads. Around them the landscape was enclosed in a fairly tarnished frame of autumn. The rusty gold of the sycamores, hickories, and poplars still clung to the branches; the maples were like a dying flame in the woods; the russet and crimson leaves of the oaks would not fall until the first snow, and a few clusters would linger on until the earliest foretaste of spring.

While she waited there, in a soundless whisper of time, it seemed to Roy that all the murmurous echo of life had paused. October waited; the passing clouds waited; and even the earth appeared to wait, as if it were slowly spinning down in a universe which also waited in

vain. Only on a near hill to the right, where a silver mountain stream rushed down in a cascade of foam, splashing, sparkling, rippling, singing on its way, did the stillness seem to breathe and awaken from immobility.

The door of the house opened and shut, and presently the aroma of coffee floated across the bright grass and the fallen leaves. Craig collected himself with a jerk, and she watched him lift his hand to brush the rumpled hair back from his forehead. It was a nice hand, she found herself thinking, with golden brown freckles on the back and thin, sensitive fingers.

"Smells as if it were all right," he said happily.

"Are you hungry?"

"Aren't you?"

"Starving."

"Are you glad you came?"

"What do you think?"

"I'm not thinking. I hate to think when everything is so—well, so exactly right. Let's take it as it is, and not worry."

While his gaze held her, she was aware of a sudden vibration. For months she had felt that she was pushing with all her strength against life, that she was sunk in the hollow of a wave which would presently break over her. Then, in a single instant the wave had receded, and she was floating at ease on a level tide. The strain, too, the hard thrusts, the constant pressure, had ended. She could remember, now, without that tight ache in her throat.

"Here's the coffee," Craig said, and his laugh was light-hearted and boyish. Then, as the man put down a red tin tray on the table, and neatly arranged the coffeepot and the loaf of bread and pat of butter, Craig became casual and friendly. He had a pleasant way with strangers, and an inveterate curiosity about the world. In a few minutes, talking at random, he had drawn out the major events in

the man's life, as well as his views on the political outlook and the danger of foreign entanglements. The only flaw in Craig's magnetism, Roy told herself, watching him, was that he appeared to be equally without effort and without discrimination. She had seen him scowl on serious occasions, and again, when there was nothing to be won or lost by amenities, he would set out whimsically, she told herself, to charm the very birds from the trees. Today he was at his best, and she wondered idly whether the contradiction in his features gave him that air of mystery and vagueness. He's lovable, she thought; almost any woman might fall in love with him.

"How do you make out here?" he was asking with unassumed interest. "You've a view all right. There's your choice between the Blue Ridge and the Alleghanies. But what about the land? Do you manage to do any farming?"

While he poured out the coffee and they sat drinking it from heavy cups, the man answered Craig's questions, and pointed out his small hill farm in the distance. "That's my place over yonder," he said. "Belonged to my great-grandfather; and his father fought in the Indian wars and the Revolution. Yes, sir, we're Valley folk, and we've always made a fair sort of living out of the land. But now, with taxes so high, ready money ain't easy to come by, and it's hard to scrape up enough to raise our crops. That's why I started this filling station, and then, when folks began wanting a bite to eat, we thought we'd try our hand at an eating place. Mighty few tourists want to pay the high hotel prices, and in summer we can't find near enough tables to seat 'em. . . ."

A car went by in the road, then slowed down and backed up, sounding a horn as it approached. "Somebody needs gas." The man broke off abruptly, and turning away, hurried over the stretch of grass and weeds to the red pumps in front of the service station.

[241]

"I like that chap," Craig said, pouring coffee into her empty cup. "This isn't half bad, is it? But it's funny using condensed milk in the country."

"The butter's fresh, anyway. I suppose the tourists got all the other milk. But do you suppose he'd rather have a view than a cow?"

"I doubt if he's ever looked at the view. I never knew a mountaineer who wanted to look at a mountain, except when he was down in the low country."

"You're always so interested in people," she said sympathetically, "as long, of course, as they don't belong to your own circle."

He shook his head. "I haven't any circle, and if I had, I'd do my best to break away from it. By the way, I meant to tell you I'd had a talk with that colored boy, Parry Clay, while he was washing my car. There's good stuff in that boy."

"I wish Uncle William would help him. It would mean so much to his mother, and she was my mammy."

"It doesn't matter, because I'm going to see that he gets a chance. If it's my one good deed, I'm going to see Parry through college, and after that, if he still keeps ahead, to Howard University."

"Can you afford it, Craig?"

"Oh, I can afford it. I can always afford what I want."

"I know what that means. You'll go without something else that you don't want."

"Well, that doesn't do any harm. Have you noticed that we've eaten the whole loaf and emptied the coffee-pot? Are you ready for more?"

"I'd rather stop again, farther on."

They left the table and walked slowly down the hill to a stream fringed by willows. The narrow valley was radiant with the leaves on the trees, the leaves in the air, the leaves on the earth. Far away, the mountains were darkening to purple, but bright wedges of sunshine were

[242]

driven into the shallow loop of the hills. A thought flashed through her mind and was gone. If only it wouldn't end! If only I never had to go back!

"What are you thinking?" he asked. "There was a shadow over your face."

"I was wishing that things could last. I don't want to go back."

"I was wishing that too."

"But it can't last. Has anything ever lasted?"

"It might," he answered thoughtfully, "if we tried to make it—if we could follow the moment."

"I wonder . . ." she began, and felt again that vague stir of expectancy.

"If we were really sensible," he burst out, "do you know what we'd do?" She did not speak, and his words came in a breathless rush, as if he were driven by some blind motive. "If we were really sensible, we'd take our lives in hand and make them do what we want. We need each other—we're happy together."

She smiled at him, but her smile wavered. "Yes, we're happy."

"Then why can't we act like rational creatures? Why do we turn and go back to unhappiness?"

"Because it will go on in spite of us or anything that we do. I mean the unhappiness. . . ."

"But it needn't go on for us. What we ought to do is to keep straight ahead. I can find a road that will take us to Washington, and we could stay there, or somewhere else, until we can be married. For once in our lives, why can't we do something that's decisive—that's final?"

She looked at him gravely, neither consenting nor refusing, while the faint quiver of longing (was it joy? was it fear?) awoke in her nerves. In the fugitive sunshine his face was transfigured by emotion—or was it merely excitement?

"But it isn't real, Craig," she said presently. "You want

[243]

it, and so do I, but it isn't real. You're trying again to re-treat from life as it is."

"We could make it real. What does anything matter as long as we're happy together? We have everything we need."

That was true, she assented. They had everything but the one thing that she and Peter had found and lost. And that one thing alone made the whole world of difference. "No, it isn't real." She frowned, and a scornful little laugh turned into a sob. "You're asking me to run away with you before you've even told me you cared."

"But I do care. I love you. You know that. And, be-sides," he added furiously, "I want the kind of love that gives security."

She shook her head. "None does that. There isn't any security in love. When security comes in, love changes to loving-kindness."

"Well, I want that. Oh, Roy, I want you! I want you to save me from myself."

"Nobody can save anyone else." God knows, she thought, I've learned that much.

"Don't you want to come away with me, Roy?"

A moment slipped by before she answered. "I want love. I need love so desperately that I suppose I'll always miss it. But I want it real. I hate shams. Oh, how I hate shams!"

"This isn't a sham. It is real."

She laughed again. "As far as it goes."

"It will go as far as we let it. Aren't you coming? Why do we always spoil things by trying to reason them out? Why do we cheat ourselves by putting off and hanging back from the one perfect time?"

"Is there ever one perfect time?"

"You know there is." Oh, yes, she knew, she knew, her heart told her.

"This is our chance to break away, and to start over again, from the beginning."

"But we might not find what we're looking for."

"That would depend on us. At least there would be protection."

"In marriage?" Her eyes were wide and stormy with pain.

"In our marriage," he answered.

Looking away from him, her troubled gaze came to rest on the drifting shadows of clouds. She had believed, too, when she was married to Peter, that there would be protection in marriage. Less than three years ago, she had believed that; and today she stood stripped, not only of her faith in love's permanence, but of every other romantic illusion. Nothing, not even the inner structure of life, could ever become again what it had been then.

When she turned back to him, her eyes were smiling, though her lips were still trembling. "You're a dear, Craig," she said, "but I'm selfish. I'm not satisfied with security. I want happiness."

"Well, we'll find it. We can find anything if we're together. God knows it would be easy to love you."

"You want to love me, I know. But when you love me too much to want to love me, I may be willing to go with you to Washington—or anywhere else."

"Then it's settled. If it can't be today, it will be tomorrow. Let's make it Christmas or the New Year."

"No, not then. We're going to leave happiness free."

"Well, what about April?"

"No, not April! Never, never, April again!" It seemed a dream now, that other marriage in April. She remembered the faces in church, the scent of lilies and gardenias, even a crushed spray in the aisle; but not the look in Peter's eyes, not the luminous joy in her heart. "If we

care enough when summer comes," she said slowly, "then I'll marry you."

He kissed her quickly. "Wait and see, darling. You'll make a man of me yet."

She smiled brightly. "I'm a substitute for war, anyway." It was a mercy, she told herself, that she was still able to laugh, and even to find life amusing. In a little while, the past would be over, for good and all; even as a bitter memory, it would be over, and she could begin to be happy.

VII

THE winter was mild, with snowdrops and crocuses blooming in January; but throughout February and March, light flurries of snow came spinning out of the north. Swift, silent, dissolving, the flakes whirled down and vanished as soon as they touched earth. From the window of the living room, the world looked, Roy thought, as if it were made out of swansdown. In the white stillness, through the hurrying snowflakes, the street and the bared branches of trees and the solid fronts of the houses appeared as fugitive as shapes that float between waking and sleeping. Only when a horn tooted, and the lights of a car crashed through the pallid dusk, did the scene and the March afternoon wear a look of reality.

Time is like that, she thought; time drifts over us and obliterates everything we have been, everything we have known. And we go on repeating ourselves; after a war to end war, we are now talking of war again. Only last summer she had felt that she was bound to the past, that she could never forget. Yet her will had been stronger than memory, and she had thrust out of her life the old unhappiness. Her days were peaceful now; so were the long nights. It was easier to command her thoughts, and she had lost the panic terror of her uncontrolled dreams. She could fall asleep without the fear of a sudden awakening, alone in a black and unreal universe, at the stroke of three; without, too, that desperate and despairing search, through this unreal black universe, for something precious which she had lost and could never recover. It was even possible to speak of Peter, or to hear his name mentioned, and not to feel again that violent shudder of recollection, that swift upward springing and downward

sinking which was, and yet was not, the hunger of passion.

At such moments, it seemed, her heart would unguardedly open above a secret well of bitterness, and then close, in a despairing quiet, over the shaken depths. All that was now ended. She had fought and won; and she knew that it was not her own strength alone, it was partly Craig who had saved her. What she had felt with a single flash of penetration on that August afternoon was a fundamental truth of emotion. It takes love, she had said, to kill love. Anger does not kill love; jealousy does not end it; even hatred does not kill love. Only another love can destroy love utterly. There were fleeting instants still when impulse would slip control, and a satirical voice in her mind ask: Did you love love, or did you love Peter? Is Craig merely a different image that love wears? Is love immortal, and does only the object of love change and vary? This year you love Craig, and last year you loved Peter; yet the love was different. Never again, she knew, could she feel the first springtime ecstasy of the heart. That was over forever. First love could come but once, in a single way. It might change, but it was powerless to repeat itself. I loved Peter, she thought, because I needed him with my whole nature. I love Craig only because he has need of me. I love love because in the world we know it is the only reality left.

A man came through the falling snow in the street. As he approached, he seemed first to be merely a fantastic shape, as unreal as the shrouded outlines of branches. Then he pushed aside the moving veil, and she saw that it was her father, with his head slightly bowed and his hat drawn down to keep the flakes out of his eyes. One of his hands, which clutched a folded newspaper, was holding tight to the front of his overcoat. Something pathetic and forlorn in his stooped figure, some touch of loneliness in his walk, brought into her young eyes a film of

tears. He needs a new overcoat, she said to herself, and then: But he never buys anything for himself. I wonder whether he really minds going shabby?

He mounted the steps; she heard the front door open and shut, and then the sound of a chair pushed aside as he stopped to take off his overshoes. A minute later he entered the room, shivering a little, and slapping his reddened hands. "A fire would look cheerful," he said. "Don't you miss the open fires in the old house?"

"I was just wishing that we could afford them here."

"If we could, where would we put them? Not in that imitation fireplace."

"You look so cold and tired, Daddy. Let me get you a drink."

"There isn't any whiskey. That's a luxury I've done without."

"Craig left a bottle, in case we needed it."

"We got on very well without it—at least my father and mother did."

"They didn't live at this time."

"Yet we, too, had our troubles." Nearly fifty years ago! Again he heard that old shot under the willow, and he felt an icy hand clutch at his heart.

"Anyway, it's different with us. We can't stand up without something to brace us. At least, people like Craig can't."

"He isn't nearly so jittery as he used to be. You've done a good job for him, daughter."

"I think I have helped. He is the kind of person who has to be helped."

"That means a great deal. And now, I'd better go down and have a poke at the furnace."

"Oh, Daddy, can't you ever stop thinking about the furnace?"

"Somebody has to think about it, Roy. It won't take more than a minute."

As he turned quickly, a red-hot twinge of pain shot through his left leg, and he stood waiting while the hurt gradually eased away. If my legs go back on me, he thought, I don't know what will become of us all. Roy was already in the dining room mixing his highball; and he stifled the groan on his lips as he limped slowly into the kitchen and then down the dim steps to the furnace room. The cellar smelled stuffy and musty and curiously depressing. When he had filled a scuttle with run-of-the-mine coal from the bin in one corner, and shaken down and carefully packed the furnace, he found himself wondering how on earth he could manage if his legs actually went back on him. As long as I can get about, he thought, remembering his father, I can keep going.

In the kitchen Virgie sat composedly peeling potatoes. "The house was getting chilly, Virgie," he said.

She gazed at him placidly, with a knife poised in one hand and with a half-peeled potato in the other. "Yas, suh, I reckon hit wuz."

"Hadn't you noticed it?"

"Naw, suh, I ain' felt nuttin'. I'se jes' been settin' here, right close up ter de range." She finished the potato and observed, conversationally, as she tossed it into the pot, "You certny do take on ovah dat ole furnace, Mr. Asa. I wonder hit don't wear you out."

"It does, Virgie, I'm quite worn-out this minute."

"You sho' do look peaked. Whyn't you lay down and res' yo'sef befo' dinner?"

"It's just my legs, Virgie. I've always depended on my legs to see me through, and now they're giving out."

"Naw, dey ain't, suh. I know whut I'se talkin about, an' all yo' laigs need is fuh you ter lay off'n um."

"I shouldn't wonder. But has everything been all right today?"

"I ain' sayin' dat, not ef'n you ax me, suh. Miss Lavinny, she's been moughty complainin', but de times dey

is er heap quieter den dey use'n ter be when Miss Stanley an' Mr. Peter wuz wid us."

"Well, I'll go up and rest. I have a kind of gone feeling inside."

"Dat's yo' stomick cryin' out, suh, an' I'll hurry up jes' ez quick ez I kin. Mr. Craig said he wuz comin', but he al'ays gits here befo' he knows I'se good an' ready. Miss Lavinny bought an ole hen ovah de 'phone dis mawnin', but she's jes' ez tough an' stringy ez ef'n she wuz an ole rooster."

In the living room Roy gave him his highball, and while he sipped it slowly and nibbled at a biscuit, an agreeable warmth began to stir in his hands and feet. I had no idea I was so chilled, he said to himself, and continued aloud: "The heat will come up in a few minutes. It had got very low, and Virgie was busy about dinner."

Roy brought a coat from the hall and spread it over his knees. "Take a bit more, Daddy," she begged. "You look less blue already."

"Yes, I needed it." Resting his head against the high back of the chair, he looked at her through a pleasant haze.

"Warm now?" she asked, and he answered happily, "Yes, I am warm now."

Roy had switched on all the lamps, and the shaded glare made a pool of brightness against the winter scene in the street. Snow was still falling; the trees and houses were mantled; but now and then the glimmer of a passing car, like the frozen wings of a giant moth, flitted under the pallid boughs.

"I hope it won't last," Roy said, glancing out of the window. "I hope we shan't have to pay a man to clear it away."

"No, it will be gone by tomorrow. Hadn't I better go upstairs now to your mother?"

"Wait awhile. She doesn't need anything as much as

you need a rest. Aunt Charlotte has given her a bigger electric pad, so she doesn't complain of the cold."

"Have you talked with her since you came in?"

"For a few minutes. But I couldn't stay. I cannot," Roy said firmly, "listen to any more talk about Stanley."

"Has she begun again?"

"She has never left off."

"I suppose it eases her mind."

"I don't care. I won't listen. No matter what she says, I will not listen to anything about Stanley." Her face flushed, and an angry gleam shone in her eyes. "What is over, is over. Stanley and—and Peter have gone out of my affairs for good."

"You're right, my child," he replied, putting down his glass and sitting erect in his chair. "You were never more right in your life."

"Can anybody stop Mother?"

"I doubt that. But we can shut it out. You must stop your ears when she talks."

"She will ask me questions. Can't I forgive Stanley? Can't I see how she's suffered? Won't I remember that she's my sister? No, I haven't forgiven her. I can't see what she's suffered. I do not remember that she's my sister. . . ."

"That's natural, daughter, I know. But your mother is not herself. She's an ill woman. She's ill both in mind and body."

"Is she really so ill? I mean, really . . ."

"In her nerves she is. It may be partly imagination, but it's what life has done to her—and to the rest of us. She has never had anything she wanted. She has never done anything she wanted to do."

"But why not? Why didn't she try?"

"She couldn't in the world she lived in. The system was not right for her. She ought to have been a man, and she wasn't even a successful woman. She wasn't pretty as

a girl. She lacked charm. She wasn't feminine. She made
no appeal."

"Yet you fell in love with her."

"Yes, I fell in love with her, or . . ." He broke off, because it was impossible to go on. He could not confess, to
Lavinia's daughter, that he had never been in love with
her mother—that no man had ever really wanted Lavinia. "You are far better off nowadays. You may think
you've never had a break, but you're better off than your
mother was."

"I hate," Roy said bitterly, "to have to live in a man's
world."

He shook his head. "It isn't always so easy on men.
There's your mother's lot, and there's mine. But, after all,
you haven't a choice, my child. There isn't any other
world unless—unless you think Stanley's world better."

"That's still a man's world. Isn't she what men want
her to be?"

"Not always, my dear. Now that you're happy again,
can't you forget to be hard?" Watching the light drift of
snow under the trees he thought at random: Is family life
at the bottom of all our troubles? And is there anything
better we could put in its place?

He felt her gaze on him, and he turned his eyes from
the window. She looked older, he told himself; the contour of her features had lost the blurred softness of
youth; but her face was more charming, more eloquent,
than it had ever been. After all, he reasoned, there is
much to be said for intelligence in a woman, especially
when experience has fined down romantic exuberance.
She was wearing her hair in a new way, with a single deep
wave brushed back from her forehead and the short curls
falling over her ears. He was not sure that he liked it so
well, but it served to define the clear curve of her eyebrows over her steady gaze. She was not beautiful, he
knew, when compared with Stanley. Roy's nose was blunt

at the tip; her mouth was wider than it should have been; and two of her milk-white teeth should have been straightened when she was little. But he had never seen a face, he said to himself, that he liked better. There was a charm in her sudden smile, in her youthful blunt profile, and even in the tiny scar, like a dimple, at the corner of her red mouth. She looks brave, he thought, and she looks honest. A man might safely trust his happiness in her hands.

"What were you thinking, Daddy?"

"I was thinking that I'd never seen a face I liked better."

"What, this old face? I've had it forever." How he loved to hear the unforced gaiety of her laugh!

"I hope Craig is good enough for you, Roy. He told me you'd promised to marry him in the summer."

"It's a long, long way to summer, darling."

"If you're happy . . ."

"Yes, I'm happy, and it's a safe kind of happiness." She smiled and then frowned. "But I'd rather not hurry. I want to wait till fall."

"Be very sure, daughter, this time."

"I was sure last time, old dear. I was entirely too sure."

There was a ring at the bell, and Roy ran eagerly to let Craig in out of the cold. With the opening door, it seemed to Asa that the driven snow invaded the house. Then the door slammed; there was the sound of cheerful voices, while Craig pulled off his overcoat; and an instant later he came with Roy into the living room. "I was afraid we were going to have sleet," he said, "but it's melting already."

"I'm glad of that." Asa stiffened, with the absurd embarassment he always felt in the presence of lovers. "I'd better be going upstairs. Your mother will be wanting her digitalis."

"Let me go, Daddy," Roy urged.

"Or let me," Craig said, with the genial readiness which in any situation was one of his most endearing traits. "Mrs. Timberlake has a weakness for me. I know," he added gaily, "because she told me so."

"Well, you can't believe everything a womanly woman tells you." Though Asa's tone was whimsical, he was asking himself whether young people who were really in love could be so casual with each other. Had love also changed? Or was it only romance that was missing? But how, he demanded in weary perplexity, how could love exist without romance or romance without love? Even when they were alone, he could still hear the sound of unconcerned chaffing; but from the bantering note he could not decide whether they called each other "darling" or "old thing." They seemed to regard the two terms as equally intimate or irrelevant. Was it all simply a part, he wondered the next instant, of the general breaking up of a pattern of life? Did it spring from some inherent distrust, not only of individual significance, but even of man's place in the universe? For it was all like that, he admitted, the intransigent youth of the present. Peter and Roy, Craig and Stanley, had each and all treated one another as if they were careless fellow travelers, to be picked up and dropped, either by accident or by design, on a very brief journey.

Lavinia was waiting for him, with an anxious expression and with her Bible open before her. "I've been anxious all day," she said. "It has been so long since I had a letter from Stanley."

"Wasn't she always a poor letter writer?"

"In the last few months she has written almost every week. But now three weeks have gone by."

"Well, I shouldn't worry. She'll write again when she wants something else."

"That's what worries me. She did ask for so many

things, and I have been able to send her only a few of them."

"Maybe you'll hear tomorrow."

"If I don't, I'll call her up. I've been trying to find her telephone number. She sent it to me in one of her letters."

"We can easily get the apartment house. Are you ready for your medicine?"

She took the glass from his hand and swallowed the digitalis with a martyred air. "Has Roy told you when she expects to be married?"

He shook his head. "Not till summer—or perhaps fall."

"She never tells me anything. I asked her, but she wouldn't tell me."

"Well, she will when she's made up her mind." Why was is that he could feel so little sympathy for Lavinia's afflictions? Was it because they had lived together too long in disharmony? Or was it that he thought of her now as imprisoned in her own morbid egoism? Turning on his way to the door, he added, "I hear Virgie with your tray, and I'd better tidy up a bit before going down."

Dinner was unusually cheerful. Craig was in one of his lively moods, and Virgie, who was a hard-shelled Baptist but enjoyed a proper joke, was constrained, on several occasions, to seek the pantry and indulge in what she felt to be a ribald sense of humor. While Asa ate his stringy fowl, and gazed thoughtfully over the depressed ferns on the table, he found himself pondering the question of time. Did time actually mean less nowadays than it meant a generation ago?

Virgie was passing the potatoes, and he helped himself absentmindedly. They were soggy, of course, and he regretted, while he prodded them with his fork, that women had allowed cooking to become a forgotten art.

"Have you ever thought of learning to cook, Roy?" he inquired. "Even the knowledge of a discarded classic may be useful in an emergency."

"Oh, but I hate it, Daddy. You aren't marrying a cook, are you, Craig?"

"You bet I'm not, darling. Why worry? There's always a restaurant, or at the worst a drugstore, round the corner."

The pudding was served and eaten, or left uneaten, and Virgie, so as to spare herself, she said, had brought the coffee in small cups to the table. Asa had just broken his lump of sugar in half when, in response to two imperative rings at the front door, he put down his cup and hastily pushed back his chair. "That's your Uncle William's ring," he said. "I'll let him in. You needn't bother, Virgie."

When he opened the door a wet wind stung his face. Snow was falling again, thick and fast, and the blown white drifts made the whole street look as if it were running away. William came in, brushing the snow from his sleeve. "It's snowing hard," he said, "but it won't stay on the ground." His face was purple, not from the cold, Asa saw, but from some inner disturbance and there were heavy pouches under the small bloodshot eyes. "I've brought bad news," William began hurriedly. "Where's Roy? I don't want Roy to hear me."

There was a distant drumming in Asa's ears. "Then we'd better go upstairs. Can you tell Lavinia?"

"She'll have to know. No use trying to put off trouble. Only I'd look out for Roy."

"Then it isn't about Stanley?" With a stab of pain, he understood how much Stanley still meant to him.

"No, it's Peter." They had hurried up the staircase while they spoke, and pausing in front of Lavinia's door, Asa listened to the hoarse rumble in William's throat while he panted for breath. "Peter's shot himself. He shot himself in the head."

[258]

"Peter has shot himself?" But it couldn't be true. Peter couldn't have ended like that. Not that virile force, that buoyant energy, all that extraordinary zest for the mere act of living!

"Stone-dead when he was found. Stanley found him."

"Where was he? When did it happen?"

But before William could answer, Lavinia's anxious voice interrupted them. "Is that Uncle William? What are you whispering about?"

"We'd better go in," Asa said. "It will have to be broken to her, and after all, it isn't as if it were Stanley."

"Good God, no," William snorted, as he shook himself and tramped into the room.

VIII

WHILE he listened to William's gruff voice trying to be gentle, Asa reflected, with the idle malice of the unguarded mind, that Lavinia shared one useful quality with the more effervescent African race. Like Virgie, whose flighty temperament was immediately sobered by the sound of grief or the sight of crape, Lavinia would have appeared to advantage in a universal catastrophe. An earthquake, Asa mused, would be the making of her character.

"But Stanley? What did he say about Stanley?" she was demanding of William.

"He had given her an injection and put her to bed. After she found Peter, she had a collapse, but she was asleep when he telephoned, and a nurse was with her."

"It seems so cruel," Lavinia said, and then more firmly, "Someone must go to her. Of course we must bring her home."

"I'll go," Asa said. "I can catch the night train." And he thought savagely: It is hell to be poor. I'll have to borrow the money from William.

"I was thinking of that," William muttered, thrusting his hand into his pocket, "and I can let you have whatever you need for the trip."

"Oh, Uncle William," Lavinia burst out, seizing his arm as if it were her only support. "If we didn't have you to turn to, what would become of us?"

"There, there, my dear niece, I'm glad to do what I can."

"But why did he shoot himself? What did they say?"

"Nobody knows. Peter had been letting down on his work. Darn temperamental chap, Spanger said, and drinking into the bargain. He imagined they hadn't been

getting on well, but he knew nothing of that at firsthand. Stanley had been nervously run down for months. She was going to have a baby, and, in some way, she managed to bring on a miscarriage. . . ."

"Oh, my poor child," Lavinia moaned. "She never told me. What else did he say? I mean Dr. Spanger."

"He asked me to break the news to Peter's mother. I stopped there on my way down. John Kingsmill is taking the night train."

"Then he will make all the—all the . . ."

"Yes, he will make the arrangements. His mother and sister wish Peter to be buried in Cedarwood."

At the mention of Peter's mother, Lavinia began to weep and Asa choked slightly. Less than a year ago Peter had seemed to him the most living thing in the world. But for an accident of the heart or the nerves, he would still be alive, he might easily have outlived the three of them for the next generation. If the color of Stanley's eyes had been different, or the curve of her mouth . . .

"I can't take it in," Lavinia murmured. "It is so terrible I can't believe it has happened." For Peter, too, had a mother.

"Things like that are happening every hour." William said in a tone of impersonal anger. "Nowadays, if a man can't dodge away from trouble, he'd as soon blow his brains out as not." He hesitated, remembering Daniel Timberlake, and continued bluntly, after a pause, "It's all the fault of this loose modern thinking." Then, wheeling abruptly, he glared at Asa, who murmured stubbornly, "I don't know, and I don't care, but we've got to do something about Roy."

"What is it, Daddy?" asked a startled voice at his back, and there was Roy looking expectantly from the hall. "Has anything happened?" Over her head, Asa could see Craig's grave features and bright roving eyes.

"Come in, my dear. We have had a shock, a very bad shock," William said. "Lavinia, you'd better tell her."

Roy turned on him in a flash. "What is it? I won't have anything broken to me."

"Wait, Roy . . ."

"Tell me. Oh, tell me. I can never go through the worst again."

Asa pushed William aside and came between the girl and her mother. He did not take her in his arms, because he saw that she was instinctively turning to Craig. "It's about Peter, darling. He died this afternoon."

She stared at him unbelievingly. "Died? Do you mean Peter is dead?"

"A few hours ago. A doctor in Baltimore telephoned your Uncle William."

Her incredulous gaze turned from Asa to William. All expression had been suddenly wiped from her face and voice. "But he can't be dead, Daddy. Peter couldn't be dead." She looked at Craig, who put his arm round her shoulders. There was no grief in her eyes, no horror even, only a profound incredulity.

"Was it an accident?" Craig asked in a level tone.

After a slight rebuff, William was again in command of the situation. This much at least, he implied, could be said for the youth of the present; it did not ask to be spared the truth of events. "No, it wasn't an accident," he answered in Asa's place.

"Then why? How . . ." Roy frowned at him in amazement. "What are you keeping back?"

For an instant William did not reply. His eyes wandered to Lavinia, then to Asa, and from Asa to Craig. Finding no help in them, he answered, with all the softness he could compress into a naturally blustering manner, "They told me he killed himself."

"Killed himself? But he wouldn't. Why on earth should he kill himself?"

"Nobody knows, my dear. Nobody will ever know."

"But he wouldn't, Daddy. He always had what he wanted. Nothing stood in his way." Still, her voice did not break. The most astonishing thing to Asa was the absence of grief in her face, the graven immobility of her attitude, as if she were not wholly there, as if some vital part of her had detached itself from her surroundings, from the immediate moment, from the actuality of time and space.

"We shall never know why he did it, darling. No one can look into a closed mind."

"He was happy. Wasn't he happy, when nothing stood in his way?"

"That, too, we shall never know."

"Then we can never know anything?"

"Not anything of the end."

Suddenly, out of the whispering stillness, Craig spoke almost fiercely. "It may have been wanting too much that killed him."

"But he killed himself." Her voice was low and frozen and remote. "Daddy says he killed himself."

"It's the same thing. He tried to kill the wanting in himself. But it's out of your life, Roy." Craig held her close in his arms. "Whatever happened, it is not a part of your life. It has nothing to do with us."

"No, oh, no." Her lips scarcely moved, but she clung to him as if she were drawing strength from his embrace. "It has nothing to do with us."

Watching her, Asa thought: If only we could spare them, our children! If only we could warn them of the danger in living! But I loved them, he told himself, and I did the best that I could. Yet his best was not enough to ward off the lightest blow of adversity.

"That is the right way to look at this—this tragedy, my dear," William was saying. "You have no reason to reproach yourself. Nothing you could have done or left undone would have prevented what happened."

"That's the horrible part, Uncle William. We're so helpless against—against the things outside ourselves."

William stared at her, as if he were seeing some awful image beyond and above her head. "There's God!" he blurted out so violently that the words sounded blasphemous.

"But it doesn't seem to matter, does it?" Roy answered indifferently. Her deep unseeing eyes were fixed on William, and her lips were so dry and hard that she moistened them before she was able to speak the thought in her mind. "Where did he—where did it happen?"

"In the apartment. Stanley was out. When she came in and went into the bathroom, she found him."

"At least he might have spared her that!" Craig exclaimed in a smothered voice.

"He was past sparing," Roy said, and added vehemently, "I'm sick to death of sparing women!"

"Well, it has nothing to do with us," Craig repeated firmly. "We're in a different world from those messed-up lives."

"Yes, we are in a different world." Roy's head was lifted, her glance was straight and unflinching, her mouth had recovered its soft outline.

Thank God, she loves Craig, Asa told himself. And he thought: Craig is right; she can take a blow on the chin. As long as she loves someone, as long as she is free to give herself, she will be safe. Are all women like that? he wondered. Is loving more necessary to women than being loved? Is it only when destiny thwarts them, and the source of being dries up within them, that they become like Lavinia, maladjusted to life?

"Thank heaven!" he said aloud. "That makes my mind easier about you."

Roy put her hand on his arm. "Poor Daddy, you are tired out."

[264]

For the first time in his life, William glanced at Asa with sympathy. "Perhaps Andrew had better go to Baltimore in your place."

"No, I am going," Asa answered stubbornly. "She is my child. You don't mind her coming home, do you, Roy?"

Roy looked at Craig. "We don't mind, do we?" she asked.

"Not now." Craig caught her hand and held it against his cheek. "Haven't we said that it has nothing to do with us?"

"It's like a bad dream," she murmured, "everything that has gone."

"That's fine," William said heartily. "What you needed, Craig, was a woman like Roy."

"I know it. I suppose I've always known it if I'd only stopped to think."

"I hope we'll all try to forgive and forget." Lavinia was making an effort to sound cheerful and practical. "We must help poor Stanley to make a fresh start in life."

"Perhaps she won't want to come home, Mother," Roy replied. "I'd never come home in her place."

"But you're so strong, dear, and Stanley is weak. She has always had to be shielded."

"Anyway, my mind's easier." Asa drew a sigh of relief. "I'll telephone to the station before I pack my bag."

"Telegraph me when to meet you," William said. "Maybe you'll be able to get a plane back." He took out a bulging pocketbook and handed a thick roll of bank notes to Asa. "This will see you through, and if Stanley needs more, all you have to do is to send me a wire." He meant it kindly; he was sincerely moved; he would have given more than money, Asa knew, to comfort Stanley. All these merits Asa acknowledged, while he found himself reflecting angrily: Is there any hell worse than poverty?

Yet how many millions of men, wearing the pavements out in their tread, would call his poverty living on easy street?

Later in the night, lying awake in his upper berth on the train, he told himself with stifled self-reproach, that he had never been sufficiently grateful to William. In spite of his arrogance and his natural parsimony, William could be counted upon to be generous in a left-handed fashion. After all, they had lived under his roof, and how could Lavinia have afforded her chronic illness without his assistance? Not that I wanted his money, Asa thought, except for Lavinia and the children. For himself, he would rather have lived improvidently, from day to day, with no care for the future. But marriage had made economic freedom too dangerous. Marriage had not only dwarfed his spirit, it had enslaved him to circumstances. For there is no freedom in human affection. In the first instant that he had preferred another's good to his own, he had exchanged a brief liberty for a permanent responsibility. Not that it mattered. His children were more to him than his individual identity. He would sacrifice both his present and his future for them; yet he had learned, with a breaking heart, that he could not protect them against fate. Time was stronger than all the love and pity of all the living. . . .

Lights flashed by, weaving a jagged pattern on the dark curtains. He drew the blankets under his chin and tried to sink deeper into an impenetrable obscurity. If only his mind would stay empty till morning, when the specters of imagination would be swallowed up in the horrors of the actuality. How could Stanley make her life over again? How could any life be made over? Perhaps he ought not to have come. Perhaps, after all, Andrew would have been better. Though he yearned over her, oppressed by the ancient burden of parenthood, he could think of no word to speak that would bring consolation.

Suddenly, out of the darkness, the dread and pain in his thoughts gathered together and were woven into a memory. There was a morning in his early childhood, before his father's failure and death, when his mother had taken him for the first time to a dentist. All he knew of such visits had been pictured in his imagination; but his inarticulate terror had lived on in some obscure labyrinth of his consciousness. All else he had forgotten. The bare structure of the incident had crumbled away, with the name and face of the dentist and the frightening buzz of his machine. That speechless terror, that dread of an unknown agony, was still hidden but alive beneath the thickening dust of years. . . .

In the early dawn the forsaken streets appeared phantasmal. The scene, he thought, might have been created in some distraught nightmare which was out of touch with existence. Was it only his fancy or had the whole world gone deranged overnight? There was barely a sign of life anywhere, not even in the languid figures sweeping trash into piles, or in the grating noises of his taxicab as it jerked over the grayish snow. When he lowered the window and leaned out, the wintry air was as dead as the chill of a vault. But this, he assured himself, wasn't the truth of things, not this airless cold, this sodden gloom, this stale odor of death. The hour would pass, and the mood with it. A sleepless night, an empty stomach, the dreary dawn, and the ruined aspect of a world that has been used and discarded—these things were the separate parts, the raw stuff, of desolation.

The taxicab stopped with a jolt. He stepped out into the dirty snow; he paid the driver; he turned and walked, with a mechanical stride, across the slushy pavement to the open door of the apartment house. A fine old Georgian mansion, he noticed casually, a relic of the lost

era of elegance which had bravely stood its ground in a later age of disorder. Mounting the steps, he paused before a row of bells and speaking tubes, and glanced regretfully up the winding curve of the staircase. There was no lift, and recalling that Stanley's flat was upstairs, he climbed breathlessly, still grasping his small traveling bag. Whatever he found at the top, he hoped with all his aching nerves that it might include a bath and a shave. All tragedy is painful, he thought, but unshaven tragedy is sardonic.

He rang the bell, and after a long wait, the door was opened by a nurse in a crumpled uniform, who received him suspiciously. "But we expected her uncle," she exclaimed in surprise.

As she drew back, he walked past her into what had once been a double withdrawing room of formal dignity and classic proportions. His disapproving look swept over the crude modern furniture and the too obvious note of decoration. Then he turned inquiringly to the nurse, who appeared plain and competent and severely professional. "Will you let me see Mrs. Kingsmill? I am her father."

"She is still asleep." The nurse glanced down at her wristwatch. "I gave her a second hypodermic at four o'clock."

"How has she stood it?"

Again she glanced at her watch as if seeking reassurance. "Not so well. It was a terrible shock."

"And she was alone?"

"Yes. Oh, yes, that was dreadful. She's very young, isn't she?"

"She is just twenty. Her birthday was a few weeks ago."

The nurse had reddish hair which she wore in a small tight roll at the back of her head. Her eyebrows were red, too, and very straight, and her wide, full mouth curved pleasantly when she smiled. She was armored, he de-

cided, in the cool judgment and the ample wisdom of one who has never known, or who has safely finished with love. But from the stiff way she moved, he suspected that her feet were hurting her. If it isn't one thing, it's another, he thought, and reflected that uneasy feet are scarcely a laughing matter.

"Twenty?" she was repeating. "Why, she doesn't look a day over eighteen."

"She is young for her age. Her mother has always treated her as a baby."

"Well, no wonder. She must be really beautiful when she is happy. Even now, she is lovely. I never saw such a skin."

"Do you think I might see her? I mean, without waking her."

"Oh, she won't wake. Not if you don't make a light. She is in terror of light. It was turned on when she found him."

"Not in the bedroom?"

"No, it was in the bathroom, at the end of the hall. The light was the first thing she noticed. She says she can't get the glare out of her eyes. It's queer what a shock can do to you."

"Yes, it's queer. I've come to take her home."

"I'm glad of that. She doesn't seem to have anybody here. I mean, of course, anybody that's kin to her. I came from Virginia myself, so I know what your kin mean to you in sorrow."

"Who has made the arrangements?"

"That's Dr. Spanger. Dr. Blaford has been down with influenza, but Dr. Spanger, from the hospital, has been like a father to her. Then there's a Mrs. Wilder, a young married woman, but she's the gay kind. She has promised to buy a black hat for Mrs. Kingsmill to wear on the train. Not really mourning, but all her hats are so—well, foolish looking, and we thought maybe in Queenborough . . ."

"Do you feel that it matters? Nobody thinks of the dead nowadays, not even in Queenborough."

"But a doll's hat, just a bunch of flowers and a bowknot. That didn't seem quite right to us."

"I suppose not. How has she taken it? I don't mean the hat, of course, I mean the—the . . ."

"Yes, I know. It was awful when I first came on the case, but as soon as Dr. Spanger could get her quieted down, he shut her up in her room while the undertaker came and took the body away. Then he told me that Dr. Kingsmill's brother was coming on and would take charge of the funeral. . . ."

While he listened to the smooth, monotonous voice, it seemed to Asa that his empty stomach turned over once, and then righted itself, in a spasm of nausea. So that was what Peter meant now, nothing more. All his physical magnetism, his vital energy, his dynamic sensuality had become simply a boxful of refuse to be carted away. "Do you think I might have a wash and a shave before she wakes?" he asked, staving off a threatening impulse to vomit.

"Oh, yes, the bathroom's all right now. Only, I don't let her go near it. I'll give her her bath in bed. The doctor will be in again on his way to his office." Her eyes sought her watch, and she added, "I was just going to put on the percolator when you rang. A cup of coffee will be ready for you by the time you're dressed."

He picked up his bag and then dropped it again. "May I look in on her for a second?" he asked a little wistfully. "I'd feel better if I could have just a glimpse of her."

She crossed the room noiselessly and opened a door at the far end. "Take a peep then," she whispered. "You won't wake her if you are quiet and don't let in the light."

IX

THERE was in the room a dimness which seemed more a partial shadow than the glimmer of daylight, and at first he saw only the bed, with its coverlet of primrose-colored silk over a child's figure. How young she is! he thought, with a catch in his throat; and how little! She was lying on her back, as straight and still as an effigy. Her head on the pillow was like the head of a doll, framed in rumpled bronze waves, and when he bent over her, he could see the faint darkness of her lashes on the pallor of her cheeks. A quiver of breath came and went through her lips, and it seemed to him that their petulant droop, of which Lavinia and he had tried so vainly to break her when she was a child, had become intolerably moving. She had never really grown up, he told himself, a little ashamed of his weakness. Her face was still the face of a sullen and disappointed child, with the dangerous appeal of an irresponsible innocence. Without warning, against his reason and his will, he felt that his heart was flooded with pity. He had been angry with her; he had even told himself that he no longer loved her; but at this instant, as she lay defenseless in sleep, he was suffocated by the longing to shield, by the savage and irrational instinct of parenthood. Swept clean by unconsciousness, her expression was as shallow, and as vaguely inscrutable, as a closed flower. He judged her for what she was, vain, selfish, unscrupulous in her motives; even so, he was ready to give all to protect her from the disaster she had provoked. . . . Without glancing at the nurse, he turned away, shut the door softly, and picking up his bag from the floor, he went about the business of dressing.

As he was finishing his breakfast, the doctor came into

the living room and the nurse discreetly withdrew. From the street below he could hear the discordant sounds of what seemed to him to be another age, another world, another life.

"I'd come to know Kingsmill at the hospital," Dr. Spanger said, hurriedly, as he shook hands, "and, I confess, his death appears simply incredible. He was one of the most gifted of our younger men. Not completely adjusted, perhaps, but with a brilliant technique. Until the past few weeks, when I noticed he was drinking too heavily, his work in the hospital had been beyond criticism. This was utterly unexpected. It has been a profound shock to us all." He was a lean, dark man, with alert, wiry movements, and features which were thin, colorless, enigmatic.

"There must have been a reason. Isn't there always a reason?"

"But a reason may be purely imaginary. Hadn't he always been uncontrolled except in his work?"

"So I'd thought. Anyway, he'd always taken whatever he wanted."

"I heard something about that. Fell in love with his wife's sister. Well, I don't wonder. She's a lovely creature, and strangely appealing. But, even nowadays, an act like that is not so easily lived down, in our profession."

"It cut them both off from their former lives. His first wife, my other daughter, is a fine woman, and very attractive. None of us could understand his infatuation, but, oh, well . . ."

"None of us ever can. Sex is a darn queer instinct . . . an inflammable substance."

"Did they seem happy here?"

"That's not easy to answer. I saw her only when she was unhappy and nervously overwrought. There was a slight operation after she had brought on a miscarriage. I've heard that they quarreled a good deal, but many

couples do that without resorting either to murder or suicide. There were financial difficulties, too, I imagine. I
should say she would be an expensive luxury for a man
of limited means. He had trouble, I know, in paying the
rent of this apartment, and I am told that he was deeply
in debt."

"No doubt." Asa glanced in disgust round the room.
"It all seems such a waste."

"That's the worst of it. Good material, a brilliant mind,
an amazing energy, all gone to waste." He drew out his
watch. Doctors and nurses, it seemed to Asa, were eter-
nally consulting their watches. "Well, I'd better take a
look at her. There was nothing I could do but keep her
quiet. The sooner she can get out of this apartment, the
better it will be for her."

The nurse appeared at the exact moment, and
together they passed into the obscurity of Stanley's bedroom. A shade was slightly raised, and a few minutes
later, Asa heard the doctor's changed voice, soothing,
caressing, infinitely consoling. He waited patiently until
the visit was over, and Dr. Spanger came out and drew
him into the hall, at the head of the staircase. "She will be
all right," Dr. Spanger declared, resuming his impersonal
manner. "I've left instructions with the nurse, and she
will give you the medicine you may need on the train. Let
her sleep as much as possible, and don't give her another
dose unless it is necessary. If you've got a drawing room,
she can lie down all the way."

"Yes, I stopped at the ticket office this morning. We're
leaving at three o'clock."

"That's right. The nurse can get her ready. Mr. John
Kingsmill is making the other arrangements. He came on
with you."

"I didn't see him."

"He telephoned me this morning. We attended to
everything here. It was a simple case of suicide. Then,

there's nothing else?" The doctor held out his hand with a dramatic gesture of farewell and relief. "You have my sympathy. I only wish I could have done more."

"You couldn't have done more. I'll leave my address with you." As he held out his card, he remembered grotesquely that Stanley had given him these cards, at Christmas, a few years before. "You will know where to reach me."

Dr. Spanger made a slight grimace which widened into a smile. "As a friend only. I liked Kingsmill, and I attended Mr. Fitzroy when he was in the hospital."

So that was over! Everything was over, at last, if only one could have patience. At eleven o'clock Mrs. Wilder floated in, like a random breeze, scattering parcels over the furniture and dropping her bag and gloves on the floor. She was a slight, trivial person, with a painted doll's face and a small bullet-shaped head hidden in a short crop of platinum blonde ringlets. Her large black eyes, heavily shadowed under plucked eyebrows, were as expressionless as glass beads.

"Oh, you're Stanley's father!" she exclaimed in disappointment. "We were expecting her uncle."

"So everybody tells me."

"Well, I'm glad somebody came. Stanley is my best friend, and I've been distracted about her. I suppose you're taking her home?"

"We're going at three o'clock. The doctor thinks it will be all right to take her."

"He would, of course. You can't imagine what we've been through. Poor darling, she was almost out of her mind. It was too awful, really, until he gave her something to quiet her." She sat down on the edge of the sofa and began to unwrap the parcels, tossing the paper and string on the floor at her feet, as she held out her purchases. "They're black, anyway. I had to go to six places before I could find a decent black hat. The nurse said it

would never do for her to go back to Queenborough wearing colors. All her hats are so gay, you know, just like poor Stanley."

"Was she gay? I was afraid she hadn't been happy."

"Oh, well, she had to keep up, didn't she? She'd been drinking a little too much, but, then, we're obliged to have something to wind us up, or we'd simply stop dead. All our crowd are crazy about Stanley."

"Did you like Peter too?"

"When he would let us. But he was snooty with our set, if you know what I mean."

"I know. Was he drinking, too, to keep up his courage?"

"He tried to cut it out, because he said it spoiled his work at the hospital. That was a part of the trouble."

"A part?"

"Oh, there were other things too. Stanley wanted so much, and Peter couldn't understand why she had to have what she wanted. Men are like that. He'd lose his temper, and fly up in the air whenever the bills came in. Then he began to spend too much time at the hospital. But when Stanley started going out with other men, he'd make scenes about that. When a man's jealous and worrying himself sick over money at the same time—well, you know, anything is more than likely to happen."

"Couldn't they have separated?"

"Why, they couldn't live so much as a day apart from each other. They even got something out of the quarrels they had, especially Stanley."

"A pretty mess they made of it!"

Mrs. Wilder frowned, and the frown did something queer to her plucked eyebrows. "They were that sort. They had never learned how to travel light."

"I thought Peter had," he said, vaguely astonished.

Her candid eyes, as empty of reserve as of delicacy, examined him wonderingly. "Peter," she remarked, with

the sharp judgment of youth, "did not have the right temperament, and Stanley is the kind that demands everything, all the time. I'm very fond of Stanley," she added confidingly, "but I'd never call her a restful person."

"And I suppose a man who is cutting up other persons needs a rest now and then." Mrs. Wilder might look like a marionette, Asa told himself, but there was sagacity under her makeup.

The nurse came out of Stanley's room and beckoned to her. "She is awake and wants to speak to you, Mrs. Wilder. There's something she would like you to do for her."

"Oh, the poor darling! I'll do anything in the world." Mrs. Wilder tripped past, and the chirping notes of her voice mingled with Stanley's smothered ejaculations.

"You may go in as soon as she leaves," the nurse said. "She never stays but a minute."

"Speaking professionally," Asa inquired abruptly, "has it ever occurred to you that love is the devil?"

For an instant, the nurse stared at him with a face like a mask. Then she lifted her wrist and let it fall before she had looked at her watch. "Speaking unprofessionally," she replied tartly, "it has."

"Have you ever wondered why people should go out of their way to make a muddle of things?"

"Some people," she retorted, "like a muddle. Pigs do." There was not the slightest hint of surprise in her tone. So detached did she appear that she might have been coolly taking the pulse of experience.

"Now there are four ruined lives," he said, "simply because two persons have bungled their small private affairs, which meant nothing whatever to the world in general or to the universe."

For the first and only time since he had made her

acquaintance, interest flickered into the nurse's expressionless face. "Were people always as flighty as they are now?" she asked. "Or is it only that nothing is private any longer?"

"Perhaps they had other excitements. Religion, for instance, and whether they would be saved or damned in eternity."

She assented with humorless gravity. "My father used to say that when the world got rid of hell, it would regret it only once, and that would be always."

"I wonder. Wouldn't a belief in humanity serve the same purpose?"

Her prim lips parted in a laugh. "Not on your life! Not if you'd ever done nursing!"

A telephone rang somewhere outside, and while she moved to answer it, she waved her hand toward the opening door of the bedroom. "Mrs. Wilder is coming out. You may speak to your daughter. Only try not to let her excite herself."

As he crossed the room, Mrs. Wilder flitted toward him, while she drew a pair of long gloves over her gleaming mauve-tinted nails. Attractive, he admitted, in spite of her artifice—or because of it?

"It wasn't anything important," she whispered, in a tone of flattering intimacy. "There're some things she'd bought and hadn't worn. She asked me to take them back for her."

A minute before, he might have said that nothing Stanley could do or not do would ever astonish him. Yet so practical and provident an idea was the last thing that he would have expected. "I'm glad she's able to think of such things," he answered, with a sigh of relief.

Mrs. Wilder raised a scrap of lavender handkerchief to her eyes, but remembered hastily that her eyelashes were too perishable for wiping. "Stanley's marvelous,

poor darling, simply marvelous," she cooed softly, "and she's the kind, too, that grief doesn't spoil. When you're as young as that, sorrow can be really becoming."

She tripped out lightly, and he went into Stanley's room and crossed the black velvet carpet to the bedside. How did Peter ever pay for this air of luxury? he asked himself, before he recalled, with a pang of sympathy, that Peter had been made to pay with his life. Someone—he couldn't recall who it was—had said that Peter was a sensual man astray in the field of science. As a failure of mere human aspiration, the defeat seemed to Asa deplorable. It was wrong; it was blundering; it was meaningless.

"Stanley," he said, for she had not turned, she had not opened her eyes when he bent over her. Very slender and straight, with her features blanched by the shock of terror or grief, and her wild curls making a burnished glow round her head, she lay almost hidden under the coverlet. "Stanley," he repeated, his voice tremulous with feeling.

Her eyelids fluttered wide, and she stared up at him as if he were a stranger. "But I don't want anybody." She thrust out her arm from the coverlet, pushing him from her.

"I've come to help you, my child. I've come to take you home with me."

Her blue eyes, darkened by pain, looked bewildered. Gazing down on her through a film, he felt that her wistful appeal was the more touching because, for the moment, beauty had been washed away by her tears. I never knew how much I loved her, he thought. Your child is still your child, no matter what happens.

"Father!" she cried out suddenly. "Oh, Father, how can I bear it?"

She reached out her arms, and dropping on the edge of the bed, he gathered her to him. "I've come to take

you home, darling. You'll be better at home with your mother."

"But why did it have to happen? Oh, why did it happen to me?"

What could he answer? What could anyone answer? She was trembling so violently that he steadied her with his arms. As a small child, she had sometimes shown this sullen despair in her face, and the recollection flashed through his mind in a searing pain. If only she could have remained a child in years as she was still in that look of incorruptible purity! Was it youth? Was it merely a physical accident? Had chance or design molded her features in their soft contour? While he watched her, he told himself that the most destructive force in life is the power of insatiable youth, of youth that has never known wisdom, of innocence that devours.

"They don't want me," she said, and her thrust-out lower lip trembled. "Nobody wants me."

"We do want you. Have your forgotten your mother?"

"Mother? Yes, I'd forgotten Mother. I'd forgotten everybody but Peter. Oh, Father, why did it happen? Why did he do it?"

"God only knows, my child. But you're going home with me."

"How can I? Oh, I can't, I can't . . . Roy hates me."

"She doesn't hate you. She is sorry for you." Was this true? he wondered. Well, no matter . . .

"I can't bear it! Oh, I can't bear to go home!"

"Everybody has sympathy for you, Stanley. You were too young to—to . . ."

"Why did he do it, Father? Oh, why did he do it?"

"That we'll never know. Try to be brave. Why does anyone do anything?"

She drew away, to the far side of the bed, as if she were straining against invisible bonds. How pathetic she looked, he thought, and how unsheltered from life! "All

I wanted was something real," she cried out passionately. "I had a right to be happy!"

"How could you expect happiness, my child, when you brought so much pain? But I don't mean to reproach you. It is all over now, right or wrong." If only that wild sobbing would end, that dragging at unseen chains!

"But he was real, Father. He was the only person that seemed alive—that seemed real. . . ."

The cry was Roy's, though Roy had never, not even in her deepest anguish, betrayed her heart so completely, or thrown herself so utterly on the mercy of life. But the tortured wail was ringing, on and on, through the hollowness in his mind. Nothing was there. Nothing was anywhere that could ease her sorrow or help her to forget. She was scarcely more than a child, yet she had the world's grief on her shoulders. Even her folly and her selfishness appeared to him, now, merely as a part of youth's desperate search for reality, for perfection.

"My child, my poor child," he began, and broke off before an advancing wave of false brightness. The nurse had entered with her professional cheerfulness and a rose-colored breakfast tray.

"Now, now, my dear, you'll feel better after you've had your nourishment." Gently putting him away from the bed, she placed the tray on a table and turned to rearrange the pillows behind Stanley's back. "Mr. John Kingsmill is on his way up," she said, "and by the time he has gone, Mattie will have a little lunch ready." With a competent gesture, she hurried him out of the room. "I'll have to give your daughter a bath and get her dressed and packed up," she added. "Mrs. Wilder is coming later to close the apartment."

"I can't—oh, I can't—" Stanley moaned; but when the nurse held a spoonful of egg to her lips, she opened her mouth as a child might have done and swallowed obe-

diently. "Oh, Father," she glanced wildly round her, "why did this happen to me?"

"Now, now, you must bear up," the nurse insisted serenely, and with the helpful tone and the words, it seemed to Asa that he had come to the end of endurance.

"Let me know when you want me," he said, as he walked slowly out of the room and away from what he felt to be the vast hypocrisy of the commonplace.

X

NOW, at last, she was safe, Roy thought; she had escaped into finality; she could drop back into the utter peace of forgetfulness. Never again would she look for him. Never again would she expect and, in her sleep, await his return. Never again would she, awake, be tormented by those fleeting resemblances in a crowd. Never again would the casual sound of his name shiver on through her nerves to some remembering center of consciousness. She was secure now from the past, from any accident of renewal; she was protected from that burning jealousy which had destroyed life at its roots. I am free to be happy, she told herself. I am free to make another life, a life wholly my own.

While she waited downstairs for her father and Stanley, she glanced about the room and the house, where nothing had changed. Yes, she was safe; yet it seemed to her that some nerve which had once been sensitive and alive had died in her memory. Peter was dead; and suddenly she felt that, being dead, he had come closer. He was in the still room; he was touching her. "You can't come in!" she cried aloud, her eyes blinded by tears. "You can't come in. You're dead. You must stay out!"

Up the street, the bare branches turned and bent in the wind, and the darkness, which had rolled down in a fog, was splintered by the glare of the arc lamp on the corner. Uncle William had gone to meet the train, and she waited, with a sickening dread, for the sound of the car and the meeting with Stanley. Of course Stanley had to come home. There was no other place for her to go, and her mother was making herself ill from anxiety. But I cannot live in the past, Roy said over and over. I must

think of Craig, and of how much more real this love is
than the other. . . . Then her mother's bell rang, and
she hurried to answer it.

"Oh, Roy, I'm so nervous. They ought to have come
more than an hour ago." Wrapped in a new purple robe,
Lavinia leaned forward, in an excitement which brought
a sallow flush to her cheeks. Her hair was combed back
from her forehead, and there was the stimulating scent of
bay rum in the air.

"The train may have been late, Mother."

"I can't help feeling anxious."

"It does no good. Uncle William went to meet them,
and he'd let you know." While she stood beside the low,
soft couch, gazing down on her mother, an unwelcome
thought darted in and out of her mind: Why do people
talk as if love were bound up in every physical tie? She
doesn't seem close to me. She doesn't even seem true.
Aunt Charlotte would call me an unnatural child, but I
don't care, I'm honest. All this softness, all this decay of
sentimentality . . . And it isn't as if she didn't have
sense. When she lets herself give up pretending, she can
be as natural and as reasonable as anybody.

"Your expression is getting too severe," Lavinia observed, as she had so frequently done, at the wrong moment. She sighed pensively, while she removed the glass
stopper from the bottle of bay rum. Her face, which had
the texture and color of sour cream, appeared to have
curdled under its puffed skin in which all the little lines
were broken and jagged.

"Isn't it time for your medicine?"

"In five minutes. The doctor changed me today from
digitalis to coramine."

As she looked at the assembled bottles, of every size,
Roy thought: How I detest the sight and taste and smell
of medicines! Maybe, after all, I am growing hard.
Mother is annoyed with me because I won't let myself be

sentimental about Stanley. "You may as well take it now,"
she said aloud, offering the glass. "I think that is the car."
Hastening out of the room, she ran quickly downstairs
and threw open the door. I mustn't feel, she said to herself: I mustn't give myself time to feel anything. "God
help us!" she exclaimed vaguely, without meaning, in a
flash of light out of darkness.

Standing in the hall, she watched the two men help
Stanley across the pavement and up the steps to the
house. At first, Roy saw only a small, mournful figure in
a black dress which was too large and a crooked black hat
with a veil slipping back over her head. Then, in the sudden blaze of the electric light in the hall, she looked down
on a pathetic child's face, with immense eyes ringed by
shadows, and a half-open mouth which appeared unable
to close over a long, sobbing breath. For an instant, Roy
held back. But the stone in her breast was swept away by
a torrent of pity. "My poor Stanley!" she cried, and running out of the door she gathered Stanley in her arms.
She is unhappier now than I am, Roy told herself as she
drew back, and the next instant: But for Craig I could
never have done it. I have Craig, but she has lost everything.

Lavinia was calling anxiously, and when they turned
quickly, they found her clinging to the banisters on the
upper floor. While she waited for them, she tottered as if
her knees were too weak to support her; and clutching at
Stanley's arm, William urged her up the stairs in a few
ponderous strides. "My poor child, my poor baby," Lavinia sobbed, pressing the girl to her bosom. Following
slowly, with one of Stanley's bags in his hand, and with
Virgie choking in suppressed excitement behind him, Asa
thought, with a barb of cynical irony: Is this the immemo-
rial or only the modern return of the prodigal daughter?
After all, was Stanley, not Roy, the innocent victim? In
the effervescent sympathy surrounding them, the solid

outlines of facts were partly obliterated. Because of Stanley's youth and her touching plight, the family, and before long the whole community, he suspected, would melt into compassion. For this emotional debauch, he told himself, it was not fair to hold Stanley responsible. She couldn't be blamed either for Southern sentimentality or for maternal hysteria. Her power was unconscious, and it sprang, he knew, from some secret malice of instinct. Her harmfulness lay not in what she had done, but in what she was and would always continue to be; she was not to be blamed that her very imperfections ravished the heart. Yet even Roy, if he could judge by her brimming eyes, had softened her harsh judgment. No doubt, it was better so. Resentments must fade and pass, or there could be no enduring peace among human beings. The old order had gone out, with its severe standards and long retributions. He glanced at Roy's pitying expression, and reflected gratefully that her new happiness was already a protective barrier between her and neglect or injustice.

Later that night, when the two sisters were alone together, Roy sat beside Stanley's bed and listened to an incoherent outburst of grief and remorse. "I never wanted to hurt you, Roy. I don't know—I never knew, even at the time, why it happened. . . . It was like lightning. It was like a storm. It was like darkness, too. . . . Oh, but I don't know. I shall never know. It seemed so wonderful, and then . . . and then why did he do it?"

"Don't talk, Stanley. Try to be quiet. If you talk, the bromide won't do any good."

"But I want to tell you . . . Oh, Roy . . ."

"Hadn't I better leave you now?"

"No, no, stay by me. I don't want to be alone. I'm frightened by the darkness. I keep seeing things in the darkness."

"Try not to think."

"But why did he do it? He wanted me with him. He couldn't bear to have me out of his life. Why did it end like this? Why? Why?"

"Perhaps he was out of his mind."

"No, he wasn't out of his mind. He did it because he couldn't live with me, and he couldn't live without me. He said that. He said that ever so often. He loved me, but he couldn't live with me."

Is she trying to torture me? Roy asked herself. Does she know what she is doing? Does she even hear the words she is speaking? But I must make myself feel nothing, nothing ever again. All that part of me is as dead as last year. Then she prayed passionately: Oh, don't let it come to life again! Dear God, let it stay dead forever! It was as if, in her consciousness, some mortal enmity lay drugged, and as if, too, a start or a shock might arouse it from sleep. Peter, who, being dead, had seemed to come closer, must be thrust out of her mind. . . . Only by refusing to let him enter, could she save herself. Only by speaking of him as of a person who had gone away a long time ago. But if he had lived—the sudden fear was sharp as a blade—if he had lived, she could not have borne it. A dark shape, like the specter of an unuttered wish, hovered over her thoughts. Was there something deep down in her that wished Peter dead? Then, as suddenly as the dark impulse had come, it was gone. I didn't mean that, she told herself in amazed horror. I couldn't be glad . . .

"But why did it happen to me?" Stanley was murmuring, in a faraway voice, as the effect of the sedative stole over her. "I never wanted to do any harm." Her head turned restlessly on the pillow, and her hair, still damp from the bay rum Lavinia had splashed on her forehead, wove a shining halo. The long curling bob, and the careless mark of an inaccurately aimed lipstick, gave her an air of surprised innocence, as of a child playing at make-

believe. She used to look like that when we were both little, Roy thought, absurd and pathetic, with the alluring softness that made grown-up persons stoop down and caress her. To Roy's astonishment, she found that her mind was empty now of resentment. No; she could not hate Stanley. Hating was too much trouble. She couldn't even judge Stanley for being what she was made. After all, if I really believed that love must be left free, Roy told herself, how could I blame them? What did Peter do but put our beliefs to the test? Where the frozen surface had been, a glow was pouring into her heart. If I were different, she thought, I might have held Peter. I might have stood in his way, if I had refused to let him go, but it would have meant keeping him against his nature. She could never have done this. Even had the power to hold him been hers, she knew that her pride, as well as her faith in life, would have preferred the loneliness she has chosen.

Stanley raised her heavy lids and stared with frightened eyes into vacancy. "Where am I?" she asked breathlessly. "Something terrible must have happened." Her face puckered in grief, and she flung out her arm with a wild gesture. "Oh, I know. I remember."

"Don't talk, Stanley, Turn over and try to sleep."

"But I'm at home. I oughtn't to have come home."

"You couldn't have gone anywhere else."

"Do you still hate me, Roy?"

Roy shook her head. "Do sisters ever really hate each other?"

"I didn't want to hurt you."

"Don't, Stanley, don't. It is over now. We have to live as we can. . . ." What did she mean? She didn't know; she didn't care; but only words, she felt, could prevent the moment from crashing into disaster.

Stanley's small, weak fingers clung to her stronger

hand. "I couldn't help it. I could never help anything. But you loved me when we were little."

"I still love you." Was that true? Did she still love Stanley? How do I know? Roy asked herself, desperately. How do I know anything? But something must be saved from the wreck of what had been everything. Something must be saved if it were only pity. Stanley had made her suffer; but, in the end, Stanley had suffered more. I did love her when we were children together, Roy thought. I did protect her because she was weaker than I. And it may be true that nothing really dies, that everything lives on in the past. Yet it is true also that I loved Peter last year, and now I love him no longer.

"I'm glad about you and Craig," Stanley said, after a silence in which she had appeared to be sleeping. "Father told me. I'm glad I didn't spoil your life."

"I thought it was spoiled," Roy answered slowly, "but I found out it wasn't—not for always."

"It's better this way. The other was all wrong. Craig never seemed real to me. But why did this have to happen? If only Peter had told me! Oh, Roy, why didn't he tell me?"

"Perhaps he couldn't. Perhaps there was nothing to tell."

After this, Stanley dropped into stillness, moaning now and then in her sleep, as a child moans in a bad dream. The only light was a pearly glimmer which drifted in from the street, and was shattered at intervals by the flashing lamps of a car. In the obscurity every object appeared remote and imponderable, as if it were only a transparent shadow of substance. Sitting beside the bed, with Stanley grasping her hand, it seemed to Roy that she could see dimly what life now was and would always be till it ended. Peter had dropped out of it, but not until he had outlived all that he meant to her, all that had seemed

[289]

necessary to her first youth, her first love. He had out-lived both ecstasy and anguish; yet the inanimate objects among which he had spent his days and nights had out-lasted him, because these endured longer than human anguish or ecstasy. Suddenly she felt, without thinking, that all this joy and pain had been borne not by her but by some other woman, who had lived and died in some other period of time.

It was late when she left Stanley sleeping and went up-stairs, to find her father waiting for her in her room. How much older he looked! We are killing him among us, she thought; we are draining every drop of his blood. And we shall never stop doing it as long as he and the rest of us live.

"I lost a button on the train," he said, looking up from the coat on his knees, "but the porter found it when we were getting off. I was afraid I'd wake Lavinia if I hunted in her workbasket." She saw that he had threaded a needle with her strongest thread and was earnestly and accurately replacing the button.

Roy stared at him in silent astonishment. Then, after a minute, she burst into the first tears she had shed since his return. Falling on her knees beside him, she hid her face in his coat and sobbed hysterically: "I can't bear any-thing more. Oh, Daddy, this is simply too much!"

"Why, Roy, my darling child!" He put the needle aside and patted her shoulders as she lay on his knees. "What is it, daughter? Has anything happened?"

"Nothing but you." Her sobbing had turned into laughter. "It is too much to see you sitting down, in the night, to sew on a button. Oh, don't, Daddy, I can't bear it!"

The old amused gleam shone in his eyes. "If I never had anything worse than that to do, darling!" In spite of his fatigue and despairing anxiety, he chuckled as he

picked up the needle. "I've got to put on this coat in the morning. It's the only one I own that's fit to be seen in. And it seems to me that a coat without a button is even more pathetic."

She struggled to her feet. "It's silly, I know, but something came over me. When I looked at you sitting there under the light, you looked so—so . . ." Seizing the coat and the threaded needle, she dropped on the foot of the bed and began to sew on the button.

He was still chuckling. "Well, I expect it looks worse to you than it does to me."

"No. It was just that I saw you had never had anything." As she wound the thread quickly round the button, and thrust the needle through one of the holes, she glanced up to meet his tolerant smile. The light shining on his hair made it look almost white (how much he had aged since last spring, she thought), and it showed the thinning place on the top of his head. While she met his gaze, she was conscious of an oddly arrested sensation, as if she were seeing things in a trance. I believe he knows us through and through, she said to herself. I don't believe things have ever fooled him a bit. Aloud she said, "If only you'd had a little happiness when you were young."

"We didn't talk so much about happiness in my day. When it came, we were grateful for it, and, I suppose, a little went farther than it does nowadays. We may have been all wrong in our ideas, but we were brought up to think other things more important than happiness."

"But what things, Daddy?"

"Oh, well, old-fogy, fantastic notions like duty and personal responsibility."

She smiled at him as she snapped off her thread. "I wonder how people first got hold of that miserable-sinner feeling. Wasn't it religion that put it over on you?"

"Maybe. But I was never bent on religion. All I felt was that I ought to do the best I could to keep things on the decent side. If you ask me why—well, honestly, I don't know. . . ."

"But the way you were always giving up things you wanted, and holding on to other things you ought to have let go—like—like husbands or wives. Just imagine!"

"I suppose they had their uses, those sanctions. It takes a lot of experiments, doesn't it, to make evolution? But I wasn't the sort to amount to much, wherever you put me. Your Uncle William told me once that I'd never get on because I had no bowels. He calls it guts now, but it all means the same thing. It's funny the way that stuck in my mind, and helped on my failure. I wasn't more than twelve, and I was trying for a better job than the one I had in the factory."

"Damn Uncle William!" Roy exclaimed, fiercely breaking her thread.

Her father clasped his hands on his knees, and she wondered whether the knuckles hurt him when he bent over. They looked swollen and slightly crooked, his hands; and she told herself, as if she had made a fresh discovery, that hands are more revealing than faces. "Did Stanley," he asked, "seem all right when you left her?"

"She'd been asleep for an hour."

"She's pretty well broken up. It isn't as if she were a strong character."

"Oh, Daddy, who is?"

"Well, you are, darling."

Roy's face darkened. "I sometimes wonder," she replied slowly, "how people live through the things that happen to them."

He put his hand over hers. "You're splendid, daughter," he said, and felt her shrink slightly away from him.

"No, I'm not. I don't care about that, but my life is my own."

"That's fine. Fight for it, and maybe you'll keep it."

She put out the hand she had withdrawn and stroked his arm. "You're going to the funeral tomorrow?"

"Your mother thinks I ought to go. She's right, isn't she?"

"She's always right about things like that." He watched her expression harden as she looked out of the window at the night sky, where a star or two shone through the naked boughs.

"You aren't taking this too deeply, are you, Roy?" he asked gently. "It isn't breaking your spirit?"

She turned her eyes from the window. "It would if I let it in. If I once let myself begin to think about it, I believe I'd break up. But I keep the thought shut outside."

"There's nothing you could have done. There's nothing to reproach yourself for."

"Oh, yes, there is. There's so much I might have done differently. But I've shut that out too."

"You had to let Stanley come home."

"I know. I don't really mind so much as I thought I should."

"She's a broken thing, and she hasn't your courage."

"Everybody keeps saying that." She flushed angrily. "It sounds as if the only good of courage is to make you pay for what other people can't—or won't—stand."

"Perhaps they don't mean it that way."

"It doesn't matter. But it's queer that nothing ever stays as it is—or was. Last summer, Stanley seemed to have everything that I wanted. And now you'd imagine that I'm happier than she is."

"Thank God you've been spared anger and hatred."

Her face brightened. "That's what Craig has done for me. I couldn't get over it so long as I felt it was my fault, because I wasn't the kind of woman to hold love. Then when he loved me, I knew it wasn't a lack in me, that Peter hadn't just grown tired of loving me. I couldn't

have borne that . . . to feel that it was because of some failure in me. It is better even to think that it was some fascination in Stanley."

What could he say to her? The right words would not come. The right words would never come when he needed them. He folded his arm about her, but she did not alter her motionless attitude. Then, after a long silence, while dumbness still held him, she leaned back against his arm and lifted and let fall his stiff fingers. "We don't have to tell each other things, Daddy," she said. "We know without telling."

In her mother's room the next afternoon, Roy tried to keep her mind away from the open grave and the slow falling, falling of earth on the life that had been Peter. All night, while she lay awake, it had seemed to her that he knocked, with the sound of earth falling and forever falling, on the innermost core of her memory. When the core was reached, when it was laid bare, he had found nothing but emptiness. But she had fought through the night till dawn had broken and her father had brought coffee. With the day, a kind of cold peace had closed over her heart. The past was over; the past was done with; the past could not ever return. At breakfast Craig had appeared, emotionally stirred and sympathetic as always. "If you could see Stanley, you would be obliged to forgive her," she said, and he replied quickly: "I've not only forgiven her. I am very grateful to her for letting me have you. But I don't want to see her." Then he had lifted Roy's face and looked down into her eyes. "If I ever amount to anything, it will be because I lost her and found you." After all, this was the best and the truest part of her life. Not that madness for Peter, who had never really loved her, but this new feeling for Craig, this steady confidence in the future and in each other. . . .

Stanley had been put to bed in her mother's room, and Lavinia, with an open prayer book in her hand, was lying beside her. Her tone, when she spoke, was solemn and reverential, but she added presently, unaware that she was thinking aloud: "I wish your father had had a new suit, Roy. That old one is so shabby." Glancing hurriedly at Stanley, who was in a profound stupor, her disordered hair straggling over the pillows, Lavinia continued in a hoarse whisper, "I can't make him spend any of Uncle William's money on himself; but he really ought to have a nice dark suit and a new black tie for the funerals in his own family.

Does she think I have no feeling? Roy asked herself, with a shock of annoyance. Does she imagine I'm made of wood, because I don't go to bed when I'm unhappy? Biting her lips, she said, after a minute, "Well, you can hardly blame him."

"I can't see why he's so terribly set against Uncle William." Lavinia's lips pouted, but she returned piously to her prayer book. For a short while she read in silence; then lifting her eyes, she sighed mournfully, "It looks as if our troubles would never be over."

Well, it did look that way, Roy assented. As with so many of Lavinia's cherished platitudes, the barb of truth was the sharpest point of offense. A clouded light sifted down from the sky, and in this light, Stanley's face was as blurred as a face seen in the rain. Yes, she must have suffered, Roy told herself with an ache of pity. She could not look this way unless she had endured the worst that could come to her. As a child and a very young girl, Stanley had always appeared, in spite of her changeable moods, to be a creature of joy—or perhaps only of gaiety, which is not joy, though it so often borrows the bright semblance. After such sorrow, what could life hold in the future? But, of course, she would get over it. People, especially the young and thoughtless, always got over things.

Broken hearts were more painful than permanent. Remorse must be harder to bear, she thought. If I felt that I had killed Peter, or made life unbearable for him, could I have lived on with that knowledge as a nightly companion? Does Stanley feel that? Was she really to blame for their love or for the end of their love? Sitting there, with her gaze on that still figure of sorrow and apathy, and yet, so strangely, of youth, too, untarnished by misery, Roy asked herself if one could find any reason—or if at any time, in any place, she could ever have found a reason or a meaning in life. It was all obscure, dark, formless; even though moments appeared to take form and glow with an inner radiance, yet in life as a whole, there was neither form nor illumination. A muddle in space, she thought, and, oh, God, *what* a muddle! She shook herself and sat up, very straight in the wan light. Another minute, and she would have slipped down into the timeless abyss; she would have plunged into that vast isolation, into the delirium of grief, of despair, of vain longing. Oh, Peter, Peter, why did I ever know you? she cried in her heart, why did I ever love you? But no, she would not go down. She would not let herself be swept back and engulfed in the past. Memories could be rubbed out. They could be lost so utterly that nothing remained of them, not even an outline. . . .

Suddenly, Stanley opened her eyes and thrust out her hands, as if she were pushing against a wall. Her gaze wandered round the room, and she began to cry soundlessly, as if unaware of the tears that overflowed her eyelids and streamed down her cheeks.

"She wants something," Lavinia exclaimed in alarm.

Roy sprang up and bent over the bed. "What is it, Stanley?" She pushed back the dampened hair which seemed to clutch at her fingers and curl round them.

For a long moment Stanley stared up at her without

recognition. "Is this home?" she asked vaguely, at last. "I must have been dreaming."

"Yes, this is home. Mother and I are with you."

"Is it Mother's room?"

"Yes, you're in Mother's bed."

"Then I wasn't dreaming. Oh, I know! I remember!" A wave of horror broke over her while she rocked from side to side in a convulsion of memory. Then the awakening appeared to fail as quickly as it had come; the opiate reasserted its influence, and a tide of apathy spread over her features. She was aware of her surroundings and of the grief she ought to feel, but she appeared insensible to the more poignant stab of emotion. What a blessing an opiate is, Roy told herself. If only the mind could be at liberty to act and observe during the while that soul and body are invulnerable to pain. "But there isn't any reason," Stanley was murmuring in a drugged voice. "There isn't any reason on earth." Her eyelids fluttered down, and then up again. "Is there ever a reason for anything, Mother?"

Lavinia yearned toward her. "Not that we can always see, darling."

"Have I been asleep a long time?"

"It will do you good. Try not to talk."

"I feel as if I'd been away—somewhere very far-off. I don't know where I was."

"You were dreaming. It will come back."

"Yes, it will come back. I wish it wouldn't. I can recollect things, but I don't seem to take them in. I feel alive only in spots."

"That's the medicine. It is good for you."

"At first I didn't know Roy. But I know her now."

"You knew me."

"I heard your voice. I knew your voice."

"Did I wake you?"

Stanley's head rolled from side to side on the pillow. "I wasn't asleep. Not exactly asleep. Not with the whole of me." She stretched out her arm, as if she were reaching for something she could not find. "Is the funeral over yet, Mother?"

"Not yet, my child. It soon will be."

"Did Father go?"

"Your father and Uncle William and Andrew and Maggie. Everyone feels the greatest sympathy. The whole town has been inquiring for you. Maggie telephoned me the flowers were simply wonderful."

"The flowers?" Stanley echoed in a deadened whisper. "Funeral flowers, and for Peter!"

"Good God, no!" Roy cried out furiously, and burst into tears.

Stanley looked at her, with dry eyes, as if she were wondering why anyone wept. "Poor Roy. I'm sorry."

Lavinia struggled down from the bed and made her way, swaying heavily, to an easy chair by the window. "Nobody holds anything against you, Stanley," she said, when she had recovered her breath. "People want to be kind. They are trying to show sympathy."

"But I don't want to see any kind people, Mother. Won't you keep them away?"

"Of course, my precious child, if you wish me to. But your Uncle William? You will let him come, won't you?"

Stanley's only reply was a languid murmur of acquiescence. She was sinking again into partial unconsciousness, and the look of returning anguish was slowly smoothed away from her features. A shaft of sunlight pierced the clouded sky, and beneath its quivering beams, her face appeared transparent and luminous and strangely unreal. "She looks so young," Lavinia said. "There's something different—I don't know what it is—in her expression." Glancing round at the clock, she added, with a gesture of relief, "The funeral must be over by now."

As the clock struck the hour, Roy looked out, through the trees, to the scudding clouds in the west. Yes, it is over, she thought: What is over can never come back; for the dead are so harmless. One can escape the dead even while one remembers them. We are safe from them. I am safe from Peter if only—if only he will stay buried and not come to life again, not even in my sleep. Poor Peter! He had only the past. The present was hers, and the future. . . .

Part Third

All Things New

I

IT'S a fine morning, praise the Lord, and a good world,
sang Minerva's heart, as she moistened her flatiron and
slapped it down on one of Miss Lavinia's old-fashioned
nightgowns. The ironing board, smoothly shrouded in a
spotless sheet, was suspended between the kitchen table
and the windowsill; and while she ironed the week's wash,
she could glance out into the backyard, which Abel had
hoed and spaded into a real flower garden. April was
closing in. You felt a touch of summer in the hot sunshine.
The wisteria on the fence and the big snowball bush in the
corner were in full bloom, and Abel's particular pride, the
Scarlet Beauty tulips, were flaunting their brilliant heads.
Some seasons the snowballs came a little late, but they were
blooming early, and all together, this spring. As the wind
raced with the tulips, they looked, for all the world,
Minerva told herself, like rows of Christian soldiers
marching as to war.

It was early yet. Six o'clock had just struck over the
town; but Abel had been up for more than an hour,
weeding and transplanting his slips. He liked to get in a
time or two in his garden before he went to work, and
after he came home from the post office, in the
eveling—no, evening. He certny did carry his years well,
did Abel. Only, when he had come down with the old flu
in the wintertime, she'd been mortally feared that he was
beginning to fail. Then it was that she had begun to tor-
ment the Throne, as her mammy and pappy used to say,
praying day and night on her knees (and it hurt her
rheumatics, too) whenever she could spare a minute to
flop down on the floor. And just as soon as she stopped
praying, there was Abel begging her to sing hymns by his
bed. "A-settin' in de Kingdom, Yas, my Lord." Abel was

a great hand for the old tunes, and he had right smart of a voice, too, whenever he let it all out. But Parry, he had to have that outlandish jazz and swing music that came blaring, fit to deefen you, over the radio.

Maybe 'twas her prayers that helped Abel, and maybe 'twasn't. Parry was certain sure his pa would have got back to health withouten her praying and churchgoing; but you could never tell how things happened, and anyway the Lord's side was the safe side. She hadn't let up, not even after Abel was out and about, because he looked so poorly and slunken that it put her heart in her mouth when she watched him trying to do things the way he used to when he was husky and strong. But after the first few weeks he'd begun to pearten up, and by the time spring was here, he was working out in his garden just the same as before he was sick. He stuck out that hoeing and weeding had picked him up, but it might have been the doctor's green physic, though Abel was dead set against it. She'd never seen Abel look spryer than he did right this minute, out there weeding round that old lilac bush. Mr. Asa let him have the lilac out of the Timberlake front yard. It was the bush Mr. Asa's ma had always been so proud of. The folks there had told Abel that it would surely die if he moved it in April; but Abel had said anything could be moved and would live if only you'd puddle it well. And, bless your life, there it was coming into bloom the next year as if it had grown right here from a shoot.

Parry had always been the lightest of her children, and the smartest too. As bright as a steel trap he was. The rest of 'em were all easygoing and sort of slow-tempered; but Parry had been nimble-witted and peppery from the start. Not a bad child. No, ma'am, he'd never given her a night's worry—not like most of these young fly-up-the-creek folks, though he was always wanting to push ahead and be somebody. Indian blood, Grandpappy had said,

that was Indian blood, way back yonder in the olden time. But Granny had made out (in the old days folks used to say she could lay spells, but there wasn't nothing in that) it wasn't Indian blood in Parry, but white blood coming out, as sure as you're born. Then her mammy had asked right sharp, "Where'd he git hold of that white blood, Granny?" But Granny she didn't say nothing a-tall, a-tall. She jest picked up a coal from the fire for her pipe and sucked in real hard, as if she was studying. That was the year Granny died, and her wits were already addled. All the answer she gave was to sort of sing aloud, the way she did when she made believe she was seeing things: "I knows what I knows, an' I sees what I sees. *Dar's a long run an' a short turn, an' de wind has full sweep.*" Naw, ma'am, nary a word would she let on. She passed away mighty soon after that, Granny did; but Minerva could see her now just as plain as the nose on your face. Grampy was lighter than Granny, and he came from over on the Bransford plantation in Powhatan County. But for twenty years before he was called away, he was butler for Miss Kate Oliver, down on James River, at Hunter's Fare.

It was the blessed truth, Minerva reminded herself, that she had a mort of things to be thankful for. Spring-cleaning was over and done with (she could never see how some colored folks, and some white, too, got along with dirt everywhere, and even, she had heard tell, with bedbugs in the ticking). But her people had been raised right. Her people didn't have truck with the no-count and the slack-twisted sort. From top to bottom, every crack and cranny in her house had been scrubbed clean, and she had soaked all the slats in the bedsteads, and stopped every chink up tight with turpentine soap, just exactly like old Miss used to do. Naw, ma'am, there wasn't a speck of dust left in her whole house, from garret to basement, and her kitchen was just as shiny as a new pin after she stopped scrubbing and polishing. She liked

things bright and cheery around her, that she did. After she had popped the dish of batterbread into the oven she had to wipe off a smeary place before she could ease her mind back to her ironing.

There surely was a pile of clothes to get through with, and she'd have to hurry, sure enough, if she wanted to have breakfast ready in time for Abel and Parry. Mighty soon now the coffee would begin to smell good and strong. She always made her coffee the old-time way, roasting and grinding her own beans, with an eggshell in the pot, or a whole egg, if she happened to have one to spare. Old Miss could never stomach this newfangled coffee, as thin and poor as leftover dregs. The old coffee-pot that Miss Charlotte Fitzroy gave to Minerva after she started using a percolator (because Yankee servants couldn't be trusted to make boiled coffee right) was on the stove now, and just as soon as the whiffs began to puff out of the spout, Abel would straighten up from his bending and sing out in his hearty way: "I smell Kingdom Come, Minervy!" But she believed in good eating, the way all her white folks had believed in the olden time. "None of these here wishy-washy po-folksy victuals for me," Granny used to say, as far back as she could make out to remember. Didn't she praise the Lord whenever she thought of her five Rhode Island Red hens and the fine eggs they were laying? When she stretched her neck out of the window, she could see the fence of chicken wire at the bottom of the yard, which saved Abel's flower beds from those clucking hens and their brazen rooster.

Yes, she'd had a good life, she said over again, while her heart sang, Hallelujah! Abel had been the right husband for her, one of the steady sort that never got into trouble. She could see him now bending and straightening his back, and feeling his pains, she knew, for neither your back nor your legs were getting limber with years. . . . Parry would never be the big man his pa was.

Abel was big and slow and easygoing, as if butter wouldn't melt in his mouth, but for all his soft tongue, he surely did have staying power. He didn't go about with a chip on his shoulder looking for trouble, and he wasn't the sort, as folks said of old Mr. William, to throw the helve after the hatchet when his dander was up; but you had to be mighty peart if you were trying to get the better of Abel. In some ways Parry took after him, and then again, he seemed more to favor her own grampy. His hair was like Abel's, just as straight as a string if you brushed it aplenty; and he was so light-colored he could pass for white any day, in the North. But he didn't hold with such doings, and he didn't aim, he said, to pass over, the way so many Yankee Negroes were doing. He talked this new-fashioned talk about being proud of his race. Any race that had gone under so often and come up still smiling was a race, he said, to be proud of. In the olden days Grampy and Granny had never heard so much carrying on about race. You were what the Lord Almighty made you, and all you had to do was to settle down in your place and be thankful if He hadn't made it a tight squeeze for you. But everything was changed now. She was raised along with her white folks, and she played with all the white children when she was little, and Mammy would have whaled the life out of her if she'd ever called her own people "niggers." Yet, to save her soul, she couldn't make out the sort of gabble, gabble, gabble they talked nowadays.

But Parry liked it, he did. Parry was all set toward the new ways and the new notions. He'd always been that-a-way, and he wan't hardly out of her lap before he began to project with book learning. She could recollect the time she found him up on the woodpile, with a book somebody had throwed in the trash can. "I'se reading letters," he had piped up at her, pointing to the print, with the book held upside down in his hands. And he kept it up

like that, sure he did, till Mr. Asa found out about it and made her send him to school. He wan't more than six or seven when he began his schooling, but he was so set on learning that he pushed straight up to the top. The teachers all knew he was bright as brass, and they were all in high feather on Commencement Day when he took every last one of the prizes. After he won a scholarship last June, he was bent on going to classes out at Makepeace College, and if he did well there, Mr. Craig had promised to help him through Howard University.

"I was thinking about a new roadster," Mr. Craig had said in his offhand, lighthearted way, "but I've a notion that Parry's future would be a safer investment." Then when poor Stanley came home and flopped down in the bed, without a morsel of spirit, just pining away to a shadow, Mr. William engaged Parry to look after her car and drive her wherever she wanted to go. He dressed him up nice too, and smart-looking; and 'twas then that Parry began saving up, so as to cut a good figure when he went on to Washington. Mr. John Kingsmill had given him a heap of Mr. Peter's clothes. They were a lot too big, but she could cut them down and stitch up as good as a man tailor. The first spare minute she got on her hands, she was going to sit right down at her machine and start right away making them over. . . .

But Stanley, poor little honey, was still wasting away. All the folks in town were good and kind to her, but the child wouldn't lift a finger to help herself, or take a bit of notice of anything that was done for her. The onliest time she ever came out of her moping was when Miss Lavinia tried to get her to see the preacher. Then she blazed up, as mad as hops, and told her ma to mind her own business and take her religion where it was wanted. And the whole blessed time there was Dr. Brompton downstairs in the parlor, waiting to come up. But she wouldn't let him. No, ma'am, she wouldn't let him set foot inside her room.

Last week, when Minerva had gone up with the washing, she had hoped that Stanley was looking a teensy bit spryer. Still, even then, she would hardly have known the poor child, lying there so pale and peaked and heart-sick, with her sunshiny hair all tangled over her head and her blue eyes, as big as saucers, a-swimming in tears. "Ain't there something I can do for you, honey?" Minerva had asked, and Stanley had sighed back, just as doleful as ever, "Not a thing in the world, Mammy." "Well, it's the Lord's hand, child," Minerva had replied, "and He knows what's best for you." But all the time she was telling herself, "It's a mortal shame, even if it is the Lord's will, and there don't seem a mite of sense in its having to happen."

It wasn't till the day after her visit, and Mr. Peter had been cold in his grave for going on six weeks or more, that Mr. William had persuaded Stanley to go out with him, in the little car he had given her when she was married. He had meant Parry to drive them; but it was for all the world like Stanley that she should do what nobody was looking for and spring a surprise on them. She'd no sooner started off, Parry said, than she began to perk up and told him it made her as nervous as a cat to have anybody else at her wheel. "You just stop and let me get there," she'd called out, as sprightly as what not, and then straight away she'd moved in front beside Mr. William, and made Parry hop over to the back seat and sit there all by himself. "Go slow, go slow," Mr. William had warned her. Her cheeks looked real pink, and she talked kind of flighty, as if something had gone to her head. . . . Lifting an iron from the stove and testing the bottom with a wet forefinger, Minerva thought gravely: Young folks in these days drink more than they used to. I hope the poor child ain't trying to drown her grief in the bottle. As pretty as new paint she was, with something wildlike about her that caught at your heart. . . .

There was a scuffling noise in the hall, and Jasper

bounced out into the backyard and wheeled in leaps and circles of joy, first to greet Abel by his flower bed, and then to the five hens and one rooster behind the barriers of chicken wire. Ecstatic barks pierced the sunny air, and Jasper's small tawny body was like an animated bronze figure. "I declare, I never saw such a dog," Minerva said aloud. "It would break Parry's heart if anything happened to him while he's away up in Washington."

Resting her iron on its side, she stood gazing dreamily through the open window, where two cardinals were pecking at seed. She saw all the little garden, radiant with April bloom, as if it were a hidden sanctuary carved out of the encompassing distractions of life. Beyond the high board fence the crowded Negro quarter was teeming with the movement and rumor of spring. She had only to open the back gate and step out into the alley, and she knew that she should find herself right in the middle of all that she, or some sure instinct, has struggled against from the very beginning of time—in the middle of poverty, and squalor, and confusion, and discord. No matter what tribulations we've had to bear, she thought proudly, we've always held up our heads with the Lord's children. Sweet Jesus, ain't we all the same in the sight of the Lord?

II

THEY are my children, but I know nothing about them, Asa reminded himself, while he looked from Roy, by the window, to Stanley, lying across the bed, as if she had been broken and flung down by a careless hand. He could not understand Roy, who was nearer to him than anyone else. He could not understand Stanley, who touched his heart with an incredible pity. In the past year, or so it seemed to him, miles of pure space, blank miles of nothing, had floated in and separated him from all those he loved most. Things had occurred which were unthinkable even now; yet all these things had their source in conflicting identities, or in that special world which enclosed these identities within circumscribed boundaries.

It was summer again. The warm fragrance of July was drifting in from the trees and the grass. But the very air of the room was heavy, he felt, with unrelated emotions. As he entered, he had been caught up and enmeshed in a whirl of vehement centrifugal forces. All the wanting in the world, he thought, and all this wanting is in conflict.

"What has happened?" he asked anxiously. "Has Stanley been hurt?"

In the flushed light Roy's profile was edged with a glimmering shadow. Without turning from the window, she answered in a subdued tone, "No, but she stayed out so long that Mother was nervous about her."

"Was she alone?"

"Yes, she wouldn't let Parry go. She will start off on these wild drives by herself, and Mother lets herself get so dreadfully wrought up. Have you seen Mother?"

"Not yet. Is Stanley asleep?"

At the question, Stanley turned over and sat up on the

side of the bed. "No, I'm not asleep, but I'm tired of being watched and waited for. I want to go and come when I please." Her hand was shaking as she pushed back the hair from her forehead, and there was a caged and defiant look in her eyes. All the apathy of her first grief had deserted her; her cheeks were burning, and her eyes shone with excitement. Though he could find no reason for the sudden shifting of mood, Asa admitted that he had never found sufficient cause for either her actions or her impulses. When the life of disconnected sensations met the shock of catastrophe, what was there to fall back upon except nothingness?

And how can one help, he asked himself, when there is no way of approach? It was like trying to express sympathy in a tongue that one did not speak and could not understand. Words are futile; signs fail; outstretched arms drop away from sheer helplessness. Yet he longed to snatch her back into safety. If only he knew where safety could be found, or had it to offer. In Lavinia perhaps. . . . Yet Lavinia's faith, though abundant, had become merely a matter of husks. She believed with conviction, but without passion; and passion alone, he had learned from Roy, could overcome and recreate passion.

"It is natural, my dear," he replied in a tone of sympathetic remonstrance, "that your mother should feel anxious about you."

"She needn't. I wish she wouldn't."

"Mothers are that way."

"They oughtn't to be. It's silly." He smiled as he watched the petulant toss of her head. Her softly tinted face was delicate and vacant. There were no depths in the startled blue of her eyes.

Roy turned from the window and looked at her. "Are you all right now, Stanley?"

"Oh, I'm all right."

"Craig is waiting for you, Roy," Asa said. "He came in when I did."

"Are you going out?" Stanley asked. "Father, do you see why I shouldn't go to a movie?"

"Would you like to go after dinner?" Roy had started to the door, but she turned and came back. "Will you come down if Craig stays?"

"No, I won't come down. I don't want to see anybody."

"I'll take you to a movie or anything else," Asa broke in quickly, "if I can find somebody to stay with your mother."

"It doesn't matter. I'll go some other time," Stanley replied impatiently. "Good night, Roy. I hope you'll have a nice evening." Her eyes followed Roy's figure through the door into the hall, and she added, after a sighing pause, "I'm glad she's happy. Somebody ought to be happy."

"She ought to be, anyway."

"I was afraid I'd ruined things for her. But it seemed all I really ruined was my own life."

"You're too young to think that. Even if one life has gone, think how many other and better lives are still ahead of you."

Her closed features seemed to bloom, suddenly, in the gathering dusk. Beauty like that, he thought, which came and went as a flare of the senses, would never lose its ascendancy over the heart. "Is that true, Father?" Her voice trembled with longing. "Is it true that everything is not finished and over?"

"How can that be, my child? At twenty, one has scarcely begun."

"I'm tired of grief," she said passionately. "I can't bear to be hurt any longer. For months I've done nothing but wish I were dead, and I'm worn-out with wishing it. I've grieved for Peter as much as I can. I can't grieve anymore. Oh, but I can't, Father!"

[313]

"Don't try to grieve, Stanley. You can't help Peter by forcing yourself to be unhappy. Nobody blames you. Let yourself be a little nicer to people, and you'll see how much sympathy they have for you."

"I can't feel the way Mother thinks I ought to."

"Don't try to. It won't do a bit of good to Peter, or to anyone else."

"I want to forget. Is it wrong to want to forget?"

"It's only natural. Why should you force yourself to be wretched?"

"It wasn't my fault. Even if I killed Peter, it wasn't my fault."

"You didn't kill him. It wasn't your fault. Peter's end was his own doing."

"I'm sick to death of it all. I want to be happy again."

"Of course, you are. Of course, you will be happy again."

"How long has it been, Father?"

"Four months. Four months and two weeks."

"That's a long time."

"It seems so when we're young and unhappy."

"And I want—oh, so terribly—to be happy!"

"You will be. You will find again everything you think you have lost."

"Then make Mother leave me alone. She likes me to be miserable. She doesn't think it is right to forget, and enjoy living."

"You don't understand her, my dear. In our day we took things harder. We thought about widowhood and, I suppose, about all other passing afflictions as tremendous disasters."

"Well, but I'm not going to sit down and fold my hands, and it simply drives me wild to stop, and to think. The only way I can bear it is by moving about as fast as I can. That's why I like to drive myself till I'm too fagged out to feel or remember. But I did care, Father. I did

care for Peter—only—only I can't stand having to suffer
like this. . . ."

"I know, my child, but I can't help getting anxious
when you are out alone for so many hours."

"Oh, please, please, please, don't fuss over me like the
rest of them. As soon as Mother stops, Uncle William
begins."

"There might be an accident."

"But there won't be. And if there is, somebody will
come by."

"What does your Uncle William say about it?"

"He wants me to let Parry drive me, or at least take
him along. But that would spoil everything. I want to be
by myself. That's the only freedom I have."

Perhaps. He could understand, for he also had
longed, in vain, for the fugitive essence of freedom.
"There isn't much freedom in either a hospital or a
grave," he said presently. "I don't know how well you can
drive."

"Oh, I'm all right. I can look out for myself."

"And for other people? That also is a rather important
lookout."

She frowned. "Mother doesn't see that she's sending
me out of my mind. I simply have to stop brooding and
get away from this house."

"How long were you out today?"

"Since breakfast. I told her I'd get lunch somewhere
on the road. I don't see why she can't leave me alone."

"That's the protective instinct, my child. Mother love
always knows best." His smile flickered and vanished.

"Did you mind when you were young?"

"I suppose I did, but my Mother was a very remarkable woman."

"That must have been worse," Stanley said. "I don't
like remarkable women."

"You might if you'd ever known any."

"Well, I don't want to; and I don't want to remember."

His laugh was tinctured with bitterness. "You needn't worry about that. Long remembering has gone out-of-style, with all other large emotions."

"Well, I'm glad. I can't live unless I go on and forget. Do you think I'm obliged to wear mourning much longer?"

"Go in scarlet, my dear, if it makes your life easier."

"I hate black. It seems to blot me out."

"Then don't wear it." He looked critically at the brilliant fairness of her coloring above the thin black dress and collar of fine white lawn which Lavinia had so patiently hemstitched. "I like you in this, but you oughtn't to be depressed by your clothes. There's enough else to dampen our joy in living. Are you coming downstairs?"

"Not with Craig. He is so tiresome."

"Roy doesn't find him so. Perhaps there's more in him than you ever suspected."

"Oh, he's good-looking in his way, and for a little while, I thought I was crazy about him. But he got tiresome so soon. I don't see how Roy can find him amusing."

"Maybe she doesn't. Maybe she isn't looking for amusement."

"Yes, they are both serious persons. That may help. Anyway, I'm glad I brought them together." Her laughter was humorless but without malice.

"Then you shouldn't mind seeing him."

"Oh, I don't mind. I see him almost every day, but he does bore me. I thought I'd broken him of all his prosy old theories. But Roy seems to encourage his wild notions about making the world over." She slipped from the bed and shook out her short black skirt which rippled in mournful swirls round her knees. "I'd really just as soon

come down to dinner. I don't want to hurt Roy's feelings."

For an instant, while she whirled in front of him, he stared at her with a smile of tender amusement. After all, an arrested mentality might possess its own special charm. "That's right," he said, turning away. "I'll expect you at dinner."

Lavinia had been dozing a few moments before; but she was awake now, and appeared hurt and resigned because he had not come to her sooner. "I don't see what kept you so long. It's almost time for my dinner."

"I was trying to persuade Stanley to come downstairs. It never occurs to her that Virgie could make out a case against bringing up trays."

"It isn't Virgie's fault. She complains all the time."

While her querulous tone rose and fell, he studied her with detached wonder. No, it isn't enough, he was thinking; family ties are not enough, nor is moral responsibility. He did not want this safe shelter, except, perhaps, in moments of weakness. Like Roy and Stanley and Craig, he also wanted the freedom to lose his head. He wanted an escape. He wanted to live, not according to a rule or a pattern, but in response to the demands of his own nature. With all its strength, his nature rejected the eternal compromise with necessity. His nature rejected this daily life with Lavinia, whom he did not like, whom he had never loved. But that in itself, he perceived, might be the answer he had been seeking. Not force of will, but weakness of character might have decreed his sacrifice to some false social security. Was his submission nothing more than the surrender of the small soul to the small gods of respectability and convention? But it will end someday, he assured himself, because he could not face the future with the door of life closed forever against

him. Someday William's wealth, or a share of it, will pass to Lavinia; and a wealthy Lavinia would mean, for Asa, the right to possess one's own soul in poverty. His job would go, too, but there is more in life, he thought, than a mean job, or even a good one. With a miraculous swiftness, the woods and the wide pastures of Hunter's Fare composed themselves in his vision. From the vacancy of the past something bright as a flame, beckoning as a promise, flashed and spun through his mind; and he thought with a rapt expectancy: Someday everything will be different. Life will be different, life will be happier, life will become what one wants, not what one fears. . . . Then the vision broke, the blown bubble melted away. Lavinia's pale astonished eyes bulged from the damaged frame of the present. "But all that is nonsense," he heard himself saying aloud. "That is pure nonsense."

"What was that, Asa?" Lavinia's startled voice broke in. "What are you thinking of?"

"Nothing, Lavinia."

"You didn't sound like yourself."

He laughed, but there was a dazed look in his eyes. "Or more like myself."

"Were you talking of Stanley?"

"Of Stanley? Yes, oh, yes, I was talking of Stanley. She doesn't like Craig any longer."

"Well, that is nonsense. Why should she dislike Craig because she treated him badly?"

"It does sound illogical. But then—" he had relapsed into his usual quizzical tone "—my logic, like my morality, is rather behind the times."

Lavinia sighed. "There isn't any least reason why they should hate each other so bitterly."

"Do they? I hadn't noticed that Craig showed any feeling one way or another. But your eyes are sharper than mine."

"No, he only avoids her, but that is what makes Stanley so furious. I believe she resents his forgiving her."

"Anyhow, it's too deep for me. I'd better brush up before dinner." Going over to the table, he measured a dose of some new medicine into a glass and, after adding a little water, handed it to her.

Lavinia swallowed the medicine promptly, though the taste was unpleasant. "I hope they won't quarrel and make Roy uncomfortable," she said, with a grimace. Then, after a moment in which she appeared to be seized by a spasm: "Oh, Asa, what are the young made of today?"

"Ask me another, my dear. But I hear Virgie."

There was a bump on the stairs; there was a clatter of dishes; there was the sound of a voice groaning in dialect.

"Virgie has her good points," Lavinia sighed, "but I do wish she wasn't so noisy."

"I suppose the quiet ones are expensive."

"Oh, of course, nobody who could afford a trained servant would stand her for a minute." Lavinia sank back with a resigned murmur. "If Uncle William ever gives me that annuity, the first thing I'll do will be to let Virgie go."

"If ever . . ." Asa began, and bit back his words with a smile. An annuity, he had long suspected, was Lavinia's euphemism for a certain solemn occasion. It would be prudent in William, he reflected, to look about him and safeguard his memory, even while he was still so successfully inhabiting the flesh.

"Oh, what lovely roses!" Lavinia exclaimed to Asa's retreating back; and wheeling quickly, he saw that her dinner tray was glowing with superb crimson blossoms.

"Minervy done sent 'em," Virgie said, while she deposited the tray on the table. "She says Abel wan't satisfied twel he done show you de best he could do."

"They're beautiful," Lavinia replied, as pleased as a girl, for she loved roses, especially when they were red. "Did Parry bring them?"

"Yas, ma'am, he's a-settin' right downstairs now in my kitchen, dat he is."

"Well, thank him, Virgie, and tell him Mr. Asa will speak to him. If he hasn't had his dinner, be sure to give him something to eat." One of Lavinia's more sympathetic traits was a feeling that the lower orders of society were permanently undernourished. Saving as she was in the externals of living, she still maintained an open hand when she dispensed sustenance either for the soul or the body.

"You'd better come along down, suh," Virgie was saying as she prepared to withdraw. "Miss Roy done tole me to hurry up dinner jes' ez quick ez ever I kin."

When she had gone, Lavinia removed the top from the cup and tasted a spoonful of cold consommé. She looked forward to her meals, and enjoyed them whenever it was possible, as one of the few sustaining pleasures in life. "I sometimes wonder," she remarked, delicately eating her soup and breaking her roll, "how housekeepers managed in the days before canned soups were invented." She paused expectantly, awaiting an answer; but the only response that came was the noisy gush of a tap in the bathroom and the tread of Virgie's hastening feet on her way to whatever private world she inhabited. . . .

Downstairs, a little later, Asa found Craig talking to Parry in the back hall. It is amazing, he thought, what a little encouragement can do for the young. The boy appeared to him to have grown up in the past few months. His look of sullen reticence had given way to a sanguine good humor, and he seemed to have cast off his encumbrances and inhibitions. "Parry has taken another scholarship," Craig said in his sympathetic voice, which was friendly without the slightest accent of patronage. "I've

just told him I'll see that he goes to Howard University next year."

"I'll certainly try hard, Mr. Craig," Parry answered, "and none of us will ever forget it." His eyes were liquid with joy, and his expression had softened from its glazed immobility.

Out of the complete dissolution of the past year, the broken promises, the wrecked hopes, Asa felt that something solid and constructive, however small, was taking shape in the present and moving on into the future. "I'm glad, Parry," he said, as indeed he was. "I like to see your mother's son go ahead." Then, as the boy turned to leave, he added, "Miss Lavinia says you must tell your father the roses are wonderful. She'd like to know what they are."

"I'll have to ask Pa, Mr. Asa. I never can recollect the names of his roses. They may be Red Radiance, but he has another kind called something like Blaze."

"Are you going home now?"

"No, sir. Miss Stanley wants me to leave her car and come back at eleven. I thought I'd go to a movie."

"But Miss Stanley has just come in."

"Yes, sir, but she wants to go out again. She said she'd put the car in the garage, but I told her I'd just as lief stay uptown and come back for it. I can get some supper at Uncle Jim's."

"Virgie will give you something. Well, I'm as pleased as I can be about that scholarship." It was only the truth, he told himself, while the boy opened the back door and went out into the yard. Irrelevantly, he added, I'd like to have given him the price of a movie; but the worst thing about being poor is not the absence of money in the bank; it is the constantly pinching lack of change in the pocket. . . .

Just as they were beginning dinner, Stanley came downstairs and slipped into the chair on her father's right. She was still wearing the thin black dress with the

lawn collar, and it seemed to Asa that she looked surprisingly fresh and young. But it is not fair, he told himself. It is not fair that she, alone of us all, should appear untouched by her sorrow. Even discontent, even anger or petulance came and went as a shadow over her features.

Virgie brought in all that was left of the canned consommé, and when that was finished, she placed before Asa a dish of lean fried chicken and corn fritters. While he carefully selected the white meat for Roy and Stanley, he thought of Kate Oliver having her frugal supper alone at Hunter's Fare.

"There's no doubt about it," he began soberly, dismembering an aged leg, while he regretted Virgie's theory that the cure for bad cooking is more cooking, "there's no doubt about it. . . ." But what, after all, had he started to say, and where could he find a safe topic? Even the prospect of war over the ocean might lead to a mild explosion between Stanley and Craig. Why should bruised emotions, he wondered, inevitably recoil into hostility? Why is it impossible for two persons who have once loved and hated ever again to be simple or natural with each other? Or was this true only of women? Watching Stanley with half-closed eyes, he asked himself if it were true, as Lavinia said, that she could not forgive Craig's failure in resentment and bitterness. A wave of pity surged through his mind, pity for Stanley and Roy and Craig and the boy Parry, as well as for all eager and thwarted youth everywhere, in any part of the world. Then the wave broke and scattered. Nothing, he reminded himself, is so helpless or so ineffectual as pity.

His gaze rested on Roy's face, and he thought: those two, at least, have found what they wanted. Craig was obviously absorbed in her, and he made no effort to disguise his casual indifference to Stanley. Asa would scarcely have recognized in him the intense but irresolute young man who had so desperately desired the wrong

woman, Roy, too, had grown gentler and less defiant in mood. She was in love again, he knew; for love alone had the power to bring that secret joy to a face, or to create a radiance which seemed to her father as burningly ethereal as light.

Well, he supposed love was important. It must be important, since it possessed this extraordinary power to ruin and, no doubt, to make lives. But he did not know. He had never known love like this, the kind of love that one read about in books and heard of in legend. . . . Stanley looked up and met his glance, and it seemed to him that the freshness of her bloom had suddenly wilted.

"Are you tired, my dear?" he asked gently.

"Oh, no, I'm not tired," she answered, with a gesture of exasperation.

"How many miles have you driven today?"

"I didn't notice. Does it make any difference?"

Roy looked at her carelessly. "Why not go with us to a movie? You may choose one you like."

"Yes, come with us." Craig glanced round with friendly unconcern. "It might make you sleep better."

There was a flicker of dislike in Stanley's eyes, as if she were forcing herself to accept an inevitable but unpleasant situation. Why does she hate him so bitterly? Asa wondered. Does she hate him because he had once loved her too much or because he now loved her no longer?

"Oh, not to a movie!" Stanley exclaimed. "You have to keep still at a movie, and I'd rather do anything than keep still."

"Maybe you'd like jitterbugging," Craig suggested flippantly. "I'm sorry that Roy and I are too sober for you. We're old and settled already."

"You always were," Stanley flashed back angrily. "You were born that way."

His eyelids dropped suddenly, and he applied himself

to his currant pudding, which, since it required few in-
gredients and little watching, was Virgie's favorite concoc-
tion. "I dare say I was," he replied in an even tone, "and
in that at least I was fortunate."

The mistake with them, Asa thought, and with the
whole of their extraordinary place in time, was that they
had never really broken through the tight shell of their
egoism. The world without them existed merely as an extension of the confusion and the thwarted longings of the
world within. Even Craig, with his easy compassion and
his earnest endeavors, was externalizing his own inner
disorder. None of them, Asa mused, has a design for living; none of them has even a definition. It isn't that they
see themselves in the terms of their age, but that they see
their age only in wider terms of themselves. Even Roy
and Craig, who were superior in so many ways to the
youth of his own period, had not yet found an escape
from the general modern dilemma. No one among them
had solved the intricate problem of how one may take
one's pleasure and still have it.

"As long as we're both settled," Roy laughed, "we
ought to be satisfied."

"Don't go out tonight, Stanley," Asa broke in. Why
was he obliged to plead with his children for their own
happiness?

"But is anybody ever satisfied?" Stanley retorted,
brushing him lightly aside.

"Some of us are." There was a roughened edge to
Roy's usually charming voice.

"I believe nobody is ever really satisfied," Stanley replied tartly.

"But that doesn't keep it from being true." Roy's hand
was trembling as she put down her fork.

"Do you think you're happy?"

"I know I am."

"And Craig's happy too?"

"You bet I am!" Craig exclaimed, with the air of a boy making a joke on himself.

"That's because you and Roy have got what you wanted." Stanley turned on him scornfully.

He met her eyes squarely, and Asa saw with relief that his restless gaze was candid and steady. "That's right. It's because Roy and I have everything that we want."

Virgie came in for the plates and carried them away with the half-emptied pudding dish. A minute later she brought in small cups of lukewarm coffee in white and green cups which Roy had given Lavinia last Christmas.

"Don't go out tonight, Stanley," Asa insisted.

"Oh, well . . ." She glanced round with her air of a lost child. "Perhaps I shan't after all."

"We must go now," Roy said, jumping up and reaching for her small beaded bag from the end of the table. "Everybody says the first part is the best."

Stanley's wandering gaze came back to her. "That's like everything else. Isn't the first part always the best?"

Why, in God's name, does she do it? Asa asked himself desperately. Why does anybody do anything? Why was acrimony more vocal than amiability? Why was life a perpetual discord when, with far less effort and less nervous waste, it might become a serene harmony? Why, in spite of every opportunity to possess and to enjoy the world, did human nature persist in acting like human nature?

"You're wrong again, Stanley." Craig had risen from his chair and was staring blankly down into her upraised eyes. "The second part is sometimes so much better that it makes all the beginning look like moonshine."

III

WHY do you act this way, Stanley? Why do you like to make other people unhappy?"

The front door had shut behind Roy and Craig. There was the sound of a car starting off from the curb. Through the open windows of the living room Asa could see two bare dark heads vanishing, in Craig's car, under the drooping boughs of the maples. "Why is it?" he repeated; and turned to look at his perplexing child in the dim lamplight, which gave him an outline, a shadow, a faint projection.

"What makes you do it?" he demanded more harshly. Anger flared up in him. He wanted to shake her into her senses, into a better mood; and at the same time he longed to see the light and color bloom again in her face, which was so empty of everything else.

Stanley's eyebrows gathered over her lowered eyes. "I can't bear it," she replied obstinately. "I can't bear to see other people happy when I'm so—so miserable." She sank into a chair and looked up at him, while the slow tears welled over her eyelids and rolled down her cheeks. "Can't you see that I have to do it or—or scream myself hoarse? Can't you see that I'll go out of my mind if I sit still and watch other people make love? Can't you see?"

He nodded, half in sympathy, half in smothered exasperation. "I can see that you're suffering. I suppose it's suffering that makes you so hard and self-centered." But she had always been like that, he reminded himself. As hard a center had been covered by her happiness as by her misery.

"I wish I could fly," she said. "I wish I were rich enough to buy a plane of my own."

"You cannot fly away from life, my dear."

"It would help. Even driving a car helps."

"And it might hurt too. You're the kind to crash sooner or later."

"But I can't just sit still and wait for unhappiness to come to an end. It takes too long to forget."

"Long? It seems to me there's no remembering in your whole generation. You needn't worry about that. The best part of your life was not, as you said to Craig, the beginning of it."

She was looking at him through a withdrawn gaze, an inward absorption, and for a moment, he wondered whether she had heard what he was saying. Then, before he could finish his sentence, she spoke in a breathless voice, tumbling her words on each other, as if they could not move quickly enough for the impulse behind them. "Were you always as hard up as you are now, Father? Didn't you ever have any more money?"

He shook his head with a wry smile. "Not to speak of. I made a hundred dollars a week once, but that was in the boom years. When the depression came, it flattened me out for good." Roy, he remembered, had asked him this question not long before—but how differently! "Your Uncle William," he continued after a pause, "would tell you that I was cut out of small cloth."

"Uncle William is big, isn't he?"

"Big enough. I've never felt, somehow, that I ever got to the bottom of your Uncle William."

She stirred impatiently. "Why doesn't he do more for us? It wouldn't hurt him to do more."

"He has done a great deal, Stanley. Not many rich relatives are so generous."

"Oh, I know, but he could do more without feeling it. He could send me away somewhere. To England . . . or anywhere. . . . Will you ask him, Father? Will you tell him the doctor thinks it is what I need?"

"Why not ask him yourself?"

"Oh, I have asked him. I ask him every time I see him. But all he says is that England may go to war. . . ."

"He is right. Nobody knows. . . . But if Hitler invades Poland . . ."

"Well, I don't care." She shook her head stubbornly. "There're worse things than war. Think what a good time so many girls had in Paris when we were fighting the last war."

"Have you ever thought what war means?"

"Oh, it's terrible, but is has nothing to do with me. And they've talked this way, now, for months. . . ."

He sighed as he turned his gaze away from her to the window. "I'm not sure," he said grimly, "that it wouldn't do you good to be caught in some actuality from which you couldn't escape."

"But a lot of people do like fighting, you know. Look at the way so many young men tried to get over to Spain. Wouldn't Craig have gone if it had lasted?"

"So he says."

"Anyhow, he wanted to go. Didn't he say that a battle for civilization was coming, and he wanted to be on the right side?"

"Well, we're not talking about Craig. Craig may be muddled, but he's fine. And aren't you all muddled? Do you know what you think? Do you even know what you want?"

"Oh, I know very well what I want."

"Can you tell me?"

"Happiness. I want happiness. . . . Oh, Father, I'm so wretched! I'm so terribly wretched. . . ."

His gaze wandered back to her and roved on again. "I don't want to preach to you, God knows, but you're suffering now from the delusion of your own importance. The world is in a state of panic. Yet you can think of

nothing but your own grief. . . . And not even of your grief—for you are trying to run away from that—but of your craving for happiness. . . ."

"Oh, but, Father, I've nothing to do with the world! I have only one life. . . ." Then her tone changed, and she looked up at him pleadingly. "Will you ask Uncle William?"

He shook his head. "I never asked him for anything in my life."

"But you might for me."

"Not even for you. Your mother is the one to speak to him."

"She won't help me. She says he is worried about his health and it would only irritate him."

"Well, I expect she knows."

"It isn't only that with Mother. She wants to keep me here. She likes to see widows mourn."

"But you aren't mourning."

"She thinks I ought to. Everybody thinks I ought to. That's what I hate in Queenborough. And the worst of it is that I can't mourn. I simply can't, Father."

He frowned over amused eyes. "It's all ridiculous," he said. "The whole social order, here, there, and everywhere, is ridiculous."

"Oh, make him let me go away, Father." She shivered as if from cold, and clutched his arm as he bent over her. "Tell him that I must go away before Roy's marriage. I can't stand a wedding."

"You won't have to look on."

"But there isn't any getting away. Weddings are all over the place. Don't you remember how it was when Craig and I . . . when Craig and I . . . ."

"I remember, but they won't be married till October. That's some time away."

"Why did they wait? They might have been married as soon as they knew they wanted each other."

"Maybe they wanted to be certain. Some people do."

"They'll never be certain. Nobody is ever certain. But they felt they had to put it off again when Peter died. . . . Poor Peter. . . . There wasn't really any sense in that. They might just as well have gone off quietly together and come back married."

"Perhaps they wanted to be proper. Some people do."

"Not Craig, and not Roy. They've never cared what anybody thought of them. . . . But you will see Uncle William?"

"I'll see him, my child, but I can't promise to ask him. And you must remember that he has many anxieties. He is concerned over this recent threat from Japan, and I imagine that William will always need as careful handling as an Oriental situation."

"What does Japan matter? Japan is so far away."

"Well, but he has all Europe, too, on his mind. Do you know what happens when a quite serious situation encounters a specially solid mind?"

"Oh, Father, won't you please try to be sensible when you talk to him?"

"I shall attempt it, my dear, even though to do that is not easy for my flighty nature."

But William was away for a month; and in all that weary time Stanley drooped and wilted while she studied her features in the triple mirror between the two windows in her room. "What's the use?" she asked her mother, who had limped in to look for her one morning. "What's the use in living when there's nothing to do?"

"Have patience, darling. Just try to have patience."

"If there is one virtue I despise," Stanley retorted furiously, "it is patience."

"What do you want to do?"

"I want to go away. I want to go somewhere I've never been before and see people I've never known."

"What good would that do you?"

"All the good in the world. Oh, Mother, if only I can get away from Queenborough, I can make a new life!"

"When you talk like this," Lavinia sighed, wiping her damp brow with bay rum, "I'm almost tempted to ask your Uncle William to send you away . . . not to England, that's out of the question, but somewhere . . . else . . . perhaps to California. . . ."

Light appeared to fall on the mirror into which Stanley was gazing. "Oh, Mother, darling, if you only would!" she exclaimed. Change or animation was the breath of life to her. Though she moved disconsolately from room to room and down the stairs to her meals, she would return flushed and glowing from the lonely drives in her car.

"Have you noticed," Asa inquired of Lavinia the next morning, when he brought her a cup of early coffee, "that Stanley is prettier than she ever was?"

Lavinia assented. "Yes, I've wondered about it. Poor child, it seems that grief isn't always unbecoming."

Asa glanced at her sharply. "If you call it grief. . . ."

"Well, don't you? She has certainly suffered." There was an uneasy note in Lavinia's voice, and she continued hurriedly: "Anyhow, I wish you'd see William as soon as he comes home. You might sound him, even if you don't ask him."

"Where has he been?"

"Charlotte told me not to speak of it, but he has gone to see some specialist in New York. She says he is very much frightened about himself."

"I thought he looked rather seedy."

"He's had that ulcer in his stomach for a long time, but he has never let Dr. Buchanan make a proper examination. Charlotte says he was afraid of what the doctor might tell him. It's queer, isn't it? A big, strong man like William, who has always been the picture of health. I

mean, it's queer that he should be so frightened of doctors."

"I suppose the stronger men are, the more they dread illness."

"Charlotte says he turns positively green at the thought of an operation. He's even given up his toddy, and for the last six months he hasn't drunk anything but milk and water."

"Well, I'm sorry," Asa said. But was he sorry? In a suffering world could he afford to waste any real sympathy upon William? Not that it mattered. For thirty years they had cultivated the pretense—he satirically, and Lavinia piously—that they both loved and respected William and would both be distressed when he died. Never once in all that time had they torn apart or frayed away so much as a shred of this pretense. He had lacked the courage, or the cruelty, to strip Lavinia clean of hypocrisy and lay bare the naked form of her subterfuge. Now, for one searing instant of truth, they looked into each other's unguarded eyes, while the screen of evasion shriveled to ashes. She will be glad when William dies, he thought; and I—I shall be glad, too; and I wonder whether even Charlotte will be sorry. For no one, he told himself, would really regret William, least of all the men he had helped to make wealthy. . . .

After that one revealing glance, Lavinia lowered her eyes and turned on a sermon over the radio. Yet why did he feel ashamed? Asa asked himself defiantly, as he left the room. Why should anybody be interested in keeping William alive?

Toward the end of August, when William at last returned, he was preoccupied neither with the Oriental situation nor the European threat of war, but with his own physical organs. After an examination and a discouraging medical verdict, in New York, he had rushed to a second

consultation in Baltimore. For months he had tried to evade a mortal disease by refusing to recognize its existence; and not until fear triumphed over his embattled will had he renounced the power of faith and invoked the concrete miracles of science. Though he feared an operation, he feared death infinitely more. That ancient adversary of life had been always his chief terror. And now, since he could no longer pretend it away, he was plunging into a desperate flight from the inevitable.

All this, Charlotte told Asa when she met him one afternoon, under a clouded sky, in a strong moist wind. "I wanted to prepare you," she said, "before you saw him. He has had a blow, and he isn't the same man." She shivered slightly from the dampness, drew her light wrap about her, and said in an uneven voice, "It is hard to believe that summer isn't yet over."

"Is the trouble more serious than William suspected?"

"Nobody knows what he suspected. He wouldn't face the symptoms until it was too late. He is so terribly headstrong, and Dr. Buchanan helped him pretend that it wasn't . . . it wasn't . . ." She still hesitated to pronounce the word lest an evil spell should be cast.

"Can they operate?"

"He doesn't know, but they say he's too old. After the examination in New York, he insisted on going to Johns Hopkins. I joined him there and talked with the doctors. He is going back in a week."

"Then he hasn't really given up hope?"

"Nobody knows. He's been in a kind of panic ever since he found out that—that it is malignant."

"Yes, yes. . . ." Here was tragedy in the midst of all the more lavish blessings of fate. A little while before, Asa had told himself that Charlotte would not regret William; but she seemed to him, while her face worked convulsively, to be heartbroken with grief and compassion. Women, he meditated, are strange beings. Had she loved William in

spite of his neglect, in spite of the brutal tyranny which he
had exercised over her life? She had aged, Asa thought,
ten years since he last saw her. Her features had fallen in,
and the sunken muscles gave to her large face an expression of hopeless desuetude, as if it were an imperfect
mask ruined in the modeling. Well, but she might have
had her own reasons, imperceptible to a spectator, for
loving her husband. Human emotions might be as inexplicable as human motives.

"Would he rather not see me?" Asa asked, while his
gaze swept the brilliant gardens in search of some hidden
strength to be wrung from external possessions. William
had had everything that other men admire and envy; and
yet here he was, at the end, defeated and destroyed, not
by any outward antagonist, but by a secreted group of
hostile cells within his own body.

"No, he expects you. But you mustn't be hurt if he
seems glum and moody. Sometimes he won't answer me
till I've asked him over and over. You know how he used
to enjoy laying down the law as long as.nobody disputed.
Now and then, he forgets and begins to bluster almost as
he used to do. But most of the time he just sits and
broods till my heart bleeds for him." Her mild eyes overflowed, and she choked over her unuttered words.

"Does he still worry over the state of the world . . .
or the country?"

"I don't believe he ever gives that a thought. Somebody in Baltimore tried to divert him by asking if he
thought there would be a war, and all he replied was, 'I
haven't thought. It doesn't matter, does it?'" She sighed
and wiped her eyes. "It's beyond belief what sickness can
do to a strong man."

Yes, it was beyond belief, Asa acknowledged. All that
will to power, that dynamic egoism, that arrogance of
success—all this was subject, now, to the unconscious energy of disease.

"Nothing seems to make any difference to him," Charlotte was muttering. "You remember how eager he used to be to get the first news from the stock market. Well, he hasn't been to his office since he came home, and when they telephone him, he doesn't pretend to be interested. Even that bad failure in New York the other day didn't make any impression."

"A death sentence," Asa said. "Yes, I suppose a jolt like that would make a man stop and think."

Charlotte turned toward the house, and he walked slowly beside her. "I never looked upon William as a pious person," she remarked in a more casual tone, "but as soon as he heard this verdict, he seemed anxious to make his peace with the next world. Only, poor soul, he doesn't know exactly how to set about doing it."

"It would be difficult, I imagine."

"Of course, you'd think it superstition. It may be, but the idea has taken hold on his mind."

"All I think, my dear, is that it might have begun sooner—or later."

She assented reasonably enough, and Asa suspected that, though she might love William, she had retained no illusions concerning him. "You mean he's been a hard man? Yes, I've spent many a sleepless night over the people he has driven to ruin and even to suicide. That was the way big business worked, he used to say, and if you were white-livered or squeamish, you'd better stay out of it. I couldn't help wondering whether that was in his mind yesterday when he sent a check for a hundred thousand dollars to the Episcopal Orphanage. It seemed so pathetic," she added with a sob, "that I almost cried." Then, as Asa could still find nothing to say, she continued in a low, panting voice: "I can't help thinking all the time that it ought to have been me. I've lived in dread for years, and I never had a pain in my breast that I didn't think of the way my mother had gone. But the doctor says

now that the stabbing pain is only chronic indigestion . . .
and poor William . . ."

Asa reached for her hand, which felt as soft and cool
and nerveless as a jellyfish, and patted it tenderly before
he slipped it under his arm. There had always been, he
thought, something touching about Charlotte. "It is often
that way," he said presently, fumbling in his mind for a
phrase so well worn that its edges were smoothed off.
"The thing we fear passes us by and strikes in a new
place." As she did not speak again until they had reached
the house, he inquired as cheerfully as he could, "Where
is William?"

"In his sitting room upstairs." Still wiping her reddened eyelids, she smiled bravely. "He is trying to
straighten out some of his affairs before he goes back to
Baltimore. I never knew before," her voice had dropped
to a whisper, "that hope fills out so much of our bodies as
well as our minds. You'd scarcely believe anybody could
fall off so rapidly."

Yes, it was true, Asa decided a few minutes later, he
should hardly have known William. From the dark sunset
a last ray of light pointed to a wasted figure sagging
against a fine Chinese Chippendale secretary. It appeared incredible that a few weeks should so completely
have crushed and deflated any man, especially a stalwart
and indomitable and gusty fellow like William. Stuffed
with wind, Asa found himself thinking.

"Here's Asa," Charlotte chirped, while William lifted
his sunken eyes and fixed a deep, panic-stricken gaze on
his visitor. The fear of death is worse than death itself,
Asa reflected as he held out his hand. If only he could get
rid of the fear, there would be nothing to dread.

"Well, I've pegged out," William said in the whim-
pering tone of a hurt child. "I've come to my end, Asa."

"And I may be run over on my way down the street,"
Asa rejoined briskly. "The doctors aren't always right,

you know," he added, on what he felt to be a note of distasteful hypocrisy. "After all, an operation isn't so bad nowadays as it used to be."

William scowled. "It ain't an operation," he retorted, with the naked candor of despair. "It's a bad end." Though he dreaded an unspeakable fate, he was stripped of the last vestige of his old blustering deception. In his hour of defeat he made no effort to avert the blow as it fell; and something vague yet majestic in his attitude reminded Asa of the brutal nobility of a wounded, dying bull.

"If the doctors decide to operate, they must see some hope for you."

"They haven't decided. If they don't, they give me a year at the most," William replied, with an aimless circular gesture, as if he were sweeping up and casting away the remains of an illusion.

"Well, doctors don't know everything. Look at old Judge Honeywell. Didn't they give him up ten years ago?"

"That's right. They know mighty little. But, somehow, what they do know for certain is always the worst. . . ." His doomed aspect was convulsed by an inward upheaval, and Asa thought for an instant that William would burst into tears. "I've done a lot of things in my life," he confessed, with a kind of sullen regret, "but when I come to look back on 'em now, I'll be dashed if I don't seem to have done most of 'em the wrong way."

"That's natural enough. All of us feel like that, I suspect, when we look back over our lives."

"It takes a jolt," William continued, as if he were not listening, "to make a man see that owning things ain't everything in the world. I've managed to pile up a good bit of property here and there; but when the time comes to go, I can't take a single piece of it with me." He broke off for a long minute, and glared at them in silence. "I reckon you two think that I believed money was every-

thing," he burst out angrily, "but you were wrong, both of you! I never set so much store by owning things. What I wanted was power. And in my part of the world, or in any part of the world, show me another thing that equals the power of money! No, sir, I'd had a hard life, and I had to get even with the people around me. I had to prove to them that I was bigger than all of them put together. If I believed in money—damn it to hell!—it was because there was nothing else to believe in."

"You've done good in your time, William," Charlotte broke in appeasingly. "I've never known you to refuse a cause you thought worthy."

"There she goes," William muttered under his breath. "Gabble, gabble, gabble. Women seem to think they can make black look white by gabbling about it."

"Well, it's true, and you know it. You aren't nearly so hard-grained as you like to pretend. You may say what you please, but the Lord knows it."

"The Lord ain't a fool, Charlotte."

"You've been generous to all of us," Asa reminded him. "I don't know how Lavinia could have managed without you. And Stanley . . . Think of the difference you have made in Stanley's life. . . ."

A scowl beetled William's fierce eyebrows. "And what good did that do anybody?" he demanded. "Not a bit. Not a bit of good in the world."

Asa shook his head, for it was all he could think of to do. "You don't know. You never can tell."

"That's true," Charlotte agreed eagerly. "I could tell you a number of things . . ."

"Gabble, gabble," William pecked at her in the manner of a plucked and enfeebled bird of prey. As he waved his splotched and stringy hand, once so merciless in its strength, a sensation of pity stabbed through Asa's fortified mind. What William had been in his prime made no difference in the final pathos of his decay. The tragic

sequence of life and death appeared to obliterate, by its magnitude, the mere personal element. Yet, after all, William had lived the life he desired; he had felt power; and he had excelled in that special spirit of ruthlessness which the youth of today so highly regarded.

"There's time enough yet," Asa suggested, "and plenty of good works lying around."

"That's why I put off the hospital," William replied, with the first sign of mastery over himself. "I told them I couldn't rest easy till I'd put my affairs in better order. It's life or death, I said, in the matter of property. That's why they let me off for a week. They were dead set against it, but I wouldn't give in," he concluded proudly, with the triumphant air of one who has bargained successfully with the Everlasting Purpose.

"He will have to stay quite awhile in the hospital," Charlotte said soothingly. "They may keep him a month or six weeks."

A crafty humor flickered in William's glance. "I've got a few matters to straighten out," he resumed, as if his wife had not spoken. "I was always so busy forging ahead that I never stopped to bother about what would come after me. It seemed to me, I reckon, that other people had to end sometime, but I'd keep going on. Then, while I was lying up there at Johns Hopkins, with nothing to bother about but my damned insides, it crossed my mind that I hadn't done a thing in the world about getting the better of the inheritance taxes. Not that you can do much. Since the government has put a tax on what we give away, there's no safety left even in trust funds. But it worried me a lot to think that, if I didn't come through, a good part of what I'd worked for and saved up would go the way those windbags in Washington wanted it to. And that, sir, ain't likely to be any way I would choose."

"Oh, William," Charlotte wailed, "what do we care what becomes of your money?"

"Do you hear her?" William inquired, with a kind of indulgent derision. "Do you hear what she says?"

"She is thinking about you."

"She's got some sense, but no business sense," William said. "Did you ever know a woman who had a grain of sense about business?"

"Well, I've known Lavinia. She has a good head for business, and puts me to shame every week."

"She's kin to me," William replied proudly. "Yes, Lavinia has a level head on her shoulders. That's why I'm going to see that she gets taken care of. She knows how to handle money without letting it slip through her fingers. To tell the truth, Asa," he continued after drawing a deep breath, "it's the thought of Lavinia that's been plaguing me. I ain't worrying about Charlotte. She will have more money than she knows what to do with, even if the government goes on robbing her as long as she lives. But I never bargained on Lavinia's outlasting me, and when all's said and done, your kin is your kin, and blood is thicker than water. You see, the way I'd fixed things was to leave the money outright to your children—and to give them just enough, but not too much, so that it wouldn't upset them. I don't hold with the extravagant ideas of young folks today, and I'd tied up pretty tight what I left. . . . But it came over me, lying up there in the hospital, that Lavinia was going to outlive me after all, and that was one of the reasons I came home. The first thing I did this morning was to get hold of Baker and make him arrange a comfortable little income for her before I died." He chuckled maliciously under his breath. "I'll feel easier, anyway, to know that she ain't counting too heavily on my death. . . ."

"You mean, then . . ." Asa's question broke off on an incredulous note. That William should voluntarily loosen his clutch on his money, and relinquish the satisfaction of doling out alms, bit by bit, was the last thing

Asa had ever anticipated. Yet, even before his mind had accepted the fact, his more impressionable senses recoiled from the shock of surprise. A wave of exultation swept over him, and he felt rather than thought: So it has come at last—freedom! I am no longer necessary. I may live my own life while I am young enough to find happiness. "You mean . . ." he jerked out and stopped, because he could credit neither his mind nor his emotion.

William thrust out his lower lip, with the spoiled pout of a child that has dropped a rattle. It was the look, Asa recognized abruptly, that Stanley had inherited as the single flaw in her beauty. "Baker is attending to it. I've told him to see Lavinia tomorrow. . . ." He sputtered angrily. "No, not tomorrow. Isn't tomorrow Sunday, Charlotte?"

"Yes, William. Tomorrow is the last Sunday in August."

"Are you sure you shan't regret it?" Asa asked.

The old man shook his head. "No, I'm not sure. I'm not sure of a thing in this world. But it won't be a big regret, anyway. The bulk of what I've made is going for something I never had, and have felt the pinch many a time of not having. You'll be surprised to hear what that is, I reckon, but it's education. There weren't many schools down in the Northern Neck when I was a boy making my way on a farm, and my eldest brother, Maxwelton, who went into the war when he was fifteen and fought four years, never got any farther than reading and writing and doing a few easy sums. You'd have thought he was a poor white to look at him, but I tell you, sir, he had some of the best blood in Virginia. Poor as Job's turkey, but his folks came over in 1619, and one of them was the younger son of an earl. Not that bragging about blood cuts any ice with me. I was never one to trade on your ancestors, good or bad. It's not blood, but

guts, that gets you on in the world, and even education can't do anything for a man if he hasn't the right stuff."

"Well, you must have had the right stuff."

"Yes, I got on, but I had a hard road. Even now, I don't like to look back on what I went through. . . ."

Charlotte, who had slipped out, came in with a glass of milk and stood patiently at his elbow. "It's time for your milk, William."

"Damn the milk!" William blustered; but he took the glass from her hand and began sipping it slowly.

"He's been better ever since he went on his milk diet," Charlotte said soothingly.

"Chatter, chatter," William snapped back, with sarcastic patience. Though he was trying to curb his biting tongue, Asa found himself wondering why marriage should so frequently develop a grated instead of a softened edge? Charlotte was the one and only human being to whom William could turn for affection or sympathy; yet her faithfulness—or was it his dependence upon her?—appeared only to have worn his tough-fibered nerves to the breaking point.

"Are you sure you won't regret what you do?" Asa repeated. "You may have many years ahead in which to think over things."

"Well, I've made up my mind. Anyway, I've made up my mind about Lavinia."

"It will mean a great deal to her and the children. But all of them, I know, would rather have you recover your health." That's not true, he thought, and then: Well, no matter. . . .

William chuckled, not maliciously, but with the aloof, impersonal mockery of an indifferent fate. "I'm not so sure," he retorted, with an impish twist to his lip. "But I'm not giving her anything to throw away on the chil-

dren. The fact is, Asa, I don't think any too well of those children of yours."

Asa shook his head. "You must remember you've done your best to spoil Stanley."

"That's right, I did," William snorted. "She was easy to look at when you were feeling hefty and strong; but Charlotte over there is worth six of her when you're down in the mouth."

"Oh, William!" Charlotte sniffed, and buried her face in her handkerchief.

"There, there," William grumbled impatiently. I'm not soft-soaping you, so you needn't begin to blubber."

Well, at least he was honest, Asa reflected, and honesty is a dignified, if not an endearing, virtue. A disagreeable old man at best, yet he had his quality. "You may tell Lavinia that Baker will stop by on Monday." William's tone had altered to one of business astuteness. "If I should go off under the knife, she won't have to worry about where her next meal is coming from. I'm not giving her money enough to hurt, but Baker will take care of her before the rest of them start wrangling over what I've done in my will. She'll be safe, even if one of these shyster lawyers gets his clutches on Charlotte. . . ."

"William, William!" Charlotte was sobbing aloud.

"I was poking fun, Lottie. I must have my fun, even with one foot in the grave." Then the old man turned back to Asa. "I always liked Lavinia," he said, "in spite of her cracked notions about sickness, when she's as strong as a mule."

"She's proud of you," Asa replied truthfully. "I believe she admires you more than she does anyone in the world."

"Well, she may have her foolishness, but she's of the right kidney. That's why I'm thinking of her and not of the young ones. To tell the truth, I'm about sick of the way the young folks are taking everything to themselves.

All I can see is that they're making a mess of the world, like their elders before 'em."

"It does look that way, but I suppose it's hard to push against the stream of your age. And isn't the age itself moving over the rapids?"

"It's all wrong," William muttered. "It's against nature, if you want to know what I think."

Well, he didn't want to know, Asa mused, not particularly, though there was nothing he could do but listen to a man who was willing to provide him with freedom and his wife with an annuity. I wonder why I've stood it, he thought bitterly. Why should his credulous generation have been left alone to hold the bag of family responsibility? Not one of these insurgent modern young would have endured thirty years of the life he had borne with Lavinia. And how did he know that this disorderly youth of the present was not wiser than he had been in his time? Right or wrong, I have finished with convention, he resolved passionately. I have finished with mistaken self-sacrifice; I have broken, here and now, with the tradition that man has made and destroyed. . . . Aloud, he said abruptly, "I wonder where they are going? To a safer place, it may be, than ours."

"Going? Who? Where?" William ejaculated. "Oh, you mean all these wild young fools of today. Well, I don't know, and if you'll take my word for it, I've stopped caring. The truth is, they've stopped being important. Stanley isn't important. That came over me, lying back there in my bed in the hospital. All this everlasting fuss about what is and what isn't right has been going on since before Adam, and it will never be decided, one way or another. Swans or geese, black or white, old or young, they don't matter. No, sir, they don't matter a jot or tittle."

"Stanley has always been fond of you."

"She's always been fond of what she could get out of

me," William replied testily. Then, after pursing his lip in a moment of calculation, he added shrewdly: "I'm wondering what she's trying to wheedle out of me now. I knew she had something up her sleeve as soon as she began to palaver over the telephone. Then, when she found out I wasn't the easy game that I used to be, I reckon she sent you up here to see what you could make of me. . . ."

"Why, William!" Charlotte gasped in distress.

"Well, I may be old, Lottie, but I'm not an old fool. . . ."

"Stanley is very unhappy," Asa rejoined defiantly.

"Unhappy?" William blustered. "Who's happy? Am I happy? Is Charlotte happy? Who'd think you were happy to look at you?"

"Well, she doesn't know that. She thinks you have everything to make happiness. She hadn't heard of your illness."

"And she won't hear of it. I won't have you and Lavinia raising any hopes of my death."

"We shan't tell her. You have a right to your secrets. Lavinia will understand."

"She'd better. Good God, rather than have those rattle-brained brats watching for my death, like kittens beside a mousehole. . . ."

"William . . ." Charlotte opened her mouth and shut it quickly again before his stare of bleak ridicule.

"You can't accuse Roy of that," Asa retorted. "Roy doesn't think about your money any more than I do. For all we care," he added, losing his head with a vague sense of astonishment, "you may give the last cent of it to the Episcopal Orphanage!" That wasn't strictly accurate, he admitted, but, then, righteous indignation is seldom literal.

A blank silence followed, while he thought with

amazement: So I've done it at last! After all these years I've let myself go! Then, as his wonder deepened, he saw a glint of humor sparkle in William's hard little eyes, and heard a subdued cynical chuckle.

"I may, may I?" the old man mumbled; "but what about education? You needn't think just because I've made fun of it . . ."

Asa laughed. "I'd forgotten education. But I don't care a rap what you do."

"You don't, eh?"

"I don't, and you know it." His voice still quivered from anger—or was it merely relief?

"Well, I know it," William growled, as if he were answering his own question. "You don't have to tell me. And, bless my soul," he resumed, after a grumbling pause, "that's the reason I like you! You may not know it, but that's why I'm doing the best I can for you in taking Lavinia off your hands. I like Lavinia. I'm fond of her in a way. She's my kin, but I wouldn't be in your shoes, not for—not for all the money I've scraped together. No, sir, I tell you now that's not the kind of job I'd have chosen."

Asa looked at him with expressionless eyes. "You chose your job, and I didn't. A man never knows. . . ."

"That's right. A man never knows; and it's a good thing he doesn't. . . . Not that I cared. Money was what I wanted, and I got it by hook or crook. But money can't buy off cancer inside of you. . . ."

"William, William . . ."

"Shut up, Charlotte. I know what I know. I'm going to face the music whenever I hear it. I'm not pretending I ain't scared, but being scared to death won't make me pull the wool over my eyes. That's what I call grit, and that's why I like this man Lavinia caught and married. He's not bright enough to set James River on fire, but he

[347]

has grit. You mark my words, when the time comes, you'll find he has more grit than all the rest of 'em put together. . . ."

Asa sprang up from his chair, because he felt that he could sit still and listen no longer. A repellent old man, he thought, but, in some queer way, invulnerable.

IV

SO WILLIAM is dying, Asa thought as he turned the corner at Westward Avenue. William, who has had —or appears to have had—everything he wanted, is dying at last. Well, everybody dies, sooner or later, Roy would remind him with the pointed mockery and unerring aim of the modern mind. And, after all, why did old people make so much fuss about death? When all was said, Uncle William had got more than he ever deserved; and it was only fair that, in his overripe eighties, he should retire from the stage, and make room for the struggling youth that had nothing to live on but the hope of an inheritance. The argument, when she came to make it, would carry conviction. That, he reflected impatiently was an annoying trait in the attitude of the present. Its eye was too sharp, and its destructive instinct too frequently sound. . . .

But when Roy and Craig opened the door on their way out, he recalled in time his solemn promise to William. "Your Uncle William has come back," he said. "I thought he looked very ill. You'd better stop and inquire for him as you go by."

"Shall we, Craig?" Roy asked.

"Not on your life, darling. I'm not after his money."

"Good for you!" She was laughing happily. "You haven't a beggar's chance of ever seeing a penny of it."

"That's right with me. Stanley has worked hard for it, and I only hope she may live long enough to enjoy it."

Asa smiled tolerantly. How cocksure they were of their new wisdom! "You may be surprised," he said, "if anything can surprise you."

"Nothing, Dad, that Uncle William could do," Roy tossed back gaily, "unless, which isn't likely, he were to turn about and begin doing good."

[349]

Asa's smile froze. "If you knew how I dislike that tone, daughter."

"Well, Uncle William isn't God."

"Someday you may be sorry, Roy."

"I'm sure to be, old dear. I'm always sorry. And Craig's sorry, too, about everything everywhere.

For a long moment, while they stood smiling at one another, Asa looked from Roy to Craig and from Craig back to Roy. The younger man still remained more or less of a mystery; and Asa had sometimes wondered whether Craig's charm concealed a deeper obscurity. It was true that Craig loved justice, that he loved truth; but did he love them enough? Was he still entangled, as the more selfish Peter had been, in a conflict of thwarted impulses and personal motives? If only he had been more high-minded or less large-hearted!

"It seems to me that we can afford to be grateful," Asa said at last—not that it made the slightest difference to him, but because he could think of no other remark that fitted so neatly into the wordless space.

"But why?" Craig demanded, in his argumentative tone. "Isn't gratitude one of the baser virtues?"

Well, that did no good; they simply couldn't connect, Asa thought. There was too wide a distance between them, and the intervening years appeared to be filled with mere vacancy. He turned back to Roy, and noticed that the scarlet feather in her hat matched the curve of her lips. It is extraordinary what happiness can do to a face, he reflected, especially that swift flamelike rapture of those who are living in the immediate moment alone. "I've had a flat life," he said to himself as they parted and he entered the house, "but when I see Roy's happiness, I know I'd go through it again."

He had intended to have a frank discussion with Lavinia before he met Stanley's reproaches; for a frank discussion with Lavinia, though seldom agreeable, was

usually bracing. But his foot had barely touched the stairs when Stanley slipped out of the living room and caught his arm in an eager grasp.

"I've been waiting for you." she whispered. "I've been waiting for hours."

"Not for hours. I came straight home, but a bus travels slowly."

"Will he do it? Will he send me away? If he won't . . ."

"Stop a minute. Let me tell you. I can't tell you if you won't listen."

"Then he won't. I might have known he wouldn't. Oh, I might have known he'd be hateful."

As they turned into the living room, she moved over to the open window, and he saw her face lit up by the flashing quicksilver gleam of a sudden shower. In that fugitive light she looked, he thought, too intensely alive. Yet she felt wasted, he knew; she felt starved for joy; she felt clipped and caged and desperate.

"Try to be fair, Stanley," he said. "Remember all your Uncle William has done for you."

"How does that help me now? If he has stopped . . . what good does that do me now?"

"He's not well. When he gets back his health, he may see differently."

"I wish he'd die. If only he'd die . . . but he won't. He'll live on until I'm old and too miserable to care any longer."

He tried to smile, but failed helplessly. "This is the first time you've been crossed. Until now you have taken everything that you wanted."

"Well, I've had to. If I hadn't taken what I wanted, how should I have got it? You have to fight for yourself if you want anything."

"Well, you can't fight your Uncle William. All you can do is to wheedle, and it strikes me he's past that sort of

treatment just now. Wait until he's himself again and feeling his oats. There are times, though you'll never believe it, when waiting is the best policy."

"You don't know," she cried angrily, and burst into tears. "You don't know how it feels to be wasting your life."

There was a sudden chill in his heart, a streak of ice, as he looked at her. With all the piled-up agony in the world, with all the pain and the bitterness and the destruction which she had caused, had nothing ever made the faintest dent in her armor of egoism? Is there any hope for humanity? he thought. Is there any hope of making a civilized world so long as we are imprisoned in a multitude of separate cells? "Why are you so sure?" he asked. "How do you know what I have felt?"

Her face quivered, and she looked up at him through a rain of tears. "You're cruel. Oh, you're cruel, all of you! Even Mother, who used to love me best, has turned against me since I came home."

The chill melted within, and the old irrational softness invaded his thoughts. She would always win in the end, not with him alone, but with other men also; and she would win, he told himself, not through strength, but through some inner weakness, whether her own or another's. "Try to be patient a little longer, and I'll see what I can do," he said gently.

"If only you knew how I hate Queenborough!"

"But it is your home. Everyone feels for you and tries to be sympathetic."

"I don't want sympathy. I want a life of my own."

"I know, my child, and I will do what I can. I will talk to your mother."

But he found, to his astonishment, that Lavinia had hardened her heart, or her mind, against Stanley. When he went into her room, she looked up from the evening paper and remarked with an undercurrent of pleasant

excitement: "Isn't it splendid about Uncle William? Mr. Baker stopped in for a few minutes on his way from the office. He is coming again on Monday or Tuesday."

"Yes, I know. William told me."

"Did he tell you how much it would be?"

"Enough to make you comfortable without spoiling your character. The bulk of his fortune, or so he hinted, is going for education. . . ."

"Education?" Lavinia gasped. "Why, what in the world? He never had any."

"That may be the reason. Don't we always value the thing we've been able to do without?"

"Maybe I can have a car, a little car," Lavinia was murmuring, "with somebody to drive it. I've always wanted a car."

"So have I," Asa rejoined tartly, and thought of the long wait and the slow journey on the trolley, winter or summer. "Anyway," he added abruptly, "you won't need me any longer."

She looked up with a laugh. "Not need you?"

"I mean . . ." He broke off, hesitated, and went on again, with one of those rash impulses which had grown on him in middle age, "I mean . . . well, I sometimes want a life of my own too. . . ."

"Why, Asa!" There was a note of ridicule in her voice. "You talk as if you were young."

"I'll never be any younger than I am now."

"Yes, I know." Her tone was more sympathetic. "It's the time of life, I suppose. That feeling comes in middle age, but it doesn't last."

He shook his head. "Even then, it may last longer than some other things. I want . . ." he began and bit back the word. "No, I won't tell you now. After all, William may change his mind in the night."

"That isn't likely." She removed her shell-rimmed glasses and folded the paper. "How I wish we could tell

[353]

the children. It might make them more . . . more . . .”

"Well, I promised William, and he has a right to keep his own counsel."

"Mr. Baker said that. It's funny the horror he has —Uncle William, I mean—of people feeling sorry for him."

"He needn't worry about that," Asa retorted. "We're too busy anticipating. If he dislikes pity, he should have seen Stanley when she thought the danger was past."

"You oughtn't to say that." Lavinia's rebuke was half-hearted, and she continued uneasily, "I don't know what to think about Stanley."

"That's not my trouble. Unfortunately, I know only too well."

"She hates Queenborough, and yet the people have all been so kind to her. It may be the Southern way—I don't know—but they seem to excuse everything because she is young and has beauty. They like beauty, I suppose, more than most people."

"When your annuity, or whatever it is, begins," Asa asked, "do you think you can manage to send her away?"

Lavinia shook her head. "Not while Uncle William is living. Mr. Baker was very positive about that. He says Uncle William's whole attitude toward Stanley has changed. I am trying to make out the cause of it. But I'm sure he thinks we've spoiled her too much."

"Even so, isn't it too late in the day—or to deep in the grave—to begin over again? I should say he had done most of the spoiling."

"I couldn't tell him that." The vein of sagacity, which so often astonished him in Lavinia, hardened her face. "The truth is, I imagine, that Stanley stirred something in him, as she seems to do with every man, young or old. He liked that when he was well, and what has changed him is simply his terror of death. He's afraid of being stirred,

because he knows it isn't good for him, and he resents it when he is expected to think of anything but his own health. Oh, I'm not talking about sex!" she exclaimed, with her natural distaste for the facts of life. "But Stanley is young and full of vitality, and she represents all the things he enjoyed most and can never, even if he holds on much longer, hope to enjoy again. This is what makes him so surly and harsh. He would rather pretend that he despises all that . . . that side of life." She fixed her protruding gaze upon her husband, who was thinking with a start of dismay: I don't really know Lavinia. I don't really know anybody, not even myself.

"Maybe if she went to see him," he said aloud, "and —and tried to be different."

"He won't let her. Not yet. She drove out to Fitzroyal this morning, but Aunt Charlotte said he was too busy to see her."

"Perhaps he was. He has a lot to do before he goes back."

"Well, Stanley came home in an ugly mood. She seems to think he is tired of giving her things."

"Maybe so. You can't blame him."

"I don't blame him, but how does that help us?" Lavinia sank her voice to a frail whisper. "The matter with Stanley is that she is never content unless she is exerting her power. I mean, her power over men. When she complains of loneliness, she means there aren't any men who amuse her. Oh, I love her. She's still my baby, but I've known other women just like her. They don't mean any harm."

"And when she wants a new life?"

"She means she wants a new love affair. Nothing else would be life. I'm not saying that she's bad. She isn't bad, and when you think how men are about her, poor darling . . ." She paused, breathed heavily with a

choking sound, and added, "What worries me most is the way she drinks in her room."

A startled look crossed his face. "I thought she had promised you to stop that."

"She did promise, but Virgie brought me an empty bottle she found in Stanley's closet this morning."

"Roy must have known."

"But she wouldn't tell. They have their own mistaken sense of honor."

"Queer, isn't it?" He shook himself as if he were discarding a load. "Well, we'll have to try some other way. There's Virgie coming, and I'd better hurry and have a wash. . . . By the way, did you get any news over the radio?"

Lavinia shook her head. "Nothing interesting. The football season opened in London today." She frowned in perplexity. "I thought it was always cricket over there."

"Well, it isn't war, anyway. There's a hope, I suppose, that Hitler is bluffing."

"Mr. Baker thinks not. . . . But here's Virgie. If you get a chance, I wish you'd speak more seriously to Stanley."

He found, however, when he tried it, that speaking seriously to Stanley was less easy than Lavinia imagined. "Aren't you taking someone with you?" he asked, as she ran past him in the lower hall; but she had only shaken her bare head and darted out of the house and down the steps to the street. He saw the sprinkling of rain on her bright hair before she slipped into her car and put her hand on the wheel. A minute later, he watched her start with a slight wavering motion, and speed by the door and up the straight street under the dripping boughs. She oughtn't to go out by herself at night. It isn't safe, he thought. But what under heaven can one do with one's children?

The next afternoon a wind from the north swept a driving rain to Hunter's Fare, while Asa and Kate fed a small blaze of resinous pine knots in Kate's living room. "It's funny to need a fire the end of August," she had said, touching a match to the lightwood, "but it takes off the dampness." Then, answering his unspoken thought, she asked in a grave voice: "Will she give you up even if she no longer wants you?" It was like that, he had found, when two persons understood each other completely. Intuition plunged deeper and straighter than the faculty of pure reason.

He stood up, with a piece of resinous pine still in his hand. "I'll go like a shot as soon as she is able to do without me."

"Will she ever be able to do without you?"

"She will." He looked earnestly at Pat and Percy, drying their wet coats before the summer flame, and they gazed back as earnestly at him. "She will whenever I lose my job, or she comes into William's annuity."

"Doesn't she need you for something more? Oh, I don't mean affection. I mean habit. I mean pride. I mean, most of all, the support of an institution."

"Damn it, I don't care! I want something of my own." His eyes roved over the book-lined walls, where the swift firelight flickered and died, over the worn easy chairs, over the orange and yellow zinnias in a green bowl on the table. "It isn't as if I had maggots in the brain, or were a pathological problem. I'm not going dotty before my time. I'm not longing to fondle flappers. I don't dream of naked furies. All I ask is what any ordinary man might expect. I want to look at the fields and trees. I want to help things grow out of the ground. I want a little freedom with you and Pat and Percy and the birds and the animals on the farm. I want, most of all, somebody I can talk to without lying. Nobody who hasn't lied con-

stantly for thirty years can ever know what a luxury it is to speak the truth now and then."

Her look was candid and tender. "What you want," she said, "are all the things that civilization denies."

"Civilization! What's that?"

"Well, then, the social order."

He laughed. "There isn't any order left, social or unsocial. I come alive in this room, on this farm, nowhere else. All I ask is a bit of living before I stay dead for good."

"Do you think for a minute Lavinia will let you go?"

"I shan't ask her. I'm going to break away if I have to walk to Reno or swim to Paris."

She smiled gently and without humor. "What will your children think?"

"What right have they to think anything? Haven't they broken with tradition? Why shouldn't I?"

"You know why . . ." She clipped off her sentence and went on in a breathless tone. "Because you and your children belong to two different worlds. What they have broken is a pattern that still holds you together. . . . Your instinct still believes in all the things they have rejected, and instinct, not reason, decides a man's life in the end. The belief your mind denies is still working in your blood and your nerves. Oh, my dear, you're trying to change the very substance of yourself, and that has never been done. . . ."

"No . . . no . . ." He caught her strong, sunburned hand and drew her nearer. "I'm only trying to be myself. I'm only trying to release something that has always been there, deep down, underneath the false surface. Do you think it was natural for me to spend my life drudging? Do you know what my secret dream has always been, and is now? Not drink, not women, but escaping from family life, and from all the cities that men have made. . . . It sounds absurd, I know, but I've dreamed for years of being a hired man on a farm."

Her smile wavered. "On this farm? Well, it needs one."

"I know it does. That is a part of my dream. I want to start in before I get too old and stiff to do a day's work."

For a long pause she looked at him without speaking. There was nothing unusual in his appearance, nothing arresting in his voice or his manner. Yet his thin, slightly stooping figure, with the drawn features, the hovering ironic smile, and the anxious, amused eyes, touched her heart to its depths. It isn't fair, she thought. It isn't fair that a man should demand so little, and yet never have even that little. He's good, she said to herself after a minute; though no man likes to be told that; and things come easier in life when one is not good. And it was true, what he said. Why shouldn't the middle-aged, especially

when they had known starvation in youth, have lives as well as the young? Why shouldn't he take his dream as his children had taken theirs?

"The farm needs you, and I need you," she said in her sympathetic voice, so eloquent with vibrations.

"You wouldn't mind what they said?"

"Why should I? I've suffered too much, and I've finished with minding. Besides Mr. Amos is getting old, and—" laughter rippled in her smile "—there a job waiting for the right hired man."

While he stood there, with his eyes on her face, his whole life, as he had lived it, seemed to fall away and apart. Except for his children, he saw, he had never had anything; and his children had belonged to him only when they were small. Roy alone had cared for him, and Roy had passed on, now, with the others. She had loved him in her way; but her own strength was sufficient for her, and he was glad that she had never needed to borrow courage. One after another, the ties had loosened, the vital bonds had weakened and failed, without giving way. And the best or the worst of it was that he felt as young, within, as he had ever felt. When he was with Kate on the farm, he could tell himself that age is a state of mind, nothing more, that time is hurrying on, and he must refuse to measure the future by a clock that has run down in the past.

A smile, half-sad, half-whimsical, softened his mouth. "But you must not think I lack the nature of a man because I am not pursued in my dreams by amorous furies."

"If you'd been a woman for fifty years," she tossed back merrily, "you would know that the nature of a man is not always welcome. There comes a time when one prefers a farmer to a lover."

"If only I may stay on, I'll stay in any capacity. It's a

queer thing, but this farm means more than just a place to me. There's a kind of rightness."

Her eyes dwelt on him thoughtfully. Though she said nothing, he could feel the warmth of her friendship mingling with the glow of the firelight. She had never been a great talker. That was one of the traits he had found most refreshing, after Lavinia's ceaseless soliloquies. Kate wasn't striking; she wasn't witty; she wasn't vivacious; and yet Kate was all, he reminded himself for the hundredth time, that he wanted from life. Some vacancy in his mind and heart was filled and was satisfied by her presence. She was the only human being who had ever given him the sense of completeness.

"As long as I am here and alive, the farm will be waiting for you," she answered, slowly, as if she were making a vow.

Though he was unaware of her hesitation, she was asking herself whether the emotion she felt for him was another aspect of love or merely the natural impulse to bring joy into a colorless life. In this calm affection there was none of that robust and vehement passion which she had known when she was younger and in love with Jack Oliver. Friendship, it may have been. Yet did one wish to give and to possess so utterly in friendship? Perhaps. She did not know. She had never been clever at analysis, at dividing facts into properties. All she knew, she told herself, was that she felt happier when Asa came, and that some brightness seemed to change or fade when he left. He fitted in, was the way she put it to herself; he fitted in with the farm, with the daily life that was lived here, with her own personality, and with the long memories of happiness in her marriage. . . . In the old days, she meditated, with her eyes on the windswept sky without, duty would have separated our lives. But what is duty nowadays except a name or an estranged shadow which

once, in some very remote past, had clung to a lost substance?

"I'm in my sixties," he said abruptly, "and this is all
I've ever known, or ever shall know, of happiness."

She withdrew her gaze from the sky. "That sounds
like the young."

"I feel that way. I'm not sure they aren't right."

"Right for what? Or for whom?"

"For themselves. Aren't they right to think first of
themselves?"

"If they're happier, yes. But are they happier?" She
put her hand on his arm. "I've never seen you in this
mood before."

"No one has. That's a part of my trouble." He bent over
and stirred the dead ashes.

"Could you have been different?" She was watching
him with a steady gaze.

A single ember flickered to life, and he prodded it
thoughtfully while he answered, "I have always been different—inside."

"Most of us are, my dear, even the youth that seems
so strange to us. Aren't we all infected, more or less, with
the distemper of our age?"

"Well, I've a right to be," he insisted stubbornly. "It's
my age, isn't it, as well as anyone's? Why do you suppose
people talk as if an age belonged only to infants and ado-
lescents? Haven't the elderly or the old any part in it? No,
this isn't a distemper, Kate. It is a revolution!"

"Then I am with you." Underneath her merriment,
she felt again that deep familiar instinct of struggle. He
was nearer the breaking point than she had imagined he
could ever come; and she would save him, she resolved,
in spite of family feeling, in spite of the will toward self-
sacrifice. Duty had done its worst with him, she thought
fiercely, duty and the sense of failure and an indomitable
tradition. "The farm will be here," she added, "and

together we can always scrape a living out of the land. One thing you may be sure of—Jack and I will never turn you away." She had spoken of Jack as if he were still alive, and Asa gave her a quick answering smile. After all, they had both loved Jack better than the whole world, better even than each other.

A glow shone in his eyes. "Then I'll cut loose," he said. "I'll tell Lavinia tonight. I've quit, and I'm through . . . somehow . . . somewhere . . . I'll be free."

V

THE road was bad, and above the lurch and heave of the omnibus, Asa's thoughts circled over and over in a constant refrain: Yes, he would tell Lavinia tonight. Somehow, somewhere, he would find freedom. A few days must pass, perhaps a week, perhaps longer; but in a little while, as soon as Lavinia was mistress of an adequate income and a more useful companion, he would make his belated but final break with the past. He was not the first man of sixty—he was by no means the first even in Queenborough—who had wanted to begin a new life and grasp at the happiness he had missed in his younger days. Many other men had felt this; many other men, and women, too, had wrought an act out of feeling and had bent circumstances—or was it fate?—to their will. Young and middle-aged and old, he saw them thronging everywhere, in every climate and country, all over the world. It was a revolt, not from a system, but from a condition of life. Not the social order alone, but a man's customary lot was the enemy. "I'll break free," he kept repeating under his breath. "I'll break free while there is yet time." He had waited patiently and very long for something to happen—something, no matter what—but now, all of a sudden, an urgent sense of panic had seized him. Life was slipping, and declining, and hurrying always faster as it departed. If he excepted his love for Roy, he had never known a moment of happiness. Not so much as a single moment that he would wish to live over again.

Then slowly the dark terror and that breathless sense of time passing had subsided. No, it wasn't too late. It was never too late while the fire of youth warmed the heart. Escape might not be easy, but at least it was possible. Con-

ventions, even those that were still valid, were not all that they used to be. Kate, in spite of her fifty years, belonged to the new order. She was as daring as Stanley, though her spirit could never lose its vital core of humanity. I am selfish, he told himself, with a queer pleasure in the sensation; but he would not make Kate unhappy, he knew, for all the selfish joy in the world. I must be free. I will be free, he resolved passionately. Nowadays, people didn't feel about institutions, or any moral symbols, as they used to feel. Yet, in the right hands, such matters could still be turned into dangerous weapons. A smile moved his lips. He could take it. He could stand up now against whatever came to him. Hadn't he lived for more than thirty years with a woman who had lost, or never possessed, a sense of humor? Other senses she had, he knew, but not that one. Well, it was over at last. He drew a long breath of relief, as if a heavy load had begun to drop from his shoulders. Yes, he would tell Lavinia tonight. He would begin another life while there was still time to make the sort of life that he wanted.

The omnibus stopped. A stout woman covered with a gay floral pattern descended before him. While he watched the bobbing purple grapes on her hat, a vague association stirred in his thoughts; but he let it slip by without trying to place it. Except for the stout woman and his own shadow in the rain, the pavement ahead of him was deserted. Then, as he walked on slowly, dreading the open door and the narrow stairs and the sound of Lavinia's plaintive voice, he saw that several cars stood parked in front of the lighted house. An instant later, with a dart of astonishment, he had recognized William's huge dark blue limousine. It couldn't be William, of course; and Asa wondered uneasily why Charlotte should have left her afflicted husband alone at night. As he stopped under the street lamp, a chill sensation wavered up from some thick obscurity into his open mind.

Something had happened! Was Lavinia enduring a heart attack? Had Stanley been hurt? A pang gripped him. It might be Roy who was hurt.

Running up the steps to the house, Asa slipped his key into the lock and entered the hall, which was empty and silent. As he hastened on to the staircase, he noticed William's gray felt hat on the table. So William had been called, probably by Lavinia, and he had come to her. Yet William, he knew, would not have come unless the appeal had been desperately urgent. With what seemed to Asa the last failing effort of youth, he mounted the stairs and rushed into Lavinia's room.

"Here is Asa at last!" Lavinia exclaimed. "Oh, Asa, if only you hadn't gone, it might not have happened!"

"What is it? What has happened?" he asked angrily, thinking of Roy. "Is one of the children hurt?"

"No, no, no." William's denial droned over his head. "The girls are all right. It was Stanley's car, but she wasn't in it. She wasn't anywhere near."

"It's too terrible," Lavinia moaned. "But we ought to be thankful."

Out of nothing, it seemed to Asa, the assembled faces swam before him, and then passed on again into nothing. He saw William; he saw Andrew; he saw Roy, with Craig standing beside her. And all these troubled faces appeared to wear exactly the same expression, as if they covered a collective anxiety, a vain endeavor to hold fast to some shifting surface of confidence. Yes, something was wrong, something was missing, something was false.

"Thankful for what?" he demanded harshly, and then fearfully, "Where's Stanley?"

"She's here. She's back here on the couch." It was Lavinia who answered; and as she leaned sideways, he saw that she had been screening Stanley, who was huddled behind her on the pillows. "It has been a shock to her. But what we have to be thankful for is that she was safe at

home when it happened. It was her car. The officers tried to make her feel less badly about that."

"The officers?" Fog closed over him, and he felt that he was smothering.

"They traced the car. It was found up the street, blocks away, in an alley near Granite Boulevard. There was nobody in it, but, of course, it had Stanley's number, and . . . and . . ."

"Yes, yes." He was looking past Lavinia's bulky shape to Stanley's huddled figure, through which long, slow shudders were running and stopping, running and stopping. Except for those recurring spasms, she looked wilted and motionless, flattened out and incredibly soft, as if she had been rained on. Her eyes stared straight in front of her, dazed and groping; and he felt that something fierce and inarticulate—was it horror? was it dread?—fluttered and died and fluttered again in the vacancy of her look. "Can't somebody tell me?" he repeated in a voice that was shrill with suspense. "Are you dumb? Are you fools?"

"Don't, Asa." Again it was Lavinia who answered. "We're trying to tell you. But I want you to understand that it might have been worse. Stanley . . ."

"Damn it all!" he burst out. "Will you tell me, Charlotte?"

But Charlotte only looked at William; and William, after a sign from Lavinia, said in a ponderous voice: "She's all right, Asa. What we're thankful for is that Stanley wasn't mixed up in it. She had used her car earlier, but she was in her room when . . ."

"When what? What happened?"

"There was an accident. A woman was injured, and her little girl was killed."

"Where was it? Who saw it?"

"It happened just within the city limits, on Granite Boulevard. Nobody saw it. Dusk had come on, and it was

[367]

raining. But one woman did see a gray sports car speeding away from the spot. She couldn't get the number, but a gray car with—with bloodstains on it was found in an alley. The police traced this car, and Stanley told them all she knew."

"I didn't know anything. Oh Uncle William, I didn't know anything!" Stanley had rolled over on her face and was sobbing wildly. Then, turning as if she were jerked into place by a wire, she sat up and moaned under her breath, "I couldn't tell them."

"There, there, darling, of course you couldn't," Lavinia said soothingly. "I wish Dr. Buchanan would come. Roy, hadn't you better give her another dose of ammonia?"

"She's had brandy," Roy whispered.

"I haven't," Stanley cried out furiously. "I haven't had anything!"

"It's natural she should be upset," William said, melting slowly and oozing into a frosty sympathy as he looked at her. "Any girl would hate to be mixed up in a thing like that. A frightful thing," he added indignantly.

"Was the car stolen? Who did it?" Asa demanded of them all—or of none of them. And with the question, he felt the whole carefully built surface of pretense ring hollow and give way underneath.

"Stanley doesn't know," Lavinia answered bravely enough. "She had a headache, and she'd come in earlier than she expected to. She had taken aspirin, and she was asleep when—when the officers came."

"Had she spoken to you?"

"No, she'd gone straight upstairs. Your head was bad, wasn't it, baby?"

"Of course it was," Stanley sobbed. "I took aspirin. I took allonal too. I slept—oh, ever so long."

"You didn't tell me you'd taken allonal, darling."

"But I did, Mother. My head was aching so I couldn't

—I couldn't . . . Then those men came, and it was so terrible. . . ." A low, wailing cry was torn from her lips. "The little girl had pinks in her hand. . . ."

"Pinks?" There was a catch in Asa's voice, and Lavinia replied quickly, rather too quickly, Asa thought afterwards, "One of the men told us. Such a nice young policeman. He said the little girl had spent the day at her grandmother's in the country. He said she had a bunch of pink flowers in her hand."

"Oh, Mother, Mother!"

"Hush, darling, you couldn't have helped it!" There was in Lavinia's voice a subdued strange note, the note of maternal passion—or was it of maternal ferocity?

"But pinks?" Asa asked over again. "Did he say pinks?"

Lavinia met his eyes with an unflinching gaze. "It is too late for pinks, Asa," she said coldly.

"It is too late for pinks." He heard his voice echoing the words, while his mind conjured up the vision of second bloomings in some grandmother's flower beds. "Then she only imagined it?"

"She imagined it after she heard the officers telling about it. You did, didn't you Stanley?" she asked, pressing her child to her bosom.

"Oh, it was my car, Mother. I might have been in it. I might have been . . ."

"But you were not, darling. No, Roy, don't give her anything more. We'd better wait for the doctor."

As Roy turned away with a glass in her hand, the shade slipped back from the lamp on the table, and the room was suddenly flooded with a harsh blaze of light. In the withering glare, it seemed to Asa that the terror in Stanley's look leaped out, like the shadow of a beast, and during the next moment lost itself in the anxious faces around her. Even before he had grasped the fact or the meaning, this shadow vanished, and the smooth surface had closed over it. Then as Craig crossed the room and

[369]

adjusted the shade, the light softened again into a mellow steadfast obscurity. Immediately, the disjoined circle bent together again, and the divided personalities, which had seemed to rush apart and away, were united in a single unbroken front of opinion.

"I wish that doctor would come," William grumbled. "The trouble with young Buchanan is that you can never get hold of him when you want him."

"Maybe we'd better stop talking about it," Charlotte suggested, with her impregnable common sense. "Maybe if we'd just let her be quiet."

"That's the right idea," Andrew assented. "If she can have a good sleep, she'll feel better in the morning. Then we'll all get together and see what we can do about it."

"Do about what?" Asa inquired irritably. "I'm tired of guessing. If the car was stolen, what business is it of ours?"

Lavinia stared at him blankly. "Stolen? I thought you knew they had arrested Parry."

"Parry?" He gazed back at her with stunned incredulity. "But it couldn't have been Parry. Parry never drinks, and he's one of the best drivers I know. It's absurd to accuse Parry."

Lavinia's face sagged and hardened. "We all felt that. None of us could believe it at first. But, Stanley—"

"Oh, Mother, I didn't. I didn't say it was Parry."

"Hush, Stanley. Try to be quiet. You had to tell them that Parry had taken your car to the garage. No matter how much you hated to tell them, there wasn't anything else you could do. They didn't blame her, of course. Nobody could," she concluded, with a vague, impersonal gesture, as if she were speaking over the heads of her audience and addressing invisible powers. "But the police insisted it could have been nobody but Parry. They were very sympathetic with us, the young one especially. . . ."

Yes, he would be, Asa thought cynically, before he repeated aloud, "It couldn't have been Parry."

"Well, they think so," William returned gruffly. "They've taken it out of our hands. You've got to remember that little girl." He snorted furiously, for he who was not lovable yet had his feelings. "Holding tight to her bunch of pinks, and smashed beyond recognition."

A high, thin scream, as frantic as the scream of a tortured animal, burst from Stanley's lips and tore on, writhing into the discordant sounds of the night.

Oh, my precious, my baby!" Lavinia gasped, bending over her. "Try to get her to bed, Roy. That must be Dr. Buchanan now." Then, a few minutes later, when the doctor hastened in, she put the girl into his eager professional arms. "Give her something to quiet her. The others will tell you."

"I've heard," the young doctor replied tenderly. "Poor girl, she's taking it hard." Picking up his well-worn black bag, which was small but of infinite capacity, he helped Roy lead Stanley away, while Asa turned back to the three men who had drawn together in a gloomy conference just inside the door.

"We've got to hear Parry's side," he said grimly.

"It's hard to credit it," Craig replied. "He's a good boy."

"We'll give him his chance," William growled between his teeth. "I believe in every man, white or black, having a chance. But if he's guilty, I hope, by God, he'll get what he deserves."

"He will," Craig rejoined. "If he's guilty, and even if he isn't guilty, this will ruin him."

"Where is he now?" Asa asked. "What have they done with him?"

"He's in jail. Minerva telephoned after they'd taken him. I'm going down there tomorrow. He must have a

lawyer. Yes, it's hard to believe," he continued slowly, "but I suppose—I suppose . . . Oh, it must have been unavoidable," he burst out. "But what I can't understand is why the fool ran away."

"Parry's no fool," Asa said.

"No, he's a smart boy," Andrew agreed, "and he knows as well as you or I that running away would convict him."

"Drunk!" William snapped tartly. "Lost his head. They all do, every one of 'em. Drink works hell with a darkie."

"But he doesn't drink," Asa answered, when the snapping had ended. "He has set his heart on amounting to something. All summer he's been studying hard and doing well. Craig was helping him."

"Well, he got it somewhere," the old man blustered. "I never saw one of his race that couldn't get drunk on a thimbleful."

"What's the use of blaming it on his race?" Craig demanded aggressively. "When you come down to facts, which is his race, anyway?"

"For God's sake!" William thundered, while a glow of rage mantled his wasted features. "Is this the time, sir, to begin airing your radical theories?"

"They aren't theories, sir, but facts," Craig flung back derisively.

"Do they matter now?" Asa pushed Craig aside and looked anxiously for Charlotte, who appeared at the exact right moment with a glass of milk in her hand.

"It's time for your milk, William," she said, and he reached out for the glass and began to sip it obediently. "I just stepped down to the kitchen," she added, apologetically, to Lavinia.

"I'm afraid it isn't as rich as yours, Aunt Charlotte, but I hope you got the top of the bottle."

"What was it," Asa inquired abruptly of Andrew, "that Stanley said when she first heard of the accident?"

Andrew shook his head. "I'm not sure what it was. She and Mother were both too upset to say anything."

"The child told 'em the truth," William mumbled between swallows. "At first she had some foolish qualms about getting the boy in trouble. But when they pressed her, she was obliged to tell 'em the plain truth. Parry was waiting in the street when she came back, and he took her car and went off in it."

"I thought," Asa dragged out the words slowly, "that she came home earlier than she intended."

"So she did, so she did," William retorted. "She came home earlier, and he was hanging about because it's Sunday evening. What's in your mind, sir?" he demanded wrathfully, resisting an impulse to bellow. "Have you any objection to your daughter's telling the truth?"

The truth, God help us! Asa thought, in a kind of dull torture. "There's nothing in my mind but the wish to help Stanley and to be just," he answered. "After all, no one has heard Parry's side."

William's explosion appeared to have drained him of feeling. With his gaze fixed on vacancy, he was muttering to himself. "I'd better be getting on, Charlotte. I've got a pain, and I'd better be getting on. Where's Charlotte?" he snapped, observing her absence.

"She's talking to the doctor," Andrew answered solicitously, for he could see that the old man was suffering. "We appreciate your coming when you're not feeling up to the mark."

William grunted. "Your kin is your kin," he replied. "It was your mother that got me here. She was crying when she telephoned me."

"It was wonderful of you," Lavinia interposed. "I can't tell you how grateful I am for your coming."

"Well, you ought to be. I'm too sick to be gadding about. Roy!" he raised his voice to a cawing note. "Tell your Aunt Charlotte I can't wait all night on her!"

"In a minute, William," Charlotte cried. "I shan't be a minute." Then, as he dragged himself out, glowering, she waddled in from Stanley's room and hastened nervously after him. "I can't stop," she called over her shoulder. "He's not feeling well. But the doctor has given the poor child a hypodermic . . . not morphine," her voice floated back, "but, he says, something new. . . ."

While he followed her hurrying figure down the stairs and outside to the car, Asa told himself irritably that women depended too much upon antidotes to reality. Morphine or "something new," it made no difference, if only it provided a brief escape from the unpleasant. When he came upstairs again, after watching William and Charlotte drive away, he met Craig and Andrew just leaving Lavinia's room.

"There's nothing more we can do," Andrew said. "Stanley is quiet now, and the doctor says we mustn't disturb her."

"Where's Roy?" Asa asked.

"Mother wanted to be helped to bed. I've a sneaking thankfulness I wasn't born in Roy's skin."

"Well, I'm going to wait," Craig insisted resentfully. "I haven't had a word with Roy since this damned accident. Nobody will get any sleep," he added in a smothered rage, "except Stanley."

"We can't all take hypodermics," Andrew replied. "Somebody has to keep an eye open."

"Oughtn't we," Asa asked, "to have a word with Parry before this goes any farther?"

"What? Tonight?" Craig glanced at his watch. "Why, it's after eleven."

"I don't care. Before I go to bed, I'm going to see Minerva and Abel."

"It will be midnight when you get over there."

"It doesn't matter. Neither of them is likely to have had a hypodermic."

"Well, I'll run you down. I suppose Roy will be up when you come home?"

"Oh, Roy will be up. But Minerva has to go out to telephone, and I couldn't get a wink of sleep until I've talked with her."

"Then I'm off," Andrew said, as they went down the steps to the street. "Maggie will come over right after breakfast, and I'll tell her," he added, with a tinge of satire, "not to let Mother forget how much she has to be thankful for."

A moment later, as Craig started his car, Asa found himself recalling that desperate drive on the night of Stanley's elopement. So short a time, and yet, for the world and themselves, a new age had set in. What is time, he thought, that we should be at its mercy? Outside the mind of man did time exist? And even in the mind of man, was there a boundary between time and eternity? Was this another Craig beside him or the Craig whom Stanley had loved? For if Craig were still the old Craig, vehement, unsettled, and rebellious, he was no longer desperate. He drove now without haste or nervousness, and the look on his sensitive face was one of confused sadness. Was he too haunted, Asa wondered, by the vision of a little girl, with a bunch of pinks in her hand, running home very happily after a day with her grandmother? And was Craig also seeing this little girl, at one and the same moment, as Stanley and as not Stanley?

VI

YES, they're still up," Craig said, when the car had stopped. "I'll wait for you out here, but don't forget that I want to see Roy."

A light shone from the lower front window, and they saw Abel's shadow rise against the blind, hesitate for an instant, and then move slowly across the room.

Without replying, Asa jumped out, flung back the gate, and went up the narrow walk, while Craig muttered despondently, "If I had my way, I'd bust up the family as an institution. . . ."

"Come in, Mr. Asa, come in." Abel held open the door and stood aside.

"I couldn't sleep till I'd had a word with you, Abel. Where's Minerva?"

"She's ironing in the kitchen. She felt she had to keep her hands busy, and there's some ironing she wanted to get through."

A new note sounded in Abel's voice, a note of apathy, of acquiescence. There is something beyond the individual, Asa thought, something remote and inseparable from the beginnings of life. With his eyes on the bare cleanliness of the room, he was aware of a reserve which he felt to be associated, in some unperceived way, with a sense of humility. A whole universe, not of life but of custom, not of reason but of psychology, divided him, he felt, from these two alien persons to whom he was sincerely attached. He had come to bring comfort, and he found himself dumb with pity.

"I had to see you tonight," he began again, and stopped because his breath failed him.

"Thank you, Mr. Asa. Minervy will want to thank you too." Abel raised his voice slightly without breaking the

deep cadence of tragedy. "Minervy, here's Mr. Asa waiting to see you."

"I'm coming," Minerva responded in a tone scarcely louder than an echo of Abel's. "The Lord knows I'm glad to see you, Mr. Asa! I was just telling Abel I knew we could count on you."

She seemed different, Asa thought, though he could not define the change in her face. "I came as soon as I could," he replied, embarrassed by the very force of his sympathy. "I was out in the country." While he held her large, smooth hand, which was developed, not disfigured, by work, his gaze wandered round the little room and lingered over her cherished possessions. He saw the crocheted mat and the bunch of garden flowers in a glass vase on the table, the speckless tidies on the backs of chairs, the three peacock feathers in a yellow bottle, and the enlarged photograph of his mother in her wedding dress over the mantelpiece. Was he a damn fool or an old fogy? he asked himself, with a choking rage in his throat. Why should these humble objects, so valueless and treasured so carefully, touch him to the quick of his nature? There was a stir at his feet; glancing down, he saw that Jasper, too, had come in with Minerva, and was gazing up at him with dark, bewildered eyes under a wrinkled brow.

"That pore dawg," Minerva said, in her native tongue. "Ain't he mighty near human?"

"He's a good dog. . . ." Asa stared at Jasper. "I'm going to see Parry the first thing in the morning," he blurted out quickly. "I want to know what he says."

Minerva looked at Abel before she answered, and when she spoke at last, her voice sounded as if it had come from another world. "Parry never said nothing, Mr. Asa."

"It was a frightful accident, but why on earth, Minerva, did he run away?"

Minerva shook her head. "Parry didn't run away, Mr.

Asa. He didn't do nothing. He wan't anywhere near." She dropped her eyes, veiling their look of hopeless sincerity, while she wiped the palms of her hands on her checked apron.

"But he took the car. Didn't he take the car?" A slow chill, a nervous dread, had started to crawl up Asa's spine. He shook himself, in a physical effort to dislodge the creeping fear or to drive it away.

"No, sir, he never went after the car. Stanley told him not to come back. Sometimes the car stayed out all night in the street."

"But I thought . . ." He stopped. He swallowed a lump in his throat. He began over again: "I haven't talked with Stanley. The shock was too much, and the doctor gave her a sedative."

"Yes, sir." Minerva was still rubbing her hands, and presently, without meeting his eyes, she lifted her apron and wiped the moisture from her face.

"When," he asked, "did you first hear of . . . of . . ."

"Not till the policemen came. They came to take Parry. He was setting right here listening in on the radio. He'd been setting here the whole evening, except when he took Jasper out for a walk before supper."

"What did they tell you?"

"They didn't tell us nothing. All they would say was that Parry had killed a little white girl and run away. They kept saying that over and over and over again, Mr. Asa." She raised her eyes and returned his gaze steadily. "One of 'em kicked Jasper," she added, "that pore dawg."

"Was he rough with the rest of you?"

"No, sir, he wan't rough. He never laid his hand on us, but he looked mean. I didn't like the set of his mouth."

"Was Parry frightened?"

Minerva hesitated, and Abel took up the question. "Who wouldn't have been, Mr. Asa? I reckon the boy was

scared clean out of his wits." He stopped and waited until
he had collected his slow faculties. "It's the Gospel truth I
speak," he said. "Parry didn't have any more to do with it
than Adam."

Dumb with pain, Asa felt the icy chill reach his neck
and begin to strangle his breathing. "Didn't you tell them
Parry had been with you?"

Minerva met his question without flinching. "I told
'em, Mr. Asa," she answered. "But they wouldn't believe
me. I'm colored."

While he stood there, gazing back into the deep silence of her look, the strangled sound of his breathing receded gradually and sank into a vast hollowness. What
was there to say? Nothing. There would never be anything. Holding out his hand, he pressed hers for a
minute, and then, turning stiffly, he shook hands in an
oddly ceremonious manner, he felt, with Abel. "I'll see
Parry in the morning," he said, "as soon as they'll let me."
A moment afterwards, he left the house as quickly as if
he were pursued, rushed through the open gate, and
jumped into the car. "You're right, Craig," he exclaimed;
"all you youngsters are quite right. It's a hell of a world!"

"Sure thing," Craig tossed back, as he lighted a cigarette, flicked the match away, and put his hands on the
wheel. "What I can't understand is why you old stagers
didn't find it out sooner." The car shot on toward the corner. "I want to fight for something," Craig said savagely,
gripping the cigarette in his mouth. "I want to fight for
something, but I don't know for what. When I look around
me, I can't see a blessed thing that's worth fighting for."

"You'll see it, my boy, after you've lost it. Before we
can romanticize the American way, we must translate it
into the American dream."

What was he saying? And what were words? Asa asked
himself. While they waited for the green light, he tried to
keep his eyes and his burdened mind on the few scat-

tered pedestrians. A girl, a boy, an old woman. Then, swiftly reversing the order, an old woman clutching a bundle, a boy dragging a small red wagon, a man fumbling in his pockets for cigarettes, a girl fidgeting with the uncurled bob on her neck. "I must see Parry," he heard his voice saying. "I must see Parry as soon as I can." The light changed, and the car sped on in the thin traffic. Not until they stopped again did he take up his unfinished speech. "I must see Parry, Craig, the first thing in the morning."

"So must I. Will nine o'clock suit you?"

"I'll have to telephone to the factory and ask."

"Well, after all, there isn't much we can do. He'll have to have a lawyer."

"You'll act for him?"

"If I can't, I'll arrange to have him looked after. . . . Had the fool been drinking? Or did he lose his head with fright and not know what he was doing?"

Again they sped to the end of a block, and again there was a heavy silence until the green light flashed out. Not until the car turned into Westward Avenue did the gathering horror in Asa's mind explode in words. "Minerva says Parry knew nothing about it."

"Knew nothing? You mean he was drunk?"

"She says he wasn't there. She says he was with her, listening to the radio the whole evening. She says he never went back for the car."

"Good God, no! Did you believe her?"

Asa choked. "I believed her," he replied hoarsely.

"But he was coming to put up the car."

"She says he wasn't. Stanley told him not to. On Sundays, and sometimes on other days, it was often left out in the street."

The car had slowed down, and Craig was gazing ahead in silence. While he slouched there, plunged in gloom, it seemed to the older man that he could hear the savage drumming of terror. But when at last Craig

spoke, his voice had dwindled into a single thin jarring sound. "Then the car was stolen. It must have been stolen."

"Yes, it must have been stolen," Asa assented.

"Did you ask what Parry said?"

"He hasn't said anything yet."

"Not even when they arrested him?"

Asa shook his head. "Minerva tried to tell the policemen, but they wouldn't listen. They wouldn't listen, she said, because she's colored."

"Goddamn it, I know!" They drove down the block and stopped in front of the house. Downstairs, the only light was in the hall; but on the upper floor the faint reddish glow of a night lamp streamed from Lavinia's bedroom. Craig sat still in the car while Asa stepped down and then turned to look back at him.

"I thought you were coming in?"

"No, I'd better get on. I'll be here again as soon as you've had breakfast." He nodded with a detached air, as if he were replying with only the outer shell of his mind. Then he started the car with an uncertain jolt, turned quickly, and drove away up the empty street.

Lavinia was asleep, or pretended to be, and Asa undressed without a sound in the bathroom, and slipped, like a bodiless shadow, between the sheets of the harder twin bed. For hours he lay awake, staring from the dark glimmer of the lamp to the pearly luster on the wet leaves and the silvery black of the night sky. When, toward dawn, he fell into a fitful sleep, haunted by dreams, it was suddenly to turn a corner in space and meet a strange little girl who offered him a tight bunch of pinks. But, when he took her hand in his hand, then the little girl shot up and changed into Stanley, while the bunch of pinks faded in her grasp, and scattered apart, and were strewn everywhither into a void. . . .

At the break of a clouded dawn Lavinia stirred and

moaned in a conscientious way before she opened her eyes. "Are you awake, Asa?"

"I'm not sure. Do you want anything?"

"It's been a dreadful night, hasn't it?"

"Pretty bad."

"I hope Stanley got some sleep." In the drab light Lavinia's face reminded him of a mask modeled in clay, and there were stained pouches under her eyes.

"Can you go back to sleep?" he asked wearily.

"I'm afraid not." She rolled her head, and waved her hand in a negative gesture.

"Well, try. It's not yet five o'clock."

For another hour they lay silent and restless in their twin beds. Then Lavinia murmured plaintively, "But I haven't closed my eyes again, Asa."

"Neither have I. Do you want coffee?"

"I was wondering whether it was too early."

"It's never too early—nor too late." He dragged himself out of bed, feeling and looking, he thought as he passed a mirror, barely more than a frayed-out rag of a man. "The next pajamas I buy," he remarked, "are going to be purple."

"Why, Asa! What are you talking about?"

"I wasn't talking. I was only thinking aloud."

"Well, you oughtn't to have such thoughts."

"Maybe not."

"I didn't even know that you liked color."

"I like a good deal, Lavinia, that, by good luck, you don't know about." He came back in his dressing gown and stopped a moment beside her bed. "Lavinia, what did Stanley tell you last night?"

"Oh, Asa, please don't! Not so early as this."

"What did she tell you?"

"Nothing. Nothing, really. You saw how upset she was."

"Do you think she told you the truth?"

"She didn't know anything. She didn't know what had happened till—till the officers came."

A wave of aversion crossed his face and was gone in an instant. "Do you believe that?"

She struggled into a sitting position and stared up at him. "What is the matter, Asa? What has come over you? Of course, I believe it. The police never questioned it."

"They wouldn't." He thrust out his hand as if he were pushing her off. "They don't know her. We do, my dear."

"Asa . . . oh, but please, Asa . . ."

"I must talk to her as soon as she wakes."

"You mustn't." There it was again in her face, the look that he dreaded, the upsurging of maternal ferocity. "You'd drive her out of her mind. The child has told all she knows. The officers were satisfied. Uncle William is satisfied."

His hard gaze probed her mind. "And are you satisfied, Lavinia?"

She flinched and shivered as if he had struck her. "Oh . . . why? why? Of course, I am, Asa. Everyone is except you. And now you . . ."

"Well, lie down, and I'll put on the coffee." He couldn't hurt her, that was his weakness. He couldn't bear hurting things. And yet, he knew that only by hurting her could he defend his own sense of right, of justice, of inward integrity. Is it true, he asked himself wearily, turning away, that there comes a crisis in life when inhumanity alone can serve the ends of humanity? Is it imperative at such moments to reach not only beyond one's lower impulses, but even beyond one's better nature? Could a principle betray one as well as an appetite? He was too old to believe that. Right was right, wrong was wrong, or his universe fell to pieces. I do not know where I am going, he thought. I cannot see a step before me; but I must go on.

The morning dragged by. Craig was late; there were matters to arrange at the factory; and it was past noon before the two men entered the jail and followed a deputy sheriff, through corridors reeking with disinfectant, to the double block of cells, at the far end, where the Negroes were kept. Here the ranker odors of Africa gripped the pit of Asa's stomach; and he was obliged to wait till the queasiness passed and the fog in his brain lifted. Outside, he had left the weather damp and sultry, with a slight cool drizzle of rain; but while he looked at the crowded dark or light faces behind the bars, he felt that all the evil smells of a sweating earth were weighed down and compressed in the smothered heat. Then, without looking for him, he saw Parry. The boy was huddled in a bunk, watching a rowdy group of Negroes play checkers with the caps of Coca-Cola bottles on a square of pasteboard. In the next bunk a half-witted old man was cackling over a new Gideon Bible held upside down. Farther away, a light mulatto was thumbing a small picture book. The noise was deafening; the light dim. Still sickened by the stench, Asa said, "We must get him out of here." Then he met the boy's eyes, and something seemed to shrivel inside him. Parry's light skin had bleached to a livid cast. His neat clothes were discolored and torn. His blue shirt, which Minerva had washed so carefully for Sunday wear, was rumpled and stained, with the collar ripped partly off. But the worst of it, Asa thought, went deeper than any surface disorder. Worst of all was the look of resignation, of defeat, of settled despair: the look of African fatalism which had surged up in a dark wave from out of the past.

"Good morning, Parry," Craig began, and the three black young Negroes, seated in a circle on the floor, glanced up and grinned cheerfully. "We came as soon as we could."

[384]

"Yes, sir. Good morning." The air of vague uncertainty, as if he were the product of some experimental species, surrounded the boy while he stood there, without advancing a step, between the young Negroes and the half-witted old man. It was the familiar sense of constraint, only worse, Asa told himself, the inability to find the exact right way of approach. How could one break down a withdrawal so remote that it belonged nowhere and touched nothing?

"Come nearer," Asa said. "I can't talk to you unless you come nearer."

"Yes, sir," Parry answered, and he moved obediently to the bars of the cage. In the light from the corridor his features appeared curiously blunted, and Asa thought with astonishment: I didn't know he was so much of a Negro. Or was it fright that had worked on the elemental strains in Parry's blood and driven them to the surface? Aloud Asa said, "I want you to tell us exactly what happened."

The boy put up his hands in an effort to pull the ripped ends of his collar together. His cuffs were torn, too, and soiled, and there were smudges of grease or dirt over his shoulders. His eyes looked dazed and bloodshot, but when Asa asked, "Did they handle you roughly?" he shook his head and answered, "Naw, sir," in a colorless voice, which had relapsed, for the moment at least, into dialect.

"Did you have a bad night?"

"Naw, sir."

"Are you sick anywhere?"

"Naw, sir."

The young Negroes on the floor burst into a clamorous bickering. "Dat's mine." "Naw, 'tain't." "Yas, 'twuz." "Naw, tain't." "Yas, suh. . . ." "Yas, suh-e-e bob, hit wuz." "De hell hit ain't!" "De hell but 'twuz!"

"I suppose it's like that all the time," Asa said helplessly to Craig; and he added, "You've got to get him out of here—quick."

"What's the matter with him?" Craig asked.

"It's the night. One night, that's enough. The trouble is, they can't take it, not the better sort. They haven't the mettle. They can't take it . . . especially," Asa's tone flattened, "when they're innocent."

"Gone soft," Craig agreed, "like the rest of us."

"Like the rest of us," Asa echoed mechanically, "too soft or too hard in the wrong spots." He turned back to Parry. "You must tell us the truth. You must tell us exactly what happened."

Parry's confused gaze wandered from Asa to Craig. In the movement, and even more in the dusky blankness, Asa noticed again the older African cast beneath the lighter surface planes of his face.

"There may be a maladjustment somewhere," Craig muttered under his breath. "But the shock, if he is innocent, was enough to have dazed him." Raising his voice above the clatter around him, he repeated after Asa, "Yes, tell us exactly what happened."

Parry looked at them sullenly, while he ran his hand over his mouth. When at last he answered, he was trying, Asa suspected, to drown both his mind and his speech in some primitive element. It was as if effort, as well as education, had failed him, and there was relief in sheer ignorance. "I don't know nothing," he said. "It's the truth, Mr. Asa. I don't know nothing."

"Tell me what you did with the car."

"I never touched it last night. I never laid eyes on it after I got it out of the garage."

"When was that?"

"That was twelve by the church clock."

"When did you go back?"

"I never went back. She told me not to. She told me she might spend the night at Fitzroyal."

Craig turned to Asa. "Would she have done that?"

Asa nodded. "With Charlotte. She wouldn't have seen William."

"Does she ever leave the car out all night?"

"Yes, we may park in the street. She does, sometimes, when she's later than she ought to be." Asa's face was bleak when he turned to Parry. "Where were you?" he asked.

"I was at home with Ma and Pa, listening in to some tunes. I was there, except when I took Jasper out before supper. I was there, Mr. Asa, when the police came and got me."

"Did you know why they came for you?"

"No more than Adam, sir, that I didn't."

"Do you think the car was stolen, Parry?"

"I don't know, Mr. Asa. I don't know nothing."

"Miss Stanley thought . . ."

A spasm jerked through the boy's muscles; his hands tightened on his torn collar; fear sprang up into the dark vacancy of his eyes. Then, suddenly, dumbness closed over him.

"Miss Stanley thought you were to come back for the car," Asa said, slowly, lingering over the words.

Parry looked down at a spot in one corner where a cockroach was crawling. His lips twitched, but he did not speak, and the muscles in his face had stopped jerking.

"Dat sho' is mine!" one of the Negroes crowed.

"Naw, 'tain't!"

"Yas, 'tis!"

"Naw, 'tain't!"

"You shet yo' trap!"

"You better lemme 'lone dar!"

The laughter sank into fierce muttering, and immedi-

ately a quarrel broke out. The half-witted old Negro scrambled to his feet, threatened the players furiously with his Bible, and began to quaver in a sexless falsetto voice, rheumy with age and grief:

"De Gospel train's a-comin',
A-comin' roun' de curve,
A-puffin' en' a-blowin',
A-strainin' eve'y nerve,
Oh, git on board, little chillun,
Oh, git on board, little chillun,
Oh, git on board, little chillun,
Dar's room fur ma-ny mo. . . ."

The thin falsetto quavered out on a thread of pain. There was a curse in a brisk youthful tone, "Gawd blast yo' stinkin' hide!" A fire engine, with whistles screaming, sped by in the street.

"Hadn't we better talk to him outside?" Asa asked, glancing over his shoulder.

Craig shook his head. "Not now. I'm coming back. I can't take the case," he added in a muffled voice, "but I'll see that he has a lawyer."

"What do you think happened, Parry?" Asa asked. "We're trying to help you."

Parry shook his head, still watching the cockroach. He was plunged now into dumbness, far below the hollow well of inarticulate understanding. But there must be, Asa told himself, some shape, if only the shadow of a substance, in that dark abyss. Was it fear? Was it suspicion? Was it a secret knowledge or a sense that denial was hopeless? The boy's mouth had tightened until it was scarcely more than a bruised slit in his face.

"It's too much for me," Craig said, with nervous exasperation. "I wasn't cut out for a lawyer."

"Can you make him say anything?" Asa asked.

[389]

"What do you want him to say?"

"Anything. He must have some idea."

"If he has, he's not talking. He doesn't believe in us."

"That's the worst." Asa turned away, and then back again. "He's lost his confidence in us—or in our good will."

Somewhere, in a distant cell, the thin chorus piped up again. Nearer at hand, there was the aimless shuffle of a rheumatic foot trying to pat and swing on a concrete floor. Then the words of the spiritual swelled and resounded.

> *"Oh, git on board, little chillun,*
> *Oh, git on board, little chillun,*
> *Oh, git on board, little chillun,*
> *Dar's room fur ma-ny mo. . . ."*

"Why's Uncle Methuselah behind the bars?" Asa asked.

Craig shrugged one shoulder. "Religious loony. They keep them here till they can ship them to the asylum.

The cockroach had turned from the corner and was scurrying desperately toward the young Negroes. It had reached the middle of the floor in safety, when an immense black hand darted out and squashed the shiny brown body. Am I going to vomit? Asa thought, in disgust with his own stomach, and asked hurriedly, "Can't you tell us anything more, Parry?"

Parry shook his head. "It ain't any use, Mr. Asa," he replied in a tone of sullen resignation. "It ain't any use in this world."

"What, Parry? What isn't?"

"Saying anything. It ain't any use."

"But why not? If you have something to say. . . ."

The boy's eyes dropped again, and he stared vacantly at the remains of the cockroach. "I don't know nothing," he repeated, with the air and in the words he would have

used as a child. "I don't know nothing about anything."

"You're sure you didn't go back for the car?"

"I never went back. That's the born truth. I never went back again."

"Well, we'll do what we can," Craig said, and held out his hand. "Keep a stiff upper lip, and we'll see what we can do." As they left the cell blocks, passed rapidly through the outer office, and ran down the steps to the street, he burst out again, as if in spite of himself, "Another life gone to smash! Good God, what a world!"

Standing beside the car, Asa lifted his head and sucked in the smell and taste of the rain. It has the taste of earth in it, he thought, and the blessed smell of the sky, or of nothing. An instant later, as he followed Craig into the car, he turned his eyes with a groping look and asked blankly, "What can we do?"

The pause was so long that he was on the point of repeating the question, when, without glancing round, while they raced toward the hill ahead, Craig answered in a tone of suppressed violence: "I don't know. I don't know anything we can do without getting her into trouble."

VII

IF HE were a different sort of man, Asa said to himself, he might know what to do and how to set about doing it. If he were like William, or even like Craig, only more so. For Craig, he felt, was made of the right substance, though he had been spoiled in the making. He had come into life at the wrong time, and under a false system. Education, which should have built character, had merely loosened foundations; and in America, as elsewhere, the seasoned timber had rotted and fallen. Craig's instincts were sound; they remained sound; but a decent world cannot be based upon instinct alone. I suppose it's true, Asa reflected, as he entered the house in the late afternoon and ascended the stairs. Goodwill isn't enough. There must be impersonality also. There must be something to lean back upon if it's only a principle.

From Lavinia's room the sound of voices floated and stopped. Always talking, he thought impatiently. Endless discussion that leads only toward endless uncertainty. William was in there (his car had stood at the door), and Andrew and Roy would be there. He wondered if Craig had come, too, and whether he had found a lawyer for Parry. Not that counsel could help the boy, unless a miracle happened. . . . But why do I yield to them? he asked irritably, passing the door as he went on to Stanley's room. Are they really stronger than I am, every one of them, even Lavinia? The old sense of failure, of inferiority, was like an odd tingling weakness in his elbows and knees. But I'm right, he persisted. I may be a failure in life, but I'm right now, and we've got to do something about it. . . .

When he opened the door, Stanley turned to him with a smile so startled and so unreal that it might have been

cast by an artificial light on her face. "Aren't you too early, Father?" she asked listlessly. "How did you get away from the factory?"

"It wasn't easy. But I've been worried about you. You mean more to me than all the factories ever built."

Her face was blank as she gazed at him. "I'm all right. The doctor has just gone. He says I'm all right." Crumpled up in her big chair, she seemed as small as a child, and even her bones, he thought, had the softness of little things. She was pale, except for her reddened lips; and her eyes looked enormous within hollows of darkness.

"You must not let your mind dwell on it, Stanley," he said. "The only way is to face the truth and have it over as soon as you can."

"Oh, I do, I do, but, Father, it is so terrible! I keep seeing . . . I keep seeing . . ."

"Will you tell me the truth, daughter?"

"But I have. I have told you."

"Not all. You haven't told us the whole truth."

With the startled light on her face, she shuddered and shrank away from him. "I've told you all I know." Hysteria was beginning again.

For an instant he hesitated. Why, when he was doing the one right thing, should he feel like a murderer? "I've seen Parry in jail, Stanley."

"Oh, don't Father! Please don't!"

"He is in hell."

"Oh, I can't bear it! Oh, Father. . . ." How often had he heard that cry from her, and how often had she escaped, by weakness alone, from the full burden of circumstances.

"Neither can Parry bear it. He hasn't the stamina."

"Will they send him to prison?"

"If they believe he's guilty, it will go hard with him."

She flung out her arms and burst into tears. "They mustn't. Uncle William won't let them."

Though his heart was bleeding for her, he repeated softly, "Will you tell me the truth, Stanley?"

"I've told you everything. I've told you all I remember." Tears ran down her cheeks, but she did not put up her hand to wipe them away. What a superb unconscious gift, he thought, she has for drama, for attitude, for expression and gesture.

"Parry says—Listen, Stanley; no, don't squirm like that, listen—Parry says he never came back for the car."

The tears froze on her cheeks. "But I told him to come."

"He says not. He says you told him you might spend the night at Fitzroyal."

"Well, I thought I might. I didn't know. . . ." Her voice rose, quivered, and died.

"Don't darling, your mother will hear you. Tell me what you did with the car."

"I left it out in the street. Oh, I told you I left it out! I never said Parry took it." She turned away from him and hid her face in her shaking hands.

"Try to tell me the truth, Stanley. It may be hard for you, but it will be a thousand times easier for you than it would be for Parry."

"Oh, don't, Father, I can't bear it! Why won't you let me alone? The doctor said I must be left by myself."

It's fear, he thought, looking over her head at the falling rain. It's fear that does most of the harm in life; and he saw all the evils in the world, the whole sinister brood, spawned by fear. Aloud he asked, "Were you alone in the car?"

"Don't . . . I can't bear it!"

"You were driving, weren't you? This is the only way, my child. You were driving and . . ."

"Don't make me. Oh, don't make me. Mother wouldn't. I want Mother. You would let them send me to prison."

"No, they wouldn't, not for a minute. . . . But it was dusk, and it was raining, and you didn't see the woman and the little girl in the street."

"I didn't, Father, I didn't." She shuddered till the chair rocked, and he drew her into his arms and held her against him.

"Then you lost your head. You were so shocked and frightened you didn't know what you were doing."

"I didn't, oh, I didn't . . . I never wanted to hurt anybody. I didn't see, Father, I didn't see. . . ."

"Of course, you didn't see. It won't be so hard, Stanley. Everybody will know it was an accident. Everybody will know that." His voice was tender; but he was haunted to despair by the image of Stanley, as a little girl, holding her bunch of pinks. It was an image that wouldn't bear thinking about, yet whether he thought or not, it was still there before him.

"Don't make me tell, Father."

"It's the only way, Stanley. It's the only way to live with yourself afterwards."

"I can't do it. I can't tell them."

"If I could take it on my shoulders, I would, darling. . . ."

"Don't make me tell them."

"It will soon be over. But, if you don't tell them, that miserable boy's life will be ruined. You're fond of Minerva."

"Mother knows it would kill me. She knows it would kill me to go through with it."

"It won't kill you. It won't be half as hard on you as keeping silent and letting that boy go to prison."

"To prison? Oh, you said they wouldn't. . . . I'd rather die than be sent to prison. . . ."

"You won't be, Stanley. It will be different for you. Everything will be made easy."

"But it mightn't be. Ask Uncle William. Uncle William

wouldn't want me to go to prison. But you don't care."
Her voice was shrill again. "You're cruel to me. You
never loved me."

"The trouble, my child, is that we've all loved you too
much."

"It's only you. The others wouldn't be cruel. They
wouldn't make me. . . ."

"They don't know, Stanley. They don't understand.
Come into your mother's room. We can ask them."

He lifted her from the chair, while she struggled out
of his arms and looked wildly round her, as if she were
seeking a place to hide. "It wasn't my fault. I never
wanted to hurt anybody."

"They will understand. All you have to do is to tell the
truth."

"But I don't know. I can't remember."

"Tell them as much as you remember."

"It was over before I knew what—what was happening. I didn't think of anything. It was just a blank
minute."

"We'll tell them that." He bent over to pick her up in
his arms. How fragile she was, how light, and how utterly
without any firmness, whether of mind or body.

Lavinia's door opened, and he heard footsteps crossing the hall. Then Andrew said, "Uncle William wants to
see you, Stanley."

"Uncle William wants to see me." Stanley sprang up
with a cry of hope. "Uncle William will help me." Breaking away, she darted across the hall to her mother's room.
"Oh Uncle William, help me!" she cried in a voice stifled
by sobs. Flinging herself on the foot of her mother's couch,
she broke into a storm of hysterical weeping.

"What is it, darling? What has happened?" Lavinia
bent over her with passionate tenderness. Then, turning
to Asa, she asked accusingly, "What have you done to
her?"

Twisting round in her mother's arms, Stanley raised her drenched face. Tears were streaming over her hollowed eye sockets, and all the bright red was smeared and splotched on her mouth. "It's Father," she said in a muffled tone. "Oh, Uncle William, make Father stop hurting me."

William was fumbling for his handkerchief. "What's the matter, Asa? What have you been doing to her?"

Standing there in front of the group, Asa let his glance travel slowly from William to Charlotte and Lavinia, and then on again to Roy and Andrew and Craig. He knew suddenly, while he looked from one startled and anxious face to another, that he was facing an intangible but wholly firm barrier. Not one of them, except Roy, and he wasn't sure about Roy, felt anything at this moment but fear of the truth, fear of certainty, fear of decision, and, most of all, fear of action. A throng of separate fears confronted him, all springing from and revolving round some central motive, some private attitude of dissimulation, some unconscious tendency to take the easiest and the most pleasant way. Feeling this, he felt also that he was no longer submissive. The instinct of failure, the sense of inferiority had evaporated. The unknown man from the depths was in command of himself and of his world. "She has told me the truth," he said. "I want her to tell you."

"The truth?" Lavinia turned on him fiercely. "You're driving her out of her senses."

"It wasn't my fault!" Stanley wailed. "I never wanted to hurt anybody."

"Leave her alone, Asa," William growled. "You'd better keep your hands off this business."

Asa glanced at him quickly. "I can't do that, William."

"We'll look after you, Stanley," Craig said. "Tell us what you know, and we'll take care of you." His voice was so roughened by pain that Asa started and looked at him

closely. The old agony of mind, raw and bleeding, throbbed again in Craig's face. Was it true that he had not entirely forgotten, that he still suffered?

Crouching against her mother's bosom, Stanley threw him a single imploring look, and lay still, a frail bundle of grief, with her wet face lifted in its disfiguring yet touching abandonment. She was apparently indifferent alike to her swollen features and to the appeal she exerted; yet Asa had never been more alive to the physical awareness, that strange sympathy of the flesh, so urgent and so unrelated to any sympathy of the mind, which she diffused as easily as she summoned, by a special gift, the charm of innocence to her smile.

"Oh, Craig," she sobbed despairingly. "Oh, Craig, you were always so good to me."

William snorted again. "Don't take it so hard, little girl. We're standing by you." He glared at Asa as if he were a dangerous opponent. "You've frightened her out of her senses. She doesn't know what she's saying."

A wordless pause enveloped them; and in this pause, it seemed to Asa that he heard the quickened breathing of eight detached personalities. Each expressed a separate identity; yet the group was held together by a single wave of emotion. "She has told me the truth," he repeated. "It will be easier for her when she has told the authorities—"

"Oh, Mother, oh, Uncle William, he wants to make me go to court! He wants to send me to prison! Oh, Uncle William, don't let him!" Stanley's cry died away and then broke out again. It was like the inarticulate moan of a small animal in a trap.

"It won't be that, Stanley." Asa felt that he was driven by a force he hated and yet could not resist. "We'll call up the commonwealth's attorney. He's a friend of your uncle's." His gaze turned to William. "You know him well, don't you, sir?"

"Well enough," William grunted.

"He will come, if you ask him?"

"Quick enough. But I ain't saying I'll do it."

"It won't be more than a fine for you, Stanley," Asa began again, "but it will mean a long sentence for Parry." He glanced at Craig almost humbly, as if he were attacking the last forlorn hope of chivalry. "Isn't that right, Craig?"

"That's right," Craig nodded. "In Stanley's case, probably, it would never even reach a jury."

"A jury!" Stanley's scream was so high and piercing that Andrew glanced apprehensively at the open window. Her body had begun to jerk up and down in a spasm of terror. As Asa moved over to her, she strained away from him and thrust out her bare arms, warding him off. "Oh, Uncle William, don't let him!" Her mouth had dropped open in the old childish habit; and while he looked at her, Asa was assailed by a wild impulse to shield her from every enemy, even from truth, even from right. . . .

"Don't touch her." Lavinia had flung herself between them.

"You know I love her. You know I'd die for her."

"Then leave her alone. Can't you see she's afraid of you?"

A cold wind swept down from some height beyond space, and rushed over him. He stood alone against his world, the only living world he knew and inhabited. When he looked at Roy, she smiled faintly and turned away to gaze out into the night, where the soft, slow, and ghostly rain of late summer was falling. Beyond the window he could see the glistening leaves and a waste of mere emptiness.

"Do you mean," his voice croaked in his ears, "that she must keep silent?"

"She doesn't know what she's saying." Lavinia faced

him defiantly. "You've frightened her till she doesn't remember."

"Do you think she could go through with it?" Andrew murmured dubiously. "Is she equal to facing it?"

"After all," Charlotte's unpolemical voice broke in, "it isn't the same thing for a boy. I'm as sorry for him as I can be. I'd do anything to help him, and I know William will, too . . . but a young girl is different. Colored people don't feel things the way we do . . . not as a young girl would, anyway. . . . Why, she's only twenty," she added briskly, clinching her argument.

"They wouldn't be hard on him." William wiped his glasses and then dabbed at his tired old eyes, which had seen too much and had stopped looking. "He could prove it was unavoidable. He could have the best counsel. It would be kept close in the family, and it would mean only a few years, at the worst, out of his life. I'd see that he—that he is provided for. No, they wouldn't be hard on him. . . ."

It's amazing, Asa said to himself, that hardness and sentimentality, as close as streaks of fat and lean, can run through a character. I shouldn't have thought he had it in him. No, I should never have thought it. . . . When no one answered, he turned to Craig. "And you, Craig?"

But Craig did not reply; and glancing at him, Asa saw that he had not heard, or was pretending he had not heard what the others were saying. Craig had drawn slightly aside, at an equal distance between Stanley and Roy, and the agony on his face was like an exposed nerve. Torn by divided loyalties, he seemed to break up and disintegrate. From his expression, he might have been driven into another sphere, or into oblivion. Nothing existed for him but his own distraught pity and the trembling figure of Stanley with that crazed look on her face.

It was Charlotte who, at last and too abruptly, shat-

tered the silence. "She ought to have bromide or something. You'd better send for the doctor."

"She isn't herself," Lavinia whispered. "Asa has nearly
killed her."

"That's no way to treat a child." William leaned over
and pressed his large, gouty hand, with its swollen and
congested veins, on Stanley's damp hair. "Her old uncle
doesn't always approve of what she does," he added, "but
when she's in trouble, she knows she can count on him."
His features hardened, and his glare shot from Asa to
Craig. "You're one of us, ain't you, Craig?" he demanded harshly. "You see how it is?"

As if the moment in which he stood were cut sharply
in two, Craig jerked upright and threw a wavering glance
round the room. "What was that? Did you speak to me?"

William scowled. "I asked you if you were one of us?"

"One of you?" His voice, flat and uncadenced, seemed
to float in from the rain. "Yes, I suppose so. I suppose I
am one of you."

"You see she couldn't stand anything more?"

"Yes, I see she couldn't stand anything more."

"Then we'll do the best we can." There was a distant
muffled roar in William's chest. "We'll do the best we can
for the boy."

"He'll be broken, in spite of everything you do," Asa
said.

Charlotte had turned away to measure a dose of bromide, and before William could answer, she pushed
between the two men and held out the glass to Stanley.
"Take this, my dear. It will help you."

Stanley thrust the medicine aside. "I don't want it."

"Take it, darling," Lavinia urged. "The doctor said
you must have it if you are upset."

"Oh, Mother, what are they going to do to me?"

"Nothing, precious. We're all taking care of you.
Uncle William will take care of you."

"And Craig?" Her eyes, wet with tears, darkened by fear, the eyes of a lost and abandoned innocence, trembled and fell as he looked down on her.

"I'll do what I can, Stanley," he answered gently. "I'll try to take care of you."

Where is Roy? Asa asked himself suddenly, for he felt that she was missing, that she was actually nowhere. But she was in the room. She was still standing apart from the others. Her face looked withered, and he thought with a stab of disbelief: She will look that way when she is an old woman. Then her pain seemed to pass into his nerves and to summon his will. They are all against me, he told himself, but I can see my way, and I must go on. They think I have lost my head, when for the first and only time in my life, I have found it. . . . He shook himself as if he were shaking rain or fog from his shoulders. This is what I am, he thought quickly. This is what I have been from the beginning. . . .

"But we can't do it," he said slowly. "You can't do it, Craig."

Craig started and looked at him. "You mean . . ."

"I mean—"

His voice was drowned in an enraged bellow from William, "Not a thing! He ain't meaning a damned thing!"

"Oh, William, be careful," Charlotte pleaded. "The doctor warned you against losing your temper."

"Temper? Who's losing his temper?"

"Well, he said excitement was bad for you."

With a final snort and splutter, William subsided into a depressed grumble. He had remembered too late that his first considerations were physical and internal.

"You mean?" Craig repeated, as vacantly as if there had been no explosion.

"I mean, we can't do it. You know we can't do it. . . ."

Craig nodded, with the dazed look of a man who has

just awakened from sleep. "I wonder," he said, and continued in a firmer tone. "Can she stand anything more?"

"She's stronger than you think. The sooner, the better. . . ."

Craig hesitated. He glanced down at Stanley, and she stretched out her arm to him. "Oh, Craig, what are they going to do to me?"

The nerve of pain jerked in his face. "Nothing, Stanley. We're going to look after you."

Watching him, while he held her hands, Asa thought: I must do it alone. Not that he cared. . . . Every decision, right or wrong, must be reached alone and enacted in complete loneliness. "Stanley," he said, leaning over her, "won't you trust us to help you?"

She recoiled with a gesture of fear and loathing. "No, not you!" she cried. "I trust Uncle William. I trust Craig. But not you."

Where is Roy? Asa asked himself, but Roy was not looking at him, and she appeared not to have heard. Her profile was outlined against the rain, and there was in her attitude something proud and desolate.

I'd better get it over, he thought. Turning away, he went out of the room; and he descended the stairs slowly, toward the back hall and the telephone.

VIII

SO IT is over, Roy thought, looking out on a world which appeared to be torn from reality. Not only her mind but her body felt bruised and aching, as if she had stumbled up from an abyss, only to find herself slipping, slipping, still slipping back into despair, into ultimate chaos. "It is in myself," she said aloud. "It is not anything outside. It is something deep down in my own nature that makes things like this happen to me. And they will always happen, no matter what I do. . . ."

For it was a bitter truth of experience, she perceived with sudden insight, that the shape of things returns again and again in the same pattern. Circumstances could leave, or appear to leave, a perpetual outline or a fixed shadow. Someone—was it Craig? was it her father?—had once told her, in a caustic mood, that love prefers weakness to strength, because it desires what it can feed on and devour. Perhaps. She didn't know. She didn't care. She was sure of one thing alone. What she was now, she would be as long as she lived. She could not break up and destroy that inward essence which was herself.

The house overhead and around her was still. The ordeal had passed quietly, and Stanley was sleeping, after a sympathetic call from young Dr. Buchanan. "I believe he is really interested in her," Lavinia had said. "I mean, seriously. He feels that she has had too much to bear." The police, too, had been sympathetic. Not that they were actually police. Two came, Roy remembered, in response to her father's message; but neither was in uniform, and one, she learned later, was her Uncle William's friend, Colonel Mosby, the commonwealth's attorney. They had made everything, especially the inquiries, as gentle as possible; and they had both chivalrously re-

gretted the necessity to release Parry and charge a young
girl in his place. Andrew said the commonwealth's attorney had a rather wild daughter, exactly Stanley's age,
and so he felt a special tenderness for the indiscretions of
youth. He implied that it was perfectly natural Stanley
should have lost her head after she thought she had
struck something, without seeing it was a child, and
should have been too shocked, when she ran away from
the scene, to know what she was doing. The doctor, too,
sitting beside the bed, with his hand on his patient's
pulse, had insisted that flight was nothing more than re-
flex action. Watching them from a corner, Roy had felt
vaguely that, by the time the questioning was over, the
three men had confused Stanley with the dead little girl.
All the horror and pity seemed, through some strange
freak of human emotion, to have veered round from the
dead to the living. If the colored boy had not run over
the child, it was, of course, a regrettable incident that he
should have been questioned and sent to jail; but, after
all, colored people were used to that sort of mistake. The
one thing nobody wants in this world, Roy had thought, is
truth. . . .

There was a slight movement upstairs, as if the pulse
of the house had quickened. She heard her father open
Stanley's door, and then shut it softly again and go into
her mother's room. A clock struck. So it was only nine
o'clock, yet it might have been any hour. When the
strokes ended, the house seemed to shrink and settle into
itself. Anything might happen here. Everything might
happen here. But the house would only breathe and stir
through its thin walls as it waited for daybreak. A new
day, she thought, will come, and there will be nothing but
empty time ahead, with flat miles all around it. . . .
There was a sharp crack in the stillness. A horn blew in
the street; a police car raced, shrieking, somewhere in the
distance. As if the sounds had wakened her out of a

trance, Roy was exhilarated by a sensation of relief, almost of hopefulness. It might not be true, after all, the thing she had feared! She could so easily have misconstrued the look on Craig's face, or only imagined it! In the morning, she might find that everything was just as it had been before Stanley came home. . . .

The doorbell rang; she went quickly to open it and found Craig standing, without his hat, in the faint drizzle. Glancing beyond him, she saw that the horizon was blotted out and the street lamps were muffled in a thin vapor, too light for fog, too misty for rain.

"I had to come back, Roy," he said. "I couldn't stay away. I had to know if it is all right."

He followed her into the living room, where she turned and looked up into his face, as if she were reading his mind and his heart. "Why did you go?"

"I had to get away. I couldn't have done anything."

The easiest way, she thought bitterly, the way of escape, the eternal way of evasion! Well, she was sick of softness, she told herself. She was sick of kind impulses that ended in cruelty. She was sick of goodwill too sapless to harden into action or character. "No, you couldn't have done anything."

"I knew you'd call me if I were needed."

"Of course . . . if you were needed."

"I thought it was better to have nobody but the doctor."

"Yes, that was better."

"It went well, then?"

"I suppose it went well. What did you expect?"

"I don't know. I was afraid it might be too hard on her."

"Nothing was hard. It was all—all so easy."

"I'm glad of that. How did she stand it?"

A vacant smile moved Roy's lips. "Beautifully. The doctor gave her more bromide. She is asleep now. Colo-

nel Mosby was sympathetic. Of course, Parry has been, or will be set free."

Craig gave a sigh of relief. "Then it's all right."

"Yes, it's all right." That queer pointed smile came and died on her lips. "It's all right, except for the little girl and her mother."

He flinched with pain. "Nobody can forget that."

"People always forget."

"Not that. Not things like that. Stanley's whole life will be saddened. After all, she has feeling. She may be wild, but she has a heart. No matter what she has done, she has never wanted to hurt anyone."

"No, I suppose not. All she wanted was to be happy."

"She is young. All young things want happiness."

"Yes." Her eyes searched his face. "We all want to be happy."

What did anything mean? Why was life not enough? Why was love not enough? How could a woman both love and hate a man? She looked at Craig's dark worn face, with the clear contour, the restless eyes, the quickly changing expression. A little charm, she thought angrily, a little charm, and one may do anything; one may devour lives and destroy institutions. But why did one love? Why did she want love and nothing else—nothing else in the world? She loved Craig. She wanted him. His love, his touch, his mere presence had seemed to revive her whole being, unbruised, unbroken, restored. That was what she now wanted from love. Her father, strangely wise, though a failure in life, had once said to her: We want to see ourselves magnified. Her love for Peter had been a fire in the blood, the first flare of young instinct. That flame had consumed and destroyed; but her love for Craig was quiet and healing. It had brought ease of mind and security for the heart.

She tried to think dispassionately, evading the issue. But everything within and without, her inner being, as well

as the room and the house and the world, wherever people lived and loved and in the end were disillusioned of love—all this was suddenly lost and engulfed in a flood of suspense that was more dreadful than certainty. It cannot be true, she thought in her desperation: I must push it away before it becomes true. If only she could push hard enough, she might thrust the unborn fact beyond some outer margin of chaos, which did not really exist as yet, and might not ever slip through the meshes of time. Then she asked herself, in a flash of astonishment, Why should I try to hold Craig, when I let Peter go without lifting this finger to keep him? Light streamed on Craig through a white shade, and she thought wearily, Why does anyone have white shades? She looked at him as if she had never seen him before and might never see him again. She saw the spare structure, in which no single line had been muddled, under his sallow skin. His nose was a trifle too long, and curved slightly; his cheekbones were high and prominent; his eyes, so startling in their paleness, were the color, she thought erratically, of rain in summer. But it was when he smiled that his features, even the flaws in them, appeared to come to life and be inevitably right and compelling. I wonder why I ever fell in love with Peter? she asked herself. I wonder why I ever found him so lovable? Her gaze wandered from Craig to the grayish blue of the walls, to the flowered chintz on the chairs and the one sofa, to the bowl of white phlox on the small table. Were they strong enough, were they solid enough, these inanimate objects, to ward off a blow which had not yet broken through into existence?

Without moving, without a gesture, without a word, they stood facing each other, in a place where there seemed to her, oddly enough, to be no external surface, only an inward depth of emotion—of quivering expectancy, of love, hatred, sympathy, jealousy, anger, compassion. . . .

Suddenly, she spoke. "Don't try, Craig. Please don't try. That doesn't do any good."

He started, and she watched his eyebrows twitch. "Any good?" His voice was spent with exhaustion or misery.

"You know," she said. "You know. . . ." Something in her heart seemed to break into flames and then go out utterly.

"I know," he replied slowly, "that you're the greatest thing in my life."

"Oh, my God!" The cry sounded as if it had been wrung from her, as if she had not even known that she uttered it. Rage was scorching her mind; yet her hands, when they gripped each other, were cold.

"Roy, what is it? How have I hurt you?" He came nearer and put his arms about her. "I have never seen you like this. I have never seen you give way."

She drew back while rage froze into bitterness. "I know. That's the way I am. That's why—"

"You've done everything for me. You've given me back my courage. You've made me over when I thought I was through. You've—"

"Stop! Oh, can't you stop? Can't you?" Her laugh had the old derisive note without the old gaiety.

"Roy!"

"I know." She shivered, and it seemed to her that every sense was sharp with fear or anguish. "Do you imagine I don't know that?"

"You know what you mean to me."

"I know that isn't any use. Nothing is any use . . . nothing . . . nothing . . ."

"I can't bear to see you like this."

She looked away from him and back again. "It isn't over with you. It has never been really over."

"You mean?"

"You know. You know what I mean."

[409]

He shook his head, but his voice was empty of life. "I know I love you."

"You love me?"

"I love you . . . I . . . ."

"Will you stop pretending! We have never pretended. . . ." Her voice was a smothered cry. "You have always been in love with her. . . ."

He frowned while his eyes darkened with pain. "I sometimes think it is hate. How do I know? It is just an ache in the nerves." He stumbled on. "But . . . ."

"But?"

"I don't know anything. I don't know what I am. I love you. I do love you. But I cannot get rid of her. I told you," he said furiously, "I couldn't get rid of her. She is in my blood. She is in my nerves. . . . I thought it was over. Goddamn me, I thought it was over! Then she turned to me. You saw how she turned to me? The very touch of her hand . . . Most of all, she needed me, and she had never needed me till—till . . . ." He broke off, plunged his rumpled head into his hands, and added in a distraught voice: "But I love you. You're the greatest thing I've ever had in my life."

"Oh, stop! Will you ever stop?" Chimes rang the hour from a church steeple, and she counted the peals as if she were to die when they ended.

"I don't blame you for despising me," he said. "You do despise me?"

She laughed. "Don't you despise yourself?"

His mouth tightened. "She is the last woman I'd ever like. I mean, really like. . . . That's what I hate about feeling. I suppose it is sex . . . but it lets you down. It has nothing to do with what you are in yourself . . . with what you stand for. . . . Or, perhaps, there is something rotten in me." He bit off his words sharply. "But there's another side to it too. She needs me. I am sorry for her. I'd like to save her from hurting herself." There was trag-

edy in his eyes. "You can't understand that, Roy. You are so fine and strong."

Suddenly, while he stared at her in amazement, she began to laugh mockingly; and this laughter, without mirth, without meaning, rang on and on, until it seemed to sink into the dulled sounds of the night and to become a single note in the world's tumult. He caught her in his arms, and the laughter was choked back, while she struggled to free herself.

"The mistake we made," she said, "was trying to understand. Love has nothing to do with understanding."

"Then how could we know each other?"

"We don't know each other. We don't know ourselves."

He nodded. "That puzzles me. I don't know what I am. I don't know what I want."

"You want Stanley." She drove in the blade, straight and deep.

"But that isn't love. I don't know what love is, but it's more than just wanting. Anyway, darling," he added earnestly, "I can't hurt you like this. I can't do this to you."

"Oh, you can, you can." Her voice was raw with pain. "I've never really mattered, except—"

"You've mattered most of all. You still matter. Nothing could ever matter so much as being fair to you. . . ."

"Fair?" The laughter began again, but she checked it by biting her lips.

"That's why I've told you. It wouldn't have been fair not to tell you."

Though the derision had died in her voice, it was still alive in her eyes and her smile. "Where, I wonder, did men find their sense of fairness?"

"I can forgive you, Roy, for—for hating me"—he made a futile gesture of protest—"but, whether you hate me or not, don't give me up."

"You mean . . ."

"I mean, marry me. I mean, help me not to be the damn fool I was born."

"You ask that?"

"Don't laugh again. If you won't give me up, I can get over this. It is either a sort of madness or—or, well, it is just pity."

"You used to pity the world, but did it do any good?"

"You have a right to say that. You have a right to say anything."

Her eyes were blazing with anger. "Are you trying to begin a better world by reforming Stanley?"

"Didn't I tell you that was madness? It's a sort of madness."

"Must we go back again? Must we start at the beginning?"

"You are right." His voice trembled. "It wouldn't be fair."

"Fair?" she asked. "Are you still talking of fairness?"

His gaze left her and swept blindly about the room, as if seeking a way of escape. "If you think I am not suffering . . ." he said.

"I've stopped thinking. I am sick of thinking." The white phlox on the table shed its petals, and she started as violently as if the silence had crashed around her.

"You blame me," he answered slowly, "but, after all, I don't want to be what I am. I don't want to act as I do. . . . Oh, that's the worst part of it! It makes us like this."

"Yes, it makes us like this." She flung out her arms and then let them fall, straight and stiff, to her sides. "It makes us feel we have to hurt something."

"Do we have to hurt each other?"

"Oh, can't you see? Can't men ever see? In love there are no friends. There are only lovers or . . . or love between enemies."

"Not with me. I could never be your enemy. I shall always love you."

"Then it isn't love. You hated Stanley when you stopped loving her."

"I told you that was madness. Do you want madness?"

She shook her head. "I wanted love when I wanted anything. But not ever again . . . not ever, ever, ever again."

"Roy!"

"Not ever again," she repeated.

"Must we quarrel? Why do women kill everything with talk?"

"How can you kill nothing?"

"Roy, you know better. I need you more than I ever did. Roy, will you help me?"

"Not anymore." Her heart seemed to pause suddenly, and then begin a thudding beat—one, two, one, two . . . "You can't hold love by helping. The only way to hold love is to destroy it." What was love, anyway, that she should have wanted it so desperately?

"You don't know what you say," he answered. "You don't mean what you are saying."

"Stanley destroyed you, but you still love her."

"Not like this. Not as I love you."

"But you want her. She is the one . . . you want."

For a long moment he was silent, while he looked away from her, through the open window. His face, though she could see it only in profile, was as revealing to her, she felt, as a wound that is probed. For all its apparent reserve, it was a face that could hide nothing.

"I tried to tell you," he said. "I owe you the truth. I want to be fair—" He jerked himself up sharply. "I mean honest. It isn't only, as you said just now . . . oh, well, wanting her. It's more as if . . . I know it sounds sentimental . . . but it's more as if pity had turned into a— into a kind of passion. . . ."

Her features, with the light withdrawn, might have floated in from the gray mist. She felt old and worn, as if she had lived through everything and had found all to be emptiness. It is not just Craig, she thought; it is the way of love everywhere, in every place on the earth. Then his words dragged her back.

"I suppose it was too soon," he said. "We try to hurry life too much, nowadays. The truth is, I longed so desperately to get over it that I may have cheated myself into thinking I had. If Peter had lived, it would not have been that way. It was only when she came back. She came back so different and so unhappy. And then this accident . . . and her loneliness . . ."

Loneliness! Roy thought. When she spoke again, her voice might have come from a stranger. "Will you go now. Will you just—go."

"But not like this. Don't make me leave you like this."

"Would you mind going—now."

"Then I will come in the morning."

"Oh, please, will you go . . ."

He stood looking at her; then walked slowly to the door; looked back again for one single hesitating instant; and went out of the room. She heard the front door open and shut softly, as softly, she thought, as if in this house there were someone dead.

IX

THERE is nothing else, Roy said to herself; and it may go on forever—this loneliness. I may live to be ninety. I may live to be the oldest human being in the world. Even then, there will not ever be anything else. . . . Last year, when she looked back, was as blank as all the other years and the days and the hours that had gone by and were now blotted out. The past, the nearest past, was empty when once it was over; it was as empty and meaningless as a slate that has been rubbed clean. No matter how vital experience might be while you lived it, no sooner was it ended and dead than it became as lifeless as the piles of dry dust in a school history book. That old childish terror, the sense of being lost in trackless space, swooped down from the clouded sky and rushed over her. She longed to escape, and in the same moment to strike back at an unseen pursuer.

The impulse died down, to spring up again with a new urgency. No, it was not Peter; it was not Craig; it was not even Stanley whom she so utterly hated. It was something older than anyone living, and more hostile. Do I hate love? she asked herself. Do I hate love, because it can ravish your heart while it wrings the blood from your veins? Yet there was no help in hating. There was nothing that she could reach by violence, and destroy. Nothing but herself, and her own pain. Nothing but the false shape of things by which she had been betrayed. . . . Her eyes burned, but they were empty of tears. It seemed to her that never again could she feel the freshness of tears, that tears were for those who still believed in life and in love.

She heard the door open and shut, and turning from the window, she saw that her father had come in.

"They have released Parry . . ." he began; and then asked in alarm, "Has anything happened?"

"Nothing that matters. Nothing that makes any difference."

"What is it, Roy?"

She tried to laugh, while a derisive voice in her mind whispered, This is the way a man looks after he has been tortured. Aloud she said in a hard-voice, "It is all over. I mean, all over with Craig."

"You can't mean . . ."

"I do. It's over. Don't look like that. It's all over."

"But you cannot, Roy. You must not. . . . Wait till all this is settled, and things have quieted down. Don't do anything rash, daughter!"

"It isn't rash. I know it. I think I've always known it deep down in my heart."

"Known what, Roy?"

"That he loves Stanley . . . that he has always loved Stanley."

"You think that because he pities her?"

"I think that because he told me."

"Told you?"

"He told me. He's just gone." She laughed scornfully. "If you had come just one minute sooner . . ."

"He doesn't know himself, darling."

She shook her head. "Do we know him any better?"

An agonized disbelief was sketched over his drawn features. "Give him time, Roy. We are living in a shocked atmosphere. Nobody is normal."

There was a discordant break in her laughter. "What good can time do?"

"You have no patience. You cannot live without patience."

For an instant, scarcely longer than a flash, she stared at him with a kind of bleak violence, as if her thoughts

were spinning round and round in endless futility. Then she burst out desperately, "Oh, Daddy, can't you see there isn't anything else?"

He moved toward her, but she drew away, sobbing wildly, without tears. "My child, my darling child, you're still so young. You're too young to see that there is as much for you as there ever was."

"There's nothing to hold by, and even if there were . . . oh, I'd hate it! I hate everything I used to believe in. I hate all the things I've thought were the right things. Nobody, not even you, told me the truth. It was all false. It was nothing but just pretending. . . . And I want to tear it to pieces. . . ."

"You are tired, Roy, and no wonder. You are unstrung, and you cannot see facts as they are."

"Oh, but, Daddy, I have felt them as they are, and I hate them!"

"That's for tonight. In the morning, you will feel differently. But, even if this has gone—and I do not believe that—you will find something better. Things go, but things come, too, at least till youth is over."

"It will happen again. The same thing, over and over. . . ."

There was a sudden chill, as icy as the clutch of a dead faith, at his heart. What power, what belief could he invoke? Had we abolished both reason and morality, to fall back upon the raw mercies of biology? In the flux of time, what was valid, what was permanent? Was there nothing he could offer her, nothing except that blind instinct for decency which mankind had picked up and lost, and picked up again, between lower and upper levels of barbarism? Was there nothing else, not even a trail of smoke from the old altars?

"You are so impatient, Roy. You never give life a chance."

"I can never keep what I want."

"But you will, my child. You will keep this—or, perhaps, something better."

"Somebody will always take it away. If it isn't Stanley, it will be some other woman like Stanley."

"That isn't true. But you cannot live, no matter how much you try, by feeling alone. Emotion will break down when you throw your whole weight upon it. . . ."

She threw out her hand, as if she were striking the air. "Just words, words. I sometimes wish we had never learned how to talk."

"I am only trying to help you."

"Stop trying. It doesn't help me. None of us is fooled by all the false faces we make. That is what I hate most about the kind of world we are living in. I's a sham, through and through, from the top to the bottom. I want to strike back at it. I want to pull it down, and destroy it. I understand poor Mother now, and why she—"

"Roy, it's life you are fighting against. Try not to wear yourself out."

She turned on him furiously. "I think it's all rotten," she said. "I think it's all just a rotten mess, through and through."

"Roy, Roy! Only a few months ago you told me you were greedy for life."

Standing there, in the white glare of the lamp, it seemed to him that all living was merely a conflict within a conflict. Was existence only a perpetual building up and tearing down? Was the struggle in any one soul simply a small reflection of an eternal warfare? Was each little world, at war with itself, ringed round by larger worlds at war with one another?

"I was then," she said. "I didn't know."

"Do you know now? Do any of us know better?"

"I know enough." Her voice trembled in her throat. "Oh, Daddy, I know enough."

"It isn't all like this."

"I don't care. I don't want anything else. I can't help it. I'm sick of trying to be brave. I'm sick of being sensible."

"Just because this has happened?"

"Just because life is this way."

"But it isn't. If only you would trust life. If only you would trust Craig—"

"Don't say it. I know what you are going to say, and I'm sick of it."

"Will you wait till tomorrow? Will you try to put off thinking tonight? Everything may be changed by tomorrow."

"It won't be. Not tomorrow. Not next year. Not ever again."

"You know what pity will do to Craig. Didn't I tell you once that he could be betrayed by his good impulses?"

She laughed, and he shivered slightly. "Yes, I know. He wants a world war because Stanley has killed somebody."

"That isn't like you. Don't be unfair."

"I want to be. I'm sick to death of fairness!"

He looked at her closely, and she saw the dark puffs under his eyes. He looks destroyed, she thought, but she felt no impulse to spare him. Only by hurting, by tearing down and apart, could she assuage this gnawing agony in her mind.

"I never knew till now," he said slowly, "that Craig means more to you than Peter ever did."

She hesitated an instant, while her eyes seemed to grope through the dark rain which had begun to fall in a blown curtain beyond the window. "It's something more," she answered, with a catch in her breath. "It's more than Craig. It's more than Peter. . . . Oh, I could never make you understand . . . but it's everything. Most of all, it's the belief in myself. It's the belief in something more

than myself. . . . Oh, Daddy, if you don't see . . ." Her words dropped back into silence, as if she had struck against some impenetrable barrier of understanding.

"I do see, my child. I see because I have been there myself. But that was in another life, and then things were ordered differently."

Her eyes blazed. "You just waited? You had patience?"

"We waited, whether or not we had patience."

"And what did you get from it? What good ever came of it?"

He shook his head, while his forehead creased in perplexity. "I don't know. I'm not sure that we have anything."

"You have Mother, and the life she has led you."

"Well, I suppose she was waiting too. That was our trouble. We were always waiting for something better to come."

"And it never comes."

"That depends. . . . No, you may be right. Not much that we wanted ever came our way."

"That's why I won't wait. That's why I'll never, never have patience."

The puffs under his eyes broke up into fine wrinkles. "But is your way any better, my dear? What does not waiting bring you?"

As if his words pierced some fog of thought or sensation, she stood motionless, with her wide-open, bewildered gaze searching his features. Then, collecting herself with a passionate gesture, she cried desperately: "I don't know! Oh, I don't know, but I'm going to find out!"

Her look startled him with its wildness. "What is it? What are you looking at?"

"Nothing, nothing. Only I won't be like you! I won't lie down and allow life to walk over me. . . ."

He stretched out his hand, and then let it drop wearily. "There are times, my dear, when none of us can do any-

thing else. We must take what we have to—or what, else, is the use in things?"

She shook her head. "Why do you think there has to be some use in things?"

"I don't know." He hesitated, as if he were trying to think of an answer. "But it is there. And even if it isn't, a decent human being can't go about making trouble."

"All I know," she said defiantly, "is that I've finished. I am through with everything I've ever known; and I'm glad of it." Her voice rose. "I don't care if I do make trouble. I don't care whether I'm decent. I don't care what I am. I've finished for good."

"You can't, Roy. You wouldn't be happy."

"Happy? I don't expect to be happy. That's another thing I'm through with—looking for happiness."

He gazed at her hopelessly. Was she seeking in him the strong man who had, for one miracle of psychological time, dominated William, dominated even Lavinia? "Wait just one night, my child. Give us just one night to think of something to do for you."

"I can't wait. I've borne it as long as I can. I've stood Stanley as long as I can. I've stood Mother. I've stood family feeling." She moved toward the door. "Daddy, I'm going!"

"Not tonight, Roy! Where can you go tonight?"

"I don't know, and I don't care. But I am going."

"Not in this rain."

She laughed tauntingly. "This rain?" she repeated. Then, with a swift gesture of repulse, thrusting away all that she had ever known and loved and valued and lived by, she broke free from his detaining grasp and ran out of the room.

In the hall she saw her hat and her small red handbag, still lying where she had tossed them when she came home in the afternoon. Picking them up, she thought vaguely: I may never come back. An instant

later, while she slipped into her summer coat and adjusted her hat, she added to herself: I may need a hat. I may need a coat, too, where I'm going. Then, clasping and unclasping her handbag: And you can't go anywhere in this world without money. Well, her week's salary was still there, and her checkbook. . . .

"You can't go, Roy, not like this." Her father had followed her into the hall. He was trying to hold her back. He was pleading with her to listen to reason. "You can't go tonight, darling. . . ."

She pushed him away from her. "You can't stop me."

"I can try." He went toward the door, barring her way. "You don't know what you're doing."

"I know better than you do. You can't stop me."

He stood aside. "No, I can't stop you. Oh, but, Roy, Roy . . ."

Only her defiant laughter, mocking with pain and as free as the wind, answered him. While he tried to hold her, she opened the front door, slipped through, and shut it behind her.

As Roy fled out into the wet streets, she heard the door open again; and her father's voice called to her. He would follow her, she knew, until she was lost from him. He would search for her in the night and the rain; but she was younger and quicker, and he could never keep up with her. Oddly enough, the thought of his desperate search left her unmoved. He was, at the moment, only a part of it all. He was a part of the life that had hurt and betrayed her. He belonged to the world she had once loved, and now loved no longer; that world of solid institutions, of firm hypocrisy, of infirm human relationships. For a block his voice followed her. Then the call wavered, and sank, and was left behind in the darkness.

X

SUDDENLY her pace slackened. Her rage was spent, and her energy faltered and gave way. Life might go on without truth or justice; but at the moment, she felt only that her body was sore and aching. She must have walked miles, she thought, and when she looked at the street signs, she discovered that she was in an unfamiliar part of the city. "I can't think," she said aloud. "I can't feel. . . . But I cannot go back. I cannot ever go back."

Rain was falling more heavily. There was a rush of wind and a pattering sound under the trees. Beyond the dimmed lights the horizon was wiped out by low-hanging clouds, and above the clouds was endless obscurity. The street, running straight and steep, stretched up into blankness. Overhead, boughs tossed and moaned as the summer leaves were torn away and flung into the gutters. Somewhere, very far-off, bells were ringing the hour; but she lost the strokes and could not pick up the numbers before the long chiming had ended. Once, when she passed an open window, she heard a radio playing swing music. In a crowded room young people were dancing. Is it late? she wondered. No, it is not late. . . . And Father is still looking for me. She felt only a dull resentment at the thought that he was searching for her in the rain.

Glancing about her, she saw that she had entered a public square; and while her tired legs seemed to give way, she quickened her dragging steps and hurried toward the shelter of a pavilion, just as a fresh gust of wind and rain whipped into her face. A group of persons had already gathered there, on the benches, under the damaged roof. In one corner a pair of young lovers pressed closely together, the girl shivering in a summer dress, the boy holding his straw hat upside down on his

knees. Through shafts of rain splintered by the light from a street lamp, she saw their rapt faces, now dimmed, now illuminated, transfixed by a single expression of stunned ecstasy. His arm was about her, and now and then, they would turn and look with a furtive joy at each other. Oh, no, not that, Roy thought. There must be hardness somewhere in life. There must be coldness. There must be some spot so empty that love is, at last, over and done with. . . . Beyond them, on the next bench, a man sat huddled under an open newspaper, which he was holding against the rain. But she turned away quickly, because, for a single vague impression, something in his careless attitude had reminded her of Peter. . . . On the other side, nearer the dripping boughs, two men were talking excitedly, while they brushed the water from their sleeves with hands which seemed to become animate or inanimate as the light flashed or faded.

"A fellow over the radio tonight sounded serious," one of the men was saying. "It looks now as if war might come any minute." He was stopped by a strangled cough, while the rickety bench shook and creaked an accompaniment.

"You're telling me!" his companion rejoined, in a voice which sounded eager and half-ashamed, as voices sound at a prize fight or in a street accident.

"That's right. I'm telling you." Again the first man broke off, and the cough racked his chest. "I'm telling you Hitler's gone too far this time. He has got to be stopped."

"Well, it's all right with me. Anybody's welcome to stop him that wants to take on the job. I say, we call that last war the First World War now, don't we?"

"Calling it that doesn't make it either the first or the last. You haven't got a radio in your home, have you?"

"We had one, but this summer I was fool enough to

lend it to my married daughter. Look here, that's a bad cough you've got. You ought to do something about it."

"It's got worse since I came out. I had a touch of flu or something, and this damn rasping has never let up."

"It doesn't pay to let a cough hang on. After I had flu last winter, my wife mixed me a bottle of whiskey and rock candy to keep in my pocket. Whenever I began wheezing, I'd take a big swallow, and it broke up that cough right away."

"I'll try it. The doctor gave me cod-liver oil, but I've finished the bottle."

"You'd better be getting in as soon as this shower holds up."

"I didn't have an umbrella, or I'd have gone on. It wasn't raining when I left home. But it's mean weather we've had ever since last Friday."

"The rain is holding up now. I'm going your way. We can get a bus at the corner. Ever think you'd like to have a secondhand Ford?"

"Or a firsthand one. I wouldn't haggle about which. . . . Do you trust the President when he says he's going to keep us out of war?"

"That sounds pretty old. No, sir, I stake by chances of our keeping out on the Middle West. The South will always try to butt in on any fight. There never was a Southerner yet that could keep his shirt on in a scrimmage. But the Middle West likes to sit tight."

Clutching his coat collar together, the man with the cough stumbled slightly against Roy as he followed his companion out of the pavilion and down the steps. He has a kind face, she thought idly, and she hoped his cough would be cured. But why was she sorry for him, and not for her father, who was missing her and still looking for her through the night? Was that because nothing mattered, not even that people, everywhere, were trying to destroy happiness?

The lovers rose, still whispering and holding hands, and went down into the darkness under the dripping trees. A minute later, the huddled figure in the corner moved, and the attitude that had reminded her of Peter was broken. The man's head was still turned away, and all she could see, when she glanced at him, was the muffled contour of a young face. Why was it that she could still be reminded of Peter? Or was Peter, safely dead now, the only living figure that remained in her world? When the man spoke suddenly, his voice startled her by its strangeness. He was not a Southerner. She was not sure that he was an American.

"Oughtn't we to be going too?"

She laughed. "There's no place to go."

"Don't you live here?"

"Yes, I live here. That's why I have no place to go."

His head turned, and from the shadows in the corner, she could feel that he looked at her. "But you must have a home?"

"Not, now. Not after tonight."

"Well, it's a beastly night." Without moving nearer or glancing at her again, he held out a package of cigarettes. When she refused, he lighted a fresh cigarette for himself and smoked slowly.

"Are you a foreigner?" she asked, not caring, not even waiting for his reply, as she started to rise from the bench. I must go on, she told herself, as if she were driven by something apart from her own being. I cannot sit here in the rain, alone in this square, until morning. If I can find a bus or a taxi, there must be a train going somewhere. But where? She could find a job in New York; but she needed dry clothes even more than she needed a job.

"Why do you ask that?" the man said. "Don't I talk like an American?"

"I just wondered. There's something about your voice . . ." As if it mattered! As if anything mattered! "You're only a boy."

"I'm twenty-four. I was born in Canterbury."

Born in Canterbury, she thought, and yet miserable! "How long have you been over here?"

"Six years. That's why I have learned to speak American. I spent three years at the University of North Carolina. Then I got a job as secretary to a professor. I've been doing historical research . . ."

"And they let you stay on."

"Nobody bothered me. I came as a student. I'm not important. I'm not dangerous."

"Are you still English?"

The shadows stirred and then settled round him. "Till a few weeks ago, I thought I was more American than British. I was taking out my first papers. Then, when the chance of war came, I felt I wanted to go back. . . . I don't know what it is. I went through too much over there ever to be romantic about old England. . . . Oh, I don't know. . . ."

For the first time, she became aware of him, less as a person than as a bundle of confused impulses. There was comfort in the presence of other misery; and she could feel, through some obscure perception, that he had been and probably was still miserable.

"I was in a devil of a hole." He scowled down at the dirty floor, where a flash of light picked out in turn a trodden banana peel, the scattered stubs of cigarettes, the sodden ends of ice-cream cones, a child's deflated toy balloon. Though she could see only one side of his face, she decided that he had a nice ugly profile. I am glad he is unhappy, she thought. I wish the whole world were as wretched as I am. I am worn out with unselfishness.

"A hole?" she echoed vaguely. A moment more, and she would get up and go away and never see him again.

[428]

"You wouldn't understand. I suppose I am too simple."

"You ought to have learned about us by this time."

"Just enough to pick up the manners and the slang. My mother was an American."

"Don't worry. You'll catch on in time."

"Not in a million years! But I'm going back. I'm part American, but not quite—and I'm not all British. But twenty-four hours after Hitler went on the rampage, I gave up my job and began to get ready. . . . You're tired?"

"Yes, I'm tired." When she tried to smile, the muscles of her face ached with the strain, and she thought bleakly, Smiling used to be easy.

"I'm sorry. I ought to have known better."

She hesitated and turned back to him. "What will you do if war doesn't come?"

"I don't know. It's coming."

"I believe you want it to come. Oh, but I know how men are about war!" Yes, she knew. If a finger ached, men wanted to plunge into a battle. But what of women? If a revolution broke out tonight, she thought bitterly, I'd be in the thick of it!

"Why are you here?" she asked, without interest. "I mean here in Queenborough?"

"I'm on my way to New York. The boat sails on Saturday, but I wanted to come sooner. A friend asked me to stay with him in his flat. His wife is away, and when I got here, I found a note telling me he had gone to join her in New York. I've been here two days, and I've had the devil of a time. If only I'd had a living soul, man, woman, or dog, I could speak to. . . ."

"Two whole days," she said, "and you've just moped?"

"I tried going to a movie, but I couldn't put my mind on it."

"How long have you been sitting here?"

"I'm dashed if I know! The others scurried to shelter after I came."

"Well, there's no use in this. I'm going somewhere."

"Are you going home?"

She shook her head, and then dropped back on the bench. "No, that's one place I'm not going. Not tonight. Not ever again."

"I wish you'd let me talk to you. Did you ever feel you had to talk or blow up?"

"I'd rather keep things to myself. It isn't easy to blow up."

"I could do it. But you're shivering. You ought to go in."

"I know. I'm going to dry myself in the train or at the station."

"What train? Where do you want to go?"

"I don't care. The first train that goes to New York. But do you know where we are?"

"I know. I'm staying just a block down the street. You can't go much farther. What do you want to do?"

She frowned. "There's only one thing I want to do, and that's to smash something."

He laughed. "You mean punch somebody's head?"

"No, nothing solid. I want to smash something that has to do with tradition or institutions or convention—or—or love. . . ."

"That's too large an order." She could feel his gaze searching her face as she moved nearer the light. "The best thing you can do is to buck up and get dry."

She stiffened angrily. "I wish you'd go. I'd rather you would go away."

"You can't stay here all night."

"I can if I choose. Anyway, you have nothing to do with it."

Without turning his head or looking directly into her

face, he said slowly, weighing each word as he uttered it: "If you'll come with me, I'll mix you a hot drink, and you can dry your clothes. . . ."

She stared at his dim profile. "With you? To your apartment?"

"The thought came to me. Doesn't it sound sensible?"

"Sensible?"

"I'm on the second floor. You have to walk upstairs. They haven't a lift. I suppose you wouldn't want to come, would you?"

Her eyes widened. "Do you know how it feels when you don't want, or not want, anything?"

"Then you wouldn't mind?"

"Or not mind anything?"

"There's nothing to be afraid of . . ."

"That's the worst," she answered. "Not any longer to be afraid."

Without replying, he held out his hand, and she walked beside him down the steps of the pavilion, out of the square, and across the street to the opposite corner. It was like walking in a nightmare, she thought, when rage has subsided into an apathy more dreadful than rage. At the instant, it seemed to her, she was destroying something she both loved and hated, some lost essence of harmony, some precious meaning in life. But she longed, even now, to suffer still more intensely, to drive the blade yet deeper into her heart.

"You're coming with me?" he asked.

"I don't care. It doesn't matter."

"Look out! You're headed straight for that puddle." For the first time he laughed. Not a bad mouth and chin, she thought, and the side of his face that she could see looked intelligent.

"There's a nip in this wind," he said.

"Is there?" Her eyes were on the pavement.

"Hadn't you felt it?"

"Not especially." She laughed. "I'm not feeling just now."

As he quickened his pace, she fell into step with him, and together they walked by the slopping puddles and under the drenched branches. Without speaking again, they turned into a side street, so deserted and melancholy that it looked as if life had abandoned it. At the end of the first block, he hurried her toward one of the old houses which had been divided into apartments. In the distance, a clock was striking, and she thought: It's after midnight, and I am going home with a strange man I met in a strange street. Was this the worst of life, or nearly the worst, to revenge oneself upon all that one has loved and hated and valued in another world?

XI

THE house stood behind a brick wall, with an iron gate which opened into a brick-paved yard. There was the pungent scent of a sycamore. She raised her eyes and looked into the dappled boughs of a giant tree. A lamp on the corner cast a greenish luster on the dripping leaves overhead and upon the mossy bricks underfoot. As she went up the shallow flight of steps into the house, she noticed a list of names and a row of speaking tubes by the door. Glancing up the well of the staircase, she thought vaguely: I wonder if Mother ever knew the people who once lived in this house? If they could see me now, what would they think of me? From a globe under the ceiling, where the plaster appeared to be crumbling, an unnatural light sifted down on the tessellated floor of the entrance. Outside, in the city, were no noises. When she paused, all the movements and rumors of living seemed to have stopped.

Ahead of her, she saw that her companion was holding open the door of an apartment. As she followed him into the private hall, he went in front to switch on a light; and in a few minutes he came back with a bathrobe of Turkish toweling over his arm. "These are Mary's things," he said. "Her name is Mary. I mean, my friend's wife. She doesn't go in for finery. There is not much hot water, but the bathroom is at the end of the hall."

When Roy came back, wearing Mary's blue cotton pajamas and striped bathrobe, he took her soaking clothes in a bundle; and presently she heard him in the kitchen moving about. He has never taken off his hat, she thought. I suppose he doesn't know any better. Not that it mattered. Not that anything mattered. . . .

While the thought was still in her mind, he brought

her two aspirin tablets and a drink of brandy without water. "Mary doesn't drink," he said, "But I found this on the shelf with the medicines."

Roy laughed and pushed it away. "I don't want it. And, for God's sake, don't offer me aspirin. That is too much like Daddy."

"You've got a bad chill. This will warm you."

She swallowed half the brandy and gave back the glass. "Aren't you going to drink it?"

"Not now. I used to drink, but I've stopped."

She smiled faintly. "Do you always wear your hat in the house?"

For an instant he hesitated. Then he jerked off his hat, and she saw, when he turned toward her in the light, that all the left side of his face was made horrible by a grotesque purple scar. "Now you know why," he said.

She looked at him steadily. "Was it an accident?"

"It was a train wreck, in France. I was smashed up when I was five. My mother was badly burned getting me out. . . ."

"Oh, but surgery could have helped you."

"Not for this. Not when it is like this. But now you know," he repeated, with a kind of dulled resentment. "Now you know why I've never had anything I didn't pay for. . . . I mean, from a woman."

She turned away from him into the living room, and fumbled for a cigarette in her bag. Her knees were trembling, and she dropped down on a hideous black sagging sofa, which stood near the front window. He also is an outsider, she thought, striking a match: He has no place or part in the world as it is. I ought to feel sorry for him, but I cannot. I cannot feel sorry for anybody or anything but myself. Even her rebellion was stonyhearted. Passion had died down into numbness. Beyond the window, she could see the dark trees, glimmering with rifts of light which splintered down through the thick

leaves. Rain was still falling, and in the branches there was a soft rustling sound. After the torrid air of the past week, the sycamore appeared to lift its boughs and toss them, thirstily, toward the closed sky. A rich earthy smell was wafted up from the ground; this scent mingled with the odor of mothballs which clung to the furniture and the rugs.

"Are you all right?" he asked. "You look a bit down-hearted." He had dropped into a chair; and he was now, meditatively, filling his pipe.

"I'm through," she replied indifferently. "I've had as much as I can stand—and more."

"Of what?"

"Oh, of everything!"

"I knew you'd had a blow. At first I thought you weren't quite right in your head."

She scoffed. "You needn't worry about that."

"Would you like some soup? I can get it hot in a minute."

"Soup!" she exclaimed derisively. "Are you really offering me soup?"

He looked at her without smiling. "Is anything the matter with soup? Have you had dinner?"

"Dinner? Good God, no. Don't let's talk about dinner."

He smoked. She picked up a fresh cigarette. "I can tell you something," he said. "It may astonish you, young woman, but you don't know what trouble is. If you want to learn, I am the one to teach you what trouble is."

"No, thank you. I've had my share."

Rain was pouring in gusts, billowing in curved waves on a high wind. While the waves flashed by the window, now dark, now bright, it seemed to her that the trees and the sky and the world beyond were all dissolving into water and flowing away. Only one lamp, under a dusky shade, was left on; and in the faint glow she studied what she could see of the man's features. He is shy and sensi-

tive, she thought; he is as sensitive as a burned child.

"So you're going," she said; "you're going to fight in a war that may never come."

He chuckled, in his odd humorless way. "But it is coming." In his slouching attitude and his dim profile, there was something deserted-looking, she thought, as if this man also had been rejected by life. Happiness may have picked him up, perhaps, and then cast him aside. He is yet another one of the disowned, Roy said to herself. He is more unhappy than I am. . . .

"Do you know what's wrong with us?" he demanded abruptly. "In the first place, we ought never to have learned to think, nor to read and write, though that makes less difference. We're not simple enough. We go about creating the stuff of misery, because we aren't like the run of people."

"Even if you're right, there must be someplace for persons like us."

"There isn't, not unless it's the battlefield; and then all we can do is to get ourselves killed."

She laughed resentfully. "For women, there isn't even a battlefield. There's only the maternity ward."

"You don't mind my talking?"

"No, I don't mind. Was that why you spoke to me? I must have looked like a drowned rat." She tucked her feet under her and leaned back in a soft hollow at the end of the sofa.

"We were all like rats, weren't we, huddling together?"

"You might have spoken to one of the others."

"I had to choose between the man with the cough and you. We can't count the lovers. Lovers are all more or less mad."

"Aren't you, too, perhaps, a little mad?"

"More than a little. I was mad about a girl in North Carolina. . . ."

"Don't tell me. I'm sick of other people's emotions. If

there's still another woman who had driven a man distracted, I am the one living person who doesn't want to hear about her."

He stared at her over his pipe before he remembered to turn away his scarred profile. "It was a bit of luck," he said, "that I spoke to you. I might have fallen in with, well—with some damn fool."

"So might I," she replied flippantly. "But what were you saying?"

"Are you sure you're not sleepy?"

"I'm not sleepy, but I'm not awake. I'm not anything. You haven't told me yet why you're going back."

"I don't know. Something is taking me. My grandfather was killed in South Africa. My father, in spite of his failings, was never a shirker. I suppose we all follow a psychological track. Something in us points the way, and we stumble blindly along it. . . . But I'm not boring you?"

"No, you're not boring me." We have nothing to give each other, she thought, nothing but a moment of pity. We are like two strangers who come, by separate ways, from opposite ends of the world, and linger for a little while when they meet, where two empty roads cross. They could not ever know more of each other than the way hands can touch and again drop apart.

Curled up so primly under the striped bathrobe, she choked back a burst of hysterical laughter. All this, she said to herself, is of a piece with my commonplace destiny. I might have been murdered. I might have fallen among thieves—or far worse. Instead, I met a decent boy, by a chance which might have been called almost conventional. I was brought, not to a house of disrepute, but to a homely middle-class flat. I am wearing the plain cotton pajamas of a respectable woman, named Mary, who does not drink whiskey and who, apparently, does not use powder or rouge. And I have been dosed with a thimble-

ful of brandy from a medicine cabinet. I suppose it is hard to avoid decent people, she thought. The world must be full of them. . . .

Then, to her amazement, the man put down his pipe and buried his face in his hands. "I am lost," he said in a muffled voice. "I am utterly lost. . . ."

Was he a little mad or merely honest? Repressing a shiver of aversion, Roy leaned toward him. "I wish I could help you. . . . And I can't even help myself!" Pity can be alive, she knew. Pity can be a slow torture. But she had finished with pity.

At the window a blind flapped. She could hear the rocking of the trees and see the rain driven outward, with a swirling motion, into the darkness. Through currents of wind and of water a street lamp flickered, and vanished, and flickered again. Is it raining in Canterbury? she wondered. Is it raining in London and in Paris, while the world waits for the sound of a dominant voice on the air or the crash of a bomb?

Aloud she said: "It was hot last week, and may be hot again tomorrow." And then, breathlessly, "Isn't there anyone close to you? You must have someone you like. . . ."

He looked up. "Only my mother. Since she died, three years ago, I've been drifting."

"And your father is dead too?"

"He left us when I was a little chap. After that wreck, my mother was never the same, and he got tired of her. He was a painter. He went off to live in an art colony in Paris. I never saw him again. My mother brought me up till I was old enough to go to school. She worked to support us. I never saw anybody work harder, day and night, at her sewing. Then she sent me to school, and school was a kind of frigid hell for me, where everything was cruel, and nothing was human. Particularly the boys. They

[438]

ragged me. They called me Scarface. I've never forgotten. I sometimes dream of them, even now. That was
the first time I'd been away from my mother. She stood
for safety. I never felt safe except when I was with her.
I used to dream of being hunted by boys—always by half-
grown boys. Mother would come and drive them away."
He stopped and shook himself, as if he were waking
from a nightmare. "And then she died. . . ."

"You poor kid," Roy said. She ought to be sorry for
him; yet she could feel with her mind alone, and knowing
is not feeling. "I wish I could help you," she repeated,
and told herself that the words were empty and meaningless.

"If only I could feel safe," he said desperately. "If only
I could feel safe from fear."

"Fear? But you're going to fight?"

"It's not that. It's not fear of war. I'm not afraid of
anything real. I'm going partly because the actual fear
may drive the false fear away."

"That sounds absurd."

"I've gone rotten. I've split up inside. Oh, the doctor
has a name for it! He is the only person who knows. It
isn't the kind of thing you can talk about."

"I know," she said; but she had known nothing like
this.

"I may really be going mad— No, don't draw away. I
am not dangerous."

"That's silly. Why should I be afraid?"

"It's agony to be alone. Yet I'm always alone."

"But you have courage. You are going to war if it
comes."

"That may save me. Fighting something solid.
Fighting what others are fighting. Not alone. Not alone,
against half-grown boys. Then, when it is all over, I shall
not be by myself. There will be other poor devils even

worse off than I am. This is the first time I have ever felt I was needed . . . that I belong with the living . . . that I am not drifting outside. . . ."

"That may save you," she said. "At least you can believe—if it is only that the struggle is worthwhile."

He was murmuring under his breath. "To find something bigger than life . . . bigger than death . . ."

When she did not answer, he left his chair and dropped on his knees by the sofa. His head rested against her, and she felt her whole body stiffen with repulsion and draw quickly away. Then, conquering her aversion, she bent over and laid her hand on his thick chestnut hair.

Presently, while she sat motionless, the sympathy flowing through her fingertips eased, little by little, the throbbing bitterness in her mind. She could feel the tormented egoism, the wounded vanity slowly ebbing away. It will not last, she thought; but while it does last, this is happening to me, not to any other woman. He needs love more than I need love. It would be charity to give him love; but I can feel for him only pity and aversion. Even so, I can be gentle to this stranger, because I could never, not in a thousand years, come to love him. . . . His head was buried in her lap, and she felt, rather than heard, the vibrations of his smothered voice. He was going to war, if war came, because he longed for, and had never had, a share in the world of human beings. And now, in this one moment out of life, he was turning for safety to a woman whom he had met, by mere chance, in the muddied, rain-sodden streets. He has been always looking for his mother in some other woman; and he will never find her. Poor kid, it isn't a lover he needs but a mother. While he talked on and on, she asked herself whether she could move her aching body without frightening him back into despair. Would the night in this room, with the driving rain outside and the flapping shade and the smell of the

drenched sycamore, outlast, in memory, all the happier
nights and days that she had known?

Suddenly the light changed; a watery dawn filtered in
through the leaves of the sycamore. I must go, Roy
thought, starting up. I must go before he awakes. What
has been, is over. Words, like acts, become stale when
they are repeated. Sliding her bare feet to the floor, she
went into the bedroom. She looked at the boy, as he lay,
flung down on Mary's bed, with the unshielded candor of
sleep in his face and in his attitude. His scarred profile
was hidden; and he appeared merely ordinary and defenseless. By next year he may be dead, Roy told herself,
but the thought was empty of feeling. And she did not
know even so much as his name! Well, she felt no wish to
know his name; but she would always remember him. He
was not a man to her, but a meaning in life. He was
barely more than a crossing road, or a door in the wall of
the present.

Turning away without a whisper of sound, she stole
out of the room and across the hall into the kitchen,
where her clothes hung, on a clothes rack, in front of the
cold gas range. Her coat was still damp, but the other
garments were dry; and it seemed to her that one and all
wore a desolate air, as if they were a part of herself that
she had cast away and forgotten. Slipping out of Mary's
pajamas, she thought: I had stepped out of my own life,
but I shall be myself again as soon as I have put on my
own clothes. Sitting on the edge of a kitchen chair, she
pulled up her stockings. They were stained with mud and
had run a ladder over the calf of her right leg. One may
violate tradition, but not the power of inanimate objects.
The broken heart still dressed and undressed; and to the
physical needs of the body, the rebellious mind still submitted. I thought I had broken away, she said to herself:

I thought I had escaped from what I was: that was only a thought: and thoughts are not real. She hung her damp coat over her arm, picked up her bag, and opened the door into the hall. Had she merely thrown off her identity for a few hours of the night, and slipped back again into that same identity as soon as the crack of dawn split the darkness?

Stealing softly down the stairs, she opened the outer door and passed from the second flight of shallow steps into the paved yard, under the spreading boughs and the strong-scented leaves of the sycamore. Rain had stopped, but the sky was still clouded; and the yard and the street outside were muffled in silence. It was the hour between dawn and day, when life has reached its lowest ebb and the movements of earth seem to pause. When she shut the iron gate behind her and walked out into the shadowless street, she felt that she was entering a dead city. Nothing stirred there, not even the wind. There was not a sound in the air. Even the milk wagons had not started their early round.

At a distant corner, she stopped and looked back up the steep hill, and over the climbing rows of shuttered, dilapidated houses. The street had appeared unfamiliar, she saw now, because it ran through an old quarter, which was rapidly crumbling. Straight ahead, over that hill, and yet another, and then yet another hill, began the modern Southern city. In that direction, if she persevered, she could find a new railway station and the trains to the North. Minutes crept by while she stood there. The light altered and deepened; presently she heard the earliest clop-clop of the milk-wagon horses. Day was at last beginning. And with the coming day, all that she had denied and had rejected in the night would return. A sharp physical clutch, an inner emptiness attacked her like nausea. The street waited. Steep and straight, it was leading toward something or nothing.

[442]

"Yet where am I going?" she asked herself, with a start. "What do I want? What am I trying to find?"

Everything, in that fresh early light, appeared changed. She felt a sudden surprise, as if she had over-taken time and were walking into a new age and a new world.

XII

"I AM chilled to the bone," Asa said aloud, as he filled the percolator and set it over the flame. But it was the chill of apprehension, he knew, for the air was not cold, and the prospect of clearing skies stayed uncertain.

A sleepless night, harassed by dread, had left him aching in mind and body. Then at daybreak, Lavinia had demanded her coffee; and he had turned out of bed, washed casually, and flung on his clothes. After taking up Lavinia's tray, he had swallowed a cup of coffee and eaten the buttered crust of a stale roll. While he sat now watching a stray cat on the fence, he began telling himself that Roy would, of course, come home; and that when she came she would be both empty and wet.

She will come back, he insisted. Don't people always come back? Yet suppose, for a minute, that she does not come back. . . . The phrase drummed through his thoughts. To ask such a question was leading him nowhere; but the dark possibility still hovered on his mental horizon. If she were not home again by the end of the day, he knew, he should be obliged to drag in the others . . . and dragging in the others, especially Lavinia, who had eyes and ears for Stanley alone, would involve them, one and all, in the usual family discussions. It would mean, too, sharing Roy, and her need of him, with Lavinia and with William, perhaps even with Craig. . . . Already his Sunday with Kate on the farm was receding. Not that his hope of freedom had vanished. That hope had merely flitted on, still within reach, just a little farther away, and diminishing slightly, but not ever disappearing. Perhaps if he had been another man, and more ruthless . . .

But who knows what is strength and what is weakness?

He thought of the boy Parry, whom he had taken from jail and carried home to Minerva. Minerva and Abel both wept, and Jasper became frantic with joy; but Parry either answered in monosyllables or said nothing. He stood just inside the door of Minerva's living room, and muttered sullenly: "I'm crawling, Ma. I never was lousy before."

"Don't you worry, son," Minerva said. "I've got a big tub of hot water, and I'll put in plenty of turpentine. Your pa and I can smoke out your clothes in the outhouse."

She pushed a chair toward him, but the boy stepped quickly aside. "I can't sit down in here, Ma. I'm crawling. You'd better keep Jasper away from me. Jasper never was lousy." When he moved, it was to take his handkerchief from his pocket and carefully wipe his moist face and hands. He seemed to feel dirty, and his skin looked more bluish than yellow. There were smudges of brown under his eyes and in the hollow of his cheeks, as if his darker blood had risen to the surface and seeped through. His attitude appeared to be beyond rage, beyond resentfulness, beyond everything but bewilderment.

"Did they treat you rough, son?" Abel asked.

The boy shook his head, and began wiping the back of his neck.

"You must brace up, Parry," Asa said. "After all, it is over now, and it might have been so much worse."

"That's right, son," Abel agreed. "We've got to thank Mr. Asa."

What had they heard? Asa wondered. How much did they know? In their shut-in look, he could read nothing. There were facts or suspicions that even Minerva would never confide to him. Parry's eyes rolled toward him, but there was no gratitude, there was no expression of any kind in their look. "Thank you, Mr. Asa," he said obediently.

"What he needs," Asa remarked cheerfully, "is a square meal. Have you eaten anything, Parry?"

"Naw, sir." Parry swallowed hard, as if to dislodge a lump in his throat. "I mean, no, sir."

"I've got the stove hot and ready," Minerva broke in. "I've laid in some strips of middling, and I'm going to make a real dish of batterbread."

"That sounds fine, Minerva." Though Asa's voice was jocular, he told himself that it was a false jocularity. "Well, you must put it all behind you, Parry," he added, after a pause. "Don't forget that you are going to be a first-rate lawyer some day."

Parry avoided his gaze. "I'm not so sure, sir," he replied. "I'm not counting on that."

Well, he had done the best he could, Asa told himself. The pity was that a man's best is so often inadequate. While he looked at Parry, he had the feeling that he had wasted his effort against a force which was soft, elusive, and yet utterly impenetrable. A single lost illusion! A solitary error of justice in a world where justice is even rarer than mercy! How could an incident like that, barely twenty-four hours in jail, have completely knocked the spirit out of a boy who was so nearly white? I suppose they are all natural-born fatalists, Asa decided; they have accepted defeat. Yet this explanation, plausible as it sounded, left his question unanswered. . . .

Why, he wondered a little later, should the beaten look in Parry's face still disturb him? Was it because he had seen at least a reflection of this look in other and in nearer faces? He had seen this look in the face of Lavinia, who had nothing. He had seen this look in William, who had won and lost everything that he wanted. Yet again, Asa had seen this look in Charlotte, and in Craig, and even in Stanley. From all these human beings, the things that had appeared beautiful or desirable, and assured,

had been withheld or finally taken away. Life had defeated them. Oh, well, but after all was it life? Or was this
sense of puzzled failure nothing more than the despond-
ent mood of an age that is finished? . . . Only Roy, because of her gallant heart, was still unconquered. Only
Roy . . . and, perhaps . . . he did not know, but,
perhaps Asa. . . . Both had lost; yet both, he felt, would
begin again, and would fight on toward an end which
they could not see. . . .

A cloud of steam gushed from the percolator, and the
kitchen was steeped in a stimulating aroma. Rising from
his chair, Asa refilled his cup and sat down again to stare
vacantly at the backs of houses which were no longer
sleeping. The daylight had grown stronger. Rain was not
falling, but the sky was still overcast. In the watery air,
which seemed liquid, objects were swimming. Grass,
weeds, the green bench, the back gate, the white and gray
cat on the fence—all these now appeared to be vaguely
shifting their outlines. Only the tall trees stood motionless.

Sitting there at the kitchen table, Asa told himself that
the moment for which he waited was at hand. If Roy
made a new place for herself, and Lavinia no longer required him, he might at last begin to live what he called
in his thoughts a life that was real. While he tossed out
crumbs to early sparrows, he felt that the life he had lived
in the past had been, not his own, but the life of another
man, and that this other man was a stranger, who spoke a
strange language.

He had shared his intimate being with no one, not
with Roy, not even with Kate, because the core of oneself
is inviolate. Always it had been like this; always it would be
like this. He breathed deeply, with a sense of elation. But
I have a right to my own one life, he thought. A quivering wire seemed to snap apart. I have as much right as

anybody to a life of my own. . . . It was at this moment
that he saw the gate slowly open, and Roy came in from
the alley.

"Roy!" he cried. Then, as she reached him, he
brought her into the kitchen and pushed her into a chair
by the table.

"Drink this coffee. You look famished."

She gazed at him with empty eyes. "I can't stay. I came
back for my clothes." She showed him her torn stocking.
"You can't go anywhere without clothes."

"You must rest first. I'm not trying to keep you. Only
go to bed and sleep, and let me bring up your breakfast.
Go to bed before Virgie comes."

Her face was drawn with fatigue, and he watched the
quivering of her lips when she tried to speak. "You don't
know where I've been. . . ."

He put his hand on her shoulder. "I don't need to
know. I know you."

She swallowed the coffee, and then stood up and
moved away from him. "You can't make me stay. Nobody
can make me stay."

"I'm not trying to make you stay. Your life is your
own, and all, or most of it, is still before you. . . . You
must get some sleep. You must come to yourself
again. . . ."

She lifted her heavy eyes and looked into his face. She
flung out her hand and began to cry under her breath.
"Oh, but, Daddy, I want something to hold by! I want
something good!"

He gathered her into his arms. "You will find it, my
child. You will find what you are looking for. It is there,
and you—if not I—will find it."

Her hands clung to him. "Oh, but, Daddy, you are
good!"

"Don't say it! I am not good. . . . I have never pre

tended to be good. . . . You are coming down with a cold. I must put you to bed."

"You will stand by me? I want you to stand by me."

"I will, Roy, as long as you need me." But she would not need him for long. Youth, he told himself, has no finality. In seeking and in finding there is not ever an end, nor is there an end in seeking and in not finding.

Looking up at the closed sky, once again he had a vision of Kate and the harvested fields and the broad river. Still ahead, and within sight, but just out of reach, and always a little farther away, fading, but not ever disappearing, was freedom.